THEY MADE HISTORY

THEY MADE HISTORY

by
Claud Golding

SIENA

This edition published and distributed by Siena, 1998

Siena
13 Whiteladies Road
Clifton
Bristol BS8 1PB

Cover photographs courtesy of Mary Evans Picture Library

All rights reserved. This book is sold subject to the condition
that it shall not, by way of trade or otherwise, be lent, resold,
hired out or otherwise circulated in any form of binding or
cover other than that in which it is published and without a
similar condition including this condition being imposed on
the subsequent purchaser.

A copy of the British Library Cataloguing-in-Publication Data
is available from the British Library

ISBN 0-75252-828-9

Printed and bound in the EC

CONTENTS

Cornelius Vanderbilt

In 1810 a youth of 16, living on Staten Island, New York, bought a small sailing boat which was going cheap. He acquired it primarily for pleasure, but one day it occurred to him that the little craft would earn him some pocket money.

He let it be known that he was willing to carry farm produce and passengers between Staten Island and New York. There was a rush to use this new carrier service, and soon young Cornelius Vanderbilt had to buy other sailing boats.

In two years Cornelius was doing a profitable business carrying supplies to fortifications in New York Harbour and adjoining waters.

It was in this way that the famous Vanderbilt family founded its fortune.

At the age of 23 Cornelius recognized the possibilities of steam-driven vessels. He sold his sloops and schooners, and from 1817 to 1829 was captain of a steam ferry between New York and New Brunswick.

The next twenty years of the life of Cornelius Vanderbilt was a period of progress. He developed an extensive carrying trade along the coast in a fleet which became so large that he was known as the "Commodore."

In 1849 the Nicaraguan Government were willing to grant a charter to any carrying concern for a service from Greytown, on the Atlantic, to San Juan del Sur on the Pacific, by way of the San Juan River and Lake Nicaragua. Vanderbilt got the concession.

In addition, he used this route for a monthly steamship line between New York and San Francisco. By 1855 he had taken a bigger plunge and established a freight and passenger line between New York and Havre. He offered to carry free the United States mails, and this drove out of business his only rival, the Collins Line. At that time the Cunard vessels were being used in connection with the Crimean War.

Vanderbilt's service continued until 1861 when he sold his steamships and entered the railway business. In 1857 he had become a director of the New York and Harlem Railway, and six years later he became its President. He greatly improved this railway service, which operated between New York and Chatham Four Corners, in Columbia County.

Next he acquired a controlling interest in the Hudson River Railway, of which he became President in 1865. He was far from satisfied, however, and he made efforts to get a grip on the New York Central, running between Albany and Buffalo. He succeeded after three years, and combined that railway with the Hudson River under the name of the New York Central and Hudson River Railroad. He became President of the amalgamation.

In 1873 he acquired the Lake Shore and Michigan Southern Railway, which resulted in a through line being established between New York and Chicago.

When Vanderbilt died on the 2nd of January, 1877, he had the controlling interest in the New York Central and Hudson River, the Lake Shore and Michigan Southern, the Harlem, and the Canada Southern railways, as well as holdings in many others. His fortune was estimated at about 100,000,000 dollars, the bulk of which he left to his son, William Henry.

During the course of his life he gave away vast sums to charities.

The Vanderbilt family emigrated from Holland to America about the year 1650 and settled near Brooklyn. About sixty years later the family became domiciled in Staten Island.

The second important member of the family was William Henry Vanderbilt, son of Cornelius, who was born in 1821. The elder Vanderbilt put his son to work as a clerk in a New York banking house, where he remained for three years ; then his father bought him a farm of 75 acres on Staten Island.

In 1860 William Henry was appointed receiver of the Staten Island Railway, and was elected President two years later. He introduced a line of ferry boats between the Island and New York.

William Henry now followed much the same career as his father. He became vice-President of the Hudson River Railway and of the New York Central and Hudson River Company, succeeding his father as President a few years afterwards.

William Henry died in New York on December 8th, 1885,

his fortune at the time of his death being estimated at 200,000,000 dollars.

When the obelisk known, like London's, as the Cleopatra's Needle was taken from Egypt to Central Park, New York, he defrayed the expense, about 100,000 dollars. Some of his benefactions amounted to half a million dollars.

For many years William Henry Vanderbilt was engaged in struggles with one railroad company or another. Pittsburg, the great steel centre, was in an invidious position with other cities in the 'eighties. The Pennsylvania railroad had a monopoly of western Pennsylvania, and while such cities as Cincinnati enjoyed "competitive" rates for the carriage of produce and manufactured articles, Pittsburg paid full rates.

In 1883 Vanderbilt met Andrew Carnegie and disclosed a plan for a railroad to run parallel to the Pennsylvania company's system.

"What do you think of the scheme, Carnegie?" asked Vanderbilt.

"I think so well of it," the other replied, "that I and my friends will raise 5,000,000 dollars as our subscription."

Vanderbilt agreed to put in a further 5,000,000 and work was began immediately. Roadways were levelled, tunnels excavated and the building of bridges begun. But the Pennsylvania company did not intend to take it lying down.

One morning Vanderbilt found workmen busy on the western shore of the Hudson River, directly opposite his own New York Central, laying a new line to extend from New York to Buffalo, and duplicating the Vanderbilt system all the way.

This inaugurated the most famous railway battles in the history of the United States. Finally the rivals had to get together, and this they did in the yacht of J. Pierpont Morgan. A settlement was arrived at whereby work was suspended on both new railways, and Pittsburg did not get its cheap rates.

William Henry's eldest son, Cornelius, became assistant treasurer of the Harlem Railway in 1865 and treasurer in 1867. After the death of his grandfather he became first vice-president of the New York Central, and held high offices in other Vanderbilt interests. He died in 1899 and his benefactions, too, were extensive.

George Monk, Duke of Albemarle

General George Monk, first Duke of Albemarle, found it difficult to keep out of trouble. He began early as a youth when he thrashed the under sheriff of his native county, Devonshire, for a wrong done to his father.

Things becoming too hot for him in Devonshire, he joined the Army and received a commission. He resigned following a quarrel with the civil authorities, where the regiment was stationed on the Continent.

Nobody, however, could keep Monk down for long. He became a lieutenant-colonel, fought on the Scottish border with great bravery, and saved the English artillery at Newburn, although he was out of ammunition.

When the Irish rebellion broke out, he was colonel of Lord Leicester's regiment. Leicester gave him the post of Governor of Dublin, but Charles I overruled the appointment, and Monk gave way with good grace.

Arousing the suspicion of some of the high officers in the service of Charles because he refused to take the oath to support the royal cause in England, Monk was arrested and sent under guard to Bristol. But he secured an interview with the King, and so impressed him that Monk was given a command in the forces sent over from Ireland during the English Civil War.

He was taken prisoner at Nantwich in 1644, and for the next two years was in the Tower, where he found it difficult to live because of his straitened circumstances.

When the Parliamentary Army began to secure the upper hand, Monk's experience in Ireland was remembered. He was released and invited to take service in the Army against the Irish rebels. He accepted, and took the Covenant. For two years he rendered great services to his new masters.

Soon after the execution of Charles, however, the Parliamentary cause began to go badly in Ireland. Monk lost one town after another, until he had to conclude an armistice with the rebel Owen Roe O'Neill. Most of his army went over to Royalists, he alone remaining faithful to the Government.

Monk next saw service with the Ironsides in Scotland; he was left to complete the submission of the country. His health broke down soon afterwards, and he had to go to Bath to recuperate, but in November 1652 he became an admiral, and served with Blake and Deane in the Battle of Portland.

On the death of Deane he was in complete command, and in the third battle between England and the Dutch achieved a complete and decisive victory.

On his return to England, Monk appears to have made an alliance with a certain Anne Clarges, daughter of a farrier in the Savoy in the Strand. She was formerly married to Thomas Radford, also a farrier. They lived at the Three Spanish Gipsies, in the New Exchange, Strand, where she sold cosmetics. She was also a sempstress, and taught plain sewing to young girls.

It was in this capacity that she became acquainted with Monk, and used to mend his garments. In 1649, she fell out with her husband, and they ceased to live together. There is nothing in the parish register to show that her husband died, but in 1652 she was married to General Monk at St. George's Church, Southwark. It was said that her first husband was alive at the time.

The next year she gave birth to a son, who was named Christopher.

The father of Nan Clarges had his forge on the site of No. 317, on the north side of the Strand. Her mother was one of five women barbers, and was celebrated in her day.

Historians are not inclined to flatter Nan : one describes her as being a person "of the lowest extraction, without either wit or beauty." Another asserts that "she was not at all handsome nor cleanly," while Pepys describes her as "ever a plain, homely dowdy."

Nan is said to have exerted great influence over Monk, and upon his being raised to the Dukedom of Albemarle, her father is supposed to have erected a maypole in the Strand to celebrate his daughter's elevation in the social scale.

Soon after his marriage to Nan, Monk returned to Scotland, beat down an insurrection, and for five years was governor of the country.

He was ruthless in extermination of opposition, and was particularly severe on the Anabaptists. Although he carried out his duties thoroughly on behalf of Cromwell, there is a suspicion that he was an opportunist. In or about the year 1654, it is said that he proposed to Charles II his restoration.

When, a year later, he received a letter from Charles II he, for reasons best known to himself, sent it to Cromwell, who, on receiving it, remarked :

"There be that tell me that there is a certain cunning fellow in Scotland called George Monk, who is said to lye in wait there to introduce Charles Stuart; I pray you, use your diligence to apprehend him, and send him up to me."

Monk continued to command the Parliamentary forces in Scotland, saying nothing, but awaiting events. In July 1659 Charles II made him tempting proposals, but he refused to accept any bribe ; with his uncanny grasp of affairs he realized that the time was not yet ripe.

Then he received tidings of Booth's rising on behalf of the King in Cheshire, and was almost on the point of issuing a manifesto when he was restrained by his customary caution. It was not before further news was received that Booth had been defeated.

The next move on behalf of the King was the declaration by Fleetwood and Lambert against the Parliament, but both were surprised when Monk did not join them, and actually took measures to oppose them. He crossed the border with a part of his army and held Lambert at bay until the latter's men had drifted away through lack of pay.

Monk received the commission of Commander-in-Chief of the Parliamentary Army, crossed the Tweed on January 2nd, 1660, and began a march on London, disbanding the rest of Lambert's army, and entering the City on February 3rd.

No one seems to have known Monk's object. He kept his own counsel, and his men followed him whether he was Royalist or Parliament bent. At one time he appears to have encouraged the Royalists of the City, and at another advised submission to the Parliament, but he still refused to take an oath against the King.

There was evidence, however, that his feelings were moving definitely Royalist when he advised Parliament to dissolve, and yet again he acted on behalf of Richard Cromwell when he removed the gates and portcullises of the City. This was a bad move, for not only the city was annoyed, but his own army by no means supported the action.

Nevertheless, he was able to put down the opposition, and immediately got into communication with Charles II, enforced the dissolution of Parliament, and imposed another on the country which was distinctly Royalist in colour. He advised the King to return, and when the new Parliament declared in favour of Charles, the Restoration was a certainty.

Monk was made Gentleman of the Bedchamber, Knight of the Garter, Master of the Horse, and Commander-in-Chief, raised to the peerage with the titles of Baron Monk, Earl of Torrington, and Duke of Albemarle. He was also granted a pension of £7,000 a year.

For a time he led a quiet life, but later was again in harness against the Dutch, who he defeated, and when the Great Fire of 1666 broke out he was in charge of the City of London.

In 1667, when the Dutch fleet sailed up the Thames, Monk was ill, but he hurried to Chatham to meet them. He died on January 3rd, 1670, "like a Roman general with all his officers about him."

His wife, the former Anne Clarges, died soon afterwards, and both were buried in Henry VII's Chapel, Westminster Abbey. Clarges Street, Piccadilly, was named after her family.

Margaret Roper

Night after night a woman waited in the shadows of London Bridge with her eyes fixed on a gruesome relic suspended from the top of a high pole.

July had given place to August. Yet the head of Sir Thomas More still swung like a pendulum from the mast, buffeted by the weather.

The bridge guards had been in no hurry to lower it. Thus it had remained for more than a month, a warning to other "traitors," and an example of the cruelty of Henry VIII. True, he had stepped in at the last moment and prevented More's body from being drawn and quartered; but that was no consolation to the victim.

Margaret Roper, eldest daughter of Sir Thomas More, had pleaded for her father's head, so that it might be buried with the other remains. The authorities had refused her request. Hence her vigil at London Bridge.

It was customary to lower heads at night, so that they might be washed away by the tide.

Margaret had determined that the whole of her father's body should be placed in the family tomb in St. Dunstan's

Church, Canterbury. She had succeeded in getting her father's remains exhumed from the grave in the chapel of St. Peter's ad Vincula in the Tower and conveyed to her home at Chelsea.

The September nights were cold, and Margaret began to fear that she would no longer be able to keep watch. At last the time arrived when none of the guards cared about preserving the "traitor's" head. The alert Margaret was there to prevent it from plunging into the water, and, wrapping the precious burden in her cloak, she hurried home to Chelsea.

She enclosed the head in a leaden box, and conveyed it privately to the family burying-place.

She had been careful not to tell anyone of her intentions, but spies gave her away. She was summoned before the Council, where she boldly told the truth, and maintained that she had a right to her father's remains.

The King ordered her to be imprisoned, but this failed to terrify, and after she had suffered with calmness for a period she was unexpectedly released.

Her stepmother and the rest of the household were still suffering from the grief of the loss of the head of the house. They were now on the verge of starvation.

Sir Thomas's property had been confiscated by the King, the widow being allowed out of the proceeds an annuity of £20. The household was broken up, and Margaret Roper withdrew to her own house to devote herself to her children.

Margaret More was married in her twentieth year. Two other daughters also married, and all of them lived with their father, Sir Thomas, at Chelsea. In addition, the Chelsea *ménage* included a poor relation of the family, brought up from childhood.

This happy state of affairs came suddenly to an end when More, having expressed his opinion about Henry's divorce of Catherine of Aragon, and refusing to take the Oath of Supremacy, was convicted of treason.

There is no more pathetic scene in history than the last farewell of father and daughter, as Sir Thomas was being led away to the Tower.

He was about to be taken inside when Margaret Roper forced her way through the officers and halberdiers, and clasped him round the neck.

"Here the weakness of nature overcame him," writes a contemporary historian, "and he wept as he gave his blessing, and uttered his Christian consolation. The people wept, too ; and his guards were so much affected that they could hardly summon up resolution to separate the father and daughter !"

"Let Margaret be allowed the liberty of being present," pleaded More, when he was told that he was to be executed on a certain day. "Permit my child's eyes to see the last of her father."

On Margaret's last visit to her father More asked her about Anne Boleyn.

"The Queen has never been better," she said.

"Never better, you say, Meg. Alas ! it pitieth me to think into what misery, poor soul, she will shortly come. These dances of hers will prove such dances, as with them she will spurn our heads off like footballs ; but it will not be long ere her head will dance the like dance."

William Roper, the husband of Margaret, was the author of the biography of Sir Thomas More. He was the son of John Roper, prothonotary of the King's court, and belonged to an ancient family of St. Dunstan's, Canterbury. Apart from the biography, there is little to record of William Roper, for much of his celebrity came to him through the brilliance of his wife. The biography, indeed, was partly written by Margaret.

She was a woman of extraordinary talent and courage. When More's first wife died he married a second time, but, in later years, Margaret was the hope of the family.

"You dear Margaret," wrote More to her on one occasion, "have never been a loiterer in learning ; but you are so modest that you had rather still accuse yourself of negligence than vainly boast of ignorance."

At this early period Margaret had made her mark in literature. Many of her Latin epistles, poems, and orations had been freely circulated and appreciated. She composed a treatise "Of the Four Last Things," which was so cleverly conceived that even her father had to acknowledge its superiority to his own work ; it caused him to abandon a discourse he had prepared on the same subject.

She translated the *Ecclesiastical History of Eusebius* from Greek into Latin. Years afterwards this was translated into English by her own daughter, Mary.

Erasmus called Margaret "the Honour of England," an allusion to her virtues and learning.

William Roper was one of the commissioners appointed by Queen Mary to extirpate Protestantism. It can only be assumed that Margaret would have prevented this had she been opposed to it. In the absence of any protest on her part, there is little question that the More family were bigoted in a religious sense.

The family had high ideals, and were deeply sensitive of their own morality, as is shown by the inscription on the tomb of Roper and his wife. Translated from the Latin into English it is as follows :

"Here lieth interred William Roper, Esq., a venerable and worthy man, the son and successor of the late John Roper, Esq.

"Also Margaret, his wife, daughter of Sir Thomas More, knight, once High Chancellor of England, a woman excellently skilled in the Greek and Latin tongues. The above-mentioned William Roper succeeded his father, John Roper, in the office of prothonotary of the High Court of King's Bench ; and after having discharged the duties of it faithfully fifty-four years, he left it to his son Thomas. The said William Roper was liberal both in his domestic and public conduct, kind and compassionate in his temper, the support of the prisoner, the poor and the oppressed.

"He had issue by Margaret, his only wife, two sons and three daughters, whose children and grandchildren he lived to see. He lost his wife in the bloom of his years, and lived a widower thirty-three years. At length (his days being fulfilled in peace) he died, lamented by all, in a good old age, on the 4th day of January, in the year of our redemption 1557, and of his age, eighty-two."

Catherine de Medici

When Catherine de Medici, a beautiful and bewitching girl of 16, entered the port of Marseilles to become the wife of the second son of the King of France, she had already made a resolution that one day she would become the most important person in France.

Born at Florence in 1519, she was the daughter of Lorenzo de Medici, grandson of Lorenzo the Magnificent. Having lost her parents, she was brought up in the care of her uncle,

Giulio de Medici, afterwards Clement VII, who, when she had just completed her thirteenth year, arranged for her betrothal to Henry, the son of Francis I.

For thirty years Catherine contented herself with the modest position at the French Court to which she was relegated, as she was not regarded as of royal birth.

At last Catherine's star came into the ascendant. Death had taken away all rivals. Since the daughter of the House of Medici had arrived at the Louvre, the Dauphin had died, leaving no child. Then the death of her father-in-law, Francis I, placed her on the throne by the side of her husband, Henry II. Thus she had the crown, but she was denied the kingdom.

Diana of Poictiers, Henry's mistress, stood in the way of Catherine's advancement, for she more than divided the influence which should have belonged to Catherine as a wife.

At last her husband died, and Catherine shed no tears.

Her next rival was Mary Stuart, heir to the throne of Scotland, who became the wife of the reigning monarch, Francis II. When Francis became insane, Mary became the most popular figure of the Royal circle in France, and Catherine had to wait still longer for her ambitions to be realized.

Seventeen months after his accession, however, Francis died, Mary went home to Scotland as Queen of Scots, and once more Catherine began to hope. Again she was denied by the assumption of power by the Triumvirate, which took over the complete control of the country.

Anyone but Catherine de Medici would have given up the attempt and retired to live in seclusion. But she was not made that way, and she still awaited her opportunity.

The assassin's pistol broke up the Triumvirate. At last the way was open, and as soon as her son, Charles IX, ascended the throne at the age of 11, she asserted her authority and declared her independence of the scheming Guise family who had ruled the destinies of France.

Catherine had studied closely all the parties by which France was divided. She was a clever dissembler, had a capacity for intrigue ; and was careful not to be too obvious in her schemes.

As she had outlived all her rivals at Court, the Huguenots were now the only party that she had to fear. The Guises had tried to keep this powerful party under. Should she do the same, or should she offer to compromise with them ?

Catherine considered this problem for a long time. At last she decided that she could never hold the same views as the Huguenots. All the traditions of her house were against the reformed religion, and she could not permit France to become Protestant, for the country would more than likely find itself at war with Italy and Spain.

But the faith of the Huguenots was spreading, and it could not be ignored. They had powerful friends in England and Germany who had no intention of allowing them to be suppressed.

Coligny was the most powerful general on the side of the Huguenots, and Catherine had no one his equal. A fight with him might spell defeat for herself.

These were the problems which Catherine de Medici had to solve, and to solve quickly.

The Huguenot army was inferior in numbers to the Roman Catholics, but the Huguenots were determined fighters and well organized.

Catherine decided that she must conciliate the Protestants, and, at the same time, try to reduce their numbers and weaken their influence. Their privileges must also be curtailed, so that in a few years' time she might fall on them, either by declaring war suddenly or carrying out a comprehensive massacre.

In pursuance of this scheme the Huguenots were surprised with gracious looks and soft words. At the same time they received no important benefits from the Queen-mother dictator.

There were no open hostilities, but murder continued all over France, and it is computed that 3,000 Huguenots were disposed of in this way.

Catherine now began to mould her son, Charles IX. In point of intellect, he was far superior to his brother, Francis, who had been regarded as an imbecile. She had him educated by a Florentine whose character was notoriously corrupt.

In the summer of 1565 Catherine and her son made a royal progress through the country with a brilliant retinue of princes of the blood, officers of state, and lords and ladies of the Court. The inhabitants of the provinces turned out in their thousands to witness the wonderful cavalcade as it passed them.

By means of this progress Catherine was able to judge the

relative strength of the two parties in her domains. She used smiles in some quarters, and frowns in others. She intimated her disapproval of the action of the Huguenots in destroying stone images, and drew her son's attention to this "sacrilege." The Huguenots had, in fact, been thorough in their destruction of the property of the monasteries. They had sacked holy buildings, destroyed church furniture, crosses, and other things which they believed to be idolatrous.

The young King readily assimilated all that Catherine intended, and this undoubtedly inspired his policy in later years.

Catherine also ascertained the opinions of neighbouring sovereigns on the question of Protestantism, and then came to an understanding with them about the procedure to be adopted.

The Council of Trent, whose sittings had just come to an end, had recommended a league among Roman Catholic sovereigns to suppress the reformed opinions. Philip of Spain took the lead, and Catherine went to Bayonne to discuss matters with him. Instead of seeing the King, however, she had an interview with the Duke of Alva, who was fanatically opposed to the Protestants.

Some historians assert that it was at this interview the Massacre of St. Bartholomew was decided upon.

It must be said in favour of Catherine that she was in favour of milder methods, but Alva insisted that "they ought by severe remedies, no matter whether by fire or sword, to cut away the roots of the evil."

"The Kings of France and Spain at Bayonne," declares Tavanne, in his *Memoirs*, "through the instrumentality of the Duke of Alva, resolved on the destruction of the Huguenots of France and Spain."

It is said that the massacre was fixed to take place in the following year, 1566, but the secret came out, and Coligny took precautions by strengthening his forces.

During the next five years there was both open and surreptitious warfare between the two parties with patched-up truces.

The massacre eventually took place in August 1572. Catherine was the chief instigator, for right up to the last moment Charles was reluctant to give the necessary order.

Thus Catherine herself gave the signal—the tolling of

the bell of St. Germain l'Auxerois. The King tried to stop the slaughter, but it was too late.

Soon after the massacre Charles was struck with remorse. He could not efface the awful scene from his memory, and this is believed to have hastened his death.

He was followed in the kingship by his brother, Henry III, Catherine retaining much of her former power. She died on January 5th at Blois, leaving the kingdom in a state of anarchy.

The Retreat from Kabul

The retreat of Napoleon from Moscow has no more distressing features than the evacuation of Kabul by the British forces and their allies in January 1842.

To explain the presence of this army in Kabul it is necessary to go back to the year 1809, when, as a result of the intrigues of Napoleon, the Hon. Mountstuart Elphinstone had been sent to Peshawar to make a friendly arrangement with Shah Shuja, who was then in power.

Elphinstone was well received, and Napoleon's advances were rejected. The fall of the Emperor in 1815 removed all danger from that quarter.

In the "thirties," however, another factor was introduced into the situation. Russia and Persia began intriguing in Afghanistan, and the Persians followed up by besieging Herat. Meanwhile a change had occurred in the control of the country. Shah Shuja had been ousted, and Dost Mohammad ruled at Kabul.

Lieutenant Alexander Burnes (afterwards Sir Alexander Burnes) was sent to Kabul to try to make a treaty with Dost, but the terms demanded by the latter were not conceded by the British Government, who decided upon the rash solution of restoring the unwanted Shah Shuja, who had remained a refugee in British territory. Ranjit Singh, King of the Punjab, agreed to co-operate in the restoration of Shah Shuja, but eventually changed his mind and actually prevented the British expedition from passing through his territory.

The Persians began their siege of Herat in November 1837. Behind the walls of that city, however, was a young officer in the service of the East India Company, named

Eldred Pottinger. As a result of his advice, the garrison was able to resist the attack of 40,000 troops from Persia, directed by Russian officers, for a period of ten months.

Meanwhile the Persians and the Russians entered into negotiations with Dost Mohammed, who was hostile to Sadozai Kamran, ruler of Herat.

Having been disappointed in his demands of Britain, Dost was disposed to listen to them.

This was the situation in Afghanistan when the British Government decided upon a move to checkmate the increasing power of Russia and Persia, and to restore Shah Shuja. It was intended that Herat should become a buffer state and that the Sikhs should be confirmed in their rule of Kashmir and Peshawar. Thus, in July 1838, a three-party agreement was signed between the Governor General, Ranjit Singh, and Shah Shuja.

The Russian and Persian attack on Herat failed, but this did not stop the British march on Kabul. From start to finish the expedition met with great difficulties. It was deficient in transport and food, and only by dogged perseverance did the British troops march through the Sind deserts and the passes.

Kandahar was reached without a shot being fired, and in this city Shah Shuja was crowned in May 1839. Other places were taken by storm, and finally Shah Shuja made a spectacular entry into Kabul.

Dost Mohammad surrendered, and was sent to India.

The war was now thought to be at an end, and Sir John Keane, the British commander, returned to India with a considerable part of the force, leaving 8,000 men, besides the Shah's army, with Sir W. Macnaghten as envoy, and Sir A. Burnes as his colleague.

For two years Shah Shuja and his allies held Kabul and Kandahar. But the cost of keeping the troops at Kabul caused concern in England. The allowance to the local chiefs were reduced, and the British occupation gradually became unpopular.

From the beginning there had been insurrections, and at last, on November 2nd, 1841, a revolt broke out at Kabul, and Burnes and other officers were massacred.

It was now found that it was more difficult to get out of Kabul than in.

It was impossible to send relief forces to the city in time, and the British in Kabul were left to look after themselves.

The commissariat fort was captured by the Afghans, no effort apparently being made to save the provisions.

On November 23rd, the British were defeated on the Behmaru Hills with consequent demoralization and hunger. Akbar Khan, one of Dost Mohammad's sons, frustrated every attempt on the part of the British to obtain supplies.

On December 11th, Macnaghten, realizing that it was hopeless to defend the city any longer, promised to evacuate Kandahar and to leave Kabul in three days, on his being supplied with provisions for which he was ready to pay.

The compact was broken by the Afghans, Macnaghten was murdered, and Lady Macnaghten and ten other women had to seek shelter in Akbar Khan's camp.

On January 6th an army of 4,500 men, with 12,000 camp followers, began its disastrous retreat from Kabul. The country was under frost and snow, and the refugees were harassed by the implacable Afghans.

At the end of the first day's march they had traversed five miles through snow dyed crimson in many places by the blood of the injured. They were forced to camp in the snow without shelter, and with little food to eat. Early next morning they resumed their flight. Apart from the military, who kept their ranks, it was a disorderly rabble.

Women with children plodded on among the refugees, while the natives attacked on every side, causing enormous casualties.

At the end of the second day they had marched ten miles, and as darkness came they once more encamped on the snow. Elphinstone, the commander, and other chief officers lost time in attempting to negotiate with the Afghan chiefs, and particularly Akbar Khan. The native chiefs had no control over their followers, and negotiations broke down.

On the third day the retreating force passed through the Koord-Caubul Pass, a narrow defile in which they were subjected to fire on all sides. About 3,000 are said to have perished at this spot. Another night of exposure followed.

On the fourth day a further attempt at conciliation resulted in Akbar Khan taking over the care of the women.

The remaining soldiers, paralysed with cold, could hardly

hold their rifles. Scores were butchered, being too weak to resist.

Two more days passed, and the force was reduced to a mere handful. The bedraggled remnant halted at Jugdulluck and General Elphinstone and two other officers gave themselves up as hostages for the safety of the troops.

This sacrifice was in vain for, still harassed by the natives, the column found themselves blocked by a barrier at the end of the Jugdulluck Pass. Here the whole of the remainder were butchered, excepting about a score of officers and forty-five soldiers. Soon even this little force was reduced by massacre to six officers, who arrived at a village sixteen miles from Jellahabad in a deplorable condition.

On January 13th, the garrison of this fortress saw a man approaching the walls, riding on a mangy little pony, which was barely able to walk. The man was completely exhausted, and when he was lifted from the animal's neck he was stiff with cold and almost insensible.

The man turned out to be Dr. Bryden, the only survivor of the force that had left Kabul a week before.

The only others saved were the officers who had given themselves up as hostages, and the women in the care of Akbar Khan.

St. Distaff's Day

*"Deceit, weeping, spinning, God hath given
To women kindly, while they may live."*

In this distich Chaucer is not flattering to women. It indicates, however, that spinning was the chief manual occupation of the sex in the Middle Ages.

Every woman was expected to spin. If she did not she was suspect.

"It stoppeth a gap; it saveth a woman from being idle," is the comment of an old chronicler.

Unmarried women, who had more time on their hands than their married sisters, were expected to keep at the distaff at all hours of day. Hence the word "spinster" became a recognized term for the unattached female, and the word "distaff" became another name for a woman.

There was a period of the year, however, when women put down their distaffs and had a holiday. This was at Christmas time. But it must be admitted that there were many other duties thrust upon them, for the Christmas and other festivals entailed a lot of work.

January 7th was the first free day after the twelve during which these celebrations continued, and it was on that day that women went back to the distaff, or were supposed to do so.

In practice they did not, for St. Distaff's Day, as it was called, seemed to be a sort of "day after," when, in view of the festivities and rejoicing of the previous fortnight, it was difficult to resume work with any enthusiasm.

The ploughmen being indisposed to begin their labours, and the women doing so half-heartedly, the day was generally spent in fun. The chief prank of the men was to set alight the women's flax, while the latter retaliated by flinging pails of water at them.

In time St. Distaff's Day developed into a day of sport as a preliminary to the resumption of work on the morrow. Herrick describes the day thus :

> *Partly work and partly play*
> *You must on St. Distaff's Day ;*
> *From the plough soon free your team ;*
> *Then come home and fother them :*
> *If the maids a-spinning go,*
> *Burn the flax and fire the tow.*
> *Bring in pails of water then,*
> *Let the maids bewash the men.*
> *Give St. Distaff all the right :*
> *Then bid Christmas sport good night,*
> *And next morrow every one*
> *To his own vocation.*

Evidence of the early use of the distaff and spindle can be traced on the monuments of Egypt and in ancient literature. In every country these implements were regarded as symbolic of women, and they must have appeared simultaneously with the efforts of the human race to clothe themselves.

The flax or tow was held on the distaff, and the twisting was effected by a spindle, which was a loaded pin or stick, the former being under the arm and the latter hanging loose and revolving in the fingers near the ground. The thread was wound on the spindle as it was made.

In earliest times no one could make a living out of spinning thread, but it was necessary for every woman to take a hand. It was a job for the farmer's wife and her maids after the ordinary work of the day was finished. In Scotland in Burns's day it was common for young girls to carry their spinning outfit, or rock, as it was called, when going to parties, and such a party was called a rocking.

In some countries the spindle was a perforated stone called a whorl. According to Stow, the historian : "About the twentieth year of Henry VIII, Anthony Bonvise, an Italian, came to this land and taught English people to spin with a distaff, at which time began the making of Devonshire kersies and Coxall clothes."

The art of spinning, though widely practised, remained unprogressive for centuries.

The process of spinning with distaff and spindle was as follows. Some twisted fibres were first attached to the spindle, and a rotary motion was given to the latter by rolling it against the thigh, or by twirling it between the fingers and thumb of the right hand, after which the fibres were drawn out in a uniform strand by both hands. When the thread was strong enough, the spindle was suspended on it until a full length had been drawn and twisted. This was then wound on the body of the spindle, and the operation was repeated.

The word "spindle" is now used for a definite length of linen yarn, namely, 14,400 yards.

Although this process was simple, yarn made in this way was equal to that made by machinery in these days.

In India a pound of cotton could be spun into a thread nearly 250 miles long. This was done with a bamboo spindle not much larger than a darning needle.

There is no definite evidence as to when the spinning-wheel took the place of the distaff and spindle. It is believed that a wheel was invented by a citizen of Brunswick in 1533, although there is no doubt that a wheel of a kind existed before that date, according to manuscripts in the British Museum. The Brunswick invention was worked by the feet.

B

Spinning with the wheel was one of the chief occupations in nunneries, although the religious houses continued to work also with the distaff and spindle long after the wheel was invented.

About the time of the change from the distaff to the wheel the word spinster as applied to single women of rank was condemned. According to a sixteenth century lawyer : "If a gentlewoman be named spinster in any original writ, etc., appeale, or indictmente, she may abate and quash the same" ; but another lays it down that "It is the addition usually given to all unmarried women from the Viscount's daughter downward."

It would appear that women above certain rank objected to the term spinster on the ground that spinning after about the fifteenth century was done by women of humbler stations of life, and it was no longer a pastime for gentlewomen.

Before the spinning-wheel became extinct some wonderful feats were achieved with it. In the year 1745 it is recorded that a woman of East Dereham, Norfolk, spun a single pound of wool into a thread of 84,000 yards in length ; that is eighty yards short of forty-eight miles. This was alluded to in the proceedings of the Royal Society.

After that time, however, a Norwich woman spun a pound of combed wool into a thread of 168,000 yards, and then, from the same weight of cotton, another thread of 203,000 yards, or more than 115 miles !

The art of spinning in its most primitive form was continued in Italy until the middle of last century.

Mary Russell Mitford

Dr. George Mitford and his little daughter, Mary, were one day walking about the streets of London, wondering how long it would be before they were reduced to starvation. Mitford's practice was gradually dwindling, and the dingy apartments in Westminster might soon prove too expensive for his income.

During their walk they came to a lottery office. The doctor determined to try his luck, but the child insisted that they must have no other ticket than that numbered 2224.

That particular ticket was obtained after much difficulty. It drew the prize of £20,000 !

The day was the little girl's birthday. She was then ten years old.

Years afterwards that child, famous as Mary Russell Mitford, the authoress, wrote :

"Ah, me ! In less than twenty years, what was left of the produce of the ticket so strangely chosen ? What, except a Wedgwood dinner service that my father had ordered to commemorate the event, with the Irish harp within the border on one side, and his family crest on the other ?

"That fragile and perishable ware long outlasted the more perishable money. Then came long years of toil and struggle and anxiety, and jolting over the rough ways of the world, and although want often came very close to our door it never actually entered."

Dr. Mitford was a strange character. He spent his wife's fortune in raising a troop of volunteers during the time of the French revolution when Napoleon threatened to invade England. Dr. Mitford defrayed the whole of the cost of equipment and training and in a few years he had run through about £40,000 and reduced himself to penury.

From a large house in Lyme Regis, Dorset, Mitford and his young daughter came down to lodgings in Westminster. The lottery prize was not the only luck that fell to Mitford. There were several bequests from relatives, but these were also dissipated.

At last father and daughter took a small cottage at Three Mile Cross, near Reading, for three months, hoping that in the meantime their fortunes would improve. They remained there for thirty years.

Mary found it necessary to work to keep herself and her father. It was in this extremity that she began those sketches which formed the first series of *Our Village*.

Like many other works esteemed in these days, *Our Village* was not at first popular. The sketches were declined by the editor of the *New Monthly Magazine* and several other editors. At last, however, the *Lady's Magazine* published them, and in 1823 they were collected in one volume.

The first series of *Our Village* was followed by a second in 1826, and others in 1828, 1830, and 1832. By this time Miss Mitford was 46.

Her mother had died in 1830, and in 1842 she lost her father. She now left the cottage at Three Mile Cross and took another at Swallowfield, about three miles farther south. Here she wrote her later works.

In her youth Miss Mitford had been ambitious to become the "greatest English poetess." Her first publications were *Miscellaneous Verses* (1810), *Christine*, a metrical tale (1811), and *Blanche* (1813).

Her play *Julian* was produced at Covent Garden in 1823, *The Foscari* at the same theatre in 1826, and *Rienzi*, regarded as the best of her plays, produced in 1828, had a run of thirty-four nights.

Her drama *Charles the First*, was refused a licence by the Lord Chamberlain, but was eventually played at the Surrey Theatre in 1834. *Belford Regis*, a novel which dealt with the neighbourhood and society of Reading, was published in 1835.

Whether Miss Mitford ever married is a mystery. According to her own correspondence she was never even in love. But the following extract from a letter which Mrs. Hofland, a great friend of the authoress, wrote to an acquaintance, seems to indicate a marriage :

In plain English, my dear Mrs. Hall, this is the fact, not communicated to me by her, for she has not told any living creature —for what reason I do not know, but I conjecture that it may not interfere with the arrangements respecting her forthcoming tragedy. . . . The marriage and all the arrangements have been kept a profound secret ; and they are gone to his seat in Northumberland. They are perfectly suited in age, he is a man of great abilities, and proud of her fame ; so that there is every prospect of happiness. No woman wanted a friend more or deserved one better, and I sincerely thank God she has found such a friend.

Mary Russell Mitford died on January 10th, 1855, and was buried in a corner of the churchyard of Swallowfield in a spot that she had chosen herself.

Her family name was originally Midford, but there is no evidence about when it was changed. Mary was born on December 16th, 1786, at Alresford, in Hampshire.

In her *Recollections of a Literary Life*, Miss Mitford gave a few personal recollections. She mentions her grief at leaving the little cottage at Three Mile Cross, where she had lived for thirty years. "In truth," she adds, "it was leaving me ; it was crumbling about us."

To this small abode came Haydon, the painter, Talfourd, the engineer, and many well-known people of the time who had heard of her literary and dramatic successes. They were surprised at the small cottage with its tiny garden. She described it as "the snuggest and cosiest of all snug cabins." But those who visited her failed to see any beauty or comfort in it.

Metropolitan Railway Opened

Dire consequences were prophesied when the first underground railway in London was projected.

Objections came from all quarters. Engineers declared that the roofs of the tunnels would collapse under the weight of street traffic.

Houses bordering the railway, they said, would be shaken, and their inhabitants poisoned by the sulphurous exhalations from the fuel with which the boilers were heated.

At last, in 1860, when the traffic problem was becoming acute, the scheme was launched.

The Great Western Railway put down £200,000. The City Corporation, at their wits' end to remedy street congestion, promised a similar sum.

A company was formed, but their shares were soon at a discount. It was not until the railway was near completion that they recovered.

When the railway was opened the shares soared.

The line extended only from Bishop's Road, Paddington to Farringdon Street.

It was opened for a trial run on January 9th, 1863, and to the public on the following day.

It was estimated that 30,000 people were carried on the first day.

"Indeed," says a contemporary chronicler, "the desire to travel by this line on the opening day was more than the directors had provided for, and from nine o'clock in the morning till past midday, it was impossible to obtain a place in the up or Cityward line at any of the mid-stations.

"In the evening the tide turned, and the crowd at the Farringdon Street station was as great as at the doors of a theatre on the first night of some popular performer."

In the course of a year nearly 10,000,000 passengers were carried by the Underground. Within two years this number was doubled.

Numerous difficulties were encountered in the building of the railway.

"The meandering stream" of the Fleet ditch gave the engineers much trouble. It had to be crossed three times.

New types of engines were necessary. Stations then had to be opened to daylight. Trains had to be lighted by gas, and a special system of signals had to be installed.

In the neighbourhood of King's Cross, the Fleet ditch broke into the tunnel, while another problem occurred at Portland Road station, used by visitors to the Zoo.

"It is a peculiarity of this district," says the chronicler, "that, between the semi-circular enclosure of Park Crescent and the quadrangular space within Park Square, a tunnel under the new road has been for a long time in existence as a means of uniting the two enclosures.

"This was familiarly known as the 'Nurserymaids' Walk,' and was the means by which the children of the residents in Park Crescent could avail themselves of the extra accommodation afforded them by the enclosure of Park Square.

"Such was the resistance offered by the inhabitants of this part to the progress of the railway, that ascending and descending gradients, to the extent of 1 in 100 had to be introduced so as to carry the line under the subterranean thoroughfare, for the benefit of the nurserymaids and children of this highly genteel neighbourhood."

Between Euston Square and King's Cross a tunnel three-quarters of a mile in length was built, but before the latter station could be reached the Fleet ditch—used as a sewer—had to be carried through an aqueduct, a wrought iron tube, a dozen feet in diameter, embedded in brickwork.

On the City side of King's Cross station a short piece of tunnelling carried the line under the Fleet ditch for the second time. The ditch had to be diverted for the third time by a tube at Farringdon Street station.

The sewer at this spot broke bounds three times during the course of the work.

The success of the Underground Railway was such that a few years later it was extended towards the City. By 1875 it had reached Liverpool Street, and in 1876 Aldgate.

The rails on the Metropolitan line were originally laid on the mixed-gauge principle. The rails were made of steel-surfaced iron, but were later replaced by rails made entirely steel. The broad gauge lines were afterwards taken up, the narrow gauge only being used.

There were two types of engines on the Metropolitan line. In one the steam came through the chimney in the ordinary way ; in the other the steam was condensed in tanks placed on each side of the locomotive.

The carriages were large and roomy, and forty feet long.

There were first-class carriages, carrying sixty people, and second and third with accommodation for eighty people.

The gas for lighting the carriages was carried in long indiarubber bags, within wooden boxes, arranged on the tops of the carriages.

"The light thus afforded to the passengers is so bright as to utterly remove all sense of travelling underground, and entirely dissipate that nervousness which the semi-obscurity of ordinary oil-lighted railway carriages gives to the sensitive during their transit through tunnels on other lines."

As to the signalling, our recorder remarks that it was so simple as "to require no exercise of skill on the part of the signalman, but rather to bring the official working them down to the level of the unerring machine upon which he has to operate."

Ventilation of the underground railway was a problem, not only at the opening of the line, but for years afterwards. Instead of coal the Metropolitan Company used coke, burnt in ovens for a long time to remove all trace of sulphur.

There was one part of the line, however, that could not be rid of foul air. It was between Portland Road and Gower Street stations.

For a long time the engineers were unable to overcome this difficulty. Then it occurred to them that the tube of the old Pneumatic Despatch Company could be used.

In 1874 the scheme was worked out and proved successful.

Lord Eldon

Lord Chancellor Eldon had a quaint wit.

"Many absurdities have been noticed in Irish Acts of Parliament," he once declared; and then added: "But perhaps none greater than what, I think, may be found in an English Act of Parliament.

"There was an Act for rebuilding Chelmsford gaol. By one section, the new gaol was to be built from the materials of the old gaol; by another, the prisoners were to be kept in the old gaol until the new gaol was finished."

Lord Eldon records in his memoirs how he won a case, while on circuit, which looked certain to be lost.

"Bearcroft came down to the assizes at Carlisle with a special retainer of three hundred guineas, in a salmon fishery cause. I led the cause on the other side; and at our consultation on the previous evening, we agreed never to ask a witness a question except in the language and dialect of Cumberland, which Bearcroft could not understand.

"Accordingly, when I began to cross-examine his first witness, who had said a great deal about the salmon, good and bad, which the fishery had produced in different seasons, I asked whether they were obliged to make 'ould soldiers' of any of them. These words puzzled Bearcroft, and he applied to me to give him an explanation of them.

"I told him that a counsel from London town could not surely be at loss for the meaning of language; and that, at any rate, it was not my business to assist, in the leading of a cause, my adversary. He then applied to the judge for an explanation, who told him he could give him none.

"The jury were astonished that neither judge nor Bearcroft had wisdom enough to understand what they all so well understood. We got a verdict, and Bearcroft swore that no fee should ever tempt him to come among such a set of barbarians as the Cumberland men again."

Eldon explains that an "ould soldier" was a salmon caught out of season, when the flesh is white and, after curing, acquires a colour "like a soldier's old red coat half worn out."

Eldon was once junior to a well-known counsel, when the latter began an argument which was against the interest of his client. After a few minutes Eldon realized that his senior was pleading the cause of the opposition. He whispered to him that he must have forgotten for whom he was employed.

"He gave me a very rough and rude reprimand," relates Eldon, "for not having sooner set him right, and then proceeded to state that what he had addressed to the court was all that could be stated against his client, and that he had put the case as unfavourably as possible against him, in order that the court might see how very satisfactorily the case against him could be answered; and, accordingly, very powerfully answered what he had before stated."

Lord Chancellor Eldon was one of the most popular men to sit on the Woolsack in the nineteenth century. He was born plain John Scott, and was the son of a coal-fitter in Newcastle. He received his early education at Newcastle Grammar School, and was intended to follow the occupation of his father.

He was rescued from this humble career, however, and he went to Corpus Christi College, Oxford. He took his bachelor's degree, and planned his studies with a view to entering the Church.

But his plans were changed entirely by his falling in love.

He was present at a ball at Newcastle when he saw Bessy Surtees, the daughter of a townsman. In a few days they eloped to Gretna Green and were married over the anvil on November 18th, 1772.

The relatives on both sides viewed this with displeasure, for it seemed that all hopes of Scott's advancement in the Church were destroyed.

Thus he turned his attention to the law, and entered the Middle Temple in January 1773. He lived at Oxford, and devoted himself to his legal studies.

He came to London in 1775 with no more than a shilling or two in his pocket. In February of the following year he was called to the Bar.

For a time he got little employment. He borrowed money from his brother to go on circuit, and one year he had to give up the circuit altogether, because he could not afford it.

On the morning of March 14th, 1781, four or five men called at his house at Newcastle, and woke him up. They told Scott that the Clitheroe election case was to be heard next morning before a committee of the House of Commons, and that the counsel originally engaged could not attend.

B*

One counsel had refused the case because he was not prepared.

"What, then, do you expect me to do ?" asked Scott.

They answered that they did not know. However, Scott agreed to take the case, and was given fifty guineas to go on with.

In addition, there were ten guineas each day, and five guineas every evening for a consultation. At the end of fifteen days, the counsel who had refused the case turned up.

The members of the committee thereupon put their heads together, and then one of them got up and said : "Mr. Scott opened the case, and has attended it throughout, and the committee think that, if he likes to reply, he ought to do so. Mr. Scott, would you like to reply ?"

Scott replied that he would do his best. He did, and was beaten by only one committee vote.

In 1783 Scott became King's Counsel, and at the age of 33 was elected Member of Parliament. In 1788 he became Solicitor-General and in 1793 Attorney-General. In 1799 he was elevated to the peerage under the title of Baron Eldon. In 1801 he received the Great Seal for the first time, but resigned on the death of Pitt in 1806.

In 1807 he was back on the Woolsack and held the position until the Liverpool administration broke up in 1826, having held it in all 24 years and 23 days, a record since the Norman Conquest.

Eldon died on the 13th of January, 1838 in the 87th year of his age. He had held the position of advocate, politician and judge, but it was as an advocate that he shone most brilliantly.

Lord Eldon's anecdote book contained many amusing stories.

"Attending a cause in the Court of Exchequer" [he relates] "a part of the ceiling fell down, and alarmed the judges, counsel, etc. Mr. Gryffid Price, an honest but excellent and warm Welshman, turned to me, and said in his familiar way, 'My dear Jack, what an escape ! Who could have expected that we should all have been delivered ?'

"He hated a pun, and particularly a bad one ; and I thought nothing could have restrained my Welsh friend's wrath when I said, 'My dear Price, you make more than enough of this. Ought not you, as an experienced lawyer, to have been aware that sealing (ceiling) and delivery always go together ?"

Charles Price

When Charles Price, the notorious criminal, was found hanged against the door of his cell in Tothill Fields Prison in January 1786, London breathed a sigh of relief.

Price was one of the cleverest rogues who ever worked the confidence trick.

It is estimated that he relieved various members of Society of over £100,000.

His audacity was remarkable. After his arrest he wrote a letter to a man whom he had defrauded of £2,000, recommending his wife and eight children to his protection.

Charles began his depredations early in life. He was born in 1730, and by the time he was 20 he had broken his father's heart.

He was only 12 when he worked his first coup. His father was an old-clothes dealer, and young Charles conceived the idea of making money by selling a coat which Price Senior had in his shop.

He ripped off the gold lace and took the garment to a Jew. The Jew was a buyer. But it was unfortunate that the Jew should offer the coat for sale to Price's father.

Young Charles had taken the precaution of wearing his brother's clothes when visiting the Jew.

The coat was recognized by Price Senior, but it was Charles's brother who got the blame.

Charles Price continued his frauds, but at last they were discovered by his father. Young Price became apprenticed with a hosier in St. James's Street, Piccadilly.

Price then robbed his father of a suit of clothes, disguised himself, and sold it to the man for whom he was working.

He assumed the name of Henry Bolingbroke, Esq., again in disguise, and bought the clothes, credit being allowed.

When young Price was asked to take the suit to the fictitious address of "Henry Bolingbroke," he kept it.

Price determined to establish a brewery. In 1775 he advertised :

"Wanted.—A partner of character, probity, and extensive acquaintance, upon a plan permanent and productive. Fifty per cent, without risk, may be obtained.

"It is not necessary he should have any knowledge of the business, which the advertiser possesses in the fullest extent.

"But he must possess a capital of between five hundred and one thousand pounds to purchase materials, with which to the knowledge of the advertiser a large fortune must be made in a very short time.

"Address to P. C. Cardigan Head, Charing Cross.

"P.S. None but principals, and those of liberal ideas will be treated with."

The advertisement attracted the attention of the celebrated comedian, Samuel Foote. He advanced £500, expecting to get a brewery. He got nothing, and retired from the scheme a sadder but wiser man.

Price gave up floating businesses, and in the guise of a Methodist preacher swindled many people.

Smuggling was his next activity   He set out for Germany and made about £300 from defrauding the Customs. Then he was thrown into prison.

Returning to England he opened another brewery at Lambeth, where he married. But again he had to decamp, and went to Copenhagen.

Denmark was not so profitable and he came back to England.

He then turned himself to forgery, and thus achieved immortality as one of the most artful and the most successful of imposters.

In 1780 he assumed the name of Brant, and engaged a young, honest fellow as servant for the purpose of passing off his forged notes.

All the transactions with his man, Samuel, were carried out in the disguise of an old man. By using high-heeled shoes and a tight suit he gave the impression of being taller than he actually was.

To pass off the forged notes, Price bought lottery tickets. Samuel had disposed of £1,400 worth of this paper when he was arrested.

Though an innocent party, Samuel got twelve months' imprisonment. Price disappeared and nothing was heard of him until 1782.

He then came out in another disguise and got into touch with a certain Mr. Spilsbury, who had taken a large number of his false notes.

Price and Spilsbury were sitting one day in a coffee-house when the conversation turned upon the forged notes.

Spilsbury related how he had been defrauded.

"Dear me ! Is it possible that such knavery can exist ?" exclaimed Price. "Did the Bank refuse payment ?"

"Oh, yes," replied Spilsbury. "It was on the faith of the Bank of England that I and a great many others were induced to take them. They were so well done that the nicest judges could not have distinguished them."

"What a complete old rascal," said Price. "He must have been an ingenious villain."

The fraud which landed Price at Bow Street Police Court was cleverly thought out.

Price called at the offices of a City merchant and stated that while in Amsterdam he had been charged with a message from the merchant's agent.

The Dutch agent had been swindled out of £1,000 by a certain Mr. Trevors, who frequented the Royal Exchange, and the merchant was asked to use his good offices to obtain a refund of the money.

Price posed only as the bearer of the message, but in conversation remarked that he knew Mr. Trevors, and gave the merchant a description of him.

Next day the merchant went to the Exchange, and, seeing a man whose description tallied with that given by Price, engaged him in talk, and afterwards invited him to his house to dinner that night.

The dinner over, the merchant taxed Mr. Trevors with the fraud. It was admitted, and Trevors offered to pay £500 on account. Trevors produced a £1,000 bank-note and asked for the change. The merchant gave him a cheque on his banker for £500, and Trevors departed.

When the note was presented it was found to be a forgery, and when inquiries were made the whole story proved to be fictitious.

Mr. Trevors was Price.

When Price was arrested he denied all the charges, hoping to bluff his way out of a conviction.

Notwithstanding his numerous disguises, many witnesses were able to come forward and identify him.

Price chose suicide rather than the gallows.

An investigation of Price's effects disclosed many interesting articles of disguise. There were two artificial noses, and a large quantity of clothing to suit all ages. Two counterfeit plates were also found.

Edmund Spenser, Poet

"He died for lacke of bread in King Street."

That, according to Ben Jonson, was the end of Edmund Spenser, poet, author of *The Faerie Queene*, one who was entitled to rank with Chaucer, Shakespeare and Milton.

King Street was a narrow thoroughfare which ran parallel to the present Parliament Street, Westminster. In Spenser's time it was the residence of many distinguished persons, but its tributaries were the resort of the Elizabethan underworld.

Thus the poet who had sung the praises of Elizabeth was allowed to die in poverty on the 16th of January, 1599.

The blame did not rest with the Queen. It is probable that Spenser for the time being had chosen to live in seclusion.

This is confirmed by the statement of Jonson that Lord Essex, the Queen's favourite, sent the poet a number of gold pieces, which were returned by Spenser with the plea that he "had no time to spend them."

The breath had barely left Spenser's body when everyone rushed to do him homage.

His remains were carried from King Street to Westminster Abbey, the funeral expenses being defrayed by the Earl of Essex.

"His hearse," writes Camden, "was attended by poets, and mournful elegies and poems, with the pens that wrote them, were thrown into the tomb."

He was laid beside Geoffrey Chaucer in the Abbey.

Twenty years later Anne Clifford, Countess of Dorset, caused a tablet to be raised to his memory with the inscription : "Edmund Spenser, the prince of poets in his tyme, whose divine spirit needs no other witnesse than the works which he left behinde him."

Spenser left his wife and two sons penniless. The widow petitioned the Queen for a pension, with what result is not known. She, however, married again.

Nothing can be said definitely about Spenser's parents. He was born in 1552 in "East Smithfield by the Tower." He was of gentle blood, but there is no evidence as to which family of Spensers he belonged. The only fact which emerges is that his mother was named Elizabeth.

There is no record of his school days.

In 1569 Spenser became a student at Pembroke Hall, Cambridge, and took his bachelor's degree in 1573, and M.A. three years later.

Leaving Cambridge, he went to the North of England, where it is thought he fell in love with his "Rosalind" of *Shepherd's Calendar* and other pastoral poems.

Presumably "Rosalind" was the lady whom he depicts in various roles as "a lowly maiden," or "a gentlewoman of no mean house," but whether her name was Rose Lynde, Eliza Horden, or Rose Daniel, can only be conjectured.

It seems certain, however, that his advances, if he ever had the courage to make them, were rejected, for she chose another.

Spenser returned to London in 1578, when a mutual friend introduced him to Sidney, afterwards Sir Philip.

Similarity of temperament brought about a friendshp and Sidney introduced the poet to his uncle, the Earl of Leicester, who employed Spenser as a secretary.

In 1579 the *Shepherd's Calendar* was published over the signature of "Immerito," and dedicated to Sidney, though the latter's name was not mentioned. It is thought by some critics that Sidney was the author of the poem.

In the meantime, Spenser had already made voluminous notes for his *Faerie Queene*.

In 1580, through Leicester's influence, he was appointed secretary to Arthur Lord Grey of Wilton, who had been given the post of Lord-Deputy for Ireland. In August of that year the poet went with his patron to Ireland.

Within six months Spenser was appointed Clerk of Decrees and Recognisances in the Court of Chancery. Soon afterwards he obtained a lease of the lands of the abbey and manor of Enniscorthy from the Crown.

In 1588 Spenser was made clerk of the Council of Munster, a post in which he was engaged in awarding to deserving Englishmen estates forfeited by the rebel Irish.

The poet himself managed to salvage about 3,000 acres of land in the County of Cork, including the castle and manor of Kilcolman.

The castle was in the midst of romantic scenery in a plain watered by a lake and bounded by mountains. It was an ideal spot for creating *The Faerie Queene*.

Once Spenser was visited by Sir Walter Raleigh, to whom he showed the first part of the poem. Raleigh was charmed. He introduced Spenser to Queen Elizabeth, the poet coming to London for the purpose.

He was permitted "at timely hours" to read portions of the poem to the Queen, who declared it to be of "wondrous worth."

In a long letter to Raleigh, Spenser explained the "general intention and meaning" of the work, which was "to fashion a gentleman or noble person in virtuous and gentle discipline."

The first three books were published in 1590, and were received with wonder and admiration. Elizabeth gave the poet a pension of £50 a year, and often had him at Court.

Meantime Philip Sidney had been killed, and Spenser wrote a pastoral elegy in his honour.

In 1596 a collection of poems appeared. They were apparently works Spenser had written as a youth.

Two years before he had returned to Ireland, where he married an Irish girl. Nothing is known as to her antecedents. Spenser describes her as "a country lass" and beautiful. "An angel," he called her.

It is believed that her Christian name was Elizabeth, and that Spenser married her in the summer of 1594.

There is a suggestion that this was Spenser's second marriage. In the register of St. Clement Danes, under date August 26th, 1587, there was an entry of the baptism of "Florence Spenser, the daughter of Edmund."

Some historians produce this as evidence of a former marriage, arguing that Spenser would naturally live close to his friend and patron, Essex, while Florence was the name of the wife of his friend, Lord Grey.

In Ireland Spenser found himself in the midst of a lawsuit with Lord Fermoy, who alleged that the poet had "entered into certain lands of his lordship."

Fermoy won his case, and was awarded the disputed property.

In 1595 Spenser returned to London with his wife, and next year the fourth, fifth, and sixth books of *The Faerie Queene* were published, as well as a new edition of his preceding books. Other poems were published at the same time.

Spenser returned to Ireland in 1597. He was recommended for the office of Sheriff of the County of Cork.

When Desmond's rebellion broke out Spenser's castle was burned and sacked. Spenser and his wife escaped, but their new-born baby was burned to death.

Destitute, they fled to England, and it is thought that they tramped their way to London.

The additional books of *The Faerie Queene* were published in 1609, after the poet's death.

The Seven Smugglers of Sussex

In the middle of the eighteenth century the Sussex coast was infested with smugglers whose activities were not always confined to defrauding the Customs.

They went about in gangs to the terror of their neighbourhood, and took dire vengeance of anyone giving information against them. A Customs officer who may have succeeded in obtaining a conviction against any of their number was often found dead afterwards.

One of the worst cases of murder of a Customs officer occurred in 1748, when William Galley of Southampton was done to death in a diabolical manner. A shoemaker named Daniel Chater, of Fordingbridge, was also murdered on the grounds that he was about to give evidence against one of the smugglers who had been arrested.

Galley and Chater were on their way to a Justice of the Peace at Stanstead, Sussex, for the purpose of giving evidence against a man named Diamond who was committed to Chichester gaol on suspicion of breaking into the King's warehouse at Poole.

They reached an inn called the White Hart, at Rowland's Castle, kept by a widow named Elizabeth Payne. From their conversation she learned of their errand. She immediately sent a message to two men who lived near by, named William Jackson and William Carter. Five other men were also attracted to the inn.

Carter called Chater into the yard and asked him where Diamond was. Chater said he believed he was in gaol, and that he was going to appear against him under compulsion by the Customs authorities.

Galley now went into the yard, and was followed by Jackson, who struck the other a blow in the face and knocked him down. Soon afterwards the rest came out of the inn, and the cry was raised : "Hang the dogs."

They overpowered Galley and Chater and put them on a horse, tying their feet below. They had not gone far when the smugglers began to whip the prisoners. Twice Galley and Chater fell off the horse, and were allowed to dangle head downwards while the whipping proceeded. Soon the captives were so weak that they could not sit on the horse. They were then placed on separate horses each before a smuggler, the flogging being continued.

At last Galley fell off the horse, shrieking : "I fall ! I fall !"

One of the smugglers named Richards pushed him, and Galley struck the ground heavily and died.

They picked up the body and placed it on a horse and proceeded towards the Red Lion at Rake. They went in and had some liquor. Then Richards and a man named Sheerman carried Chater to an old mill and chained him inside. Carter compelled the landlord to lend spades and show them a place which had previously been used to bury smuggled tea. Here they buried Galley.

They remained at the inn all day, and at night went to their homes. On Thursday they met again and brought with them seven more smugglers. They held a discussion, and it was decided to kill Chater.

The inhuman wretches began to torture the man, slashing him across the face with a knife. At last, when Chater was insensible and covered with blood, they put him on a horse and carried him to a well. Fastening a noose round his neck, they lowered him over the side. Finally they let go the rope and Chater fell to the bottom. To hasten his death they threw down a large quantity of big stones.

The wretches then returned home and began to boast what they had done.

The authorities got busy, and a diligent search was made. Some of the smugglers were taken up on suspicion and examined in the presence of the Commissioners of Customs. They turned King's Evidence.

It was not until January 16th in the following year that six men were indicted for the murder of Daniel Chater. They were Benjamin Tapner, John Cobby, John Hammond, William Carter, Richard Mills the elder and Richard Mills the younger. William Jackson and William Carter were indicted for the murder of William Galley.

When the trial came on, the evidence was so conclusive that the jury brought in a guilty verdict in a few minutes.

The men were ordered to be executed on the following day, and the sentence was carried out in each case, except in that of Jackson, who died in prison on the evening of the day he was condemned.

They were hanged at Chichester on January 18th, before a huge crowd of people.

Carter's body was hanged in chains near Rake, in Sussex, Tapner on Rook's Hill, near Chichester, and Cobby and Hammond at Cesley Isle, on the beach where they had sometimes landed their smuggled goods, and where they could be seen from a great distance in both directions.

In the pocket of Jackson was found a relic bearing the words, half in Latin and half in French: "Ye three holy kings, Gaspar, Melchior and Balthazar, Pray for us now, and in the hour of death. These papers have touched the three heads of the holy kings of Cologne. They are to preserve travellers from accidents on the road, headaches, falling sickness, fevers, witchcraft, and all kinds of mischief, and sudden death."

The body of Jackson was put in a hole near the place of execution, together with those of the two Mills, father and son, there being no friends who claimed to take them away.

A stone was erected at the spot, with the following inscription :

"Near this place was buried the body of William Jackson, who, upon a special commission of Oyer and Terminer, held at Chichester on the 16th day of January, 1748-9, was, with William Carter, attainted for the murder of William Galley, custom-house officer; and who likewise was, together with Benjamin Tapner, John Hammond, Richard Mills the elder, Richard Mills the younger, his son, attainted for the murder of Daniel Chater; but dying in a few hours after sentence of death was pronounced upon him, he thereby escaped the punishment which the heinousness of his complicated crimes deserved, and which was, the next day, most justly inflicted upon his accomplices. As a memorial to posterity, and a warning to this and succeeding generations, this stone is erected, A.D. 1749."

Jackson was a native of Hampshire, and had a wife and large family. William Carter was a thatcher; the two Millses were horse dealers, Tapner was a bricklayer, and Cobby a labourer.

In every case the men had deserted their legal occupations to follow the life of a smuggler.

The Story of Miles Coverdale

On the east side of the Communion Table in the Church of St. Magnus, London Bridge, there is a Gothic panel on a black slab let into the wall, with a representation of an open Bible above it, and having the following inscription:

"To the memory of Miles Coverdale, who, convinced that the pure word of God ought to be the sole rule of our faith and guide of our practice, laboured earnestly for its diffusion; and with the view of affording the means of reading and hearing in their own tongue the wonderful works of God not only to his own country, but to the nations that sit in darkness, and to every creature wheresoever the English anguage might be spoken, he spent many years of his life preparing a translation of the Scriptures.

"On the 4th of October, 1535, the first complete printed version of the Bible was published under his direction. The parishioners of St. Magnus the Martyr, desirous of acknowledging the mercy of God, and calling to mind that Miles Coverdale was once rector of their parish, erected this monument to his memory, A.D. 1837.

" 'How beautiful are the feet of them that preach the gospel of peace, and bring glad tidings of good things.'— Isaiah iii, 7."

Miles Coverdale derived his name from the village of Coverdale in Yorkshire, where he was born. He therefore hailed from the same county as Wycliffe, the "Morning Star of the Reformation." The year of Coverdale's birth is given as 1488.

Coverdale appears to have become an active reformer after having spent a period with the Order of Augustinian Monks. His activities attracted the attention of Thomas, Lord Cromwell, with whom he became a great favourite, and he is believed to have been shielded from persecution by that minister of Henry VIII.

In 1532, however, he went abroad, and assisted Tyndale in his work in translating the Bible. In 1535 his own folio translation of the Bible, printed, it is believed, at Zurich, with a dedication to Henry VIII, was published. This was the first English Bible allowed by royal authority.

The reception of this book at the English Court is marked by an interesting incident.

The English ecclesiastics were by no means favourable to the work and, at first, there was considerable criticism. Henry ordered several bishops to read it through. They kept it a long time before delivering their opinion. At last the King demanded its return and a decision on the advisability of making it of universal application. The bishops reported that there were many faults in it.

"Are there any heresies in it?" demanded the King.

They replied that they had found none.

"Then," said the King, "in God's name, let it go abroad among my people."

There is a difference of opinion as to whether Coverdale's translation was his own idea or whether he was employed to do the work. According to an affidavit, signed by a certain Emanuel van Meteren in May 1609, he was brought to England in 1550 by his father "a furtherer of the reformed religion, and he that caused the first Bible at his costes to be Englisshed by Mr. Myles Coverdal in Andwarp, the which my father, with Mr. Edward Whytchurch, printed both in Paris and London."

A record of this affidavit is given in the registers of the Dutch Reformed Church, Austin Friars, London. This agrees with a statement by a certain Simeon Ruytinct in his life of Emanuel van Meteren, that Jacob van Meteren, Emanuel's father, had produced at Antwerp a translation of the Bible into English and had employed for that purpose "a certain learned scholar Miles Coverdale."

Others declare, however, that the Bible in which Meteren was interested was either Matthew's of 1537, or the Great Bible of 1539, and not Coverdale's of 1535.

The printer of Coverdale's Bible is believed to have been Christopher Froschouer of Zurich, who printed a later edition in 1550. The printed sheets were bound and distributed by James Nicolson, the Southwark printer.

Coverdale's first Bible was a small folio in German black lettering, with the title "*Biblia, the Bible; that is, the Holy Scripture of the Olde and New Testament, faithfully and truly translated out of Douche (German) and Latyn into Englishe, MDXXXV.*"

Coverdale never claimed to have translated the Bible without assistance. In his dedication to Henry VIII he makes it clear that he had five assistants or used five sources, and in the Prologue he thanks "The Douche (German) interpreters."

Coverdale's Bible was the first in which the non-canonical books were separated from the canonical books. The former were placed at the end under the title of "Apocripha."

In 1537 appeared what was known as Matthew's Bible. It was produced by the London booksellers Richard Grafton and Edward Whitchurch. There is little doubt that Matthews was a *nom de plume* for someone else. It is thought that it may have been John Rogers, a friend and fellow-worker of Tyndale.

It was not really a new translation, but a compilation from the Bible of Tyndale and Coverdale. The author took complete books from both versions and made them into a composite Bible. It is, however, from Matthew's Bible that later revisions have been made.

About the year 1538 Coverdale went to Paris to superintend a new edition of the Bible then being printed there by order of Francis I. Nearly all the 2,500 copies of the edition, however, were seized by the Inquisition and burned. Only a few escaped.

The copies that were rescued enabled Grafton and Whitchurch to produce in 1539 what is called Cranmer's or the Great Bible.

In August 1551 Coverdale was appointed to the see of

Exeter. While in that office he preached frequently in the cathedral and in other churches in that city.

He also preached on occasions at St. Paul's Cross, London, where he was fond of telling his hearers the anecdote concerning Henry VIII's acceptance of his Bible.

On the accession of Mary, Coverdale lost his see and was thrown into prison.

He was released after two years, and then went to Geneva, where he assisted in producing the Geneva translation of the Bible, which was completed in 1560.

When Elizabeth became Queen, Coverdale returned to England, no doubt expecting to be restored to his see. But it was considered that he had imbibed too freely the principles of the Geneva reformers, and he got no preferment, other than the rectorship of St. Magnus, London Bridge, close by the spot where the Great Fire of London began in 1666.

The patronage of this living was in the hands of the Bishop of London.

Before Coverdale went to the parish the church was much neglected, and the services badly performed. The priests and clerks spent the time of Divine service in taverns and ale-houses, and in fishing and in "other trifles."

Coverdale restored a semblance of order, but was compelled to resign the parish in 1566, two years before his death, which took place on the 21st of January, 1568, owing to ill-health.

Edward Pellew Viscount Exmouth

The *Dutton* lay wedged in the rocks under the Citadel at Plymouth. Tremendous seas battered her sides and tore down her rigging. More than 500 men and women crowded to the rail, waiting for rescue.

They had seen their officers pulled ashore by rope through the angry seas, but only a slender hope remained of any of the lower ranks reaching shore alive, for the ship's timbers were cracking and the deck was awash.

Helpless spectators on the Hoe urged the rescuers to greater efforts, but they were afraid of being lost themselves in the panic that was now gripping the troops on board the *Dutton*.

At a moment when despair had reduced everyone to impotence a coach drew up on the Hoe, and a man in naval uniform jumped out.

The man was Captain Sir Edward Pellew.

He took in the situation at a glance. He saw the confusion on board the *Dutton*, and noted the officers standing on the Hoe.

"Get back to your ship!" he exclaimed. The officers refused.

Seizing a rope Pellew made it fast to himself and plunged into the sea, and was pulled out to the wreck.

The rescue of the 500 passengers and crew is one of the most thrilling episodes in the history of the British Navy.

Long afterwards, when Pellew was commanding the fleet off the Scheldt, he wrote a letter to a personal friend who had asked him the true facts concerning the *Dutton*. Fifteen years had passed away, and Pellew's version of the affair had never been published.

Even now he was reluctant to tell the part he had played in the rescue of the men. He wrote:

Why do you ask me to relate the wreck of the Dutton *? A lady and I were driving to a dinner-party at Plymouth when we saw crowds running to the Hoe, and learning it was a wreck I left the carriage to take her on, and joined the crowd.*

I saw the loss of the whole five or six hundred was inevitable, without somebody to direct them, for the last officer was pulled ashore as I reached the surf; I urged their return, which was refused, upon which I made the rope fast to myself, and was hauled through the surf on board, established order, and did not leave her until every soul was saved but the boatswain, who would not go before me. I got safe, and so did he, and the ship went all to pieces; but I was laid in bed for a week by getting under the mainmast (which had fallen towards the shore), and my back was cured by Lord Spencer, having conveyed to me by letter his Majesty's intention to dub me Baronet.

No more have I to say, except that I felt more pleasure in giving to a mother's arms a dear little infant only three weeks old, than I ever felt in my life, and both were saved. The struggle she had to entrust me with the bantling was a scene I cannot describe, nor need you ; and, consequently, you will never let this be visible.

It was not until the death of Pellew that this letter saw the light.

This action was characteristic of Captain Pellew. He had already saved several seamen from drowning by leaping from the deck of his ship.

Edward Pellew was born at Dover in April 1757, and began his career at sea in the frigate *Juno*. He served in the American revolutionary war, and was present at most of the encounters in that disastrous campaign. He was a lieutenant in the frigate *Apollo*, and was promoted to the rank of Master and Commander, first of the *Hazard* and afterwards of the *Pelican* sloop of war. He was advanced to Post-captain in 1782.

On the outbreak of war with France in 1793 Pellew was appointed to the frigate *Nymphe* at Plymouth. He recruited his men from Cornwall, his native county.

The *Nymphe* fell in with the French frigate *Cleopatre* and chased her through the night. In the morning the French captain, Jean Mullon, bore down on the *Nymphe*.

When within hail Pellew advanced to the gangway, removed his hat and shouted : "Long live King George," to which his men responded with cheering. The French captain replied with "*Vive la Nation*," and was seconded by his men.

The fight began, and finally the *Cleopatre* was captured, her captain being killed. Pellew put into Portsmouth, buried Mullon at his own expense and, on learning that the Frenchman had left a widow without means of subsistence, sent her a considerable sum out of his slender purse.

As an acknowledgment of this, the city of Paris presented the freedom of the city to Captain Pellew.

Pellew was presented at St. James's Palace and received the honour of knighthood. The *Dutton* rescue brought him a baronetcy.

Pellew was one of the most successful officers during the wars with France. While in command of the *Indefatigable*, as Commodore of the Western Squadron, he captured two French frigates. Soon afterwards he drove a French admiral's flagship ashore and took the admiral and crew into Plymouth.

In 1798 he captured fifteen enemy cruisers. In the following year he quelled a mutiny in his ship by grappling with the ringleader, eventually driving the men below decks.

In 1799 he co-operated in the landing of the French royalists in their expedition to the Morbihan. In 1801 he received the honorary rank of Colonel of Marines, and was elected to Parliament for Barnstaple.

On the resumption of hostilities against France, Sir Edward was appointed to the *Tonnant* and was in charge of five ships of the line. Soon afterwards he was advanced to the rank of Rear-Admiral and given the command in the East Indies. There he remained for five years, securing important advantages to British commerce by restraining the enemy cruisers.

He became Vice-Admiral and returned to Europe, and in 1810 he was appointed to the chief command of the fleet watching the French force in the Scheldt.

At the end of the war in 1814, Admiral Pellew was elevated to·the peerage under the title of Baron Exmouth of Cantoneign, with a pension of £2,000 a year. He was invested with the ribbon of the Bath and in the following year he received the Grand Cross of that Order.

With the reappearance of Napoleon on the throne of France he was given the Mediterranean command and kept the French fleet from co-operating with Napoleon.

His next, and one of the greatest of his exploits, was to force the Dey of Algiers to release several hundred Christian slaves. For this service he received the dignity of Viscount.

In 1827 Lord Exmouth was appointed for three years to the chief command at Plymouth. At the end of his three years' service he received the honorary rank of Vice-Admiral of England. He died on January 23rd, 1833, at his house at Teignmouth, Devon.

Frederick the Great

Frederick the Great, King of Prussia, born January 24th, 1712, had no brains as a youth. At least, that was the opinion of his father, the elder Frederick, who declared : "My eldest son is a coxcomb, proud, and has a fine French spirit that spoils all my plans."

Frederick William I brought up his son with extreme severity so that he might become a great soldier and "acquire thrift and frugality."

This procedure was not at all to the liking of young Frederick. He detested the military exercises which he was compelled to undergo, and preferred the tuition which he received from a Frenchwoman, Mme. de Roucoulle, which mainly concerned literature, a subject for which the coarse King had little use.

In addition, Frederick acquired a taste for music, learned Latin secretly against the wishes of his father, derided religion, and refused to learn to ride and shoot.

He despised German habits, and his feelings were shared by his sister, Wilhelmina.

The life of young Frederick was one of continuous antagonism to his father, who introduced a regime for the boy with the object of breaking his spirit.

One day the boy was seen playing the flute accompanied on the piano by a young girl. The girl was publicly flogged through the streets of Potsdam by the executioner.

At last the Queen decided that the time had come to take action, and made arrangements for him to seek refuge in England with George II. Only the boy's sister and two lieutenants were in the plot for smuggling him to England.

The King heard of it, and finding that the boy had already left the palace, sent soldiers after him, and he was caught just as he was entering his carriage to take him to Saxony.

One of the lieutenants escaped, but the other was brought back to Potsdam, handcuffed to the prince. Each was thrown in a separate dungeon, and when Wilhelmina implored her father to release her brother, she was thrown from one of the palace windows.

The King had now firmly made up his mind that his son would die on the scaffold, and believed that such a fate for his offspring would be an intervention of Providence for the security of the country.

He was certain that his son would be no good. "He will always be a disobedient subject," he said, "and I have three other boys who are more than his equals."

So the father prepared to execute his son.

The captured lieutenant was sentenced by court-martial to imprisonment for life. The King, however, changed the sentence to one of death, and the lieutenant was executed in Frederick's presence.

At last the prince was saved by the intercession of the Emperor of Austria, Charles VI.

It was then reported by the prison chaplain that the prince

had now had a change of heart. He was released from solitary confinement and sent to work in the auditing office of the departments of War and Agriculture at Custrin while the pardon was being granted.

"The whole town shall be his prison," the King wrote, "and I will give him employment from morning to night in the departments of War and Agriculture of the Government.

"He shall work at financial matters, receive accounts, read minutes, and make extracts. . . . But if he kicks or rears again, he shall forfeit the succession to the crown, and even, according to circumstances, life itself."

When Frederick, unknown to his father, fell in love with Amelia, the daughter of George II, his father, who had actually arranged for him to marry her, cancelled the marriage because the prince had been in correspondence with the English Court.

In addition he cancelled the marriage that had been arranged between his daughter, Wilhelmina, and the Prince of Wales.

Young Frederick gradually fell in with his father's wishes. He began to see there was no option, his father being determined to have his own way. On November 30th, 1731, he was allowed to appear in uniform, and in the following year he became a colonel of the regiment at Neuruppin.

In 1733 he married the Princess Elizabeth Christina, daughter of the Duke of Brunswick-Bevern.

He was granted the estate of Rheinsberg, near Neuruppin, and although the marriage which had been arranged for him by his father was an unhappy one, he was more content than he had been at any period of his life.

He and his wife lived apart, and it is said he treated her very harshly and brutally.

He became King on May 31st, 1740, and began to rule with much more feeling than his father. All religious opinions were allowed, torture was abolished, treason cases were conducted with strict justice. While he ruled himself, he would always allow people to state their wrong personally to him.

When the Emperor Charles VI died in 1740 he immediately made military preparations for the conquest of the three Silesian duchies which Prussia had always asserted were hers by right.

He invaded Silesia with an army of 30,000 and gained a victory against the Austrians at Mollwitz. Being under the impression the battle was lost, he left the field early, which gave rise to the belief that he lacked courage.

A second victory was gained at Chotisitz in May 1742, and Maria Theresa agreed to the Peace of Breslau which put Frederick in possession of Silesia. When the Prince of Friesland died without heirs he also took over that country.

At the age of 33 Frederick was the most important sovereign of his time. He administered the country himself, his ministers being puppets.

The economic development of Prussia continued apace. Agriculture improved, the burden of the peasants was lightened, and the army was increased to 160,000 men.

He lived alone in a mansion which he gave the name of Sans Souci, and rose regularly in the summer at five, and in the winter at six, devoting himself to public business until eleven.

From 1756 to 1763 his energies were directed to the conduct of the Seven Years' War, in which he pitted his strength against almost the whole of Europe.

Though the resources of the country were sadly depleted by this war, he was able, through the peace of Hubertushof, to maintain the status of Prussia, and to obtain recognition for Prussia as one of the great powers of the Continent.

From this time it was inevitable that there would be a final struggle between Prussia and Austria for the supremacy.

Immediately after the conclusion of peace Frederick set about putting the country in order to enable it to recover from the terrible loss it had sustained.

Some states were relieved of taxation for a period, big landowners were given free issues of corn to replace that which had been destroyed, and a great deal of money was spent in the erection of new houses to replace those razed to the ground.

The coinage was restored to its proper value, and the Bank of Berlin was founded.

His excise was on French lines, and while the system resulted in a big revenue, there was much corruption by the French officials. This resulted in criticism of the King which he took in good part.

One day, while riding along the Jager Strasse, he came upon a crowd of people.

Turning to the groom, he said : "See what it is."

"They have something posted up about your Majesty," reported the groom.

Riding up to the poster, the King found a caricature of himself in "melancholy guise, seated on a stool, a coffee-mill between his knees, diligently grinding with the one hand, and with the other picking up any bean that might have fallen."

"Hang it lower," said the King. He beckoned his groom and ordered him to lower the poster, "so that they may not have to hurt their necks about it."

The result was exactly as the King had anticipated. The crowd gave him a hearty cheer, tore the caricature into pieces, and as the King rode away cried out : "Frederick for ever."

The King was meticulous in regard to the administration of justice, although he disliked formality.

In one case, described as "the Miller Arnold case," he dismissed the judges and condemned them to a year's fortress arrest because he considered that they had not done justice to a poor man.

He liked to be described as the advocate of the poor, and was greatly pleased at the answer given to him by a miller whose windmill stood on ground which was required for the King's garden.

The miller refused to sell it. "Not at any price ?" suggested the King's agent. "Could not the King take it from you for nothing if he chose ?"

"Have we not the Kammergericht (Court of Appeal) at Berlin ?" was the retort, and this became a popular saying.

Frederick died at Sans Souci on August 17th, 1786, through exposure to rain during a military review. He left Prussia in a much stronger position than when he began to reign.

The Treasury was full and the Army considerably increased in strength.

He was careless of his personal appearance, was somewhat stout and below medium height. During his later years he was content with an old blue military uniform, the breast of which was usually browned with snuff.

Saint Paul's Day

The commemoration of the conversion of St. Paul was one of the most important Church festivals in the Middle Ages. The Apostle was regarded as the patron saint of London.

Tradition relates that St. Paul visited Britain and actually preached to the Druidic worshippers, whose London headquarters were on the site of the present St. Paul's Cathedral on Ludgate Hill. There is no definite proof of this.

It is supposed that the earliest building on this site dedicated to St. Paul was founded by him. On the other hand there is reason to believe that it was in existence before the Christian era, and was originally used either for the worship of Diana or for Druidic services.

In 1316, ox heads, sacred to the goddess Diana, were found during excavations on the south side of St. Paul's. At other times the teeth of boars, and other animals and a piece of buck's horn, with pieces of vessels that might have been used in heathen services, have been discovered.

According to Flete, the Westminster monk, who relates that Londoners returned to the worship of pagan gods during the fifth century : "Then were restored the whole abominations wherever the Britons were expelled their places (by the Saxons). London worships Diana, and the suburbs of Thorney (Westminster) offer incense to Apollo."

Whether St. Paul came to England or not, it is certain that the see of London was in existence in the second century, long before the arrival of St. Augustine. There is no mention until the sixth century, however, of a church of any magnitude on the site of the cathedral dedicated to St. Paul.

St. Paul's Cathedral was apparently a magnificent edifice in the days of William the Conqueror. Some of its valuable possessions were seized by his reckless followers. On the day of his Coronation, however, he granted a charter securing the church's property for ever, and insisted on the restoration of all the stolen property.

The church then in existence had been built by Ethelbert, King of Kent. It was burned down in the later years of the Conqueror, and a new one was begun by Bishop Maurice.

The main building was completed in about a century and

has been described as "so stately and beautiful, that it was worthily numbered among the most famous buildings."

In 1221 a new steeple was finished, and in 1240 a new choir.

It was about this time that the celebration of St. Paul's Day became attended with considerable festivity. In the reign of Henry III (1222) the observance of St. Paul's Day as a holiday was referred to in the Council of Oxford, and a great deal of money for the building of the church was raised by the granting of indulgences.

The subterranean church of St. Faith was begun in 1256, and at last the structure was completed. Thus it remained until the Great Fire of London in 1666.

In the reign of Mary (1555) St. Paul's Day was observed in London with processions. According to an entry in the *Grey Friars Chronicle* :

"On St. Paul's Day there was a procession with the children of all the schools in London, with all the clerks, curates and parsons, and vicars, in copes, with their crosses ; also the choir of St. Paul's ; and divers bishops in their habits, and the Bishop of London, with his pontificals and cope, bearing the sacrament under a canopy, and four prebends bearing it in their grey *amos* ; and so up into Leadenhall, with the mayor and aldermen in scarlet, with their cloaks, and all the crafts in their best array ; and so came down again on the other side, and so to St. Paul's again.

"And then the King, with my lord cardinal, came to St. Paul's and heard masse, and went home again ; and at night great bonfires were made through all London, for the joy of the people that were converted likewise as St. Paul was converted."

During Mary's time, too, a quaint custom was observed. It arose from an undertaking made in 1375 by Sir William Baud when he was permitted to enclose twenty acres of the Dean's land. Baud contracted to present the clergy of the cathedral with a fat buck and doe yearly on the days of the conversion and commemoration of St. Paul.

"On these days" [relates the old chronicler] "the buck and the doe were brought by one or more servants at the hour of the procession, and through the midst thereof, and offered at the High Altar of St. Paul's Cathedral. After which the persons that brought the buck received of the Dean and Chapter at the hands of their Chamberlain, twelve pence sterling for their entertainment ; but nothing when they brought the doe.

"The buck being brought to the steps of the altar, the Dean and Chapter, apparelled in copes and proper vestments with garlands of roses on their heads, sent the body of the buck to be baked, and had the head and horns fixed on a pole before the cross, in their procession round about the church, till they issued at the west door, where the keeper that brought it blowed the death of the buck, and then the horns that were about the city answered him in like manner; for which they had each, of the Dean and Chapter, three and fourpence in money, and their dinner; and the keeper, during his stay, meat, drink, and lodging and five shillings in money at his going away, together with a loaf of bread, having in it the picture of St. Paul."

St. Paul's was associated with many events that did not harmonize with its sacred character. It provided entertainment for the citizens in the shape of plays. If a civil war were pending, or the citizens were called upon to defend themselves against rebels, the people would flock to the church to display their martial spirit and present banners to their champions.

When Louis of France came to London in 1216 to assist the people of England against their own King John, the English barons swore fealty to him in St. Paul's. When Henry VI and Edward IV were fighting for the crown, each went to St. Paul's to declare himself head of the kingdom.

The body of Richard II was displayed to view in the church. If there were a stroke of business to be done, the bargainers would go into St. Paul's Walk in the interior of the Cathedral and settle the matter. The Walk, in fact, became a parade like a seaside promenade. It was here that benefices were sold, lawyers consulted, and payments made for goods supplied.

Thus, during the day, the cathedral was a strange sight.

"At one time," [writes a contemporary historian] "in one and the same rank, yea, foot by foot, and elbow by elbow, shall you see walking the knight, the gull, the gallant, the upstart, the gentleman, the clown, the captain, the appel-squire, the lawyer, the usurer, the citizen, the bankrout, the scholar the beggar, the doctor, the idiot, the ruffian, the cheater, the puritan, the cut-throat, the high men, the low men, the true man and the thief; of all trades and professions some; of all countries some. Thus while Devotion kneels at her prayers, doth Profanation walk under her nose."

c

Australia Day

The average Briton seems to take little interest in the fact that on January 26th, 1788, the first official batch of colonists landed in New South Wales, established the township of Sydney, and thus founded the colony now known as the Commonwealth of Australia.

A few Australian flags will be flown to-day; there will be a commemorative service in St. Clement Danes Church. Beyond that—nothing. One of the brightest days in the calendar of the Empire is almost neglected.

It is 149 years since Australia was founded. Next year perhaps some more notable commemoration will be arranged to celebrate the 150th anniversary.

On May 12th, 1787, a number of vessels known as the "First Fleet" set sail from Plymouth bound for New South Wales. It was a much more ambitious outfit than that which sailed from the same port 167 years before, when about a hundred souls went to colonize America.

In the "First Fleet" were the armed brig *Supply*, the transports *Alexander, Scarborough, Charlotte, Friendship, Lady Penrhyn,* and *Prince of Wales*; and the victualling ships *Borrowdale, Golden Grove,* and *Fishburn,* loaded with tools and supplies.

Primarily the expedition was organized to settle convicts at Botany Bay; but it was not long before this aspect of the scheme was lost in the more important one of adding a new and great country to the British Crown.

The expedition was in command of Captain Arthur Phillip. On arrival at Botany Bay, Phillip was to become captain-general and governor-in-chief of New South Wales. In his ship the *Supply*, in the capacity of lieutenant-governor designate, was Major Robert Ross, in command of 197 marines.

The vessels must have presented an extraordinary spectacle. The decks were crowded with pens containing sheep, hogs, goats, puppies, kids, turkeys, geese, ducks, chickens, pigeons, cattle and horses.

There were 771 convicts, of whom 192 were women and 13 children. There were 252 guards and officials, 210 seamen of the navy, and 223 merchant seamen.

The voyage to Botany Bay took eight months and one

day, and the distance sailed was 15,063 miles. The ships, except by arrangement, had not lost sight of each other for an hour, although nine of them were merely small merchantmen, and they had sailed in unknown waters.

The death rate was low, despite the fact that the ships were crowded and their passengers belonged for the most part to a sickly and unhealthy class.

The success of the expedition was due solely to Phillip, who had insisted upon an adequate supply of good provisions, and who took note of every detail.

In the Historical Records of New South Wales there are many references which purport to be the musings of Phillip, who foresaw something more than a mere convict settlement in Australia. Here are some of them:

"I would not wish convicts to lay the foundations of an empire. . . . The laws of this country will, of course, be introduced in (New) South Wales, and there is one that I would wish to take place from the moment His Majesty's forces take possession of the country: That there can be no slavery in a free land, and consequently no slaves."

The expedition reached Botany Bay on January 18th, 1788, and a party went ashore in command of Phillip. It is recorded that they were met by a number of natives, who responded to his signs of friendship by throwing down the weapons and taking presents of beads and maize.

The low-lying bay was examined and Phillip came to the conclusion that it was unsuitable for a settlement. He therefore left Ross in charge, and set out to examine what was known as Port Jackson, a name given to the place by Captain Cook a few years before.

Phillip's journal records that they came to "a bay or harbour in which there appeared to be a good anchorage," and he selected a cove for landing which he named Sydney Cove, in honour of Lord Sydney, the British Home Secretary.

On his return to Botany Bay on January 24th, he was surprised to find two French ships, the *Boussole* and *Astrolabe*, also on a voyage of discovery. He avoided them, and two days later a party was landed in Sydney Cove. The British flag was unfurled, the guns fired salutes, and toasts were drunk all round. The proclamation of the colony took place on February 7th.

At the outset Phillip found that it was not to be an easy

matter to settle comfortably at Sydney. The soil was poor and there was not enough labour to make the settlement self-supporting. In a letter to the Under-Secretary of the Admiralty, Phillip says : "If fifty farmers were sent out with their families they would do more in one year to render the colony independent of the mother country than a thousand convicts."

In that letter was the first suggestion of an emigrant scheme.

Phillip himself lived in a canvas house he had brought out with him. Later a stone house was built for him in what is now Bridge Street. The other officers had stone houses, and the convicts had log huts plastered. Barracks were built for the soldiers, and a hospital was put up.

The log huts were whitened with pipeclay, large quantities of which were found in the neighbourhood of the cove.

According to early charts of the settlement these first settlers kept close to the cove, the waters of which then reached as far as Bridge Street. The only source of water supply for many years was the Tank Stream.

One of the greatest difficulties was food. Famine was always a possibility during the intervals between the arrival of supplies. In June 1790 starvation seemed certain for the whole community. But help came in the nick of time through the arrival of the *Lady Juliana* from London with a cargo of flour and a consignment of prisoners.

The attitude of the natives was another problem. Phillip did all he could to conciliate them. But small parties of settlers were murdered, and the governor had to send out punitive expeditions, much against his will, to stop the massacres. At the same time he forbade "all persons not expressly ordered out for that purpose ever to fire on any native, except in his own defence, or to molest him in any shape."

Phillip divided the settlement into four sections, and set up courts of civil and criminal jurisdiction, which sometimes brought him into conflict with Ross.

His next move was to establish farms and confer grants of land on various settlers and officers. Phillip, desiring to return to England, embarked on December 11th, 1792, and on arriving home was awarded a pension of £500 for his services.

Phillip died at Bath on August 31st, 1814.

The credit for the settlement and development of Sydney

is due to Phillip. He made the settlement self-supporting by developing agriculture and turning an otherwise disorderly mob into a community of sober and disciplined people.

Between the departure of Phillip from Sydney and the arrival of Lachlan Macquarie in 1810 the growing town was neglected by the authorities and the inhabitants. In August of that year Macquarie issued instructions about the width of streets and the nature of buildings. He divided the town into five separate districts, erected watchhouses, and gave names to the streets, which had hitherto been called "rows."

In September 1788 the population of Sydney was 933. In July 1804 it was nearly 7,000. In 1851 it had risen to 53,924, and in 1925 the city and suburbs held nearly a million people.

Thomas Paine

January 29th, 1937, was the bicentenary of the birth of Thomas Paine, the rationalist and free-thinker, and the man who was partly responsible for the separation of the United States from Britain.

In the year 1774 Tom Paine, to dodge his creditors, went to America. He became editor of the *Pennsylvania Magazine*, which supported the revolutionary principles of young America. For nearly two years he studied the question of the relations between the colonists and the Mother Country. Then he produced his pamphlet, *Common Sense*.

Undoubtedly this work echoed the sentiments of the majority of Americans, but it was the first outspoken declaration of that sentiment. Up to that time, despite the fact that the war had been going on for many months, no man had voiced a policy of separation.

Common Sense went right to the point, and showed in the simplest but strongest language the inevitability of a definite break between the two countries.

Within five months Congress, on the motion of John Adams, declared : "The exercise of all powers of government must be under authority from the people of the colonies, for the maintenance of internal peace, the defence of their lives, liberties and properties, against the hostile invasions and cruel depredations of their enemies"—phrases which seemed to have been lifted from *Common Sense*. General

Washington admitted that the pamphlet worked "a powerful change in the minds of many men."

Paine was the stormy petrel of two revolutions. Not long after the affairs of America had been settled satisfactorily for the colonists, there were rumblings of trouble in France.

When the revolution broke out in that country, Paine stirred up the Paris "citoyens" with his cold logic, and took a leading part in the revolution as a member of the Convention. Finally, falling foul of Robespierre, he escaped the guillotine only with difficulty.

Paine's writings were certainly revolutionary in an intolerant age of Toryism. To-day, however, his famous *Rights of Man*, which sent Edmund Burke into paroxysms of rage at the time of the French Revolution, would be regarded as no more than a mild radical opinion.

He was branded a blasphemer, and was described by contemporary historians as "that foul man Tom Paine."

The political jobber, William Cobbett, called him a "base, malignant, treacherous, unnatural and blasphemous" individual—an admirable example of a pot calling a kettle black.

Thomas Paine was born in Norfolk, and was the son of a Quaker father and a Church of England mother. At the age of seven he records he was already questioning the truths of Christianity.

He was brought up in his father's business of staymaker, but soon left the paternal fireside to try his luck in varied and numerous ventures.

At times he was a privateersman, storekeeper, tobacconist, schoolmaster, exciseman, and political pamphleteer.

In 1766 he was a teacher of English in an academy in Goodman's Fields, Whitechapel. A year later he was at a school at Kensington, and, at the same time, preaching at Moorfields.

He went to Lewes, Sussex, and there joined the Whig Club, becoming one of its cleverest members in debate. He gained a livelihood as exciseman.

Paine got into debt and had to hide from his creditors. Eventually he lost his job through being absent from duty.

By this time Paine had married twice. His first wife died, and his second was separated from him.

He came to London, met Benjamin Franklin, who painted

in rosy hues the possibilities in America. Franklin provided him with letters of recommendation to his son-in-law, Richard Bache, and other leaders of social life across the Atlantic.

For his activity in connection with the American revolution—he actually fought with the colonists—he was rewarded with the post of Secretary of the Committee of Foreign Affairs, and received a grant of 3,000 dollars and an estate near New Rochelle. The states of New York and Pennsylvania also made him monetary awards.

In 1779 Paine was in trouble through publishing State secrets. His estate was forfeited, and he had to resign his post. Later, however, he became clerk of the Pennsylvania legislature, and went with Colonel Laurens to France.

In 1787 Paine came to England, and received a great welcome from the Radicals.

Soon afterwards Edmund Burke published his famous *Reflections* on the French Revolution, to which Paine replied with his *Rights of Man*.

This work was regarded as seditious. Paine wrote : "The heads stuck upon pikes which remained for years upon Temple Bar differed nothing in the horror of the scene from those carried upon pikes in Paris."

One day, while Paine was in a publisher's shop in St. Paul's Churchyard, William Blake, the painter and author of *Jerusalem*, rushed in and cried, "You must not go home or you are a dead man !" A warrant was out for Paine's arrest.

Twenty minutes after Paine had left Dover the warrant arrived there for execution by the officials of the port. He never returned to England.

In 1792 his trial took place in his absence, and he was sentenced to outlawry.

He was elected to the National Convention by the Department of Calais, but when the Girondins fell, Paine was imprisoned by Robespierre.

On the downfall of the "Sea-green Incorruptible," Paine returned to his seat in the Convention, and remained until its adjournment in October 1796.

Before his imprisonment he had published the *Age of Reason*, written from the point of view of a Quaker who did not believe in revealed religion.

Paine returned to America, where he was not at all well received because of an attack he had made on Washington's military policy and other activities. He retired to his estate at New Rochelle, and there he died on June 8th, 1809.

Eight years afterwards Paine's corpse was disinterred by William Cobbett and brought to England. Cobbett judged that there might be money in displaying the mouldering bones of the rationalist. But no one seemed desirous of gazing upon the relics of the author of the *Age of Reason*, and the corpse remained in Cobbett's garret in Bolt Court, Fleet Street, London, for fourteen years, from 1819-33.

Where the bones were finally deposited has never been ascertained.

Hannah More

In Wrington Churchyard, near Bristol, there is a stone slab on which are the names of five sisters. Included is that of Hannah More, the authoress and dramatic writer. All these sisters were endowed with more than ordinary talent, but Hannah was the cleverest of them all.

She was an acquaintance of Dr. Johnson, Oliver Goldsmith, Sir Joshua Reynolds, and Edmund Burke.

The whole career of Hannah More is an example of what can be effected by a woman who was neither high-born nor wealthy, nor beautiful. It is true that her dramas never kept the stage for any length of time. Nor were her poems more than trifles, but her writings on moral and religious subjects gained a world-wide reputation.

She wrote one novel, *Coelebs in Search of a Wife*, which appeared in 1808, and enjoyed such a popularity that Hannah More's share of its publication was £2,000. It ran through twelve editions in as many months.

This novel was written during a period of ill-health. "Never was more pain bound up in two volumes," she herself writes. Although she lived to a great age, she was always delicate and a sufferer. In one of her letters she says that she suffered under more than twenty mortal disorders.

Hannah More was born on February 2nd in 1745 in the hamlet of Fishponds, about four miles from Bristol. Her father inherited "great expectations," as Hannah herself puts it, but he was reduced to a comparatively humble position of master of the Free School at Fishponds.

In 1757 they opened a boarding school at Trinity Square, Bristol, in which Hannah, then 12, and her four sisters were teachers. The family attracted notice, and the school flourished, and eventually became one of the most famous in the west of England.

Hannah produced a poem at the age of 17 called "The Search after Happiness."

In 1777 her tragedy *Percy* was performed at Covent Garden

Theatre, Garrick writing both the prologue and the epilogue, and taking the principal part in the play. Afterwards she wrote other plays, but with indifferent success.

In those days it was a passport to society if one had written even a tolerable poem, and Hannah More soon found herself in the circle of the great writers, actors, and painters, and a correspondent of Horace Walpole.

At the age of 40 Hannah More began to take life seriously. She doubted whether the existence she was leading, though it was blameless, was consistent with Christianity.

At last, in 1786, she withdrew from what she called the world, and she and her sisters spent their time in philanthropic work.

The district around Bristol Hannah described as a "moral desert." Nevertheless, they set to work. Neighbouring farmers had no idea of education. Parents in many cases refused to send their children to school unless they were paid to do so.

But the sisters persevered. Schools were established. The sick and aged were visited. Under Hannah More's system prejudice broke down. Her small establishments for the ailing or the ignorant became large institutions.

In 1800 Hannah More built a house at Barley Wood, near Wrington, and she occupied it for thirty years. In her garden were urns commemorating friendships. One was inscribed, "In grateful memory of long and faithful friendship," to Beilby Porteus, Bishop of London. There was another to John Locke. In 1802 her sisters went to reside with her, and they all remained together until death divided them. Mary died in 1813, Sarah in 1817, and Martha in 1819. Hannah was then left alone.

She had eight servants, who appear to have turned the place in her absence into a house of entertainment, for they spent their mistress's money in orgies that gave Hannah's home a bad reputation. At last she had to leave the neighbourhood and go to Clifton. "I am driven like Eve out of Paradise, but not by angels," she remarked as she left the house for the last time.

In 1788 Hannah More published the first work which indicated her change of habit. It was called *Thoughts on the Manners of the Great*. Three years later she produced *An Estimate of the Religion of the Fashionable World*, and in 1799

Strictures on the Modern System of Female Education. This latter work attracted so much attention that it was said Hannah More was about to be made the governess of the Princess Charlotte of Wales.

This plan was never realized, but in 1805 Hannah published *Hints Towards Forming the Character of a Young Princess.* Her next work was the novel, and in subsequent years her writings included *Practical Piety, Christian Morals,* and *Essays on the Character and Writings of St. Paul.*

Among other claims which Hannah More had to be remembered is that she was one of the earliest writers of tracts for popular circulation, and her *Shepherd of Salisbury Plain* is regarded as one of the best of these.

Hannah's friend, Sir Joshua Reynolds, painted her portrait, which represented her as small and slender with delicate arms and hands, large dark eyes, and a beaming, intelligent countenance. She also sat to other artists, among them Opie, whose portrait is that of a plain woman of middle age.

Hannah More died at Windsor Terrace, Clifton, Bristol, on September 7th, 1833. She left a large fortune. But as she had no relatives and no immediate friends in want, her money went to augment the funds of public charities, particularly those of Bristol.

Hannah More was a confidante of Horace Walpole. The latter was a martyr to gout, and had deposits of chalk in his fingers. "Yet," records Hannah, "neither years nor sufferings can abate the entertaining powers of the pleasant Horace, which rather improve than decay; though he himself says he is only fit to be a milk-woman, as the chalk-stones on his fingers'-ends qualify him for nothing but scoring."

"A finger of each hand has been pouring out a hail of chalk-stones," he tells Hannah; "and the first finger which I hoped exhausted, last week opened again, and threw out a cascade of liquid chalk, exactly with the effort of a pipe that bursts in the streets; the gout followed, and has swelled both hand and arm."

Hannah More was a keen critic of her contemporaries. She writes of her own time:

In vain do we boast of the eighteenth century, and conceitedly talk as if human reason had not a manacle left about her, but that philosophy had broken down all the strongholds of prejudice, ignorance, and superstition; and yet at this very time Mesmer has got a hundred thousand pounds by animal magnetism in Paris, and Mainanduc is getting as much in London.

There is a fortune-teller in Westminster who is making little less. Lavater's physiognomy books sell at fifteen guineas a set. The divining-rod is still considered oracular in many places. Devils are cast out by seven ministers; and to complete the disgraceful catalogue, slavery is vindicated in print, and defended in the House of Peers.

St. Werburgh

Many eligible young Saxons offered their hands and hearts to Werburgh, daughter of Wulfhere, King of the Mercians, but she replied with a blank refusal to them all.

Werbode, a favourite in her father's court, was turned down with scorn. He is the villain in the traditional story of St. Werburgh.

Werburgh, patroness of Chester, was one of the earliest and most celebrated of the Anglo-Saxon saints. She lived in the seventh century and was a moving spirit in the establishment of nunneries in England.

Her father, Wulfhere, had embraced Christianity, but with little enthusiasm. His wife, however, had her daughter educated under the influence of the church.

There were three sons, Wulfhad, Rufinus, and Keured, and Werburgh was the only daughter. The princess had a reputation for sanctity from her childhood and, declaring that she would consecrate her life to the church, she made it clear that she was not in the marriage market.

Werburgh was beautiful, and her resolution was a blow to the young knights in her father's court. Werbode, in particular, was disappointed, for, having her father's approval to his suit, he considered himself betrothed to her. He forthwith began to scheme the downfall of all those opposed to him, including the Queen.

But fate interposed to safeguard Werburgh.

At this period there are said to have been five bishops' sees in Mercia—Chester, Lichfield, Worcester, Lincoln, and Dorchester (Oxfordshire). Lichfield was the nearest to the court of Wulfhere, which was established at Stone, in Staffordshire.

To the see of Lichfield came St. Chad, or Ceadda, who had been appointed Bishop of the Mercians. He built an oratory at a place called Ad Barve, or "At the Wood," where he spent much of his time. One day, while hunting, Wulfhere's sons Wulfhad and Rufinus found him there and, according to the legend, were converted by the conversation of the bishop.

Werbode learned of the visits of the two sons to Chad's headquarters, and went to their father with malicious stories. He obtained an order from the King to put the young men to death.

No sooner was this barbarous act achieved than Werbode was poisoned by an evil spirit, and, it is said, died in a delirium.

King Wulfhere was now overcome with remorse, and became an earnest Christian. With her father's consent, Werburgh became a nun and entered the monastery of Ely, which was in charge of her cousin Etheldreda. Here she became celebrated for piety, and performed many miracles.

In 675, Ethelred, brother of Wulfhere, succeeded to the Mercian throne. He immediately recalled Werburgh from Ely and entrusted to her care the establishment of nunneries in Mercia. With money supplied by the King, she founded establishments at Trentham and Hanbury (near Tutbury), in Staffordshire, and Weedon in Northamptonshire. She controlled them all at the same time.

Werburgh died at Trentham on February 3rd, 699. In her last moments she asked that her body should be buried at Hanbury.

The people of Trentham, ignoring this last request, attempted to obtain possession of the saint's remains with a view to burying them in their own neighbourhood. But once again fate intervened, and the people of Hanbury were able to get possession by a miracle, and carried the body for burial in their church.

During the Danish invasion years afterwards, the body of St. Werburgh was taken for safety to Chester, and placed in the abbey church, now the cathedral. From that time she became the patroness of Chester.

Certain details of the story of St. Werburgh are told both by William of Malmesbury and a Chester monk named Henry Bradshaw. A work by the latter was printed in 1521.

It is written in verse, and it described many posthumous miracles performed by St. Werburgh. One story tells how the dead saint was responsible for putting out a terrible fire that was consuming the City of Chester.

The citizens were powerless. According to Bradshaw:

Some cried for water, and some for hookes dyd call;
Some used other engins by crafte and policy;
Some pulled downe howses afore the fire truly.

But it was in vain until someone thought of the relics of St. Werburgh.

They addressed their prayers to her, and the monks brought out her shrine and carried it in procession through the burning streets. This foresight, says the legend, had the desired effect. The flames immediately began to subside.

In the ninth century a community of secular canons, in honour of St. Werburgh and St. Oswald, was formed at Chester under King Athelstan, and soon grew into note. At the Norman Conquest, William the Conqueror deprived this establishment of much of its lands, and the Norman Earl of Chester, Hugh Lupus, removed it entirely and replaced it by a Benedictine colony from Bec, in Normandy.

He richly endowed the Benedictine brotherhood, and his countess, Ermentruda, and his numerous tenants followed his example.

The abbey became very rich. It possessed much land, manses, chapels, churches, woods, and tithes, with the privileges of fishing with one vessel and ten nets, and all the profits of what was known as the Feast of St. Werburgh.

At this feast, which was held before the abbey gate, were the stalls of merchants, who brought wares imported from all countries. The goods were sold beneath coverings of reeds, which the monks were empowered to collect from the marshes.

Outside the abbey, too, was erected the movable theatre for the performance of the Chester mysteries, said to have been invented by a monk belonging to the abbey. According to old manuscripts relating to these mysteries, still in existence, these plays included twenty-four mysteries representing subjects taken from the Bible.

Malefactors attending the fair were allowed sanctuary for the time being, and could not be arrested unless they committed some new offence. This regulation naturally drew to the fair a rough crowd which, one would have imagined, would be detrimental to the proceedings.

On one occasion, however, it proved of service, and actually saved the city.

Randle the Third, Earl of Chester, was besieged in his castle of Rhudland by a Welsh army, and was in danger of being overwhelmed.

A messenger was despatched to his constable, Robert de Lacy, who was attending the fair. De Lacy collected a numerous body of minstrels, musicians, thieves, and other malefactors, and marched them to the relief of Randle.

It is said that the Welsh saw from a distance this extraordinary army and, not knowing of what it was composed, raised the siege and retreated.

From that time this event was celebrated by a parade of minstrels, a ceremony which continued until the middle of the eighteenth century.

The Trial of John Berry and His Confederates

The middle of the eighteenth century saw an alarming increase in crime. England was enjoying a short spell of peace, and many of those who came back from the war took to burglary, robbery, and forgery for a living.

But there was another factor which swelled the criminal calendar. A method adopted by the magistrates to reduce the number of malefactors actually increased them. Runners, commonly called thief-takers, were appointed to bring in criminals, and these men were paid certain fixed sums in the event of a conviction.

They were not content to carry on their work legitimately. They amassed money by inducing young men to commit crimes, or by bringing false accusations against them and securing convictions by manufactured evidence.

One of the most notorious of these thief-takers was Jonathan Wild, the Bow Street runner. But he had many imitators. One was John Berry, whose activities took place about forty years after Wild.

Berry, who lived in Hatton Garden, Holborn, conspired with James Egan, a shoemaker, Stephen M'Daniel, a publican, and James Salmon, a breeches maker, to accuse innocent people of crime and so secure the rewards offered.

On one occasion they persuaded two victims, named Newman and Marsh, to join them in a highway robbery. The men were executed.

A man named Tyler was met by one of the gang, who said that he would make him a present of a horse, as he had no further use for the animal. Tyler took the horse to an inn in Smithfield, to be looked after until he had a stable for its use.

He was immediately seized by Egan, who took him before the sitting alderman. He was committed to Newgate, and soon afterwards hanged for stealing the horse.

In 1753 they charged a man named Woodland with felony and he was committed and sentenced to death. He was, however, reprieved and transported.

Many others fell victims to these rogues. At last they were discovered and punished.

Running short of money, they were induced to bring into the gang a man named Blee, who was instructed to persuade two boys to join with him in a robbery.

They all met at a public-house called the Sir John Old-castle, in Islington, and arranged for the robbery to be committed at Deptford. The inhabitants of Deptford had offered a reward for the arrest of any highwayman or footpad, in addition to the allowance made by the authorities.

They then separated, and met afterwards at the Bell Inn, Holborn. It was now decided that Salmon should make two pairs of breeches, and put them into a bundle with a distinguishing mark ; that he should have in his pocket a tobacco-box, with his name on the lid, and various other articles that could be readily identified.

It was arranged that he should be robbed by Blee, who had yet to find two willing boys. There proved, however, no difficulty about this.

About nine o'clock on the following Monday morning Blee took the boys to a public-house in Little Britain, where they had bread and cheese and beer. From this place they went to the "Bell" in the Borough. Here the two boys, John Ellis and Peter Kelly, recognized Berry, who was sitting in the bar, as a thief-taker, and mentioned the fact. Blee had difficulty in assuring them they had no cause to fear.

They now went to a house in the Borough Market, where

Blee got the boys drunk, and afterwards they went to Deptford.

While they were in the Ship public-house at Deptford, Salmon came in and pretended to be drunk. He supported himself by the counter, and said that he was going to London.

It was getting dark when Salmon left. A few minutes later Blee and the two boys followed.

They overtook Salmon near a milestone on the London road.

"There is the old breeches-maker that was so drunk at the Ship," whispered Blee. "Let's clean him out."

Kelly asked Salmon what he had under his arm. The latter began to whine, and remarked that he would give them everything if they would leave him alone. He delivered the bundle to Blee, who gave it to Kelly. He handed over his money, which was in a tin box. They then searched his pockets and took his tobacco-box.

Blee took the boys to a lodging-house in Kent Road. In the morning they went to the Spread Eagle in the Borough Market, and Blee left, telling the boys he was going to find an old clothes dealer who would buy the articles they had stolen.

He returned to the public-house with Egan, who offered five shillings for the goods, and gave a shilling on account. Egan then left.

About an hour afterwards M'Daniel appeared and said he had a warrant for the arrest of Ellis and Kelly. He seized the boys and tied them together with rope. Salmon was brought in and identified his belongings. Whereupon the boys were taken before a magistrate at Greenwich, who committed them to Maidstone gaol.

On the way to Maidstone, the boys apparently became friendly with the constable in charge of them, and told him how they had been tricked by Blee.

Inquiries were made, and it was soon found that Blee and M'Daniel were acquainted. Blee was arrested, and before the magistrate at Greenwich confessed to the whole transaction.

The trial of the two boys was allowed to go on, and Berry, Salmon, M'Daniel and Egan appeared as witnesses. Immediately after the jury had pronounced a verdict of guilty the whole four were arrested. Confronted with Blee they stoutly maintained that the whole story was a fabrication. Later, however, each asked to be allowed to stand as evidence for the crown, but the police deemed that the testimony of Blee was sufficient to secure their conviction.

They were brought to London and charged with being accessories before the fact. This charge failed on an interpretation of the law, and a further charge of conspiracy was brought.

They were found guilty at the Old Bailey and were sentenced to be punished as follows : Berry and M'Daniel to stand on the pillory, once at the end of Hatton Garden in Holborn, and once at the end of King Street, Cheapside ; Salmon and Egan were to stand once in the middle of West Smithfield, and the second time at the end of Fetter Lane, Fleet Street. All were to be imprisoned in Newgate for seven years and at the end of that time, to find sureties for £1,000 each for their behaviour for the following seven years.

M'Daniel and Berry were severely treated by the crowd when they appeared on the pillory, and the reception accorded to Egan and Salmon in West Smithfield was one of the severest ever known from London people. After about half an hour of pelting from the enraged mob, Egan died. The sheriffs then thought it time to remove M'Daniel, who was taken to Newgate.

All three survivors, however, had been so roughly handled that they soon died in prison.

Holloway Prison

Strangers who pass along Camden Road, London, regard with curiosity a large building which looks like a medieval castle.

It is, indeed, a copy of Warwick Castle, but it is neither old nor romantic. It is just a prison—Holloway prison for women convicts from all over England. It holds about 400 women, but it is seldom, if ever, full.

Every class of woman offender is sent to Holloway. Within this prison walls are white-haired old women and others young and attractive ; some are in for serious offences, others for simple misdemeanours.

Holloway has not always been a women's prison. It

was originally built as a house of correction, known as the City Prison, for male and female prisoners sentenced at the Old Bailey and the Mansion House or Guildhall justice rooms.

It was also the debtors' prison for London and Middlesex.

It originated from the old Giltspur Street Compter, a debtors' prison and a house of correction which stood near St. Sepulchre's Church, Holborn. The Compter was pulled down in 1855. Meanwhile Holloway Prison had been opened on February 6th, 1852.

Holloway Prison was built in 1850 on land originally bought by the City Corporation as a cemetery during the cholera epidemic of 1832, and it has an area of ten acres. The boundary walls of the prison are nearly 20 ft. high, and built in the castellated style which gives them an imposing appearance. There are strongly fortified gateways, and the embattlement extends throughout all the wings, which are six in number.

In the middle of last century the prisoners were employed in various ways according to a mixture of the separate and associated systems.

The architect of this "castle" was Mr. J. B. Bunning; the prison cost £105,000 to build.

It is fire-proofed, ventilated by a 150 ft. shaft, and is supplied with water from an artesian well carried 300 ft. down into the chalk. On each side of the gatehouse are buildings of red brick with stone dressings, which serve as residences for the governor of the prison and the chaplain.

The gateway tower resembles the approach to a grand medieval castle. It was built after a model of the principal front of Warwick Castle.

On the right of the entrance is the wing originally devoted to women prisoners only, nearly a hundred being confined there at one time. Twenty years after the prison was built the number of women had considerably diminished.

On the other side of the doorway is a lofty hall. This was used as a reception room for prisoners; on the left of the hall is a room in which prisoners were weighed and registered. Here also were kept photographs of all the prisoners confined in Holloway, with the details of their crimes.

At the end of a corridor are the four principal wings, lettered A, B, C, and D. One was set apart for prisoners never before convicted ; another held tradesmen, mechanics and persons who had hitherto been in a respectable position in life. A third wing was confined to prisoners convicted of petty offences, and the fourth was used for old "lags."

There were 349 cells, 289 for men and 60 for women. Sixty others were set apart for "debtors."

The water for the prison was pumped from the well by a treadwheel.

In those early days the prisoners were engaged in brick-making in the grounds at the rear. They were allotted a certain task to perform during the day. If they exceeded this amount of work they were allowed to participate in the profits of their labour.

About twenty years after the prison was built a report was published on its administration. It showed that the number of prisoners admitted in 1874 was 1,572. The greatest number in the prison at one time was 275 men and 35 women.

It was disclosed that the prison was partly self-supporting. Mat-making had realized £1,225, oakum-picking £111, brick-making £442, and gardening and pig-breeding £83. Shoemakers and tailors earned £43, and other industries produced £52.

The prisoners worked from 5.30 in the morning to 8 o'clock in the evening. Out of this period one hour was set aside for exercise, one hour for chapel service, and two hours for meals. During the year under review seven prisoners had proved refractory and had to be put in irons, and eighty men and one woman had to be placed in the dark cells.

Two services were held in the chapel every Sunday, and one on Good Friday and Christmas Day. Uneducated male prisoners received two hours' education weekly in classes, and in certain cases special instruction in their cells. The women received four hours' instruction weekly.

All this, of course, is now changed. There are now classes for the women nearly every night, and there is a singing and dramatic class. Some of the prisoners are allowed to cook for the other inmates. The labour is divided according to the state of health of the prisoner. The weak get sewing ; others work in the laundry, or make clothing for the Borstal boys ; others scrub and clean.

The appearance of the women prisoners in Holloway differs little from that of the inmates of Poor Law institutions, except that they are always neater. All the women wear the same kind of clothes—white caps with frills, and blue or grey cotton dresses.

The average number of women in Holloway is now about 300, and the number of girls has been reduced to less than a dozen. This reduction in the inmates of Holloway is due, of course, to the probation system, for the vast majority of girls charged at police courts are never sent to gaol.

The Portland Vase

On February 7th, 1845, an act of vandalism occurred in the British Museum which shocked the art world.

The beautiful Portland Vase, with a history dating back to the beginning of the Christian era and possibly earlier, was smashed in a fit of frenzy by a man named William Lloyd.

The attendants heard a crash as they were conducting people out of the museum just before closing time. Rushing up they found the vase and its glass case lying on the floor in fragments.

The vase was reputed to be worth thousands of pounds, some estimates of its value reaching six figures.

It belonged to the Duke of Portland, who had lent it to the museum.

Generally believed to have come out of a sarcophagus discovered in the sixteenth century near Rome, it was made of wonderful dark blue glass, with opaque white glass figures decorating the outside.

For a century it rested in Barberini Palace, and for that reason was often known as the Barberini Vase.

In subsequent years it changed hands several times before it ultimately reached the British Museum.

Through a legal anomaly the man who had caused the catastrophe could not be proceeded against for smashing the vase. He was prosecuted for breaking the glass case in which the vase was enclosed.

Lloyd was fined £3, and being unable to pay the fine

went to prison. A few days later someone paid the fine and he was released.

Now, without a close scrutiny, it is difficult to tell that the vase was ever in pieces, for it was put together with remarkable skill by Mr. Doubleday, of the British Museum.

The age of the vase is not definitely known, but it is believed to have been fashioned years before the legions of Julius Caesar overran this country.

A comparison between the vase and specimens recovered from Pompeii indicates a similarity.

The sarcophagus in which the relic is supposed to have been found was in an underground chamber under the Monte del Grano, and two and a half miles from Rome. A cast of the sarcophagus is in the British Museum, the original being in a museum in Rome.

The wooden coffin is decorated with pictures illustrating the story of Achilles, and from the headdress of a female figure it is assumed that the period belongs to that of the Severi, about A.D. 200, and that the tomb was that of Alexander Severus and his mother Mammea.

In this sarcophagus, according to general belief, the vase was discovered, full of ashes, but, although it is certain that the coffin was found in 1582, there is no certainty that the vase was in it.

Until the close of the eighteenth century the vase was an ornament in the Barberini Palace, and then was bought by Sir William Hamilton, who disposed of it in 1785 to the Duchess of Portland.

It was placed in the British Museum by the fourth Duke of Portland in 1810.

It is said that the Barberini family were compelled to sell it because of a bad run of luck at cards by the then head of the family.

James Byres, the antiquary, had the vase in his possession a short time before it was acquired by Sir William Hamilton, and it was then that a mould was made of it. Sixty casts were taken, which were sold at ten guineas each.

There appears to have been some secrecy regarding the purchase of the vase by the Duchess of Portland.

Horace Walpole was somewhat exercised about its disappearance, for when, after the death of the Duchess, its location was known, he wrote to the Countess of Upper

Ossory telling her that the vase, "which had disappeared with so much mystery, is again discovered, not in the tomb, but in the treasury of the Duchess of Portland."

In a further letter to the Countess he described the Duchess as "a simple women, but perfectly sober, and intoxicated only by *empty* vases."

After the death of the Duchess the vase was sold by auction and bought by the third Duke of Portland for 980 guineas.

It was described in the sale catalogue as follows :

Lot 4155.—The most celebrated antique vase, or Sepulchral Urn, from the Barberini Cabinet, at Rome. It is the identical urn which contained the ashes of the Roman Emperor Alexander Severus and his mother, Mammea, which was deposited in the earth about the year 235, after Christ, and was dug up by order of Pope Barberini, named Urban VIII, between the years 1623 and 1644. The materials of which it is composed emulate an onyx, the ground a rich, transparent, dark amethystine colour, and the snowy figures which adorn it are in base-relief, of workmanship above all encomium, and such as cannot but excite in us the highest idea of the arts of the ancients.

The vase was offered for sale in London in May 1929 by the Duke of Portland, and was withdrawn after a final bid of 29,000 guineas.

Bishop Hooper

A few years before his martyrdom, John Hooper, Bishop of Gloucester, wrote to his friends on the Continent :

The last news of all I shall not be able to write. For there, where I shall take most pains there shall ye hear of me to be burnt to ashes . . . and that shall be the last news, which I shall not be able to write unto you, but you shall hear it of me !

It was a tragically correct forecast, for Hooper was burned at the stake in the presence of the people of his own see.

Hooper can be regarded as the first Nonconformist. In

addition to his hatred of Popery, he was uncompromising in his objection to certain ritual in the Protestant church. His consecration as Bishop of Gloucester was almost prevented by his refusal to wear the episcopal robes, particularly the rochet. He also refused to take the Oath of Supremacy in the terms in which it was couched.

His puritan friends, Bucer and Peter Martyr, as well as Cranmer and Ridley, tried to persuade him to give way, but it was not until he found himself in the Fleet Prison, London, that he consented to a compromise.

His consecration as bishop took place in March 1551. Gloucester was such a poor see, "a pittance for so great a clerk," that in the following year he was also declared Bishop of Worcester, and Hooper laboured in the two dioceses, out of the revenues of which "he pursed nothing, and in his palace was a daily dinner for so many poor people in succession."

Hooper was born in Somersetshire about the year 1495, and was educated at Oxford. He took his degree at Merton in 1519. According to some writers he joined the Cistercian monastery at Cleeve in his native county, but appears gradually to have accepted reformed beliefs.

The controversy regarding the old faiths attracted the inquiring nature of Hooper, and in a letter to a friend on the Continent he records how the writings of the Reformation scholars were inducing in his mind a feeling of doubt.

When Hooper became chaplain to Sir Thomas Arundel, the latter sent him to Bishop Gardiner of Winchester for what was described as "theological adjustment."

Gardiner was the last man to whom Hooper should have been sent, for he was one of the most bigoted of the Catholics. As was to be expected, he failed to convert his pupil. He commended Hooper's learning, but "bore in his breast a grudging stomach against Master Hooper."

Hooper ultimately fled to France, where he became a still more ardent Protestant.

Two years after the accession of Edward VI, he returned to England and became Bishop of Gloucester. He distinguished himself by his eloquent preaching, his zeal against Popery and his superintendence of the schools.

An old chronicler writes of him : "He left neither pains untaken nor ways unsought, how to train up the flock of

Christ in the Word of Salvation, continually labouring in the same. He was impartial to all men, as well rich as poor. . . . In every corner of his house was some smell of virtue."

But Gardiner had not forgotten his stubborn pupil.

Edward VI died in 1553, and the Roman Catholic Church was re-established under Queen Mary.

Hooper was now one of the first to be questioned about his faith. He was ordered to go to London for trial. He refused, saying : "I am called to this place and vocation, and I am thoroughly persuaded to live and die with my sheep."

Soon he was seized and taken to London.

On January 28th, 1555, Hooper was brought before Bishop Gardiner, with Rogers, Vicar of St. Sepulchre's, London ; Rowland Taylor, Vicar of Hadleigh, Suffolk ; Saunders, Vicar of All Hallows, Bread Street, London ; and Bradford, a Prebendary of St. Paul's.

They were put through a gruelling examination on the questions of transubstantiation and the Pope's supremacy. All gave unsatisfactory replies.

Again Hooper was thrust into the Fleet Prison. There his bed is described as "a little pad of straw, with a rotten covering."

He remained in confinement for six months, but stead-fastly refused to give way. Then he was deprived of his bishopric.

Early in 1555, the fires of martyrdom were kindled and Bishop Gardiner, the chief persecutor of the "heretics," con-demned Hooper with the other stubborn clerics.

Hooper had expected to face the flames side by side with Rogers ; but the latter went to his martyrdom first at Smith-field. On the following morning Hooper began his journey to Gloucester, where he was to die.

Three days afterwards, at night, he was led through the streets of his own city. It may have been intended to spare him the publicity. If that were the case, his captors must have been surprised at the number of citizens who stood silently watching him pass.

The sixty-year-old priest walked painfully into the house appointed for his temporary prison, for sciatica had seized his legs.

On February 4th, he was formally degraded of his offices,

and at eight o'clock on the morning of February 9th, he was conducted to the scene of his martyrdom.

The stake had been placed close to the end of the cathedral in which his voice had been so frequently heard.

It was market-day; but market-sellers deserted their stalls, and the beasts in their pens, neglected by their keepers, were startled into mournful cries by the huge crowd that had gathered.

It is said that no less than 7,000 people were present to see the last moments of their bishop.

Hooper walked slowly through the streets to the market-place. The sciatica pains had increased, and he was no longer able to walk without the aid of his staff. Yet he contrived to maintain a serenity at which the people marvelled.

Hooper was forbidden to speak under a threat of having his tongue cut out.

They led him to the pole and shackled him. He knelt and prayed.

Then they thrust a box in front of him which contained a scroll with a Royal pardon.

To stoop and pick up the box would have saved him from the flames. But Hooper merely glanced at it, and shook his head.

The flaming torch was brought. But all efforts to light the faggots were unavailing.

"Bring dry faggots!" cried his persecutors. For the others were too green or had become damp through exposure to the weather. New ones were brought.

At last they were kindled, and a huge volume of smoke obscured the martyr from the eyes of the crowd.

Then the smoke was wafted away by a strong breeze, and Hooper was seen moving his lips in prayer. Gradually the flames rose to his legs.

"Good people, give me more fire, for Christ's sake!" exclaimed the tormented bishop.

A boisterous wind now sprang up and fanned the flames. Says the old historian: "He died as quietly as a child in his bed."

Hooper was the author of many treatises, and is described as "a tolerable philosopher but better theologist."

The quarrel which Hooper began in connection with vestments prevailed for centuries.

The Exploits of William Parsons

Towards the close of the year 1750, the London-Windsor road was the scene of the operations of an intrepid highwayman, named William Parsons. The exploits of Dick Turpin, so exaggerated in fiction, were as nothing compared with those of Parsons.

He was an educated man of good family. When ultimately he was "turned off" at Tyburn on February 11th, 1751, he had crowded more adventure into his short life of 34 years than any other highwayman of his time.

The tragedy behind the ruin of his life was his father's indifference to the welfare of his son.

Young William took the first downward step while at Eton College. It was the petty theft of a copy of Pope's *Homer*, which he filched from a bookseller named Pote. Although disgraced, William was not expelled. His father, however, never forgave him and, convinced that his boy would be a rogue all his life, in the absence of stern discipline, sent him to sea.

Parson's ship, under sailing orders for Jamaica, was detained at Spithead. Rankling under what he believed to be injustice, the lad deserted and made his way to Bishop's Waltham, ten miles from Portsmouth.

He ingratiated himself into the society of the place, fell in love with the daughter of a physician and secured her promise to marry him.

But this little romance reached the ears of Sir William Parsons, his father, who hurried to Bishop's Waltham and stopped the match. He railed at the boy, but an uncle who had accompanied Sir William induced young Parsons to return to his ship.

In due course the vessel arrived at Jamaica, where William promptly deserted, shipped himself on a man-of-war, and returned to England. His first act was to go to Bishop's Waltham.

By this time his father had determined to have nothing further to do with his son, but when William reached the house of the girl he was surprised to find his uncle there. The uncle had kept an account of William's movements.

Once more William was dragged from the arms of his lady love.

His uncle secured him an appointment as midshipman in H.M.S. *Romney*, bound for Newfoundland. On his return to England William learned that his relative, the Duchess of Northumberland, had revoked her will in his favour.

When this news came to the ears of the rich friends of his family William found himself repulsed by everyone except a certain Mr. Bailey, who endeavoured to effect a reconciliation between son and father. To some extent he succeeded, and again William was sent abroad.

He obtained an appointment under the Governor of Fort James, on the River Gambia, but he had not been there more than six months before he disagreed with Governor Aufleur and declared his intention of returning to England.

The Governor instructed the guards to prevent his leaving. Notwithstanding, Parsons hid aboard a home-bound vessel.

When Parsons arrived in England his uncle invited him to stay at his house. There he remained for three months, until a woman servant complained of his attentions and he had to leave.

Thrown on his own resources he slept in a hay-loft in Chancery Lane and lived by begging.

At the beginning of the winter his father came to London, and William called on him to ask for forgiveness. But his stepmother declared that she would not have him in the house.

He went into St. James's Park, intending to throw himself into the pond. Suddenly, however, he thought of a ruse to obtain money.

Pretending that he was entitled to a legacy, he called on several shopkeepers and obtained credit for clothes. With these assets he managed to get into gay company.

Soon his creditors began to press him. He was saved from ruin by meeting a young woman who had lately received a bequest of a large sum of money. He made love to her, and the marriage took place on February 10th, 1740. Parsons was then twenty-three.

His relations were now satisfied with the connection he had made, and appeared to forgive him the past.

A few weeks after the marriage he secured an appointment as ensign in the 34th Regiment of Foot, and discharged his debts.

He occupied a luxurious house in Poland Street, where

he resided for two years, during which time two children were born.

From this time all might have been well with Parsons, had he not lived in a style far beyond his means. He kept three saddle-horses, a chaise and pair and several unnecessary servants, and frequented gaming houses.

He was promoted to lieutenant and was sent to France. But he was accompanied by a notorious gambler whom he believed to be a friend. He got into further debt, and was forced to sell his commission.

On his return to England, his creditors pressed him, and he was forced to adopt an alias—Captain Brown. They discovered his hiding place, but he managed to get on board the *Dursely* privateer as a captain of marines.

His service was of short duration. Becoming ill he was landed. His means were soon exhausted and he drew bills of exchange on three merchants in London, on which he raised £60. Forging the signature of a London alderman, he obtained £100 from a merchant at Plymouth.

He had now definitely embarked on a career of crime. With a woman accomplice, whom he represented as an heiress, he applied to a clergyman to be married. The ceremony was about to begin at an hotel where the couple were staying, when Parsons discovered he had forgotten the ring. He obtained one by misrepresentation from a jeweller in the town. Then he and the woman decamped, leaving the clergyman awaiting their return.

Parson's exploits now followed one another with great rapidity. Among them was a fraud on a military officer, which netted the rogue £40 and a horse which he sold in Smithfield.

He then began to accept bribes for laying information against Jacobites. Several inoffensive gentlemen were punished, two losing their military commissions.

Among his frauds was the counterfeiting of a draft in the name of the Duke of Cumberland for £500, another on Sir Joseph Hankey and Co. for £500. A widow, named Bottomley, was robbed of military hats worth £60 which Parsons sold to a Jew for £30.

The authorities were now close at his heels. Fearing arrest, he managed to get himself taken into custody as a person disaffected to the king, which kept him in the house of a king's messenger for eighteen months.

He next went to Holland and remained several months. On coming back to London he was fortunate in a series of gambling bouts and made enough money to last him a year.

He soon resumed his career of crime, however, but was caught with a forged draft, and was convicted at Rochester Assizes. He was sentenced to transportation for seven years. He served as a slave in Maryland, but was released through the intervention of a man who took him into his house.

He repaid this kindness by stealing a horse. For several weeks he held up people on the road, and, having obtained sufficient money for his passage to London, he sailed to England.

He hired a horse, rode to Hounslow Heath, and began his career as a highwayman. His exploits during the next few months caused a sensation. All efforts to capture him were in vain. His description was circulated all over the home counties. For several years, however, he made regular appearances on the roads.

At last he was caught. His father endeavoured to secure a pardon without result, and Parsons was hanged at Tyburn on February 11th, 1751 for returning from transportation.

Benvenuto Cellini

No man ever applauded himself so much as Benvenuto Cellini.

If the stories he tells in his autobiography are true we see a picture of an individual, unscrupulous, immoral, and bombastic.

He had an amazing egotism which runs through the pages of this work. He exaggerates his own bravery and introduces incidents of self-heroism which never could have occurred.

He gives himself a halo by insinuating that he was a special ward of the angels.

Giovanni Cellini, and his wife Maria Lisabetta Granacci, had been married eighteen years before they had a child. Then three were born in quick succession. Giovanni did not mind if the third were a boy or a girl. When it proved to be a boy he named it Benvenuto (Welcome).

Benvenuto was a wilful boy. His father desired him

to follow his own profession of musician and maker of musical instruments.

At fifteen, Benvenuto decided to do nothing of the kind. He preferred design and metal work.

Old Cellini gave way, and his son was apprenticed to a goldsmith.

Already Benvenuto had established himself in his native place as a formidable youth by taking part in a fight with a number of companions. He was banished to Siena, where he worked for Francesco Castoro, another goldsmith. Thence he went to Bologna and continued in the same craft.

After a visit to Pisa, he ran away to Rome at the age of nineteen. He set up in business. His first production was a silver casket, and his second some silver candlesticks.

The Bishop of Salamanca ordered a vase. This was executed with such skill that it drew the attention of the Pope, Clement VII.

There is still in the Vienna Museum the gold medallion "Leda and the Swan," cut in hard stone, which Benvenuto sculptured soon afterwards.

It was about this time that trouble occurred in Rome. The city was attacked by the Constable de Bourbon, and Cellini, with a gang of young Italian bloods, supported the Pope.

In his autobiography Cellini does not forget to claim a big share for the defeat of the Bourbon. He declares that it was he who shot the French leader.

According to his account cauldrons of molten metal were poured upon the heads of the attackers at his instigation. He, too, was responsible for the preparation of the arquebuses which shot down the invaders.

These exploits in Rome resulted in a reconciliation with the magistrates of Florence who had exiled him, and he was able to return to his native place.

He began work on some gold medals, including "Hercules and the Nemean Lion" in gold repousse work, and "Atlas Supporting the Sphere" in chased gold.

Later he returned to Rome, where he found conditions more to his liking. But he was soon again in trouble and fought many duels.

Following an affray with a notary, Ser Benedetto, he had to bolt from Rome.

A number of cardinals used their influence to get him a pardon on the elevation of Paul III to the pontifical throne. He was reinstated into favour.

He had to leave Rome again through the plotting of a natural son of the Pope, but it was not long before he was back in favour.

Francis I of France invited Cellini to Paris to carry out certain work. He took a house at Fontainebleu and remained in France for some time.

Returning to Rome at the age of thirty-seven, he was imprisoned on a charge of having stolen during the war gems from the pontifical tiara. He had spent a period in prison in the Castle of Sant' Angelo and then escaped.

He was captured and treated with great severity, daily expecting to meet death on the scaffold.

Powerful friends interceded and eventually he was released. He went again to France, where he became involved in political intrigues. He believed the Duchess d'Etampes to be working against him at the Court of Francis I, and though he frequently sought revenge he found it a more difficult matter to get rid of his enemies in France than it had been in Rome.

After five years he returned to Florence, and produced some of his best work.

He soon fell foul of Baccio Bandinelli, a rival sculptor, who accused him of immoralities. This was not a new charge. Cellini does not apologize for the way in which he treated some of his models. On the contrary, he relates some of these incidents with gusto.

One day he found his model Caterina in the arms of one of his friends, Pagolo Miccieri. Cellini drew his sword and clutched the man by the throat.

Then he called a notary and insisted that the couple should be married at once.

Cellini's autobiography is a work of strange adventures, stories of love affairs that are sometimes revolting, and of murders committed with complacency.

There are stories of the practice of the Black Arts, of a legion of devils which he and another evoked in the Colosseum after one of his numerous mistresses had run away back to her mother.

He asserts that once he found an extraordinary halo of

light surrounding his head, and saw visions of angels who assured him of their protection. ·

Cellini began to write his autobiography in 1558. During the war with Siena he was appointed to strengthen the defences of Florence.

He died unmarried at Florence on the 13th of February, 1576. All along he had supported a widowed sister and her six daughters.

One of Cellini's grandest works is his famous bronze "Perseus With Head of Medusa," in the Loggia dei Lanzi, Florence.

James and Horace Smith

When Drury Lane Theatre was rebuilt in 1812, following a fire that destroyed the old building, there appeared an advertisement in the newspapers offering a prize of money for a poem to celebrate the occasion.

Among those who sent in efforts were James and Horace Smith, who immediately found themselves famous. The idea had occurred to these brothers that they should write a collection of poems, imitating all the leading poets of the time. James wrote the imitations of Wordsworth, Southey, Coleridge, Crabbe and Cobbett; and Horace wrote those of Byron, Scott, Moore, Monk Lewis, and Fitzgerald.

There was sarcasm, humour and pathos in these productions. But not one of the poets parodied took offence. On the contrary they were all pleased and, having all these great men behind them, the Smith brothers became "lions" at once.

Crabbe, always a temperamental man, was the only one to criticize the Smiths, but his criticism was mild. "There is a little ill-nature—and I take the liberty of adding, undeserved ill-nature—in their prefactory address; but in their versification they have done me admirably."

The Smith brothers were a modest couple. They had no intention of revelling in society. They had no literary vanity, and they shrank from the eyes of admirers.

When the well-known society hostess Lady Cork wrote to them and requested their presence at her evening entertainment, James Smith wrote expressing their regrets. They could not possibly accept the invitation, he said, for his brother Horace had engaged to grin through a horse's collar at a country fair; while he, himself, was due to dance a hornpipe at Sadler's Wells Theatre that same night.

The brothers were the sons of a successful attorney, who became Solicitor to the Ordnance, and who discouraged the early tendencies of James and Horace towards literature. James, born on February 16th, 1775, went into his father's office and succeeded him as Solicitor to the Ordnance. Horace became a successful stockbroker. In his youth he was a friend of the poet Shelley.

Both young men contributed to periodicals, and in 1807, when he was twenty-eight, Horace even published a novel called *Horatio*. It was not until 1812, however, that they became famous for their *Rejected Addresses*.

The poems were supposed to be the productions of unsuccessful competitors for the Drury Lane prize, and they were to be spoken at the opening of the theatre. The address actually spoken, however, was written by Lord Byron.

The *Rejected Addresses* went through twenty editions up to the middle of last century.

James Smith was contented with this triumph, and never put his pen to anything elaborate afterwards, but he continued to contribute to periodicals. Horace remarks that James was "fond of his ease," and never courted further popularity. Horace, on the other hand, became a man of letters.

James wrote a number of pieces for the comedian, Matthews, who used to say of him : "He is the only man who can write clever nonsense." James lived among the wits, particularly those associated with the drama, but, as one of his friends remarked, "He ever preserved the dignity of the English gentleman from merging in the professional gaiety of the jester." His humour was always friendly and without sarcasm or satire.

Horace eventually became an author by profession. He had a quaint and humble way of dealing with editors. The following is a specimen of one of his letters regarding a rejected manuscript :

I am sorry you should deem the smallest apology necessary for returning my MS., a duty which every editor must occasionally exercise towards all his contributors. From my domestic habits and love of occupation I am always scribbling, often without due con-

sideration of what I am writing, and I only wonder that so many of my frivolities have found their way into print.

With this feeling, I am always grateful towards those who save me from committing myself, and acquiesce very willingly in their decisions. In proof of this I will mention a fact of which I am rather proud. Mr. Colburn had agreed to give me £500 for the first novel I wrote, and had announced its appearance, when a mutual friend, who looked over the MS., having expressed an unfavourable opinion of it, I threw it on the fire, and wrote "Brambletye House" instead. Let me not omit to mention, to the credit of Mr. C., that, upon the unexpected success of that work, he subsequently presented me with an additional £100.

Between 1825 and his death in 1849, Horace Smith published several novels. The best of them is *Brambletye House*.

It was said of Horace and James that "One was a good man, the other a good fellow."

Neither brother was rich, James as Solicitor to the Board of Ordnance could never have amassed money. His whole capital amounted to about £3,000 which he invested in an annuity, and then died three months after it was bought.

Horace was twice married. He left a daughter by his first wife and two daughters by his second. He lived at Brighton during the later years of his life and was seldom seen in London.

He was always generous, and it is recorded that he once helped Leigh Hunt with a sum of money when he was pressed by his creditors. But Shelley, his friend, who had pleaded with Horace on behalf of Leigh Hunt, never realized that the money given to Hunt was nearly all Horace Smith's little capital.

During the later years of his life James Smith was an invalid, and when he attended the "evenings" at the house of Lady Blessington, the leading hostess of the time, he wheeled himself about the room in an invalid chair. He was in perpetual pain, but nevertheless made himself agreeable and pleasant to all the guests, and never lost the merry twinkle in his eyes.

James died on December 24th, 1839, in the 65th year of his age, and he was buried under the vaults of St. Martin's Church, London. Horace died on July 12th, 1849, aged 69, and was buried in the churchyard of Trinity Church, Tunbridge Wells, where a gravestone inscription testifies to his benevolence.

James lived at No. 18, Austin Friars, in the City of London. After he had been many years a resident there, another James Smith came to live in the same building. The second-comer called on the author and suggested that, to prevent inconvenience, one or the other should leave, and hinted that he would like to stay.

"No," said James, "I am James the First, you are James the Second; you must abdicate."

Towards the end of his life James lived in Craven Street, Strand, which then, as now, was tenanted by solicitors's offices. A friend who called on James noticed that the street gave a view of the Thames, and propounded the following epigram referring to the river and the solicitors :

"Fly, honestly, fly to some safer retreat,
For there's craft in the river and craft in the street."

To which James retorted quickly that there was no need for honesty to make such a sudden exodus, for

"The lawyers are just at the top of the street,
And the barges are just at the bottom."

There is no memoir of Horace Smith, but he wrote a biography of his brother, James, to preface an edition of the latter's collected writings.

Russian Gunpowder Plot

On February 17th, 1905, the Grand Duke Sergius of Russia was murdered. On the same day twenty-four years before, Tsar Alexander II and his family were nearly killed by a bomb which exploded in the Winter Palace, St. Petersburg.

Within a month after the latter event the Tsar was killed as he was driving in his carriage.

All these events were associated with revolutionary activity that lasted from the year 1880 to 1905, when the revolution came to a head.

Alexander II succeeded to the throne in 1855 on the

death of his father, Tsar Nicholas. As Alexander was known to be pacific, it was expected that he would refrain from attempts to enlarge the frontiers of his country, and Europe fully expected a change of the aggresive policy of the previous emperor.

Instead, he immediately issued a proclamation in which he declared his intention of following in his father's footsteps and continuing the Crimean War. Finally, he was compelled to make a humiliating peace.

The people of Russia began to clamour for reforms. They instanced the cases of the western nations and demanded similar constitutions. It seemed that for the first time in history public opinion was unanimous.

This enthusiasm for reform even affected the Emperor himself, and, after a short period of consideration, he began a series of drastic reforms. One of the most important of these was the emancipation of the serfs. Others, regarded by most people as of equal importance, were the reorganization of the administration of the law and the institution of proper local government.

All these were quickly accomplished. The serfs were no longer subject to tyrannous landlords, and civil and criminal law courts on French lines were introduced. Means were also taken to develop the great resources of the country. Europe had a vision of Russia at last awakening from her traditional sleep. But nothing of that kind occurred.

Corruption and abuses soon reappeared. Industrial enterprises did not seem to be able to make headway. The Press, which had been given full liberty, now took every licence.

Alexander now dropped his efforts, and the Government made it clear that the period of reforms had come to an end. There was an immediate outcry from young Russians of good families. At first it was confided to students, but gradually secret associations were formed and the police had to interfere.

But the propaganda continued with no great success until the agitators made an appeal to the poorer classes, and spread rumours to the effect that the landlords had refused to carry out the reforms laid down by the Tsar.

A secret terrorist tribunal was formed; many well-known officials were condemned to death, and in some cases the sentences were carried out. These acts of terrorism had the opposite to the desired effect, and repeated attempts were made to assassinate Alexander.

On February 17th, 1880, an explosion occurred in a guardroom filled with dynamite and gun-cotton under the dining-room of the Winter Palace at St. Petersburg. The Tsar and family escaped through being a little late for dinner. Eleven soldiers were killed and forty-seven wounded.

A revolutionary named Hartman who had a house near the palace was arrested in Paris three days later, and four days later St. Petersburg was placed under military rule.

Hartman was expelled from France and took refuge in England. In the following May a trial of several Nihilists took place. In November some of them were condemned to death and others imprisoned for the explosion at the Palace.

Notwithstanding the terrorism Alexander was willing again to consider reforms and had approved a new plan on the morning of March 13th, 1881. That afternoon, however, he was assassinated.

The next emperor, Alexander III, was a reactionary. He refused to grant any new liberties and those already arranged were curtailed.

The revolutionary movement reached its worst phase following the disasters of the war with Japan in 1904. On July 14th of that year the Minister of the Interior, named Plehve, was assassinated. A meeting of local councils was now held, and it was decided to approach the Tsar for the reform of the whole Russian system, and for the institution of a representative national assembly.

The deputation laid their views before Prince Mirski, the new Minister of the Interior. The Tsar gave way on certain points, but new reforms affecting the peasants and workmen did not fully satisfy public opinion. There was, in fact, no promise of constitutional government.

The Tsar was inundated with petitions urging a national assembly from nobles and the professional classes. These petitions were backed up by general strikes and outrages which culminated in the murder of the Grand Duke Sergius on February 17th.

Prince Mirski resigned and his resignation was followed by a manifesto which reaffirmed the principles of autocratic government. This brought a further outcry, and finally a promise by the Tsar that he would summon representatives of the people to examine the question of new legislative proposals.

A commission of inquiry was appointed, with the Emperor as president, to find means for carrying his promise into effect. It seemed as if everything would now be satisfactorily settled. On August 6th, the new law was promulgated. It was then found that the new Duma would have no power to make laws, its only function being to examine legislative proposals, the Tsar still retaining the right to pass them into law.

There was a furious agitation. In September there was a general strike. For several days the whole industrial machine of the country was at a standstill, and there was no communication with the outside world.

At last the Government were forced to give way, and at the end of October, the Tsar issued the famous manifesto promising Russia a liberal constitution. The Government were certainly panic-stricken and were ready to agree to anything to prevent a revolution. But they were dilatory in carrying out their proposals, and preparations were soon begun for armed rebellion.

At that time, there was already an organization of workers in existence ready to take over the reins of Government and exercise their power on behalf of the proletariat.

The revolutionaries, however, were not so strong as they had believed.

Mutinies occurred at Sebastopol and Kronstadt, and in December much street fighting took place. All these outbreaks were ruthlessly put down, and in the end the revolutionary movement degenerated into spasmodic outbreaks of mass meetings and the wagging of red flags.

Despite the agitation, the Tsar kept his promise to convoke a legislative assembly, and on May 10th, 1906, the first Duma was opened by him. But it proved so hostile to the Tsar and Government that it was dissolved on July 23rd.

A second Duma met on March 5th, 1907, but it proved to be incompetent and it was dissolved in three months. A fourth was convoked for November with a wider representation, and other drastic changes were made in the electoral machinery.

Meanwhile, however, the revolution was beginning to take a Marxian aspect, and with the outbreak of the Great War, the "proletariat" seized their opportunity.

The Murder of Amelia King

It is easy to commit a murder, but the disposal of the victim's body offers all sorts of difficulties. The inability to dispose of the body of a murdered woman brought Theodore Gardelle to the gallows in 1761.

It is doubtful whether Gardelle was really guilty of murder, but his attempts to get rid of the remains piecemeal sealed his fate.

Theodore Gardelle was an educated Swiss and an accomplished painter. In 1760 he took lodgings at a certain Mrs. King's, in Leicester Fields, London.

The train of circumstances which led to his execution began on the morning of Thursday, February 19th, 1761, when Gardelle sent the maid to buy a pennyworth of snuff.

The girl went to her mistress, who told her that she could not go on the errand as there was no one to answer the front door. But the girl, anxious to get out, replied that "Mr. Gardelle would come down and sit in the parlour until she came back."

She then went to Gardelle and he agreed to be on the spot in case of visitors.

The girl went on her errand and left him in the parlour. A few minutes later Mrs. King came down and began to chaff Gardelle about a picture of her which he had painted. The painter took it as an insult, and said to her with considerable warmth, "You are an impertinent woman!"

Mrs. King flew into a rage, stepped up to Gardelle and struck him a blow on the face. She attempted to repeat the assault but Gardelle caught her by the shoulder and pushed her from him.

She tripped over a carpet, fell backwards, and struck her head against an article of furniture. Gardelle tried to raise her, but she pushed him away, and threatened him with the law.

Gardelle ignored the threat and again tried to lift her up. Once more the woman thrust him back.

Gardelle, according to his own evidence, now appears to have lost his head. Seizing an ivory comb which tapered to a point he struck her with the instrument to stifle her cries.

He then placed her on the bed, and drew the bedclothes over her. He regained the parlour and then swooned.

When he came round he found that the maid had returned. Meanwhile the woman had ceased to cry.

When Gardelle appeared he told the maid that a man had called, and that her mistress had gone out with him in a hackney coach.

The maid went up to her mistress's chamber and found the door locked. She was surprised, but she made no comment.

Meanwhile Gardelle made several excursions to the room in which Mrs. King lay dead, and decided that he would have to get rid of the girl. At last he gave her her wages and took receipt, and she departed.

Left to himself he proceeded to divest the corpse of its clothes and put them in a bag.

On the following morning several inquiries were made for Mrs. King, but Gardelle declared that she had gone away to Bath. So far there were no suspicions that a murder had been committed.

On Saturday, a man named Mozier, an acquaintance of Mrs. King, who had arranged to take her to the opera, called at about three o'clock in the afternoon and Gardelle told him that Mrs. King had gone to Bath.

Gardelle now introduced into the house a woman named Sarah Walker as a charwoman for daily work. In another room of the house lived a man named Pelsey who became curious about Mrs. King's absence, but Gardelle told him the same story, namely, that the landlady was at Bath.

It is strange that Gardelle should have chosen the city of Bath as the temporary residence of his victim, for it was the bath in the house which eventually gave him away.

During the week which had passed since the death of Mrs. King, Gardelle had endeavoured by various means to get rid of the body.

On the Thursday which began the second week following the crime, the charwoman reported that she could not get any water from the cistern, and she had recourse to the large water-tub used as a bath in the back kitchen. She pulled out the spigot, but only a small quantity of water ran out.

She fetched a chair and, using a poker, prodded the

inside of the tub and discovered that there was something soft in the water. By pressing down the obstruction she succeeded in getting a small quantity of liquid.

She told Pelsey of her difficulty and they agreed to examine the water-tub more closely at the first opportunity. Later that evening they found that it contained blankets, sheets, and coverlet of a bed. They returned the articles to the tub and began to keep watch on Gardelle.

Next day they saw him wringing out the clothes, and they reported his strange actions to a Mr. Barron, an apothecary in the neighbourhood. Barron went to Mrs. King's house and asked Gardelle where she was. Gardelle appeared to be in considerable confusion, but repeated that she had gone to Bath.

Steps were now taken to trace the maid who had been dismissed, and in view of her evidence Gardelle was taken into custody and brought before Sir John Fielding, the Bow Street magistrate.

A search of the house disclosed many tokens of the guilt of Gardelle, who eventually confessed. The body, however, was still to be found.

On the following Monday a carpenter and bricklayer went to the house to make a search. Pieces of the woman's body were found hidden in all sorts of places. There had been a fire in the garret and some half-consumed fragments of bones were recovered. In the chimney were other bones.

A man named Perronneau then came forward and told the police that Gardelle had left with him a small box. This was opened and found to contain a gold watch and chain, a pair of bracelets, and a pair of earrings, all of which were known to have belonged to Mrs. King.

Gardelle was sent to New Prison, where he attempted to commit suicide by swallowing opium. A further attempt to take his own life by swallowing a dozen halfpennies also failed to kill him.

On March 2nd he was brought to Newgate and a strict watch was kept on his movements. A month later he was tried at the Old Bailey. In his defence he insisted that he had intended no malice to the woman and that her death was caused by the fall.

He was convicted, however, and sentenced to be executed on April 2nd.

When he was asked why he did not attempt to make his escape before being arrested, he declared that he remained at the house to prevent an innocent person being charged with the murder. He added that he had no desire to rob Mrs. King, but had removed her trinkets to lend colour to the story that she had gone to Bath.

He was executed on April 4th, 1761. In the Haymarket, near Panton Street, close to the house where he had murdered the woman, the cart conveying him to Hounslow Heath halted for a few minutes. It was soon surrounded by an unruly crowd, and but for the activities of the police Gardelle would have been lynched.

His body was hanged in chains on Hounslow Heath.

Voltaire

Voltaire was amongst the most misunderstood men in history. Because of his unremitting attacks on Christianity an impression has been left in the lay mind of a sinister individual actuated by some devilish influence.

That he did try to cast doubt upon the Scriptures goes without saying. "Write what you will," said an opponent on one occasion, "you will not destroy the Christian religion."

"We shall see about that," was Voltaire's reply. This was not the boast of an egotistic man ; he believed he could do as he said.

Where Voltaire erred was in thinking that the falseness of the religion of his day was typical of Christianity, as exemplified by the superstition, hypocrisy, and intolerance that ruled everywhere, disgracing the French nation, its government and Court.

He was not a revolutionary, but his theories did much to provoke the revolution, for, in exposing the condition of the Romish Church of his day, and modelling the French mind to his own unbelief, he paved the way unconsciously for the atrocities and blasphemies of the revolution.

Voltaire, born February 20th, 1694, began life as Francois Marie Arouet. The de Voltaire was assumed by him in after life on his being left the family property.

His father, Francis Arouet, was treasurer of local revenues, and his mother, Margaret Aumart, belonged to a noble family of Poitou.

Because of the feeble constitution of the infant, the baptismal rites were not performed for months after his birth. His father, a man of means, was able to give his second son a liberal education, and although not an eminent scholar, he assimilated enough knowledge for his literary work.

He was instructed by tutors in a Jesuit college, and it was here that his first heretical tendencies began to show themselves.

One of the masters, it is said, predicted that the boy would become an advocate of deism as opposed to the doctrines of the Church, and when a friend of the family, Abbe Chateauneuf, in common with other well-known pillars of the Church, deliberately avowed his own unbelief, the seeds thus sown in the mind of Arouet grew into a strenuous opposition to orthodoxy.

He was to be found in the salons of Paris, where his literary aptitude and advanced opinions made him welcome. Already many were indignant at the hypocrisy and licence which prevailed at the court of Versailles, and were working for the removal of all religious beliefs.

But Voltaire did not go to the lengths of some who were professed atheists ; he took his stand upon deism, and it was as a deist that he attacked the revelation of the gospels.

The fascinations of Paris were dangerous for the youth, and his father hastened to remove him from temptation by obtaining for him an appointment in the suite of the Marquis of Chateauneuf, the French Ambassador at The Hague.

Having a flirtatious tendency, young Arouet soon became entangled with a woman. This caused his speedy return to Paris.

It was about this time that he conceived the ideas for two of his most noted works, the *Henriade* and the *Age of Louis XIV*, who had lately died, disgraced in the eyes of the people.

Soon after the king's death several pamphlets of satirical nature insulting to the king's memory were published. Arouet, who had already become widely known as a wit, was accused of being the author of some of them.

Merely on suspicion he was committed to the Bastille, where he did much writing. His release was obtained by the Duke d'Orleans, and at the age of 24 his tragedy *Œdipus* was produced.

It was this play which embittered him to society, for before it could be performed in Paris he had to submit to its being altered to suit the prevailing taste, thus embodying principles to which he could not honestly subscribe.

He became the object of malice on the part of his rivals, and when his second play was a failure they were overjoyed.

In 1722 Voltaire visited Holland and called upon Rousseau. A short friendship ended in jealousy and an antipathy on the part of Rousseau which lasted for years.

Two years later appeared the first French epic poem, *Henriad*. It was first printed in a correct form in London and was dedicated to Caroline, the wife of George II.

Soon afterwards Voltaire was again in the Bastille for some vague offence, and at the end of six months' imprisonment he was ordered to leave Paris.

He came to England, and soon expressed his admiration of the civil and religious liberties of this country. He became acquainted with many of the leading English writers and was particularly drawn towards Newton, Bolingbroke, Pope, and others.

Here Voltaire was free to take his stand for the principles of deism, despite the ridicule of the atheists. During his stay in England he wrote the tragedy *Brutus* and another tragedy which was never performed.

Having private means, Voltaire was not subject to the whims and fancies of rich benefactors, and could propagate his beliefs with independence. The theatre, however, was the only safe method of doing this, and he used it at every opportunity.

The play *Zaire* he composed in little more than a fortnight. It was a success, but he also met with failures.

While in England he collected material for his life of Charles XII of Sweden, and also for his *Lettres sur les Anglais*, which, published at a later date, gave the French an idea of the liberty of conscience enjoyed by Englishmen, as compared with the conditions in France.

La Pucelle was a piece which sent Voltaire's opponents frantic. Before it was published his enemies learned the theme and declared that it was an offence against morality.

It was in connection with the criticism of this work that Voltaire declared that he would kill Christianity.

Discussing the way in which people were sent to the Bastille for little or no offence on false commitment orders, Voltaire once asked :

"What do you do with those who forge *lettres de cachet* ?"

"Oh, we hang them," was the reply.

"That is well so far," said Voltaire, "until we come to the time when we hang those who write the genuine *lettres de cachet*."

Which indicates the extent of Voltaire's prejudice against officialdom.

By this time Voltaire was beginning to realize that his enemies were determined to get rid of him by fair means or foul.

He was continually persecuted, so that his work was beginning to suffer, and finding a kindred spirit in the Marchioness du Chatelet, a learned woman and a philosopher, they decided upon living together in a retreat that was not quite so irksome.

In a quiet spot on the borders of Champagne and Lorraine Voltaire wrote an exposition of the discoveries of Newton in astronomy and optics, but he could not obtain permission for the publication of the book.

He then produced among other works his history of Charles XII of Sweden, and made preparation for his history of Louis XIV, and the essay on the manners and spirit of nations.

While at Cirey, too, he began a correspondence with Frederick the Great of Prussia, who was himself ambitious in the literary field, and was particularly anxious for fame as a writer of French.

Asked to criticize some of Frederick's work, it is to be feared that Voltaire gave a too-glowing account of the MS. This led to a friendship, which was often prejudiced by egotism on both sides.

In 1746, he was admitted a member of the French Academy. About this time he lost his collaborator, the Marchioness, and following this misfortune he returned to Paris, and resumed his labours, producing the plays *Semiramis*, *Orestes*, and *Rome Sauvee*.

Having to put up with the persecution of his literary

rivals, he accepted again the proffered friendship of Frederick the Great and went to Berlin, and they became boon companions.

But the two men of the same vain temperament could not agree for long. There was mutual disgust, suspicion, and even hatred, and Voltaire had to leave Berlin in a hurry, with Frederick doing his best to stop his escape.

Paris would not have him, so he was compelled to live at Ferney with his niece, Mme. Denis, a widow without children.

Many of his noted writings were composed at his Ferney retreat. In 1757 he edited an edition of his complete works, but continued to vent his dislike of Christianity, in which he was completely unrestrained, and often descended to the worst vituperation, all of which made a lasting impression upon French democracy, and earned the enmity of the aristocracy and the Church.

The theatrical circle of Paris was always his friend, and with this support he ignored his literary rivals who had coalesced with Jesuits and profligate courtiers to attack him.

He returned to Paris, and there he received so great a reception from the theatres that he was induced to declare : "I shall be suffocated under the weight of these offerings."

But the excitement and exertions began to tell upon him, and he died on May 30th, 1778, in his 84th year.

Eugene Beauharnais

Towards the end of 1795, a 14-year-old youth, an *etat-major* in the French army, presented himself before the great Bonaparte and demanded the return of his father's sword, which had been taken away and stored when he was guillotined.

The boy was Eugene de Beauharnais, the son of Alexandre Beauharnais, who was executed for treason in June 1794.

"He was a handsome boy," says Napoleon in his *Memoirs*. Which may have caused a reflection in the mind of Napoleon that such an attractive boy must have an equally attractive mother.

And so it proved.

Napoleon gave instructions for the sword to be handed to the boy. Next day Mme. Beauharnais caused her name to be written in the General's visiting book. A few days later she made a personal call. Soon afterwards he was invited to her house to dinner.

Napoleon sat next to her and was charmed.

"I invited her to dine with me," says the great man, adding, "at last things took their course in such fashion that we fell in love with each other."

A marriage was arranged, and Josephine Tascher de la Pagerie became Mme. Bonaparte, and afterwards Empress of France.

Young Eugene was gratified, for, to quote Napoleon again, "he was already looking forward to becoming my adjutant." But he could not as yet imagine himself as an Emperor's stepson.

When Bonaparte was appointed to the command of the army of Italy, he married Mme. de Beauharnais a few days before setting out. He appointed Eugene as his aide-de-camp, and the young man followed the General some time later.

Eugene was only sixteen when he was sent on an important mission to the Ionian Islands, which, in consequence of the Treaty of Campo-Formio, had come into the possession of the French.

In 1798 Eugene accompanied Bonaparte in his expedition to Egypt and soon became distinguished for valour and zeal.

On November 8th he entered Suez at the head of the advanced posts, and for this was awarded the rank of lieutenant.

Some months afterwards Jaffa was stormed, and again Beauharnais was one of the foremost in the operation, and received the capitulation of the prisoners. At an attack on St. Jean d'Acre he was wounded.

On October 19th, 1799, he returned to France with Napoleon and was made captain of the Chasseurs of the Consular Guard.

Next year he accompanied Bonaparte in the Italian campaign and was present at the battle of Marengo, where again he distinguished himself. He was now promoted rapidly.

When, in 1805, Napoleon assumed the dignity of King of Italy, Eugene, then only 25, became his viceroy. He introduced numerous improvements in the social and civil institutions of the country and won for himself the popularity of the people.

In January 1806, Eugene married the Princess Augusta Amelia, daughter of the King of Bavaria. To celebrate this occasion Napoleon declared him to be his adopted son, under the title of Eugene Napoleon, hereditary prince of France. He also received the title of Prince of Venice, and heir-presumptive to the crown of Italy.

For three years there was uninterrupted calm in Italy. Then Austria became alarmed at Napoleon's successes, and prepared to invade Italy with an army of 100,000 men. To oppose this large force the Viceroy had no more than 60,000. Padua quickly fell into the hands of the Austrians, who, however, were afterwards defeated at Caldiero where Eugene had hastily thrown up defences.

Meanwhile, Napoleon was securing victories elsewhere, and this served to discourage the Austrians and encourage the Italians. Soon an army arrived to assist Beauharnais, and, dividing his forces into three corps and placing himself at the head of one, he defeated the Austrians at St. Daniel Malborghetto and forced his way through the mountain passes of Carinthia. Thus he effected a junction with Napoleon's army at Ebersdorf.

In his bulletin Napoleon referred to Beauharnais as having "exhibited during the campaign all the qualities which belong to the greatest captains."

Under orders from the Emperor, Eugene invaded Hungary, and won the battle of Raab against the much superior army of the Archduke John. Soon afterwards he won another battle at Wagram.

Eugene's rapid promotion and success was exciting jealousy among the other members of Napoleon's family. They could see that if Napoleon died childless his stepson would take his place as Emperor.

With crafty cleverness they began to attack Josephine, and finally secured a divorce between her and Napoleon.

Eugene was now faced with a difficult decision. He was fondly attached to his mother, but Napoleon insisted on his being the mediator in accomplishing the divorce. As Chancellor of State he was also compelled to announce the Emperor's decision to the Senate.

Eugene saw that it was useless to resist the Emperor's

demands and he carried out the delicate negotiations to the best of his ability, even to placing the act of separation before his mother.

In 1812 Eugene took an active part in the campaign in Russia in which he commanded the Fourth Corps of the Grand Army.

In the following May, Eugene was once more in Italy, where it seemed his presence was indispensable to prevent the continual inroads of the Austrians.

In January 1814, an army composed of Neapolitans, English, and Austrians began a march on Upper Italy.

Eugene secured his last victory against Bellegarde. But Napoleon himself was no longer victorious, and France was compelled to submit to her enemies.

Eugene was deprived of his viceroyalty, and soon afterwards he and his wife became fugitives.

After Napoleon's final defeat, Beauharnais retired to Bavaria.

He died of apoplexy on February 21st or 22nd, 1824.

The Home of the Washingtons

Many Americans who visit this country include in their itinerary of sightseeing the ancestral home of George Washington—Sulgrave Manor, Northamptonshire.

Before the ancestor of George Washington emigrated to America, about 1657, the family had lived for many generations on English soil. It was a family of some account prior to the seventeenth century. Formerly they lived in Durham and Lancashire, and it was from the latter county that they moved to Northamptonshire.

The first recorded member of the family was Lawrence Washington, whose uncle, Sir Thomas Kitson, was a wool-stapler in a large way of business. Kitson flourished during the reigns of Henry VII and Henry VIII, the success of his trade being dependent on sheep farms in the Midland counties.

Lawrence Washington, a barrister, who found the law unremunerative, became Kitson's right-hand man, and superintended the business with the sheep farmers in Northamptonshire.

Lawrence Washington eventually became Mayor of Northampton, and, identifying himself with the reformed religion at the time of the dissolution of the monasteries, he was given a grant of monastic property. The estate which thus came into his possession was Sulgrave.

The train of circumstances which brought Sulgrave to the Washington family is clearly defined. In Northampton-shire is Althorp, the seat of the famous Spencer family. The Lady Spencer of Lawrence Washington's day was a Kitson. The Spencers, moreover, were prominent in the promotion of the sheep-farming industry. Thus the connection between the Washingtons and the Spencers was close.

In addition, Dr. Layton, the chief commissioner for the dissolution of the monasteries, was rector of a near-by parish, and it is to be presumed that Layton used his influence to get the grant of Sulgrave for Washington.

For three generations the Washington family remained at Sulgrave, having attained to the highest rank of county society. Then suddenly their fortunes were dissipated, how, or for what reason, is not clear. They were forced to sell Sulgrave and move to the parish of Brington, which was nearer the Spencer family's home.

Some years later an improvement in the circumstances of the Washingtons was brought about by a fortunate marriage. The eldest son wedded the half-sister of George Villiers, the notorious Duke of Buckingham. Immediately prosperity returned.

In 1623, a Henry Washington believed to be the then head of the family, was knighted by James I. On the outbreak of the Civil War, the Washingtons supported the Royal cause, and Sir Henry was one of the most prominent of the Royalist commanders. He was leader of the storming party which attacked Bristol, and he also showed conspicuous ability at the defence of Worcester.

The exact relationship of Sir Henry Washington to the American President is not clear, and the linking up of the English and American branches is difficult. In the year 1658, however, the brothers John and Lawrence Washington are known to have been landholders in Virginia.

John established himself at Bridge's Creek, became a member of the House of Burgesses in 1666, and died in 1676. His eldest son, Lawrence, married Mildred Warner, and had three children. One of them, Augustine, married twice. By his second marriage he was the father of the famous George, who was born February 22nd, 1731.

George Washington never made any claim to illustrious ancestors. He knew little of them and cared even less. Naturally attempts have often been made to clear up the connection between George and the Northamptonshire family, and last century it was discovered that a certain Lawrence Washington, who was opposed to the Commonwealth regime, found himself out of favour and was removed from his position as Fellow of Brasenose College on the ground that he was a "frequenter of alehouses."

His son, John, shipped as a mate in a tobacco ship, arrived in Virginia and settled down.

The Washingtons do not appear to have thrived in the New World, for George's father, presumably the grandson of John, earned a living as a sailor in a merchant ship. Later he began an ironworks, and then took to planting and buying and selling land.

In the church at Brington, Northamptonshire, are two stones. One of them, dated 1616, bears the arms of the Washingtons, and it is assumed that the then head of the family was buried there.

The other grave appears to be that of a younger brother. It bears the family shield, but with the addition of a crescent indicating a less exalted scion of the house.

It has often been debated whether the United States flag originated in the Washington coat of arms. It is supposed that the Stars and Stripes emblem of the Republic was taken from the shield of the great George Washington. There is a similarity which cannot be merely coincidental. The stripes of the Washingtons are alternate gules, red and white as are those of the American flag.

Moreover, the Washington stars are five-pointed, as is the case in the United States flag.

In 1911 a movement was begun to produce a permanent commemoration of the hundred years peace between Great Britain and America which followed the treaty of Ghent in 1811.

A British-American peace committee was formed, and, as one of the peace memorials, it acquired Sulgrave Manor. It is a small manor house with about nine acres of land and it cost £8,400 to buy. The funds were raised in England by public subscription.

The original building belonged to the Priory of St. Andrew's, Northampton, from which it was obtained by gift of Henry VIII at the time of the dissolution.

On the south porch of the Manor are the Washington arms, and on the front gable are the Royal Arms of the Tudors.

About seven years ago the Manor House was restored in order that it might be a really effective "place of pilgrimage for Americans in England and the symbol of the kinship of the two peoples."

The house was enlarged to what was believed to have been its original size, and rooms which had hitherto been closed to visitors because of dilapidation were thrown open. These reconstructions were carried out mainly through funds raised in the United States.

In the restored kitchen is an old meat-jack with its steel framework used to work the spits on which meat was roasted.

Sulgrave is said to be one of the few places in England in which a meat-jack can be seen in its proper position.

The Comedy of "Romeo" Coates

One of the most eccentric of the quaint characters who frequented London society in the days of the Regency was "Romeo" Coates.

He appeared suddenly in the West End in 1810 apparently from the West Indies. He was wealthy, of middle age, dressed well, sometimes showily, and wore a coat with an unnecessary amount of fur.

Having plenty of money he found it easy to get into society and at evening parties, he was usually to be seen with buttons and knee-buckles studded with diamonds.

His Christian name was Robert; the "Romeo" was gratuitous because of his extraordinary performance in *Romeo and Juliet* at the Haymarket Theatre.

London was curious about Coates's antecedents, but he remained a man of mystery. When, therefore, the management of the Haymarket Theatre announced that Coates would appear in the part of Romeo, it was expected that there would be a full house.

Coates was advertised on the play-bill as an "amateur of fashion" who had consented to perform "for one night only." It was an open secret that he had acted indifferently at rehearsals. Thus instead of a tragedy, patrons of the Haymarket expected a comedy. Their hopes were realized.

Coates appeared in a grotesque garb. He wore a cloak of sky-blue silk, covered with spangles, red pantaloons, a white muslin vest, and a wig of the Restoration period. On his head was an opera hat.

An outburst of laughter from all parts of the house greeted his advent on the stage. Before he had opened his lips, there was the ominous sound of a garment being rent. His pantaloons much too tight for him, had burst down the seams.

When he began to speak the uproar increased, for Coates had not the faintest idea how to act. His voice was too affectedly guttural, and he was blatantly vulgar to "Juliet." His rendering of the balcony scene was too comic for the pit and balcony, who shrieked their amusement.

The piece was never completed. The curtain was rung down amidst the jeers of the audience.

One can easily imagine that this initial experience of the histrionic ability of Robert Coates was sufficient for the management of the Haymarket Theatre. There is evidence, however, that "Romeo" put on an even more amusing performance at the same house. On this occasion he appears to have hired the theatre for his own pleasure, as he termed it.

For this display public excitement was intense. Neither Garrick nor Kemble could have caused so much enthusiasm. Every single seat in the place was occupied. The whole of fashionable London was present in anticipation of an entertaining evening. In a stage box sat the actor's notorious friend, Baron Ferdinand Geramb.

Coates had advertised himself to give a performance of Lothario. He was dressed in velvets and silks, and a hat covered with diamonds. Immediately he was seen on the stage there was crowing from every quarter. This was in allusion to the large crowing cocks which appeared on his crest.

It was a very angry Lothario who faced the audience. He drew his sword and challenged the unruly spirits in the gallery to mortal combat. Immediately there was a cessation of the uproar as if the audience had been impressed by Lothario's bravery. Then, in order to annoy spectators, he approached the Baron in the box and began to converse with him.

Very soon there was a demand for Lothario to begin his business.

The sequel is graphically told by a writer in the *New Monthly Magazine* of 1827 as follows :

At length he commenced : his appeals to the heart were made by the application of the left hand so disproportionately lower down than "the seat of life" has been proposed to be placed ; his contracted pronunciation of the word "breach," and other new readings and actings kept the house in a right joyous humour, until the climax of all mirth was attained by the dying scene of "that gallant, gay Lothario" : but who shall describe the grotesque agonies of the dark seducer, his platted hair escaping from the comb that held it, and the dark crineous cordage that flapped upon his shoulders in the convulsions of his dying moments, and the cries of people for medical aid to accomplish his external exit ?

Then, when in his last throes his coronet fell, it was miraculous to see the defunct arise, and after he had spread a nice handkerchief on the stage, and there deposited his head-dress, free from impurity, philosophically resume his dead condition. But it was not yet over, for the exigent audience, not content "that when the men were dead, why there an end," insisted on a repetition of the awful scene, which the highly flattered corpse executed several times, to the gratification of the cruel and torment-loving assembly.

"Romeo's" love of notoriety was not confined to the Haymarket Theatre. He had designed a curiously shaped carriage, in which he drove two white horses about Hyde Park daily. More than anything, the coach resembled a cockle-shell. On the vehicle and harness appeared his crest of two cocks crowing.

Wherever he went the street urchins ran alongside the equipage crying "Cock-a-doodle-do !" the while Coates risked a serious accident by leaning out to cut at the boys with his whip.

In 1821, "Romeo" Coates was exceeding gratified to receive an invitation to a reception at Carlton House given by the Prince Regent.

His extraordinary egotism was equal to overcoming

any trepidation he might have felt through his ignorance of the procedure of being presented at Court. He had never met the Prince Regent, and he was astonished that he should have been one of those chosen to meet the Bourbons from France in whose honour the reception was to take place.

The fame of his cockle-shell carriage, his reputation on the stage, and his intimacy with the great wits of the day, was nothing to this new access to fame.

He took every precaution to discover the necessary comportment. He visited the best tailors, and ordered the richest velvet. Diamond buttons were affixed to his Court dress. He attended a barber daily in order to get a semblance of neatness in his grisly but scanty locks.

The great day arrived. The cockle-shell carriage received a final overhaul and cleaning, and at the appointed hour "Romeo" Coates descended from the vehicle at the door of Carlton House. He entered the palace without question when he presented his ticket, but a second scrutiny by the Prince Regent's Secretary disclosed that the ticket was a forgery.

Coates had no option but to retrace his steps to the street. His coach had been driven off and he had to make the journey to his home in Craven Street in a hackney coach.

Next day London had a good laugh. The ticket had been forged by Theodore Hook, notorious for his practical joking. He had imitated one of the Lord Chamberlain's tickets; had put on a scarlet uniform and delivered the invitation himself at Coate's house. Having been one of those invited to the fête, Hook had been a witness of Coate's discomfiture.

But when the affair came to the knowledge of the Prince Regent he sent his secretary to the residence of Coates to apologize for having turned him away. The Prince invited Coates to come and look at the State rooms. Romeo went and was accorded a pleasant reception.

After having been the fun and sport of the West End of London for several seasons, Coates went to Boulogne where he settled and induced a woman to marry him.

Strangely enough, however, he met his death in London, for while on a visit to the City that had laughed at him he was knocked down by a vehicle and killed on February 23rd, 1848. He was seventy-six years old at his death.

The Conversion of Ethelbert

Because Ethelbert allowed St. Augustine to land in England and preach Christianity to the inhabitants of Kent, he has come down in history as a great king.

Actually Ethelbert had no great say in the matter, for Augustine had landed and established a headquarters before the King was aware of the fact.

The Venerable Bede the Saxon historian remarks that Ethelbert had heard of the Christian religion, having "a Christian wife of the Royal family of the Franks, called Bertha, whom he had received from her parents on condition that she should be permitted to practise her religion with the Bishop Luidhard who was sent with her to preserve her faith."

From which it seems likely that the pious Bertha had been negotiating with Rome unknown to her husband. Thus it was a woman who was partly responsible for the introduction of Christianity—or rather, the Roman version of it—into England.

It is not at all certain, though, that Ethelbert first heard of Christianity from his wife, for there had been Christian establishments in the country long before the arrival of St. Augustine.

Thus, on the authority of Bede himself. "There was on the east side of the city (Canterbury) a church dedicated to the honour of St. Martin, built whilst the Romans were still in the island, wherein the Queen, who, as has been said before was a Christian, used to pray."

The mission of St. Augustine was to the pagan Saxons, the invaders, who, in thrusting the early Britons across the Welsh border, had demolished all their Christian institutions, and established the worship of their own gods.

It was in the old church of St. Martin, one of the earliest churches of the Britons, that St. Augustine and his followers met to sing, pray, and to say Mass.

To quote Bede again: "When he (Ethelbert), among the rest, induced by the unspotted life of these holy men, and their delightful promises, which by many miracles they proved to be most certain, believed and was baptized, greater numbers began daily to flock together to hear the word, and forsaking their heathen rites, to associate themselves, by believing, to the unity of the church of Christ."

It is recorded, however, that Ethelbert, unlike many of the other Saxon Kings who embraced Christianity, did not force his subjects to be baptized.

Ethelbert reigned "fifty-six winters" and his dominions extended to the Humber, during which time Christianity spread all over the country.

On June 22nd, "in the nineteenth year of the reign of the most pious Emperor Mauritius Tiberius, in the eighteenth year after his Consulship," the great Pope Gregory sent a letter of approval to his new convert, King Ethelbert. An extract from this message is interesting as showing that the end of the world was regarded as imminent.

Says Pope Gregory : "We find in the Holy Scripture, from the words of the Almighty Lord, that the end of this present world and the kingdom of the saints is about to come, which will never terminate. But as the same end of the world approaches many things are at hand which were not before—namely, changes of air and terrors from heaven and tempests out of the order of the seasons, wars, famines, plagues, earthquakes in several places."

The Pope hastens to assure Ethelbert, however, that these things "will not, nevertheless, happen in our days, but will all follow after our days." He continues : "If you, therefore, find any of these things to happen in your country, let not your mind be in any way disturbed ; for these signs of the end of the world are sent before, for this reason, that we may be solicitous for our souls, suspicious of the hour of death, and may be found prepared with good works to meet our judge."

It was during the reign of Ethelbert that the murder of the monks of Bangor occurred, in the year 607. Ethelbert himself had nothing to do with the massacre, but Augustine— on the authority of Bede, his own biographer—was clearly involved.

Having converted the domains of Ethelbert, Augustine appears to have met with equal success in Northumbria, ruled over by the war-like Ethelfrid.

He was not successful in his dealings with the Welsh whose religious traditions were older than the Saxons. The Welsh refused to conform to the customs of Augustine's church. They denied that he was their archbishop. Among other questions in dispute was the date of the observance of Easter.

"The man of God, Augustine," says Bede, "is said, in a threatening manner, to have foretold that in case they would not join in unity with their brethren, they would be warred upon by their enemies . . . and undergo the vengeance of death."

A year after the death of St. Augustine, Ethelfrid, King of Northumbria, led his army to Chester, "where he slew an innumerable host of the Welsh; and so was fulfilled the prophecy of Augustine, wherein he saith: 'If the Welsh will not have peace with us, they shall perish at the hands of the Saxons'."

The Welsh had drawn themselves up in line of battle. With them were a large number of priests variously stated to number from 200 to 2,000. Observing the priests praying for the success of the Welsh soldiers, most of whom were from the monastery of Bangor, Ethelfrid exclaimed: "If then they cry to their God against us, in truth, though they do not bear arms, yet they fight against us, because they oppose us by their prayers."

He commanded the priests to be attacked and all were massacred.

Ethelbert was third of the English kings who had held the sovereignty of the southern provinces below the Humber. But, says Bede, he was the first "that ascended to the heavenly kingdom." He died on February 24th, 616, and was buried at St. Martin's, Canterbury, by the side of his queen.

He introduced into a country at that time, almost without laws, the judicial customs of the Romans, and protected the property of the church by strict regulations. He was the fifth in descent from Hengist, the Saxon invader.

There is a dispute among historians about the exact place of landing of St. Augustine. Camden declares that it was at Richborough where the palace of Ethelbert was situated, whereas others maintain it was in the Isle of Thanet. To reconcile the two versions it has been suggested that Richborough in Ethelbert's day was actually within the Isle of Thanet.

Richborough was undoubtedly a place of considerable note and probably the most important seaport on the South-

East Coast. Bede describes it as the one place of note. Camden suggests that it was cut off from Thanet by the River Wantsum changing its channel, and he gives the town's various names from the time of the Romans to his day. It was one of the naval headquarters in the seventeenth century.

It is believed that the palace of Ethelbert was on a commanding elevation, and the key of the broad river which allowed the passage of ships from the Channel and thus cut off the North Foreland. It was here that Hengist landed, and also one of the Roman invasions.

Colonel Francis Charteris

When Colonel Francis Charteris was buried in the churchyard of the Grey Friars, Edinburgh, it was with considerable difficulty that the coffin was lowered into the grave without mishap.

Charteris had such an evil reputation that the mob present at the funeral made an attempt to get at the coffin with the object of tearing it to pieces. He had committed almost every crime in the calendar before he was eventually charged at the Old Bailey on February 25th, 1730, with assaulting a servant girl.

For two years after his appearance at the assizes he had remained in obscurity in Scotland, and had then died in miserable circumstances.

Charteris belonged to a distinguished Scottish family, and was heir to an estate which his ancestors had held for 400 years. He was also related to several other well-known families in the North.

He had every prospect of rising to an important office of State, as did some of his early acquaintances. He preferred, however, to adopt a career of crime.

Choosing the Army for a profession, Charteris served under the Duke of Marlborough as an ensign of foot, but was soon advanced to the rank of cornet of horse. His subsequent activities made it clear that the Army was only a means to an end.

He was an expert gamester, and when the Army was in winter quarters he cleared many of his fellow-officers of their money by his skill at cards and dice. Having won all an officer possessed in ready cash, he would lend him the money back at what he described as the "moderate" interest of 100 per cent. The security for repayment of the loan was usually the officer's commission.

In course of time Charteris carried on such a large traffic in commissions that John, Duke of Argyle and the Earl of Stair, young men in Charteris's regiment, applied to the Earl of Orkney then in the Army quarters at Brussels, drawing that officer's attention to what was going on.

The Earl reported the matter to the Duke of Marlborough, who ordered Charteris to appear before a court-martial. An equal number of English and Scottish officers composed the court, and after a fair hearing of the case, Charteris was sentenced to return the money he had obtained by exorbitant interest and to be deprived of his commission. He was drummed out of the regiment, his sword first being broken.

Charteris was by no means abashed at this disgrace. With an impertinent shrug of his shoulders he buttoned up his coat and left the court room with every indication that he was contemptuous of the proceedings.

He left Brussels and began to walk towards Mecklin. On the way he stopped at an inn for the night.

Charteris was treated with all possible respect as an officer. He ordered an elaborate supper and then went to bed.

In the morning the landlord was called to Charteris's room by the violent ringing of the bell. Terrified that he had failed to satisfy his guest, the man entered the bedroom full of apologies. But when he heard Charteris's complaint he shook with fear, for the latter swore that he had been robbed of a diamond ring, a gold watch, and a considerable amount of money.

Charteris pointed to a broken window—needless to say he had broken it himself—and declared that the robber must have got in that way. He even suggested that the landlord himself was the thief.

The innkeeper went down on his knees and pleaded for mercy. But Charteris insisted that he would call in the authorities if he was not reimbursed for his loss.

Eventually he applied to a monastery, and several monks came to the inn to investigate. Believing Charteris to be a high personage they lent the landlord sufficient money to satisfy his demands.

Charteris then continued his journey, and at length reached Scotland. He had not been home long when he succeeded in buying another commission in a horse regiment and rose to the rank of colonel.

At this time the Duke of Queensberry was a commissioner to the Scottish Parliament, then assembled at Edinburgh to discuss the proposed union with England.

Charteris was invited to a card-party by the Duchess, and he contrived to get her seated with her back to a mirror with himself sitting opposite. He is said to have won £3000 from her by this ruse.

The Duke appears to have had a shrewd idea of what had happened, for he introduced a Bill in the House prohibiting gaming for more than a certain sum, and it passed into law.

Charteris continued his frauds at the gaming tables and lent his victims money at high rates of interest. He took bonds for the sums owing, and frequently brought these unfortunate people into the courts.

He began to lend money on mortgages, always demanding large premiums. At length he became so rich that he was able to buy several estates in England.

At the same time he became notorious for his associations with women. He employed agents to lure young girls to his house.

At length Ann Bond, whom he employed as a domestic servant, succeeded in exposing him.

Ann Bond had lived in London and left her employment owing to ill-health. She took lodgings at a private house, and after her recovery was sitting at the street door when a woman accosted her and offered her a situation in the establishment of a Colonel Harvey.

She took the place, but had been there only two days when she discovered that she was in the house of the notorious Colonel Charteris. She pleaded to the housekeeper that she was ill and wished to leave.

Charteris threatened that he would shoot her if she left his service. The same day he assaulted her and beat her with a horse-whip. Finally she was turned out of the house.

She took out a summons for attempted assault, but the grand jury held that it was not an attempt, but an actual commission of assault.

Charteris was committed to Newgate and loaded with

chains. He succeeded in buying lighter shackles and paid for the use of a room in the prison, with a servant to attend him.

Wealthy interests obtained a writ of *habeas corpus* and got Charteris released on bail.

When the case was heard every ruse was employed to prove that Ann Bond was a woman of immoral character; but she succeeded in convincing the jury of her unblemished character and Charteris was found guilty.

The usual sentence for a criminal assault of this nature was hanging, but Charteris's relatives got the case brought before the Privy Council, who were finally induced to recommend the King to grant a pardon, the Colonel agreeing to settle an annuity on Ann Bond.

Victor Hugo

Victor Hugo has been called a showman and a poseur.

It has been said that he "engineered a reputation," and that Rodin's bust of him, with its enormous brow, was not a fair delineation of his features. The fact that the first sketch of his life that got into print was written partly by his wife and partly by himself is another argument of those who would lower him in the scale of authors.

Criticism of Hugo has come mainly from his own countrymen. He lived during a time of revolution in France when individuals were not always loyal in their politics, and when the abilities of opponents were not recognized.

As Hugo himself was not consistent in his beliefs—he was successively Royalist and Republican—it is easy to understand why he was condemned on occasions by both sides.

Yet it is claimed now that Hugo was the greatest tragic and dramatic poet since Shakespeare.

Hugo was not only a prolific writer, but one of the most precocious. At the age of 14 he produced a tragedy; at 15 nearly won a prize in an Academic competition, and by the time he was 20, when he published his first set of *Odes et Ballades*, he had three times won a prize at the Floral Games of Toulouse.

Hugo, born on the 26th of February, 1802, was the youngest son of General J. L. S. Hugo, who had fought with distinction in the service of Napoleon. He was educated in Paris and Madrid. His mother was a Royalist and a Catholic, and young Hugo, being in his mother's company more than his father's, imbibed the same doctrines, only to reject them later in life, despite the fact that his first works in poetry and fiction were designed to proclaim his faith in these principles.

At the age of 21 he married his cousin Adele Foucher, and in the following year he produced his first romance, *Han d'Islande*, his second, *Bug-Jargal*, appearing three years later.

With the publication of his *Cromwell* in 1827, Hugo became one of the most conspicuous figures in France. He was the leader of the literary romanticists who protested against the hidebound conventions of the age.

His *Odes* had been Royalist and religious in their tone, and Louis XVIII had bestowed on Hugo a pension. *Cromwell* showed that he had deserted the classic and academic for romance.

In 1828 Hugo published the tragedy *Marion de Lorme*, in which he represented a king as the puppet of a minister. The work was officially condemned. Four years later *Le roi s'amuse* was prohibited by order of Louis Philippe after a lively first night on the stage. Fifty years later, on the anniversary of its first rejection, it reappeared and met with acclamation.

But it was the appearance of *Hernani* in 1830 which brought Hugo his greatest reputation and resulted in the battle between the romanticists and the classicists. The play was performed at the Théâtre Français.

The victory of the romanticists was actually gained by a ruse, for Hugo was careful to obtain as many seats as possible and pack them with his own followers. The classicists also appeared in strength, so that there were hardly any seats for the ordinary theatre-goers.

On several occasions the performance of the play led to fisticuffs between the contenders.

In 1831 Hugo published *Notre Dame de Paris*, a story of old Paris, much on the lines of the works of Sir Walter Scott. Every subsequent year an important work came from the pen of Victor Hugo.

Until about the year 1830 Hugo had been a royalist, but he now began to idolize his father's hero, Napoleon. He sat for the City of Paris in the Assemblée Constituante, where he sometimes voted with the Right and sometimes with the Left.

At last he threw in his lot with the Democratic Republicans. In his first speech in the Chamber, Hugo displayed a remarkable knowledge of Poland. His second speech, which was on coast defence, is memorable for its practical suggestions.

An impassioned appeal by Hugo on behalf of the exiled family of Bonaparte caused Louis Philippe to revoke the sentence of outlawry.

Events in France moved swiftly. The monarchy fell, and the House of Orleans fled from France. A new constitution was established proclaiming a Democratic Republic. Hugo continued to advocate his patriotic and progressive principles. A turn of the wheel might have made him president.

But within three years the situation again changed. Louis Napoleon, a relic of the Bonapartes, rose to power. In December 1851, a *coup d'état* gave him supreme powers, and he became emperor under the title of Napoleon III. With many other honourable men who had supported law and order, Hugo was forced into exile. He withdrew to Brussels, but, being ejected from Belgium, he went first to Jersey, and then settled in Guernsey, where he wrote his *Napoleon le Petit*.

Several other works appeared during the next ten years. Then in 1862 came his great romance, *Les Misérables*, and two years later, *Les Travilleurs de la Mer (Toilers of the Sea)*.

Hugo was away from his country for nearly twenty years. In 1870 came the fall of the empire as a result of the war with Prussia, and Hugo returned to Paris.

About six months afterwards he was chosen to represent the Seine in the new republic, but he soon resigned his seat on the ground that one of his speeches drew interruptions from the Right. He stayed in Paris during the rule of the Commune. He then went to Brussels, where he complained publicly against the Belgian attitude to the French Commune. He was again expelled from Belgium.

He stood for Paris in an election but was beaten, and in 1872 he published his *L'Année Terrible*, which depicted the year of the war with Prussia. It was full of condemnation of Germany and eulogies of France.

His last romance in prose, called *Quatre-Vingt-Treize*,

appeared in 1874, and a year later was published a complete collection of his speeches and addresses.

In 1876 he became a senator, and next year his *Histoire d'un Crime* was in the hands of the public. During the next five years Hugo produced several well-known works, and in 1882 came *Torquemada*, which is described by some critics as the effort of "a Hugo in decay," but by others a worthy successor to *Ruy Blas*.

Victor Hugo died on May 22nd, 1885, and was given a magnificent public funeral, his remains being laid in the Pantheon. He was regarded as the foremost man of letters of the time.

A number of works were published after his death, including the poems *Theatre en Liberte* and the unfinished poems *Dieu* and *La Fin de Satan*.

Lord William George Frederick Cavendish Bentinck

How a horse, described as Running Rein, who finished first in the Derby of 1844, was a four-year-old, has often been told, but it is not generally known how Lord George Bentinck was able to expose the fraud.

For several months Bentinck had been suspicious that the horse, Running Rein, entered in the Derby, was ineligible through age.

His suspicions began when the animal won a two-year-old plate at Newmarket in the previous year and beat the Duke of Rutland's Crinoline.

An inquiry followed this race, but Goodman, the colt's owner, was allowed to go off with the stakes. The real name of the horse was Maccabeus, which had been painted to resemble Running Rein.

Another horse called Gone Away was painted to resemble Maccabeus in case inquiries should be made.

Much of the evidence which Bentinck obtained for the exposure of the fraud came from Tommy Coleman, trainer, roughrider, innkeeper, and the originator of steeplechasing.

There are letters in existence written by Bentinck to Coleman, whom, it appears, he instructed to get all the evidence he could about the two horses.

In one of them he writes : "Find out who painted Gone Away's leg. Was it Goodman himself (the owner of Maccabeus) or William Sadler ? It was painted in London."

In another it is shown that he had traced the movements of the false Running Rein back for two years. He writes :

Can the ostler at Bryant's recollect a dirty, mean-looking little fellow, with light brown or sandy thin whiskers, with a bad knee, kicked by the horse he was leading up, stopping at the Red Lion to wait on Saturday, September 24th, 1842, and asking his way either to Haine's livery stables in Langham Place, or else to Mr. Goodman's stables in Foley Place ?

The colt he was leading was a high-couraged, unbroke or rather half-broke bay, entire thoroughbred two-year-old colt, with black legs and not a white speck about him, and a long tail.

The colt had also at the time a small scar scarcely healed up, on his near arm, just above the knee on the outside. The man and the colt were on their way to Epsom to Smith's training stables. The man's name was Richard Watson.

In furtherance of his inquiries Lord George Bentinck called on Wood, the Epsom corn merchant, who had run the horse as Running Rein, and asked him to produce the animal. It was then found that the horse, his trainer, and Goodman, were missing.

The horse was disqualified. Later it was discovered that the animal had been killed and buried. A party of men dug the body up one night, but as it was without the head identication was impossible.

Lord William George Frederick Cavendish Bentinck, born February 27th, 1802, had other interests besides sport. He was generally known as Lord George Bentinck, and was the second surviving son of the fourth Duke of Portland. He joined the Army, and was for some time private secretary to his uncle, George Canning.

In 1828, he succeeded his uncle, Lord William Bentinck, as member for Lyme Regis, and represented the constituency until his death twenty years after.

He failed to acquire a reputation in politics because of his inability to speak. He was first a member of the moderate Whig Party. Later he joined the Opposition, voted in favour of Catholic emancipation and the Reform Bill. Still later he became the chief advocate of Protection, and was able to rally round him the opponents of Sir Robert Peel.

This ability in a man who had hitherto been regarded as merely commonplace caused much surprise, but there is no doubt he was actuated by an animosity towards Peel.

He believed that Peel and his colleagues had "hounded" to the death his illustrious relative Canning, and his attacks on Free Trade were full of personalities.

On his becoming leader of the Opposition he gave up his racing interests, sold his stud, and devoted the whole of his energies to politics.

He died suddenly on September 21st, 1848, two years after he had begun to be a voice in the Commons.

It was in connection with the Derby of that year that Lord George Bentinck bewailed his luck, for he had, two years before, actually sold the winner for a small sum as a yearling.

"Never mind," said a friend, sympathizing with him.

"But I do mind," said Bentinck. "You do not know what the Derby is."

"Yes, I do," replied the friend ; "it is the blue riband of the turf."

And that title has remained to this day.

Humphrey, Duke of Gloucester

On the morning of February 28th, 1447, Humphrey, Duke of Gloucester, erstwhile Protector of England, was found dead in his bed in the monastery of Bury St. Edmunds.

Arrested a few days before for high treason under orders from the weak king, Henry VI, he had been thrown into a cell and left until a decision had been made about his disposal.

When the body was publicly exhibited to the people of Bury St. Edmunds, there were no marks of violence on it, but the belief that he had been murdered was universal.

His death ushered in the Wars of the Roses.

Shakespeare blames Cardinal Henry Beaufort, Bishop of Winchester, for the crime. Beaufort survived Gloucester only six weeks, and the poet depicts the Cardinal tortured with remorse on his deathbed. The old man of 80 is made to exclaim :

Died he not in his bed ? Where should he die ?
Can I make men live, whe'r they will or no ?
O ! torture me no more, I will confess—
Alive again ? then show me where he is !
I'll give a thousand pounds to look upon him—
He hath no eyes, the dust hath blinded them—
Comb down his hair, look, look it stands upright
Like lime-twigs set to catch my winged soul !
Give me some drink ; and bid the apothecary
Bring the strong poison that I bought of him.

If it were not Beaufort who was directly responsible for Gloucester's death—assuming that he died at the hands of an assassin—it must have been other adherents of the Red Rose. Shakespeare implicates also the Duke of Suffolk.

The end of "Good Duke Humphrey," as he was known to the people, was the signal for the opening of the great Lancaster-Plantagenet drama which bathed the country in blood for nearly 40 years until the accession of Henry VII.

Immediately after the death of Henry V, in 1422, a Council of Regency was appointed to act during the infancy of his son, Henry VI. The Duke of Gloucester was placed at the head of the Council with the title of Protector. In that Council, too, was Henry Beaufort, an ambitious and unscrupulous man whose object was to supplant Gloucester.

Failing to get his rival out of the way, Beaufort succeeded in getting the Council to agree to the coronation of the young King, then only eight years old. This meant the abolition of the office of Protector. Gloucester thus reverted to the status of an ordinary peer, but still had a voice in certain matters concerning the government of the country.

To pretend, however, that the child King did not want a Protector was absurd, and Beaufort got himself nominated to the office.

Beaufort was now virtual ruler of the country. During the next few years Gloucester did his best to curb the activities of the Cardinal, much to the latter's annoyance.

"Good Duke Humphrey" appears to have stood in the way of the unscrupulous designs of everyone else. His one object was to prevent the King from being harmed. Thus, apart from his own small party of friends, everyone's hand was against him, and it is difficult to decide which of the contending factions was most anxious to get rid of him.

He was first attacked through his wife. The Duchess of Gloucester is said to have been curious about the probable date of the King's death. She was superstitious, and it was proved that she had consulted magicians about love-philtres to secure the fidelity of her husband.

But it was also said—but not proved—that she had sought the King's death. She was accused of keeping in her home a wax figure, melting away before the fire. As the image melted, so, it was thought, the flesh of King Henry would wither, and finally he would dissolve into death.

No real evidence of this was produced. Nevertheless, the Duchess was found guilty of conspiring the death of the King, and was sentenced to perpetual confinement. In addition she was required to undergo public penances in three different places in London.

The Duchess was said to have had a number of confederates. One of them, the Witch of Ely, was burned at Smithfield, and a canon of Westminster died in the Tower. A third victim was hanged, drawn, and quartered at Tyburn.

For the purpose of her penance, the Duchess was brought by barge from Westminster to Temple Stairs, from which spot she walked with a tall wax taper to St. Paul's Cathedral, where she made her submission at the High Altar, the place being packed with people.

Another day she walked to Christ Church, Aldgate, and a third day to St. Michael's, Cornhill. On each occasion the Lord Mayor, Sheriffs and Corporation followed.

Soon afterwards she was banished to the Isle of Man. Her ghost, it is said, haunts the island to this day.

Since he had been deposed from the office of Protector, Gloucester had continued to condemn the activities of the various factions in the country. He tried to restrain those who had designs against the imbecile King. The persecution of his wife did not achieve what his enemies had desired, for he continued to expose conspiracies. In 1445 a new factor intervened in the affairs of the country. The King married Margaret of Anjou, daughter of the King of Sicily, who, in view of the inability of the King to govern—he was often insane—attempted to take over the affairs of the realm herself. Her ally was the Duke of Suffolk who had negotiated her marriage with her husband. These two formed an alliance against all other factions.

"Good Duke Humphrey" appears to have had no more respect for the principles of the Queen than he had for those of Beaufort. Thus he now had an additional enemy.

At length he was arrested, imprisoned, and, it is thought, murdered.

Both Beaufort and the Duke of Suffolk may have been implicated in his death, but the truth never came to light.

On the death of Gloucester, the Earl of Suffolk rose to supreme power. But it was not long before the Commons impeached him, and, despite the efforts of the Queen to save him, he was banished for five years. On the way to France he was stopped, brought back, and executed.

Richard Pigott

Twilight was setting in on the evening of Friday, March 1st, 1889, when the Spanish police, acting under the instruction of Scotland Yard, entered the Hotel Ambajadores at Madrid, and going up to a room on the first floor, demanded that Richard Pigott, a notorious witness in the Parnell Commission, should deliver himself into their hands.

An interpreter was sent to Pigott to let him know that the police were outside. For a moment he was staggered, and then recovering himself, he made some reference to his luggage, and stooping over a bag, took from it an object which he was apparently anxious to conceal.

A police officer darted forward : but he was too late. A shot was heard and Pigott fell to the ground with a bullet through his brain.

Thus the curtain fell upon the final act of a drama that caused a sensation in the United Kingdom for years.

Richard Pigott had given perjured evidence before the Commission of Inquiry which was instituted by Lord Salisbury's Government to make investigations into allegations that Charles Stewart Parnell, the Irish leader, had been implicated in the Phœnix Park murders of May 1882.

This commission, which began its inquiry on September 17th, 1888, sat for 128 days. More than 450 witnesses were examined, including one of the Phœnix Park murderers, to tell the stories of a whole series of murders, nearly 150 in number, that had occurred in Mayo, Cork, Galway, Kerry, and other places.

On the fiftieth day of the inquiry the evidence—much of it manufactured—against Parnell, was beginning to be questioned.

The collapse of the charges, which were based principally upon a large number of documents that had been in the possession of Pigott, followed when it was discovered that the documents were forgeries.

The following sensational story was revealed.

Mr. E. Caulfield Houston, a journalist, and a son of a prison warder, had been appointed secretary of the Irish Loyal and Patriotic Union, and considered it a part of his duty in this office to obtain proofs of Nationalists complicity in crime.

He appears to have worked on the principle that anything detrimental to the Nationalist was true, while anything in their favour was false.

He had written a pamphlet entitled *Parnellism Unmasked*, from information supplied by Richard Pigott, who was originally the proprietor of a number of newspapers subsequently bought by Parnell.

In furtherance of his attacks against Parnell, he thought it might be possible to get from Pigott additional evidence which would implicate Parnell in the Phœnix Park murders.

One night in 1885, therefore, he interviewed Pigott, whom he found poverty-stricken in a house in Sandycroft Avenue, Kingstown.

Pigott immediately rose to the occasion and promised to furnish the evidence, for a substantial consideration, of course.

Pigott went to Lausanne, to America, several times to Paris, taking care to save as much as possible out of his expenses, and making the job last as long as possible.

At last Houston, pressed by his employers, demanded the proofs. Pigott thereupon declared that in a black bag at Paris there were documents which would supply all the evidence that Houston required. These documents, according to Pigott, had been left behind by some of those concerned in the murders.

Copies of these letters were handed to Houston, and being requested to supply the originals, Pigott went to Paris and put up at the Hotel St. Petersbourg.

After him came Houston with Dr. Maguire, Professor of Moral Philosophy at Trinity College, Dublin, who installed themselves in another hotel.

Pigott appeared on the night of their arrival with the original letters, saying that he had obtained them from Maurice Murphy and Tom Brown, who were waiting downstairs, and demanding the money which he had promised for the letters, or in default the letters themselves.

Maguire and Houston retired and held a consultation and examined the documents. Maguire was satisfied and handed Houston £850 in banknotes to pay for the letters. Returning to the room where Pigott was waiting, Houston gave him £605—£500 for Brown and Murphy, and the remainder for Pigott himself.

There were no Brown and no Murphy; they were as fictitious as Mrs. Harris. Thus Pigott went away with £605 in his pocket.

Arriving in London with the letters, Houston took them to the Marquess of Hartington, who declined to give him any advice as to how they should be used. He then approached the manager of a newspaper, who took the whole story for granted, and they were thus produced before the commission.

Asked whether inquiries had been made at the time as to the origin of the letters, the representative of the newspaper admitted that they had not.

He had paid Houston £1,780 for the documents and then handed them over to the solicitors of the newspaper and to a handwriting expert.

It was on the strength of these letters that a leading article appeared in the newspaper on April 18th, 1887, as follows :

"We possess and have had in our custody for some time, documentary evidence which has a most serious bearing on the Parnellite conspiracy, and which, after careful and most minute scrutiny, is, we are quite satisfied, authentic.

"We produce one document in facsimile to-day by a process the accuracy of which cannot be impugned, and we invite Mr. Parnell to explain how his signature has become attached to such a letter."

Shortly before this article appeared Houston had disclosed where he had got the letters, and questions were asked by Parnell's counsel as follows :

"After Mr. Houston made this communication to you, did you make inquiries from other people as to who Pigott was ?"

"No," was the reply.

"What his antecedents were ?"

"No, I had no means of doing so."

Pigott went into the witness-box on February 20th, 1889. He was not prepossessing in appearance, and during his examination practically the only words that could be got out of him were, "Oh, yes."

When the question of the letters was brought up on the following morning he was deadly pale. He was soon admitting that certain statements he had made were false. He denied all knowledge of the letter that had appeared in facsimile in the newspaper.

It was then shown that he had written letters to both political parties in Ireland begging for money for services rendered, and the texts of the letters were so amusing that the Court laughed.

Whereat Pigott cried out, "This is very amusing to you, but it certainly is not to me," only to send the judges and the rest into fresh laughter.

Asked to write down the word "hesitancy", he misspelt it "hesitency", as it had been in the facsimile letter. The Court then adjourned.

When Pigott's name was called on the morning of Tuesday, February 26th, he did not answer.

"Where is the witness?" asked Sir Charles Russell, Parnell's counsel.

"We don't know," replied the Attorney-General, and immediately the public in the court cried out, "He's bolted!"

Sir Charles applied for a warrant for Pigott's arrest. This was granted, and the court adjourned for half an hour.

Pigott was last seen at an hotel in Fleet Street, where he had been staying under surveillance of the police, at eleven o'clock at night. On Tuesday he was in Paris, no one having the least idea how he had got away. He then went on to Madrid, and took a room at the hotel.

On arrival he sent a telegram to his Dublin solicitor who was staying in Lincoln's Inn Fields, requesting him "to send what he had promised" to him under the name of "Ronald Ponsonby." This telegram, of course, was handed to the police.

Immediately the London police got busy and telegraphed to Madrid, with the result already stated.

Parnell became a national hero. A great crowd cheered him as he left the Law Courts and wherever he went. The inquiry dragged on. Parnell was examined and cross-examined, but, of course, this procedure was unnecessary.

He was elected an honorary life member of the National Liberal Club, was presented with the freedom of the City of Edinburgh and was fêted everywhere.

Edmund Waller

"*Excellent as a poet, wit and orator, but he was not a worthy, honourable man.*"

Thus Bishop Burnet sums up the character of Edmund Waller.

It depends upon the point of view, Waller earned a bad reputation for instigating a plot against the Parliament during the Civil War. Naturally the Roundheads regarded him as a snake in the grass; the Royalists, on the other hand, may have admired his enterprise.

Burnet, whose *History* is not without prejudice, takes exception to the way in which Waller bribed his way to immunity after he had been charged with conspiring against the Commonwealth. But if it were merely a question of money, there are few who would not buy their own lives.

In the second year of the war between King and Parliament, two men, named Tomkins and Challoner—the former Waller's brother-in-law, and the latter well-known on the Stock Exchange—hatched a reactionary plot which appears to have had the support of many Cavalier officers and noblemen. The object of these men was to :

1. Seize the children of Charles I and keep them in safe custody;
2. Capture Hampden, Pym and other leading members of the Parliament hostile to the King;
3. Arrest the Puritan Lord Mayor of London and the committee of the City Militia.
4. Capture the outworks, forts, magazines, and gates of the Tower of London and City, and to admit through the gates about 3000 Royalists from Oxford; and
5. To resist all payments to Parliament for the support of the army of Lord Essex, the Parliamentary general.

A certain night was fixed for the coup. But while the conspirators were assembling at the house of Tomkins in Fetter Lane, soldiers of the Parliament arrived and nipped the plot in the bud. A search of the cellar of the house disclosed incriminating documents, and all the conspirators were arrested.

Tomkins and Challoner were hanged in Holborn. On the scaffold Tomkins said :

"Gentlemen, I humbly acknowledge, in the sight of Almighty God (to whom, and to angels and to this great assembly of people, I am now a spectacle) that my sins have deserved of Him this untimely and shameful death ; and, touching the business for which I suffer, I acknowledge that affection to a brother-in-law, and affection and gratitude to the King, whose bread I have eaten now about twenty-two years—I confess these two motives drew me into this foolish business. I have often since declared to good friends that I was glad it was discovered, because it might have occasioned very ill consequences ; and truly I have repented having had any hand in it."

This was tantamount to a declaration that he, Tomkins, had been induced to join the conspirators by Waller. His reference to eating the bread of the King concerned the fact that he had been secretary to the Commissioners of the Royal Revenues.

Challoner's statement also implicated Waller. He declared on the scaffold : "It came from Mr. Waller that if we could make a moderate party here in London, and stand betwixt and in the gap to unite the King and Parliament, it would be a very acceptable work, for now the three kingdoms lay a-bleeding ; and unless that were down, there was no hopes to unite them."

Waller narrowly escaped the fate of his fellow conspirators. According to Clarendon, the historian of the rebellion : "With incredible dissimulation he acted such a remorse of conscience, that his trial was put off, out of Christian compassion, till he could recover his understanding."

But there is good reason to believe that Cromwell himself caused the prosecution against Waller to be deferred, for he was a near connection of the Parliamentary general.

Meanwhile Waller paid Puritan preachers to pray for his repentance. He apologized before the House of Commons, and finally he was released, fined £10,000 and allowed to retire to France.

When he had spent all his money and was near to starvation, he was allowed by Cromwell to return to England where, to quote Clarendon, "he lived after this in the good esteem and affection of many, the pity of most, and the reproach and scorn of few or none."

Waller, who was born at Coleshill, Buckinghamshire, on March 3rd, 1605, belonged to one of the most ancient families in the kingdom. Centuries before they had held large possessions in Kent.

An ancestor, Sir Richard Waller, captured Charles of Orleans at the battle of Agincourt, and kept him at his home in Kent for twenty-four years.

Robert, the father of Edmund, married the daughter of Griffith Hampden. This Edmund was first cousin to the Parliamentary leader.

At Eton and King's College, Cambridge, Edmund Waller early showed an aptitude for writing poetry. He was returned Member of Parliament for the borough of Agmondesham (Amersham) before he was 17 years old. But the members of that Borough were not allowed to speak in the House, so Waller was forced to keep silent until the dissolution in 1622. He was, however, introduced at the Court of James I, and appears to have been a favourite.

At the age of 18 he published his first poem. At intervals other pieces followed. He wrote slowly, but always with polish.

In 1625 Waller was returned for the Borough of Chepping Wycombe (High Wycombe), but two years later represented Agmondesham with the right to take part in debates.

At 25 he married a Miss Banks, a city heiress, and retired to his home near Beaconsfield to spend his time in writing.

In a few years his wife died, leaving a son and daughter, and Waller returned to London Society. He now besieged the heart of Lady Dorothea Sydney, daughter of the Earl of Leicester, whom he calls Sacharissa. He immortalized her in a poem.

He chose the name Sacharissa because she was sweet. But even his poetry had no effect upon the haughtiness of the beauty, and Waller had nothing pleasant to say about her afterwards.

Some years afterwards, however, the two met again, and Sacharissa asked whether he would ever write nice things about her again. To which the poet replied: "Yes, when you are as young again."

Another poem, written under the *nom de plume* of "Amoret,"

was designed to capture the fair Lady Sophia Murray, but she, too, rejected him.

After the exposure of his plot he wrote a poem eulogizing Cromwell, which is supposed to be the finest of all his compositions.

On the restoration of Charles II, however, it would seem that Waller was just as ready to propitiate him as he had been Cromwell. His pen was scarcely dry from writing a glowing epitaph of Cromwell, when he produced another poem congratulating the King "on his Majesty's happy return."

In 1661 Waller again entered Parliament, this time for Hastings, and he continued to be a favourite at the court of Charles II until nearly the end of his life.

He died in his eighty-third year, in the autumn of the year 1688.

Waller is described as one of the most witty men of his time. Even Clarendon admits that "his company was acceptable where his spirit was odious."

Charles, Lord Stourton

Over a tomb in Salisbury Cathedral there was once suspended a silken cord. Time has rotted it away, and the event which it symbolized is almost forgotten.

But one can still hear the story, told in the annals of Salisbury, of the "wicked Lord Stourton," who was hanged in Queen Mary's reign for an atrocious murder.

The house of Stourton was of great antiquity in Wiltshire. The family had held great estates even before the Conqueror, and one famous ancestor, one Botolph de Stourton, was a vigorous opponent of the Norman invader.

From him came a line of knights who fought in the Crusades, and Sir John Stourton, a great warrior and statesman in the reign of Henry VI, was raised to the peerage as Lord Stourton. It is his great-great-grandson who is the "villain" of the silken cord.

In the Middle Ages the Stourton family were rigid in their adherence to the laws concerning poaching in the forests. On their property was a great deal of forest land,

and woe betide any of the poor people who killed any of the beasts of the chase.

About the time of Henry VIII there arose disputes between the common people and the noble families about the ownership of land which had been used by the former since the days of the Conqueror. The big landowners began to encroach upon this common land and enclose it for their own pastures and flocks.

The evil had obtained such proportions that in the reign of Edward VI a proclamation was issued compelling those who had stolen land to throw it open for one day in the year. In default they were mulcted in heavy penalties.

In the parish of Kilmington near the ancestral estates of the Stourtons lived a yeoman family named Hartgill. By the time that Charles, the eighth Lord Stourton, came into possession of these estates, a vendetta had been going on for many years between the two families.

Charles took up the quarrel with increased bitterness.

One day near Whitsuntide, Lord Stourton visited the Hartgills with a large crowd of retainers and complained that they had been hunting with horses and dogs on his property.

The Hartgills were apprised of the approach of Stourton and his party, and forthwith took refuge in the parish church. One of the Hartgill family, however, ran back to his house to get bows and arrows and other weapons of defence. On the way he was shot at by the Stourton retainers, but not an arrow found its mark.

Many of the villagers arrived to assist the Hartgills and, being outnumbered, the Stourtons were forced to beat a retreat. The elder Hartgills, unable to take any part in the fighting, established themselves in the tower of the church, where food was brought to them at intervals.

One of the sons, young John Hartgill, decided to go to London and lay the matter before Queen Mary and her Council. But he had scarcely left the village when the Stourtons returned to the churchyard and began a siege.

The Hartgill stables were visited and a fine hunter belonging to the head of the family was deliberately shot with a cross-bow in sight of its owner, who was looking through the church window.

The son was successful in getting the Council to move,

and a commission, led by the High Sheriff of Somerset, arrived to make inquiries.

Stourton was ordered to appear before them. His explanation was unsatisfactory and he was taken to London and lodged in the Fleet Prison. But before long he was back at Kilmington, persecuting the Hartgills, having made his escape from the prison by bribery or influence.

During the next two or three years no serious clash between the two families occurred, although there were a number of minor fights. But the Hartgills nursed their grievances and, at a favourable opportunity they petitioned the Queen for redress. Stourton was again called before the Council, when he promised good behaviour, and gave an undertaking to return any cattle which his men had stolen from the petitioners.

In response to an invitation, several of the Hartgills went to the Stourton manor to bring home their cattle. On the way they were attacked by several of Stourton's men, John Hartgill being wounded and left for dead in the road.

The matter was now brought before the Star Chamber, and Stourton was requested to pay over to the Hartgills a sum of money to indemnify them for their losses. To hurry the payment of the indemnity Stourton was again thrown into the Fleet Prison.

At length he undertook to pay and was released.

A meeting was arranged between the Stourtons and the Hartgills. On a frosty January morning they all assembled at the church. But Stourton brought with him a large party of men on horseback and foot. The elder Hartgills had again taken refuge in the roof.

Stourton sent them a message that they must come out, as the church "was no place to talk of worldly matters." The Hartgills came out of their hiding-place, but would not venture near Stourton and his crowd.

"My lord," said the old man Hartgill, "I see many of mine enemies about your lordship, therefore I am much afraid to come any nearer."

Whereupon Stourton promised that they should not be harmed.

On this assurance they approached nearer, and Stourton began a speech in which he told them that if they would come into the church house he would pay them the money.

The Hartgills refused to go into any covered place but the church.

A table was now produced and placed on the green in front of the building. On it Stourton threw a purse as if about to make payment. "The Council have ordered me to pay you a certain sum of money, and you shall have every penny," he promised.

No sooner had he spoken, however, than he gripped the arm of William Hartgill, exclaiming, "I arrest you of felony."

About a dozen of his men surrounded the other party, and buffeted them into the church house. The Hartgills were bound, and when helpless their purses were taken from them. Stourton also removed a turquoise from one of the pockets. This he afterwards gave to Lady Stourton.

This is the account of the affair given by Strype, the historian, who adds that the Hartgills, father and son, were taken to the Stourton estate, and thrust into a house. Two magistrates, creatures of Stourton, examined them, on what charge is not clear.

Afterwards they were unmercifully whipped until it was thought that they were dead. The presumed dead bodies were wrapped in their own gowns, and thrown into an underground chamber. When one of them disclosed by his groans that he was still alive, Stourton ordered one of his servants to cut the dying man's throat.

One of Stourton's men protested at the murder, but was promptly silenced by Stourton with the words . "What, faint-hearted fool! Is it any more than ridding the world of two knaves, that living were troublesome to God's law and man's ? There is no more account to be made of them than the killing of two sheep."

Thus the sinister work was finished, and a grave was dug for the two Hartgills.

But the peer could not hope to escape retribution. The whole story came out; he was arrested and committed to the Tower of London. His trial took place on February 26th, and he was sentenced to be executed. Four of his men were also convicted.

The men were hanged at Tyburn. Stourton was throttled by a silken cord at Salisbury on March 6th, 1557. He was buried in the Cathedral, a silken cord hanging in front of his tomb.

William Willett

Twenty-two years ago to-day died William Willett, a Chelsea builder, who in the year 1907 became obsessed with the idea that everyone got up too late in the summer time.

It was a pity, Willett thought, that so many hours of daylight should be wasted. The summer evenings were not long enough for pleasure and outdoor recreation. Could not something be done to transfer these morning hours to the evening?

Willett conceived the idea of putting on the clock eighty minutes. In his anxiety to conserve more than a full hour he had overstepped the mark and added another twenty minutes. If he had stipulated only an hour, it is probable that his scheme of daylight saving would have been adopted years before the measure passed the Houses of Parliament.

Willett's campaign for putting on the clock by eighty minutes cost him a good deal of money, for he footed the bill for propaganda himself.

About twelve months after he began to advocate daylight saving, he attracted the attention of the authorities, and Mr. (afterward Sir Robert) Pearce introduced a Bill in the House of Commons to make it compulsory to put on the clock.

In 1909 the Bill went to a Select Committee, but it is doubtful whether anything further would have been heard of it had it not been for the War. In 1916 an expert committee was set up to inquire into ways and means for saving fuel, and the Committee advised that Willett's scheme should be adopted.

Willett had suggested putting on the clock by eighty minutes, by four separate movements. The Committee, on the other hand, recommended one movement of sixty minutes.

On May 17th, 1916, an Act was passed and the scheme was put in operation on the following Sunday, May 21st. There was a storm of opposition.

Farmers objected to the new measure because their milkers had to get up an hour earlier to do their work. Farmers, no doubt, had a reasonable complaint, for it meant that their employees would have to get up in darkness during the greater part of the year. It was also argued that during the hay and corn harvests the labourers would be idle for an hour while the dew was dried off the mown harvest by the sun.

At the outset of the controversy that followed there was much sympathy with the farmers, but when the scheme was put to practical test it was found that the difficulties had been much exaggerated.

On May 21st, 1916, therefore, Summer Time was introduced.

At first there was much confusion and prejudice. The Royal Meteorological Society warned everyone that Greenwich mean time would still be used for meteorological observations. The Port of London Authority announced that Greenwich time would apply to movements of the tides.

The parks belonging to the Office of Works and the London County Council decided to close at dusk, which meant that they would be open an extra hour in the evening. Kew Gardens, on the other hand, ignored the daylight saving scheme and decided to close by the clock.

In Edinburgh the confusion was even more marked, for the gun at the Castle was fired at 1 P.M. Summer Time, while the ball on the top of the Nelson monument on Calton Hill fell at 1 o'clock Greenwich mean time. This arrangement was continued for the benefit of seamen who could see it from the Firth of Forth.

The time fixed for changing clocks was 2 A.M. on a Sunday.

After the War several Acts of Parliament were passed relating to Summer Time. Eventually in 1925 it was enacted that Summer Time should begin on the day following the third Saturday in April. If that should prove to be Easter Day the clock was to be put on on the day following the second Saturday in April. The date for the closing of Summer Time was fixed for the first Saturday in October.

In 1916 a nation-wide campaign was begun in the United States for the support of daylight saving. For about a year the subject was the centre of a controversy. In 1917, however, an Act was passed by Congress, to advance United States time by one hour on the last Sunday in March and to put it back by one hour on the last Sunday in October.

This Act was in force for one year from March 31st to October 27th, 1918, and it was renewed from March 30th,

1919. Meantime, however, there was an outcry throughout the continent, particularly from the farmers, and the Act was repealed on August 20th, 1919.

From that time onwards the legislation in regard to daylight saving was spasmodic, and although it was observed in the States of Massachusetts and Rhode Island and in the Metropolitan district of New York, the enthusiasm—or what little there had been—waned considerably.

Some of the large cities adopted the scheme, while others repudiated it. In the States west of the Mississippi daylight saving was rejected.

Although daylight saving was widely used in the northeast, it even there found opposition, particularly in Connecticut, where it was an offence to show anything but Eastern standard time. Later, however, a number of towns in that State observed daylight saving.

When the Bill was discussed in the House of Commons in 1925, some curious objections were raised to the continuance of Summer Time. One member said that he had received a letter from a woman who wrote: "I am the mother of nine, the last still-born owing to Summer Time."

Another member suggested that explicit instructions should be issued to the public on how and when to put clocks on. He knew of a family who sat up until 2 A.M. to make the change exactly at that time.

During the World War nearly every country in Europe adopted the device of putting the clock forward an hour to save fuel for lighting and heating. Bills were adopted by Germany, Austria, Italy, and in Scandinavia, but were not revived. France introduced a permanent Summer Time Bill in 1923. Canada, Holland, Belgium, Spain, and Portugal followed suit.

William Willett was born in 1857, and died on March 4th, 1915. He did not live, therefore, to see the result of his campaign. He was the head of a building firm bearing his name with headquarters in Sloane Square, London.

Henry the Navigator (of Portugal)

A gale blew down the coast from the Bay of Biscay and rocked the castle of King John of Portugal at Oporto.

The frail, white-haired woman raised her aching head from the pillow, and glancing round at her husband and her three sons, murmured: "What wind blows so strong against the house?"

"The north wind," replied her husband.

"Then it is the wind for your voyage," the woman said.

And then, with another effort that taxed her waning strength, Phillippa, the daughter of the English John of Gaunt, pleaded that her illness should not deter them from their contemplated crusade against the Moors.

"The Lord hath need of thy help," she whispered.

Prince Henry, the third son, gazed sorrowfully at his mother, and kneeling by the bedside placed his hand in hers.

It was his mother's inspiring words that assisted Henry in his subsequent campaigns and made him one of the most important figures in history; the man who laid the foundations and built the walls of Portugal's great colonial empire.

He was the founder of the Aviz dynasty, under which Portugal reduced Castile and conquered the Moors of Morocco, giving the country an important voice in the counsels of Europe.

While his cousin, the English Henry V, was leading his starved and ragged army to victory at Agincourt, Henry of Portugal was gaining his laurels in Morocco. Landing at Ceuta, the "African Gibraltar," he led his men with conspicuous gallantry against the black hordes.

This battle of the Cross and the Crescent is described by old chroniclers, who give a vivid picture of the struggle with the Moslems making a stand at the very walls of the city, where the Christians were held up by a negro giant "who fought naked, but with the strength of many men, hurling the Christians to the earth with stones."

Then the negro was brought down by a lance thrust, and Ceuta fell.

Having established himself at Ceuta, Henry resolved to probe the secrets of Morocco by sending ships down the west coast of Africa, across the unknown ocean where men had never sailed before.

He thus began his explorations, which earned him the surname of "Navigator," although he, himself, never sailed on the expeditions.

In the year 1415, the year of Ceuta, he commissioned a certain John de Trasto for the expedition to find a passage to India, and thus bring Western Europe into direct contact with the treasures of the East, and to spread the Christian faith.

Henry established himself at Sagres (Cape St. Vincent) and built a palace, a chapel, a study, an observatory (the earliest in Portugal), and a village for his men.

From these headquarters he sent, sometimes single ships, sometimes huge armadas, to sail southwards beyond the Cape of Nun, the utmost limit of navigation, beyond which, according to mariners, there was no return.

John de Trasto pushed the Portuguese influence to Grand Canary. This was not a voyage of discovery, for the Canarian Archipelago was well known to the French and Spaniards. It was not until ten years later that Henry really made a significant move towards a colonial empire for Portugal.

In 1424 he attempted to purchase the Canaries and began colonization. Three years later in collaboration with his father, King John, he sent out an expedition to the Azores, and was gathering information about the coast of Guinea and the interior of Africa.

In 1433 the old king died, pleading with his son not to give up those schemes which, because of previous failures, such as the attempt to round Cape Bojador, were ridiculed for their costliness.

The following year one of the prince's ships doubled the cape, and by the close of 1436 the Portuguese had almost reached Cape Blanco. In 1441 colonization was begun in earnest, and the first slaves and the first gold dust were brought back from the Guinea coasts.

In the meantime these successes were attracting the attention of merchants and seamen from Lisbon and Lagos, and hosts of adventurers offered themselves for the expeditions.

In 1443 the Prince was created a Knight of the Garter by Henry VI.

For forty years captains and crews of many nations sailed under licence from Henry. Year after year they pushed south until they had explored 1,350 miles beyond the charted world, and the North Star "was so low that it did almost seem to touch the sea."

Many strange tales were brought back to Henry the Navigator, tales of elephants and crocodiles, of natives with darts and spears tipped with poison. Some of the natives thought that the white men had been painted and often tried to rub off the paint.

Stories were told of trees whose trunks were one hundred and eight spans round at the foot, and of the discovery of the four great rivers that flowed from the Garden of Eden.

One of the most interesting stories is that which concerns the discovery of the gold country, and how the leader of the expedition, Diego Gomez, made friends with a native king who "always fastened his horse to a nugget of gold that twenty men could hardly move."

"We met," Gomez adds, "in a great wood, and he brought with him a vast throng of people with poisoned arrows, assagais, swords, and shields."

A formidable personage was this king, whose fierceness could be tempered only with the judicious use of port wine and biscuits.

The port wine, it appears, made him feel a new man, for, according to Gomez, who told the story to Henry, the king became "pleased and extremely gracious, giving me three negroes and swearing to me by the one and only God that he would never again make war against Christians, but that they might trade and travel through all the country."

All the information obtained by his navigators was sifted and studied by Henry, and gradually led to the first real map of the Old World.

Before this time maps had been either theoretical or the mere "scratchings of savages," having little regard to facts and much to legend.

But the chart of Fra Mauro, which is a scientific review of Henry's explorations crammed with detail and done on a vast scale, is the forerunner of the modern map.

Henry attended to the education and conversion to Christianity of the hundreds of black slaves whom his captains brought back to Portugal, and founded colonies along the routes of exploration. He improved the art of ship-building, and did a great deal for navigation in regard to the perfection of instruments.

Henry was one of the greatest navigators the world has ever known, but he never went to sea himself. Seated in his study at Sagres, he directed his captains through the unknown seas in search of islands, which either through intuition or deduction he thought existed.

He was stern but always generous, spending his days and often his nights at work, and following a rule of monkish asceticism.

Henry was born on March 4th, 1394.

He died on November 13th, 1460, in his town near Cape St. Vincent, and was buried in the church of St. Mary at Lagos. A year later his body was removed to a monastery at Batalha.

His great nephew, King Dom Manuel, had a statue of him erected at the church of Belem. In 1840 a monument was built to his memory at Sagres by the Marquis de Sa da Bandeira, while another statue has been placed in the Plaza Infante Henriquez at Oporto, close to the site of the palace where he was born.

The site of the palace is now partly occupied by a street officially named after him, but better known as the Rua dos Ingleses, so called because the English wine merchants who owned the port wine industry met there for centuries to transact their business.

It is not only the personal deeds of Prince Henry which will linger long in history, for the subsequent results of his labours have brought great advantages to the human race.

Only a comparatively small part of his task was accomplished by himself. For forty years after his death his successors worked for the opening out of the African, or southeast, route to the Indies, and the Prince's share has been forgotten in the glory obtained by Diego Cam, Bartholomew Diaz or Vasco da Gama.

The Story of Somerset House

Edward Seymour, the brother of Jane Seymour, wife of Henry VIII, had no scruples when he began to build a mansion on his elevation to the dukedom of Somerset.

To obtain the site and materials he appears to have been guilty of infringing both public and private rights.

The Strand Inn, the houses of the Bishops of Lichfield and Coventry, and also of the Bishops of Worcester and Llandaff, and the church and churchyard of St. Mary-le-Strand, were demolished to make way for Seymour's house.

New materials for the building of the houses of the nobility in those days could be obtained only after long delay by bringing the stone by sea. Thus, if an owner was anxious for his house to be built quickly he had little conscience about pulling down other stone buildings to get the material.

Somerset went quite far afield for his purpose. He caused the charnel house of Old St. Paul's and the chapel above it to be pulled down, and also a large cloister on the north of St. Paul's called Pardon Churchyard, which contained important monuments.

He also demolished the steeple and part of the church of the Priory of St. John of Jerusalem in Clerkenwell. When at the zenith of his power he was not averse from giving favours to the clergy in return for parcels of property on which there were suitable buildings.

According to Bishop Burnet, "many bishops and cathedrals had resigned many manors to him for obtaining his favour."

Bishop Babington, for instance, who was appointed to the see of Llandaff in 1591, which had been depleted of its property during the time of Somerset, declared that he was only Bishop of "Aff," as "Land" had been taken from him.

In addition, while Lord High Treasurer and Earl Marshal, Somerset is said to have sold chantry lands to his friends at cheap rates.

His power was already beginning to wane as the magnificent Somerset House was rising in its splendour. It was not long after he had caused his brother to be beheaded and had rifled St. Paul's churchyard and Pardon churchyard that he was committed to the Tower.

One of the grounds of complaint against him was that he had sought his own glory "as appeared by his building of most sumptuous and costly buildings, and specially in the time of the King's wars, and the King's soldiers unpaid."

. Eventually he was released from the Tower with his influence curbed. Later he was sent to the fortress again, and beheaded.

It is believed that Somerset never actually lived in the house, which was the first building of Italian architecture erected in this country.

On his death the building fell into the possession of the Crown, and was occupied for a time by Princess Elizabeth (afterwards Queen Elizabeth) and was known as "her place called Somerset Place, beyond Strand Bridge." The house later became the residence of Anne of Denmark, the consort of James I, and when the King died he lay in state there.

Then Somerset House was settled for life on Henrietta Maria, the wife of Charles I, and was refitted in 1626. Being allowed to carry on her own religion, she turned Somerset House into an ecclesiastical establishment.

After the execution of Charles I, an Act was passed for selling "several tenements in the Strand, parcel of the possession of Charles Stuart and Henrietta Maria, late King and Queen of England, belonging unto Somerset House."

The money thus obtained was to be used for the payment of the Commonwealth troops, but it appears that the property was never definitely disposed of. On the Restoration, Henrietta Maria was back in her Palace, and made considerable additions, and for the first time introduced in England the mode of inlaying floors with different coloured wood.

Pepys has references to Henrietta's house. He records that on September 7th, 1662, he was taken into her Majesty's Presence Chamber, and saw for the first time the Queen Consort, Catherine of Braganza, whom he describes as "though she be not very charming, yet she hath a good, modest and innocent look which is pleasing."

Pepys adds that the only English words he ever heard her utter were "You lie" to an accusation by her husband, Charles.

Another entry in the *Diary* states : "The Queen Mother

hath outrun herself in her expenses, and is now come to pay very ill or run in debt, the money being spent that she received for leases."

On the death of Charles II, Somerset House became the residence of Catherine of Braganza, and she lived there until her return to Portugal in 1692.

It was here that Sir Edmundbury Godfrey is supposed to have been murdered, his body afterwards being taken to Hampstead Heath and left there.

The house still continued to belong to successive queens until April 1775, when Queen Charlotte was granted Buckingham Palace, and was requested to give up Somerset House, which would be appropriated "to such uses as shall be found most useful to the public." The demolition of the buildings was begun as soon as the necessary Act of Parliament had been passed.

The new building was the work of Sir William Chambers. Although he has not gone down in history with a reputation approaching that of Sir Christopher Wren, he was one of the foremost architects of the eighteenth century.

He was appointed architect of Somerset House in 1775 while Comptroller of His Majesty's Works. By 1779 he had completed one of the fronts.

According to a parliamentary return of about 1790, nearly £370,000 was expended on the building.

No settled use appears to have been allocated to Somerset House in its early days. The annual exhibition of paintings of the Royal Academy was held there, the first taking place in May 1780, and it continued annually until the National Gallery was built.

The Society of Antiquaries, and other learned bodies, including the Royal Astronomical and the Geological Societies, also met there from time to time.

The whole of the east wing of Somerset House was left unfinished by Sir William Chambers, but was completed in 1829 from the designs of Sir R. Smirke. This part is now King's College.

At that time the Exchequer and Audit Department and the Inland Revenue, with other Government departments, had been placed there.

Sir William Chambers was born at Stockholm in 1726. He was the son of a Scotsman who had gone over to Sweden temporarily to obtain money from Charles XII for stores which he had supplied.

Young Chambers had a hankering after the sea, and started life as a supercargo in a merchant ship trading with China.

On these voyages he sketched many buildings in foreign cities, and was particularly attracted by Italian architecture. Later he studied architecture in Italy and France.

On his return to England he attracted the attention of the Court, and was appointed teacher of architectural drawing to the young Prince George, afterwards George III.

For thirty years he was regarded as the leading architect in England.

During the building of Somerset House he received £2000 a year. He was also the designer of the Royal State coach, which Walpole described as "a beautiful object, though crowded with improprieties," which cost £8000.

Many of the ornamental details of Somerset House were copied by Chambers from architecture in Rome, and he employed many well-known sculptors for the purpose.

In his capacity as architect to the Crown he was called upon to lay out the gardens at Kew, and in 1765 he published *Plans, Elevations, Sections, and Perpective Views of the Gardens and Buildings at Kew*.

Both in his writings and designs he showed a tendency to the Chinese mode of architecture and gardening. In 1771 he was made a knight of the Swedish Order of the Polar Star, and in the following year published *A Dissertation on Oriental Gardening*, which resulted in many gardens of large houses being laid out according to his theories.

He was architect of the house of the Marquess of Abercorn, near Edinburgh, and Milton Abbey, Dorsetshire.

In 1857 a new wing was built to Somerset House from the designs of the architect Pennethorne, which cost more than £100,000.

At the end of the year 1874 the wills, which had hitherto been housed at Doctors' Commons, were deposited in Somerset House.

The Department of the Registrar-General was established in 1836 by the passing of an Act for registering all births, marriages, and deaths in England and Wales after June 30th, 1837.

Before this date all registration was done by means of

parish registers, and the records were not kept in a central registry.

Parish registers were introduced by Cromwell in 1538 on the dissolution of the monasteries. This order raised a storm all over the country, for it was regarded merely as an attempt to get a census of the people to levy new taxes.

Previous to the registration of 1801, there was no official census of the population, and the only way of finding out the increase of population was by subtracting deaths from births.

As many people did not avail themselves of voluntary registration, estimates were unreliable.

Cardinal Mazarin

"Must I quit all these ?"

Cardinal Mazarin was dying. As minister of the Regency during the minority of Louis XIV of France, he had piled up enormous wealth. Around the walls of his gallery were many pictures by the great masters.

Mazarin sat in a chair, wearing nightcap and dressing-gown. He gazed wistfully at the paintings that he was destined to leave behind in a short time.

"Look !" he exclaimed to those standing round. "Look at that Correggio ! This Venus of Titian ! That incomparable Deluge of Caracci ! Ah, my friends, I must quit all these. Farewell, dear pictures that I loved so dearly, and that cost me so much !"

For Mazarin death brought two regrets—the parting with his treasures and the fact that his peculiarly handsome appearance had been dissipated by the ravages of disease. He tried to remedy the loss of his good looks by appearing rouged and painted. Often, however, he was prodigal with the vermilion to the amusement of his courtiers.

In a highly painted and powdered state he was carried one day to the promenade, where he was subjected to the ironical compliments of his friends.

Mazarin was an inveterate gambler. As he lay on his death-bed he could not resist a game of cards, his hand being held by others during the play. When the papal nuncio came to give the cardinal the usual plenary indulgence he found him still at play.

Mazarin achieved great things for France, yet he was inferior to his famous tutor, Cardinal Richelieu.

He was an Italian by birth and was born at Pescara, in the Abruzzi, on July 4th, 1602. It is generally conceded that he came of an illustrious Sicilian family, although his parents were poor.

He was educated at a Jesuits' college in Rome, and, having distinguished himself there, went to the university of Alcala to continue his studies. Returning home, he entered the army of the Pope, and served for some time as captain of infantry.

It was while he was serving Pope Urban VIII that it was discovered that he had a genius for negotiation. He was employed to negotiate with the French and Spanish generals and succeeded in bringing about the peace of Moncon in 1626.

Soon afterwards, France, Germany, Spain, and Savoy were involved in a dispute about the succession to the Duchy of Mantua. The Pope decided to mediate, and Mazarin accompanied Cardinal Sacchetti to Turin for the purpose. In 1631 he brought about the treaty of Cherasco, which established peace.

A few months before this Mazarin had met Louis XIII of France and Cardinal Richelieu. When, therefore, he was sent in 1634 as nuncio to Paris, he had no great difficulty in ingratiating himself with the French monarch and his minister.

In 1636 he returned to Rome with a mission from Louis, which included a request that the Pope should make Mazarin a cardinal. Urban refused to elevate Mazarin, and he went back to France in high dudgeon.

Three years later, however, when Mazarin had accomplished a particularly difficult task in Savoy, the Pope acceded to the request of the French sovereign, and Mazarin received his cap.

During the closing days of Richelieu, Mazarin was his firm friend and assistant, and when the former died in December 1642, he recommended to the king that Mazarin should be appointed in his place. But although he carried on the duties of prime minister, he did not receive the title during the reign of Louis XIII.

With the death of Louis there began a period of much difficulty for Mazarin. The Queen-Regent, Anne of Austria, disliked him, and immediately appointed the Bishop of Beauvais to the office of prime minister.

But matters soon began to go wrong, and Anne was only too anxious to get Mazarin back. Thus, during the minority of Louis XIV, he continued to advise the regency.

He continued on the traditions of Richelieu and prosecuted the war against Spain and Germany. Ultimately, to his great credit, came the peace of Westphalia which ended a European strife of thirty years. Through this France gained some important territorial concessions.

But the very year that the German war was terminated came the civil war in the Fronde. The Parliament of Paris and many of the higher aristocracy rebelled against the authority of Mazarin. Proclaiming an attachment to the Crown the conspirators made it clear that they opposed only Mazarin. The people of Paris joined the revolt.

Nobles and mob marched through the streets of the City and demonstrated before the royal palace. Bowing before the storm, Mazarin left Paris, threading his way through the barricades that had been erected. The revolution extended to the provinces.

But the tide again turned in his favour, and the Court returned to the City in triumph.

Mazarin, who had imposed heavy taxes on the people to cover his own extravagance, increased his demands, and the triumph of the Crown had the effect of postponing reforms for 150 years.

From this time the power of Mazarin began to grow. By subtlety and craft he overcame the efforts of his foes, and although the egotistic Louis XIV had reached his majority, Mazarin was the virtual ruler of the country.

Having quieted France from within, he declared war on Spain, by which France gained Artois, part of Flanders, Hainault, and Luxembourg. At the same time, a marriage was arranged between Louis and the Infanta Maria Theresa, daughter of Philip IV of Spain.

France was now the dominant political factor in Europe. She had displaced the proud and powerful House of Austria which had dictated policies for a century and a half.

Thus all Mazarin's plans had prospered; but France still

groaned under the tyranny of the Crown and its advisers, for both noble and peasant were abased. The throne was supreme.

The last great public work of Mazarin was to conclude a treaty with the Duke of Lorraine by which further territory came into possession of the French Crown.

Mazarin did not live to enjoy the fruits of his toils. He had made himself rich, had expended money lavishly in the acquisition of treasures. But, having climbed to the summit of his glory, he found himself facing death.

Early in 1661 he was smitten with an incurable malady, at a time when he was actually negotiating the treaty with the Duke of Lorraine. He brought home the treaty to the Louvre only to learn from his physician, Grenaud, that he had only two months to live.

But, although an Italian, he was concerned to the last about the country he had adopted and served.

He outlined a policy which he thought Louis XIV should follow, and named the ministers whom he advised the King to employ.

Mazarin died at the early age of fifty-nine, on March 9th, 1661.

Louis XIV then began to reign. He ignored the advice of Mazarin. He took over complete control. The ministers Mazarin had recommended became his puppets.

"The State, it is I," said Louis.

The Luddite Riots

One of the strangest and most foolish industrial disputes that ever occurred in England began on March 11th, 1811, in Nottinghamshire. It led to a series of riots which continued intermittently for five years, during which time a tremendous amount of damage was done wantonly.

The hosiery trade, which had suffered a depression for some years, was almost completely ruined by ruthless sabotage. As a large proportion of the population of the county were engaged in the industry, the consequence can readily be imagined.

Wages had been falling for some time, for the scarcity of work had reduced the value of labour.

At the beginning of February, ominous rumblings of discontent among the workers were heard. Employers and the authorities were alive to possible rioting, and it was arranged to employ out-of-work knitters to sweep the streets, so as to keep the men from mischief.

But it was impossible to find work for all those unemployed. In addition, a further reduction in wages for those still at work made the workers as discontented as those without jobs.

At length the unemployed lost patience, began to make threats against the employers, and finally demonstrated in the market-place of Nottingham.

Workers and unemployed came from every district around, and the situation had taken on an ugly aspect, necessitating the calling out of the military. The soldiers arrived just in time to prevent destruction of property in Nottingham. But that same night an organized scheme of sabotage was begun.

At Arnold, a village four miles north of Nottingham, sixty-three knitting frames were demolished. In the following three weeks over two hundred others were put out of action.

The work of destruction was carried out at night with extraordinary secrecy by workmen urged on by agitators. They formed a secret society, calling themselves Luddites, binding themselves by oaths, and disguising themselves to avoid detection.

The quaint name of Luddites appears to have been derived from a youth named Ludlam, the pioneer of the frame-smashing. He worked for his father, a framework-knitter, and when he was told to carry out certain work he deliberately took a hammer and smashed the frame.

The method of operation of the Luddites was to assemble in parties from six to sixty, according to the work of sabotage on hand, appoint a leader, known as the General or Ned Ludd, and to arm themselves with pistols, swords, hatchets and hammers. The swordsmen and owners of the pistols were posted at the entrance to a factory or house, while the others went inside and demolished the frames.

Later they all reassembled at another spot when, if no further destruction were intended for that night, the leader would call out the numbers—not names—of the men, fire a pistol, and dismiss the gang.

Having dispersed, they removed the black handkerchiefs from their eyes and returned home.

This "black-gang" procedure may have been rather melodramatic, but it kept the police continually on the alert and, at length, forced them to admit defeat.

Despite all efforts of the local police force, the outrages continued, and a large military contingent was brought into the neighbourhood. Two London police magistrates, together with Metropolitan constables, also arrived to assist the local civil power to discover the ringleaders.

It was decided that the only way to combat stealth was to employ stealth. A secret committee was formed of police and soldiers, and a large sum of money was allotted for the purpose of bribery to obtain information. A Royal proclamation was issued warning the offenders.

Despite these measures, the destruction went on and was even redoubled in violence.

On the night of Sunday, November 10th, a party of Luddites entered the village of Bulwell to demolish the frames of a manufacturer named Hollingworth. But, having been warned of their visit, he obtained the assistance of several friends armed with firearms.

A miniature battle took place, and one of the attackers, John Westley, of Arnold, was fatally wounded. The mob were so enraged that they resumed the attack with vigour. At last they forced an entrance, caused the defenders to evacuate the factory and destroyed not only the frames but all the furniture in the place.

On the following day they attacked a wagon-load of frames near Arnold, and a few days later went in a body to Sutton-in-Ashfield, where they reduced to ruins thirty-seven frames. On this occasion they were dispersed by the military, who succeeded in capturing prisoners, four of whom were committed for trial.

This appears to have had the effect of slowing up the scheme of sabotage, for during the next week only one frame was destroyed. A number of haystacks were burned, however, in revenge against the owners, who had been called out in the yeomanry and had assisted in tracking down the Luddites.

On Sunday night, November 24th, there was a resumption of the outrages, thirty-four frames being demolished at Basford, and a further eleven on the following day.

On December 6th an order was issued by the magistrates which almost amounted to martial law. They ordered all persons in the affected districts to remain in their houses after 10 o'clock at night. All public-houses were closed at the same hour.

During the next six days the activities of the Luddites were intensified, and about fifty more frames were destroyed in various villages around Nottingham.

A further proclamation was now issued offering a reward of £50 for information leading to the arrest of any of the offenders. But if any of the residents in the neighbourhood possessed such information they kept away from the authorities, fearing reprisals by the Luddites.

Meanwhile the men were excited to further deeds of violence.

They now began a concerted campaign of plunder of farmhouses, stealing money and provisions, and declaring that they "would not starve while there was plenty in the land."

The destruction of frames continued through February 1812, and on the 20th of this month so many people had been thrown out of work that nearly 5000 families were compelled to seek relief out of the poor rates.

The next move on the part of the authorities was to open a fund to provide money to increase the Government rewards. This resulted in the apprehension of seven of the Luddites, who were charged at the March assizes and sentenced to transportation. One of them was Jeremiah Brandreth, known as the "Nottingham Captain."

Still the outrages continued, and the Government finally considered it necessary to pass an Act making the penalty for breaking knitting or lace frames one of death.

In the following month an employer named Trentham was shot by two ruffians as he stood at his door. The wound, however, was not severe. A reward of £600 was offered for the arrest of these men, but they were never brought to justice.

There were spasmodic outbreaks of destruction until October 1816, when they finally ceased. Over one thousand stocking frames and a large number of lace frames had been destroyed in Nottinghamshire alone. At times the riots spread into Derbyshire and Yorkshire, and one or two cases were reported from Lancashire.

The movement died down, not as a result of the vigilance of the authorities, but because the perpetrators of the outrages came, in time, to see the folly of destroying the implements of their own livelihood. Moreover, the damage was a liability on the county rates.

Cesare Borgia

For utter depravity there are few worse records in history than those of the Borgias, Pope Alexander VI, Cesare, his son, and Lucrezia, his daughter.

Rodrigo Borgia, the father, intrigued and bought his elevation to Papal authority by his great wealth. At no previous or subsequent election of a Pope were such large sums of money expended in buying votes, and on August 10th, 1492, Rodrigo, to his great joy, was elected.

He adopted the title of Alexander VI, and while the smaller fry of the Church were not at first alarmed by his election, the cardinals, who knew his character, were by no means impressed.

Contrary, however, to general expectation, during the first part of his reign Alexander ruled with discretion in striking contrast with the disorderly method of government under the previous Pope.

But a man of Alexander's passions and temperament could not be expected to continue as a model ruler. Having dug himself in, he began to look round for openings in the Church into which he could place his relatives, and would brook no opposition.

He would have gone to the length of plunging Italy into war if frustrated.

Cesare was then a youth of 16, studying at Pisa. His father made him Archbishop of Valencia; his nephew, Giovanni, received a cardinal's cap, and other sons, the Dukes of Gandia and Giuffre, were given parts of Papal states, which brought a threat of war with Ferdinand of Aragon, King of Naples.

Alexander had always been ambitious for his children as

well as himself. When merely a cardinal, he had contemplated important marriages for his children.

Lucretia had been affianced to the Spaniard, Don Gasparo de Procida, but he was not good enough for the daughter of a Pope, and when Alexander was elevated the union was annulled, and she was married to Giovanni Sforza, Lord of Pesaro, the marriage being celebrated at the Vatican with great magnificence.

In the meantime the pomp at the Papal court was causing much uneasiness to the people of Rome. Finding eventually that the Pope was not to be moved by criticism, the city dropped into an orgy of crime.

Murder and robbery were committed with impunity, and a big business was done with Jews and heretics, who were allowed to enter the city on payment of large sums of money.

The Pope himself was shameless; he lived a purely secular and immoral life.

Cesare was the Pope's favourite son, and in the early part of his father's rule he lived a life of profligacy at the Vatican, and was soon known for his acts of violence.

In 1497 his brother Giovanni, Duke of Gandia, met a violent death, and the murder was attributed to Cesare. It was said that Cesare had decided to get rid of him because he was a rival for the affections of Donna Sancha, wife of Giuffre, the Pope's youngest son.

There were also rumours that Cesare and Giovanni quarrelled.

In 1497 Cesare went to Naples as papal legate and there crowned Frederick of Aragon king. The Pope now contemplated an illustrious marriage for Cesare, but the young man wished to marry Carlotta, the daughter of the King of Naples. Both she and her father refused to countenance this at any price.

Soon afterwards Cesare renounced the priesthood, and on October 1st he went to France as papal legate with a wonderful retinue. He carried with him Alexander's bull annulling the marriage of Louis XII with Jeanne of France, and the permission for the French king to marry Anne of Brittany.

In return for this concession Louis created Cesare Duke of Valentinois, and conferred on him a large pension. Cesare then discovered that Carlotta was in France, and immediately paid court to her again, but, as before, she spurned him, and eventually, with the blessing of Louis, he chose Charlotte d'Albret, sister of the King of Navarre.

There was trouble in Romagna, and Alexander conceived the idea of subduing the local despots. With the help of the French king he established a principality for himself out of the states which owed nominal allegiance to the Pope.

With an army of 300 French lancers, 4000 Gascons and Swiss, and a number of Italian troops, Cesare made his headquarters at Cesena, and attacked Imola and Forli, both of which were ultimately forced to capitulate.

The latter city was defended by Caterina Sforza, and when her domain fell she entered a convent, and died there.

On returning to Rome, Cesare was awarded a higher office of the Church, and for a time remained in the city, taking part in bull-fights and other carnival celebrations.

In July 1500, the Duke of Bisceglie, Lucretia's third husband, was attacked by assassins on the steps of St. Peter's and badly wounded. He was carried to the house of a cardinal and nursed by his wife and sister-in-law.

It was suspected that Cesare had plotted the attack, and this was afterwards confirmed when, as Bisceglie was recovering, he was murdered at the instigation of Cesare.

This crime, it is said, was not without some provocation, for Bisceglie had tried to murder Cesare first.

In October of the same year, Cesare went to Romagna with an army of 10,000 men and was received with acclamation by most of the cities. But Faenza held out, for the inhabitants were fond of their young ruler, Astorre Manfredi, a youth of 18.

In April 1501, Manfredi surrendered on being assured by Cesare that his life would be spared. He was, however, sent to Rome and murdered.

Cesare had now become the master of extensive territory, and his father created him Duke of Romagna, but he was despised by the whole of Italy because of his cruelty and immorality.

Soon the Princes began to plot against him, and risings broke out at Urbino and in Romagna, the papal troops being defeated.

The moment had come for Italy to turn against this vile family when, in the nick of time, the French king pr omised help, and this frightened the revolutionaries into coming to terms.

Two of Cesare's opponents were strangled in his own house.

As he was preparing for another excursion into central Italy, Cesare and his father suddenly became ill. The Pope died on August 18th. While Cesare was still indisposed, enemies rose up against him on all sides.

It is said that they brought about this illness themselves. They had formed a design to poison Cardinal Corneto at a banquet, but in mistake had swallowed the poison themselves.

The resulting controversy over the election of a new Pope found Cesare in the midst of the scheming, but by now he was becoming discredited. He tried to bully the Cardinals, but they refused to be intimidated, and Cesare had to leave Rome in September in the hope that the Spanish Cardinals would elect a Pope friendly towards him.

Pius III was elected, but this did not help Cesare. After a few months this Pope died, and Cesare was compelled to make terms with the next, who was the famous Julius II, who declared that Cesare must restore his territories to the Church.

Failing to give way completely, Cesare was thrown into prison, but escaped in Naples. By the order of King Ferdinand he was sent to Spain, where he was condemned to imprisonment for life.

In November 1506, after two years in prison, he again escaped and fled to the court of his brother-in-law, the King of Navarre. He took service in the king's army and, while besieging the castle of Viana, was killed on March 12th, 1507.

It is doubtful how much is truth and how much is rumour concerning Lucrezia Borgia. She was the daughter of Pope Alexander VI by his mistress, Vanozza dei Cattanei, and was born in Rome in 1480.

She had unusual beauty, but her morals were prejudiced by the licence of her father's palace. At the age of eleven she was betrothed to Don Cherubin de Centelles, a Spanish nobleman.

This was broken off and she was married by proxy to another Spaniard Don Gasparo de Procida.

But, as in the case of Cesare, this was not a union

compatible with the Pope's high station, and, when he was elected to the purple, Lucrezia was married to Giovanni Sforza.

This marriage was soon annulled by the Pope, and she was married to Alphonso of Aragon, Duke of Bisceglie, a handsome boy of 18, who fled from Rome when he was fully acquainted with the character of the family.

A year later he was induced to return and was then murdered by Cesare.

Lucrezia's next husband was Alphonso, son of the Duke of Ferrara, who married her only after a great deal of persuasion, for the reputation of Lucrezia was well known. Bribes and threats were offered and made before the wedding eventually took place by proxy.

Even then it is doubtful whether Alphonso would have had anything to do with her but for her pretty face when she arrived at Ferrara. For the next four years Lucrezia appears to have led an uneventful life, for there is an entire absence of scandal. When her husband succeeded to the Dukedom in 1505 her mode of living was without blemish.

She became interested in the arts, and devoted herself to the education of her children and to works of charity.

The only event which occurred during the time was the killing of Ercole Strozzi, who is said to have been murdered by her husband for paying attention to her.

Lucrezia died on June 24th, 1519, leaving three sons and a daughter by the Duke of Ferrara, one son by the Duke of Bisceglic, and another of doubtful paternity.

There has been much scandal concerning the morals of Lucrezia. It is probable that she was no better and no worse than many other women in Rome during that time, and but for her being the daughter of a notorious Pope she would never have been heard of historically.

It is possible, too, to say a word for Cesare. He was an adventurer with a character similar to many men who infested Italy during the time of Renaissance.

He was more successful than they at the outset because he had more brains and was the son of the Pope.

Karl Marx

There is a grave in Highgate Cemetery which will be visited to-day by scores of people who make a yearly pilgrimage there to pay their respects to a man who was the originator of theories which led to the introduction of an important force into world politics.

The inscription on the tomb records the death of four people, one of whom is Karl Marx. The others are his wife, their grandson, Henry Longuet, and their servant, Helen Dernuth.

To understand the principles of Marx and the place which his followers have assigned to him in history, it is necessary only to refer to the oration of Marx's companion and friend, Friedrich Engels, delivered on the occasion of the interment of the philosopher's remains.

It was as follows :

"The loss which his death · has inflicted upon the fighting proletariat in Europe and America, and upon the science of history, is immeasurable. The gaps that will be made by the death of this titan will soon be felt.

"Just as Darwin discovered the law of evolution in organic nature, so Marx discovered the law of evolution in human history. He discovered the simple fact that human beings must have food and drink, clothing and shelter, first of all, before they can interest themselves in politics, science, art, religion, and the like. This implies that the production of the immediately requisite material means of subsistence, and therewith the extant economic developmental phase of a nation of an epoch, constitute the foundation upon which the State institutions, the legal outlooks, the artistic, and even the religious ideas of those concerned have been built up. It implies that these latter must be explained out of the former, whereas usually the former have been explained as issuing from the latter. . . .

"Before all else, Marx was a revolutionist. To collaborate in one way or another in the overthrow of capitalist society and of the State institutions created by that society ; to collaborate in the freeing of the modern proletariat, which he was the first to inspire with a consciousness of its needs, with a knowledge of the conditions requisite for its emancipation—this was his true mission in life. Fighting was his natural element. Few men ever fought with so much passion, tenacity, and success. . . .

"Had Marx done nothing but found the International, that was an achievement of which he might well have been proud."

Since Russia became Communist, many attempts have been made to have Marx's remains removed to Russia without avail, and the grave is kept tidy by a few Germans, who have raised a fund for the purpose.

If Marx's career be studied without prejudice, it is full of interest and not without pathetic incident. Like so many other men who have made a mark in history, he suffered with ill-health. Liver trouble, considered a family disease, caused him to fear cancer of the liver. It was this which gave him such a pronounced inferiority complex.

Although his family were Protestants, they were of Jewish extraction. He had been born a Jew and could never forget it; he despised Judaism. "What is the mundane cult of the Jews?" he asked, and his own reply was "Huckstering." "What is the Jews' mundane god?—Money." And so, prejudiced against his own race, he had an additional reason for hiding himself—physically speaking—from the eyes of the world.

Perhaps the inferiority complex in relation to his breeding did not appear until later years, for there is evidence that he could be assertive as a young man.

There is, for instance, the story of his "cave-man" wooing of Jenny von Westphalen. Jenny was of high birth, the daughter of an important government official, and the belle of Treves. Marx knew that there were many far more presentable than he, but setting aside his self-consciousness, he succeeded against any number of suitors.

When the parents on both sides objected, Marx was not dismayed. He and Jenny became engaged, and eventually the parental blessing was given. This achievement filled Marx with confidence and a determination to excel in his studies at the University. Jenny was the lineal descendant of the Earl of Argyll, who was beheaded under James II.

All through life he was proud of his wife and once after visiting his birth-place, he wrote to her:

Almost everyone I meet asks me for news of "the prettiest girl in Treves" for tidings of "the queen of the ballroom." It cannot but tickle a man to find that in the fancy of a whole township his wife is enshrined as "fairy princess."

In 1836 Marx went to Berlin University and chose jurisprudence as a special study, although he was equally interested in history and philosophy.

At the university he developed Radical views, and, instead of going for his degrees, he joined the staff of the *Rheinische Zeitung*, a Radical organ. In the autumn of 1843 he went to Paris to study Socialism, and it was there that he met Friedrich Engels, the two collaborating in literary work.

They went to Brussels together and came into close contact with the Socialist working-class movement, founded a German workers' society, acquired a local German weekly, and finally, joined a Communistic society of German workers, the "League of the Just," a secret society with branches in London, Paris, Brussels, and a number of Swiss towns. In connection with this society, Marx and Engels wrote their pamphlet *Manifest der Kommunisten*, a history of the working-class movement and an explanation of the Communist standpoint.

In February 1848, the Revolution broke out in France, and after spending a short time there, Marx and Engels went to Cologne and founded a newspaper which they described as "an organ of democracy." It was published daily and Marx was the editor. When the Prussian National Assembly was dissolved in the same year Marx advocated the non-payment of taxes and armed resistance. Marx's newspaper was suspended, a state of siege was declared at Cologne, and Marx was brought to trial for high treason. He was acquitted, but soon expelled from Prussian territory.

He went to France, but was given the alternative of leaving the country or living in a provincial town. He chose the former alternative and came to England, where he remained to the end of his life.

In London he lived in poverty in small rooms in Soho, and all his children who were born during this time died in infancy. At last he obtained work for the *New York Tribune* and was paid a guinea each for his contributions.

In 1859 he denounced the Franco-Austrian war, and declared it to be a Franco-Russian intrigue ; and in the same year he sat down to write his famous work *Das Capital*, which was eventually published in 1867.

Meantime the International Working Men's Association was inaugurated in London, and although Marx was not the head in name he was actually the inspiring genius.

All its literature was written by Marx. He was more a theorist than an agitator, and was often a restraining influence against the extremists of the party, adopting a middle course of compromise which satisfied in the end both right and left.

It was probably Michael Bakunin who eventually brought about the fall of the International. Bakunin was a Russian of good family, with distinctly anarchistic views. He had been arrested in 1844 in Saxony after the Dresden rising, and condemned to death. Instead of being executed he was handed over to the Austrians, tried once more and sentenced to death. Again he escaped the death penalty by being handed over to Russia, imprisoned in the fortress of St. Peter and St. Paul, and afterwards sent to Siberia. He escaped, and reached London in 1861, and had an interview with Marx, at which the two men appear to have adjusted their earlier differences.

Bakunin was head of the International Alliance of the Socialist Democracy, which Marx regarded as a rival of the International. Marx described the programme of Bakunin as "an olla podrida of worn out commonplaces, thoughtless chatter; a rose garland of empty notions, and insipid improvisation."

When Bakunin became a member of the International there was not room for two men of such outstanding characteristics, and Marx decided to get rid of him.

The methods that Marx employed to do this were reprehensible. He declared that Bakunin had embezzled money intended for propaganda purposes, although there was not a word of truth in it. Many other accusations were made and the crisis came following the breakdown of the Paris Commune in 1871.

A congress of the International was held at The Hague, and the seat of the General Council was moved from London to New York, but it was not long before the whole thing collapsed, and in 1876 the International was dissolved at a conference in Philadelphia.

By reason of his unjustifiable attacks on Bakunin, Marx had almost become a discredited man in the Socialist movement. He returned to his scientific work, and his attempts to send the second and third volumes of *Capital* to the press, but he became very depressed, mainly because he lacked money.

It was in this connection that Engels came to his rescue.

Asked how much he required to pay off his debts, Marx replied by letter :

"I am quite overcome by your extreme kindness. My wife and I have gone into the figure together, and we find that the amount of the debts is much larger than I supposed, £210 (of which about £75 are for the pawnshop and interest)."

Engels succeeded in disposing of his business interests, paid off Marx's debts, and went to live near him.

In 1873 onwards Marx suffered from bad headaches : his liver trouble recurred. With Engel's help he went to Karlsbad in 1874, 1875, and 1876, and although he derived a certain amount of temporary benefit, he became worse year by year. The collapse of the International was a great blow ; *Capital* had not reached his expectations, while a Social-Democratic movement in Germany was started without his advice.

Then his wife fell ill and died, while Marx was suffering from bronchitis and pleurisy. Two years later his favourite daughter died, and three months afterwards on the 14th of March, 1883, Marx himself was dead.

At his funeral the only persons present were Engels and half a dozen other friends.

Admiral Sir George Pocock

One of the most daring and best-conducted enterprises in the history of the British Navy was the reduction of Havana, the capital of Cuba, in the year 1762.

War had just been declared against Spain, and Sir George Pocock, Admiral of the Blue, received instructions to proceed to the West Indies and do what he could to occupy the Spanish possessions in that quarter.

Although the Spaniards were certain that the British Navy would make an attack there, they fully expected a large squadron to be sent. Thus, when Sir George Pocock sailed with only four ships of the line, and some transports, the enemy considered that their West Indian ships were more than strong enough to cope with him.

But on his arrival in the West Indies, Sir George took

command of a formidable fleet which had been secretly concentrated in that quarter. It consisted of twenty-six ships of the line, fifteen frigates, and a considerable number of sloops of war, making together a fleet of more than fifty vessels.

On June 6th, 1762, this fleet arrived off Havana. Land forces under the command of the Earl of Albemarle, amounting to more than ten thousand men, were landed next day, and the joint operations on sea and land were immediately begun.

The result of the campaign can be seen from the following dispatch from Pocock to George III's Admiralty:

"I desire you will acquaint their lordships, that it is with the greatest pleasure I congratulate them on the great success of his Majesty's arms, in the reduction of Havana, with all its dependencies.

"The Moro fort was taken by storm the 30th of last month, after a siege of twenty-nine days, during which time the enemy lost above a thousand men, and a brave officer in Don Lewis De Velasco, captain of one of their men-of-war, and governor in the Moro, mortally wounded in defending the colours, sword in hand, in the storm.

"And on the 11th instant the Governor of the Havana desired to capitulate for the town, which was granted, the articles agreed to and signed, and we were put in possession of the Punta and the Land Gate on the 14th. With this great and important acquisition to his Majesty have also fallen twelve large men-of-war of the line, three of which were sunk, with a company's ship, in the entrance of the harbour; nine are fit for sea, and two upon the stocks; a blow that I hope will prove more capital to the enemy as they receive it so early in the war, and I may venture to say will leave all their settlements in this part of the world, exposed to any attempts that may be thought proper to be made on them. . . ."

The victorious troops discovered valuable merchandise and silver belonging to the King of Spain, and a large quantity of arms, artillery, and military stores.

No sooner did the Courts of France and Spain—who were in alliance against Britain—hear of this reverse, than they began negotiations for peace. They got very favourable terms considering that all their settlements in the West Indies were at the mercy of the British Navy.

On his return home, Sir George Pocock received the thanks of both Houses of Parliament, the City of London, and other bodies. But like many other distinguished sailors and soldiers during the Hanoverian period, he was allowed to languish under a grievance.

He took offence at the appointment of a junior admiral to the post of First Lord of the Admiralty, to which he thought himself and other admirals had prior claims. He resigned his rank and went into retirement.

Sir George Pocock, who was born on March 16th, 1706, was the son of the Chaplain of Greenwich Hospital. He entered the Navy at the age of 12 and served against Spain in the Mediterranean in 1718. After sixteen years he became first Lieutenant of the Namur, and in 1738, when war against Spain was about to be renewed, he was given command of the *Aldborough*. In 1739 his squadron made many rich captures, one ship being worth two million dollars.

In 1744 he was captain of the *Sutherland*, and next spring was ordered to the East Indies with four of the East India Company's ships under his command.

On his return he was ordered to the West Indies, and he served there several years. In 1755 he became Rear-Admiral of the White.

On the death of Admiral Watson at Calcutta, in August 1757, Pocock succeeded to the chief command in the East Indies and was promoted to Vice-Admiral of the Red.

About this time it was expected that a French squadron would be arriving in the neighbourhood of India. Britain was in process of consolidating her hold on India, and France was disputing her right.

On April 29th the two squadrons met. After a battle which lasted all day, the French retired with five times the casualties of the British. The French retreated to Pondicherry, and the British squadron returned to Madras.

On May 10th, Pocock set out for the relief of Fort St. David, then besieged by the French, but contrary winds prevented progress, and on June 6th he received intelligence that the place had been forced to surrender.

Six weeks later he came across the French at anchor near Pondicherry, but they escaped.

On August 1st Pocock once again encountered the enemy. Two days later he succeeded in bringing them to action. The French had to flee to Pondicherry, having sustained enormous losses.

Both squadrons laid up during the monsoons and repaired their damage.

On September 8th, 1759, after seeing nothing of the French for months, Pocock again encountered them at Pondicherry, and a running fight lasted until the 27th. There were a number of small engagements and two severe battles.

Finally, Pocock was able to report as follows :

"I have not been able to obtain a certain account of the enemy's loss, but it is reported by a deserter that they had 1,500 men killed and wounded, and some of their ships were very much shattered. . . .

"Our loss is very considerable, though greatly inferior to the enemy's. We had 118 men slain in action, 66 have died since of their wounds, 122 remain dangerously, and 263 slightly wounded; so that our whole number killed and wounded amounts to 569 men.

"Among the slain are Captain Michie, who commanded the *Newcastle* : Captain Gore of the Marines, and Lieutenant Redshaw, both of the *Newcastle* ; Lieutenant Elliot of the *Tiger* ; the master of the *Yarmouth*, and boatswain of the *Elizabeth*.

"All the officers and seamen, in general, behaved with the greatest bravery and spirit during the action ; and by the vigour and constancy of their fire, obliged the enemy to retreat, notwithstanding their great superiority."

The following year Pocock returned to England, and in 1761 he received the Order of the Bath, and the East India Company placed his statue in marble in their hall.

The memorable expedition against Havana was his next triumph.

After his retirement he lived in Curzon Street, Mayfair, London, and he died there on April 3rd, 1792, at the age of 87.

The Duchy of Cornwall

The 17th of March, 1937, was the six hundredth anniversary of the creation of the Duchy of Cornwall.

The first Duke was the 7-year-old Prince Edward, son of Edward III, and known as the Black Prince. His investiture took place in full Parliament at Westminster on March 17th, 1337

The Duchy of Cornwall is not the same as the County of Cornwall. The 1337 Charter granted to Edward the Black

Prince and his heirs for ever seventeen manors in Cornwall the Manor of Lydford, the Forest of Dartmoor, and other estates in Devonshire and elsewhere. Included is the estate in Kennington, London. Twenty-three Dukes of Cornwall have successively received the revenues of the Duchy.

The Duchy is vested in the eldest son of the reigning monarch. In the absence of such a son, the Crown receives the income.

Before the days of the Black Prince there was a Norman Earldom of Cornwall.

Traditionally, however, there was a Dukedom of Cornwall. In Geoffrey of Monmouth's *Histories of the Kings of Britain*, the story is told of Corineus who, after accompanying Brutus the Trojan to Britain, was granted "that share of the land, which is now called Cornwall, whether from being, as it is, the cornu, or horn of Britain, or from a corruption of the said name Corineus."

When the Saxons were conquered by the Normans, William I created his half-brother, Robert of Mortain, Earl of Cornwall. Robert began to build Launceston and Trematon Castles for the defence of his possessions.

One of the most famous Earls of Cornwall was Richard King of the Romans, second son of King John. After a crusade in Palestine in 1240, he returned to England at a time when his brother Henry III was having trouble with the barons, led by Simon de Montfort. Richard seems to have had more ambition to become a leading light in the Holy Roman Empire than to attain any particular greatness in England.

He spent a large part of the revenues from his earldom in buying for himself the title "King of the Romans." He was elected Holy Roman Emperor, and was crowned at Aix-la-Chapelle, but was unable to secure the obedience of his subjects owing to German intrigue.

At length he had to return to his native country to look after his estates. He extended his domains by securing Tintagel, Restormel Castle, and the town of Lostwithiel. He made Lostwithiel the capital of the Earldom.

His son, Edmund, Earl of Cornwall, built a range of buildings, including a Shire Hall for the holding of his Courts. The hall remained until the eighteenth century, when it was destroyed. Other buildings were used as a kind of clearing depot for the tin mines of Cornwall. Ruins of some of these buildings can still be seen.

The Earldom of Cornwall, as organized by Richard and his son, led to the establishment later of the Duchy.

The Cornwall estates were lost temporarily to Royalty when Edward II conferred the Earldom on his favourite, the Gascon, Piers Gaveston. After the Gascon's murder by Edward's barons it was taken over by John of Eltham, who was created Earl of Cornwall. On John's death Edward III decided to use the Earldom and its revenues as a means of subsistence for his son, the Black Prince, and elevate it to the dignity of a Dukedom.

The Duchy of Cornwall is distinct from the Principality of Wales. The Duchy falls to the eldest son of the reigning monarch automatically, whereas the title of Prince of Wales is conferred specially by the King. Thus it will be seen that the Duchy is held sometimes by the Duke and sometimes by the Crown.

The holder of the Duchy cannot dispose of any of the estates without the consent of Parliament. A contingency arising out of this rule arose in the days of Henry VIII when he annexed a part of the Duchy to the Crown. In return, however, he had to grant to the Duchy other lands of equal value, including a number of monastic manors, both inside Cornwall and without.

In course of time the manors in the possession of the Duchy increased to seventy-eight, more than twice the number granted under the original charter. The estates of the Duchy outside the County of Cornwall are in Devonshire and various other counties, but the richest is undoubtedly the Manor of Kennington, London.

The succession to the Duchy has not always been without its problem. In the days of Henry VII, his elder son, Prince Arthur, was the holder of the title and revenues, but on his death the question arose whether his brother Henry (afterwards the Eighth) could assume the Dukedom. The original Charter was examined by the lawyers, who finally ruled that the phrase the "eldest son" meant the eldest surviving son. Thus Henry succeeded.

Throughout the reigns of Edward VI, Mary and Elizabeth, of course, the Duchy and its revenues were vested in the Crown, as none of those monarchs had a son. Charles I was another second son to hold the Duchy. He was also Duke of York and Albany.

During the Commonwealth and the regime of the Cromwells there was no Duchy of Cornwall, the manors being sold by Parliament. On the Restoration, however, the Duchy was restored, but as there was no legal son of Charles II to inherit the title, it was vested in the Crown. Thus from the time of the execution of Charles I to the death of Queen Anne sixty-five years later, there was no holder of the title except James Francis Edward, son of James II, who held it only a few months.

During the Hanoverian period the Duchy was in the hands of the "eldest son" more than in the hands of the Crown. Edward VII before his accession, held the Duchy for nearly sixty years. It then devolved on his son, Prince Albert, and on his death, on Prince George, afterwards George V. Edward VIII became Duke of Cornwall at his birth.

It is estimated that there are about 2,000 tenants of the Duchy of Cornwall, excepting, of course, those who live on the Kennington estate. They live on about 270 farms and small-holdings.

James Bolland

One of the most notorious criminals of the eighteenth century was James Bolland, a butcher, who became a sheriff. Like Jonathan Wild, he used his official cloak to fleece his victims, and like Wild, he finished his career on the gallows.

Bolland had a shop in Southwark where he had a flourishing business. But he was an extravagant man, and, being on the verge of bankruptcy, he saved himself by selling out.

For some years he had associated with bailiffs, thief-takers, and prison officials. He saw the corruption that was going on and how easy it was to make a good income by "squeezing" prisoners.

He succeeded in getting himself nominated as sheriff of the County of Surrey, and he hired a house in Falcon Court, Southwark, fitted it up as a prison, and soon had a number of malefactors "lodging" with him.

He had no use for prisoners in indigent circumstances.

He promptly sent them to prison, expediting the process of law in order to get rid of them. Those with money he kept as long as he could, deliberately putting obstacles in the way to prevent an early hearing of the cases.

Hoping that the law's delay would eventually result in their release, these prisoners paid the money demanded by Bolland. At length, when they were completely fleeced, he saw that the law took its course.

Many prisoners of this type elected to go to prison rather than lose all their money.

One of Bolland's methods for ridding his "guests" of their money was card playing. He openly cheated them of their cash, and when they expostulated he threatened to take them to prison immediately.

Although Bolland made a big income in this way, he was soon in difficulties through his profligacy. When the demands of his creditors reached a desperate stage, he induced a friend to take a commission of bankruptcy against him, but before this could be acted upon, Bolland had secreted all his valuables. He gave notes and securities to some of the larger creditors, and through the smaller creditors secured his certificate of discharge.

Meanwhile he was carrying on systematic frauds. On one occasion he went into Oxfordshire, and bought a string of horses. Having paid for them, he expressed a desire to buy a mare, which, however, the owner refused to sell. The following morning Bolland called for the animals he had bought and took the mare with them.

The owner intended to prosecute Bolland for felony, but was persuaded to accept a bill in payment. Before the bill fell due, Bolland had gone bankrupt.

The notorious practices of Bolland were now causing uneasiness among the lawyers who employed him, so that his business dwindled. He decided to move into Middlesex, where there were more opportunities, and got himself nominated through bondsmen, as an officer to the Sheriff of the County of Middlesex.

He was employed to arrest the captain of a ship in the East India service, who owed a debt of £300. Bolland was offered a handsome commission to recover the money or secure the apprehension of the captain.

To save arrest the captain paid the debt, and proceeded on a voyage. Bolland reported that he had been unable to capture him.

A fresh writ was issued for the arrest of the captain on his return to England, and when a bailiff waited on him, the whole transaction was laid bare.

A suit was instituted against Bolland for the recovery of the £300. Bolland was arrested and taken to the Fleet Prison, but he secured his release on the grounds of insolvency.

Again Bolland got himself nominated as sheriff's officer, and he continued to carry on as before. Bolland was not the only sheriff's officer who conducted this traffic, but he was the most successful of them all.

He fleeced the prisoners, defrauded tradesmen, and lived sumptuously.

One of Bolland's ruses for obtaining money was to provide bail for rich prisoners whose relatives would have nothing to do with them. He secured the services of two men whom he clothed in good suits, and they appeared before the magistrates time after time to stand bail, giving of course fictitious names. The prisoners charged naturally paid for this accommodation.

This was a profitable scheme until his myrmidons were arrested for highway robbery and hanged at Tyburn.

The office of Upper City Marshal fell vacant and Bolland decided to purchase it, when it was put up for auction. He bid £2,400 paid his deposit, and awaited the approval of the Court of Aldermen.

But a letter was written to the Lord Mayor by an unknown person describing the character of the man who aspired to be City Marshal. There was an inquiry, and the accusations were substantiated.

Bolland's deposit was returned and he was refused the post. He threatened to bring an action for damages against the aldermen, but when he was told that they were in full possession of the facts of his past career he dropped the matter.

Bolland's activities were finally cut short through an attempt to defraud a bank.

A man named Jesson had discounted a note for Bolland. Some time afterwards they met in a tavern, when Jesson asked that the note should be redeemed. Declaring that he was short of cash, Bolland produced a note of hand given by a Mr. Bradshaw, and offered to take up the other note if Jesson would accept Bradshaw's security. Jesson agreed, and Bolland endorsed the note in the name of Banks.

Next day Jesson asked a friend named Cardineaux to discount the note he had received from Bolland. Cardineaux paid him £15 on account and asked him to call for the balance at a tavern on the following day.

Cardineaux, Jesson and Bolland met at the place appointed, and the first-named questioned Bolland about the identity of Banks, the name endorsed on the note. Bolland declared that Banks was a licensed victualler in Rathbone Place, and Cardineaux appeared satisfied.

Cardineaux took the note to his banker, who discounted it. Meanwhile, Bradshaw, the man who had originally given the name, was declared bankrupt. The bank approached Cardineaux for payment ; Cardineaux applied to Jesson, who in turn, had recourse to Bolland. Bolland refused to take up the note, and even denied that Jesson had received it from him.

But when Cardineaux pointed out that the endorsement of "Banks" was a forgery Bolland promised to pay the note when it fell due.

This, however, did not suit Cardineaux, who went to his solicitor. Bolland was arrested and lodged in the Old Bailey.

He was brought to trial and sentenced to death for forgery. On the morning of March 18th, 1772, he was executed. He was buried in Bunhill Fields Cemetery.

Sir Isaac Newton

When Isaac Newton was born he was such a sickly child that "he might have been put into a quart jug," but his physique was normal within a few years.

He was born on Christmas Day, 1642, old system, the year in which Galileo, another famous astronomer died.

Newton's father had died before his birth, and when he was three years old his mother was married a second time—to the Rev. Barnabas Smith.

Isaac was sent to small day schools at Skillington and Stoke, in Lincolnshire, and at the age of 12 went to a public school at Grantham.

He did badly at first because of an inferiority complex, and because of the persecution of one of the other boys who was a bully and the acknowledged head of the school.

Newton determined to be revenged.

He first of all challenged the boy to a fight, and, having trounced him soundly, strove successfully to surpass him in learning.

He became head of the school, and during his leisure hours made all kinds of mechanical appliances. He built windmills, water-clocks, sundials, and a carriage which could be driven by the person who sat upon it.

One of his pastimes was kite-flying. He made kites of such peculiar shapes that he attracted a good deal of attention in Lincoln.

One kite which he flew at night with a lantern on the tail caused consternation around the countryside. The local people saw the light swinging in the sky and thought it was a meteor of eccentric tendencies.

Newton was also a good artist, copied portraits and wrote verses.

On the death of his stepfather in 1656 young Isaac was taken from school to help in the management of his mother's little farm.

Although he carried out his duties satisfactorily and attended the local markets, he was more interested in science, and his books were more attractive than buying and selling farm produce.

At last his distaste for a farmer's life caused him to be sent back to school at Grantham, where he remained for nine months preparing for a University course.

He went to Cambridge in June 1661, and was admitted to Trinity College.

He bought a book on astrology which contained such puzzling diagrams that he had recourse to Euclid to assist him in understanding them. Later, he threw Euclid aside as "a trifling book," and turned to Descartes's *Geometry*.

In the summer of 1665 he had to leave Cambridge because of the plague. It is believed that it was during this year that he began to study the question of the force of gravity, and to speculate upon the problem that the same force which brought an apple to the ground governed the moon and the planets and kept them in their orbits.

In 1666 he obtained a glass prism and experimented "to try therewith the phenomena of colours." A year later he was elected a minor Fellow at Cambridge, and took his M.A., being twenty-third on the list of 148.

A temporary reappearance of the plague stopped his studies for a time, but at the end of 1668 he made a reflecting telescope over six inches long and a magnifying power of thirty-eight which showed him Jupiter's four moons and the crescent of Venus.

Next year he was appointed Lucasian Professor of Mathematics, and from this time began to communicate with the Royal Society, for his discoveries had already created much interest in the scientific world.

His reflecting telescope was sent to the Society and inspected by the King. Before the end of the year a Fellow of Trinity College had constructed an instrument which Newton acknowledged was better than his own.

Newton was elected a Fellow of the Royal Society on January 10th, 1672, and a week afterwards he offered to read an account of what, in his judgment, "was the oddest if not the most considerable detection which had hitherto been made in the operation of nature."

This was his discovery that white light consisted of rays of different colours and different refrangibility, but it was not allowed to go unchallenged.

Hook, Huygens, and several other "inferior people" so upset his tranquillity that he said he would be no longer "a slave to philosophy," but would give it up altogether, except for his own satisfaction.

He began to find mathematical theories dry, and decided to apply for the Law Fellowship. When someone else was appointed to the post Newton asked the Royal Society to excuse him from its weekly payments.

In December 1675 Newton communicated another discovery to the Royal Society. It was a "Theory of light and colours." Hook, after he had read it, declared that most of it was already contained in his *Micrographia*. Whereupon there was a controversy between Newton and Hook, which lasted for some time.

Later there was a controversy on certain principles given in Newton's *Principia*. The doctrines put forward were said to have been discovered by Leibnitz, and for two centuries there was a cleavage of opinion as to who had the prior right of discovery.

Sir David Brewster in his *Life of Newton* claims that Newton should have the credit for the invention of the method of fluxions in 1666, although the principle of it was not published to the world until 1687.

Newton was one of the deputation which protested against the granting to a monk of the degree of Master of Arts. They appeared before the notorious Judge Jeffreys, who rebuked them and remarked : "As most of you are Divines, go away and sin no more lest a worse thing come unto you."

Sir David Brewster records that "Under this rebuke, and in front of such a judge, the most ferocious that ever sat upon the judgment seat, stood the immortal author of the *Principia*, who had risen from the invention of its problems to defend the religion which he professed and the University which he adored.

"The mandate which he resisted—a diploma to a monk—was in one sense an abuse of trivial magnitude, unworthy of the intellectual sacrifice which it occasioned ; but the spark is no measure of the conflagration which it kindles, and the arm of a Titan may be required to crush what the touch of an infant might have destroyed."

Newton's efforts in connection with this protest were rewarded after the revolution by his being chosen in 1689 to sit in Parliament for the University, but when it was dissolved in 1689 he failed to obtain re-election.

His friends tried to obtain for him the Presidency of King's College, Cambridge, but in vain. Another attempt to get him appointed to the mastership of the Charterhouse School was also unsuccessful.

In the autumn of 1692 his health began to give way. For nearly a year he could not sleep, lost his appetite, and suffered with neurasthenia to such an extent that he was reported to be insane.

This belief prevailed for years and was never really erradicated, but as he wrote during this period his four celebrated letters to Dr. Bentley, and was carrying on researches of a chemical nature, there can be little truth in the story of his insanity.

Despite the discoveries which Newton had made, there seemed little inclination on the part of the Government to reward him, until his friend, Charles Montague, whom he had known as a Fellow of Trinity, was appointed Chancellor of the Exchequer.

He appointed Newton in 1695 Warden of the Mint at a salary of £600 a year. Four years later he became master of this establishment with a salary of £1,200 a year.

In the same year the French Academy elected him one of their eight foreign Associates.

In 1703 Newton was elected President of the Royal Society. He advocated the publication of the observations made at Greenwich Observatory, and approached the Prince Consort on the point, who offered to pay the cost.

Articles of agreement were drawn up, whereby Flamstead, who was responsible for the observations, agreed to supply them. In the end he failed to fulfil his contract; a quarrel followed, and Flamstead declared that Newton was his enemy.

Newton is said to have acted unjustly in the matter, and to have given way to "sudden ebullitions of temper" and "apparent perversity of conduct."

Despite this controversy, Newton was knighted on April 16th, 1705, when the Queen, with the Prince Consort was passing through Cambridge to her residence at Newmarket.

The Court was held at Trinity Lodge, and the celebrations were so extensive that the University had to borrow £500 to pay the cost.

On the accession of George I, Charles Montague was made Earl of Halifax and appointed First Lord of the Treasury. Through his friendship with Newton he became acquainted with Newton's niece, Catherine Barton, a woman of considerable beauty.

He had admired her so much that he left her the rangership and lodge of Bushey Park, with £5,000 and an annuity of £200, purchased in Newton's name.

This legacy was viewed with suspicion by many people, and Newton did not escape being involved in the suggestion that he had contrived the whole thing.

Sir Isaac Newton was a great favourite at the Court of George I, and to undermine his reputation, Leibnitz the German philosopher, charged Newton with certain offences. When the King heard of it, Newton had to defend himself.

Five papers were submitted by Leibnitz, but the trouble

was ended by the death of the German philosopher himself.

Newton was 80 when he was attacked with illness, and lingered on for some time. The fatigue of presiding at the meeting of the Royal Society on March 2nd, 1727, was the beginning of the end.

On March 18th he became insensible, and he died at Kensington on the morning of March 20th, 1727, in his 85th year.

His body, taken to London, lay in state in the Jerusalem Chamber. It was then taken to Westminster Abbey and buried near the entrance of the choir where a monument was erected by his relatives.

John Sebastian Bach

Outside a wayside inn on the Hamburg-Luneburg road stood a lad of fifteen. Hungry, weary and without money, he sniffed the seductive odours that came from the kitchen.

Suddenly two cods heads were flung through the window and fell at his feet.

With a feeling of disgust at the apparent callousness of the cooks, he spurned them with his foot. Then, as an afterthought, he picked them up, intending perhaps to hurl them back through the window.

To his surprise he found a coin in the mouth of the fish.

Without more ado he walked into the inn and had a good meal.

That lad was John Sebastian Bach.

Young Bach was then a choir boy in the Michaelis-Kirche, at Luneburg. Several times previously he had walked the thirty miles from Luneburg to hear the veteran organist, Johann Reinken, play in his Hamburg church.

He had no means of getting there but on foot, but no obstacle would interfere with Sebastian's love of music.

Bach, who was born on the 21st of March, 1685, had been left an orphan, and ill-equipped to face the world. Yet he allowed nothing to stand in the way of his ambitions.

He was 10 years old when he lost his father. The latter was one of twin brothers, who were so very much alike in voice and person that even their wives only knew one from the other by their dress. They were identical in temperament and in their musical talent. When one fell sick, so did the other, and their deaths took place at the same time.

Sebastian's elder brother, Johann Christopher, took Sebastian under his protection. He taught him the principles of music, but had little sympathy with Sebastian's aspirations. He would not allow the boy to consult his musical books.

But there was one book which Sebastian determined to consult at all costs. It contained compositions by all the best composers of the day. Obtaining the book by stealth, Sebastian copied the pieces, but as he was obliged to do it in secret, he did it on moonlight nights without artificial light. It took him six months, and at the end of that time his sight was permanently impaired.

The death of his brother left young Sebastian destitute at the age of fifteen and, in this condition, he went with a school-fellow on a 200-mile tramp to Luneburg, where he obtained an engagement as treble singer in the choir of St. Michael's. Here he remained until his voice broke.

Besides walking to Hamburg on several occasions to hear Reinken, he walked to Zell to listen to the Prince's band. At the age of 18 he was engaged to play the violin in the band of the Duke of Weimar.

Of all the musical instruments, Sebastian preferred the organ, and, after about a year, he accepted the office of organist at Armstadt. While in this situation, he would often walk many miles to hear well-known organists. Once he went to Lubeck to hear the celebrated organist Buxtehude, and was so impressed that he stayed there three months.

In 1707 Bach became organist of St. Blasius Church at Mulhausen, in which place it is believed he married his relative, the daughter of Johann Michael Bach, of Gehren, by whom he had seven children.

In the following year he returned to Weimar, no longer a fiddler in the orchestra, but as organist. His reputation as a player and composer was now spreading all over Germany. In 1717 he came under the patronage of Prince Leopold of Anhalt Kothen, who appointed him master of his chapel and director of his concerts.

About this time Marchand, a French player, challenged him to a contest to decide the superiority of French or German music, and this was arranged at Dresden before the Elector.

Marchand did not turn up and Bach gave the whole performance.

In 1722 he revisited Hamburg to hear Reinken, then nearly a hundred years old. He played before the old man, who exclaimed : "I thought this art would die with me : but here I find it has a more able representative."

In the same year Bach's first publication appeared. Although he had worked privately for many years, it was not until he was 38 that one of his works was printed.

Bach was the first to use the thumb and the fourth finger on the pianoforte keyboard.

In 1723 Bach was appointed organist to St. Thomas's School, Leipzig. His income increased by an additional appointment as composer to the Duke of Weissenfels, and through the numerous works which were now being published.

His favourite instrument, apart from his organ, was the clavichord, the forerunner of the pianoforte, on which his playing was noted for beauty of touch.

An enormous number of church compositions came from his pen at this time, including most of his motets and church cantatas.

Bach had lost his wife and married a second, by whom he had thirteen children, making a family of twenty in all, eleven sons and nine daughters.

In 1736 Bach received the further appointment of chapelmaster to the Court of Dresden, under Augustus III, King of Poland and Elector of Saxony, who had become a Roman Catholic. This gave Bach the opportunity of writing his Masses and other works for the Roman service.

He was now at the height of his popularity. He never, however, sought applause. He kept on composing, playing, and teaching.

In 1747 Bach visited Potsdam at the invitation of Frederick the Great. The evening concert was about to begin, and Frederick himself was about to play with his flute the first solo piece, when an officer presented to him a list of new arrivals in the town. On it was the name of Bach.

"Gentlemen," said the King, impressively, "old Bach has come."

A messenger summoned Bach to the palace, the composer not being allowed to change his travelling dress.

Frederick found Bach an entertaining visitor, and induced

him to play upon the newly-invented instrument, the piano-forte. Soon afterwards Bach wrote an elaborate work which he dedicated to Frederick.

He visited Berlin and then returned to Leipzig to leave the place no more. He now became blind, and six months later he died, on July 30th, 1750.

John Liston

If the biography of John Liston, the comedian, be true, he could hardly have been worse equipped for the part of humorist.

The writer, who is said to have been Charles Lamb, begins well by giving Liston an illustrious ancestry from Johan de l'Estonne, "who came over with the Norman William and had lands awarded him at Lupton Magna, in Kent."

We are told further that Liston's immediate forbears were Puritans, and that his father, an Anabaptist, was named Habakkuk.

Thereafter Lamb—or the anonymous writer—proceeds with a story of tragedy and distress.

At the age of nine young Liston was placed under the tuition of a certain Rev., Mr. Goodenough, whose death was attended with "awful circumstances."

Master and pupil were walking one day on the edge of a mining shaft when the parson allowed his curiosity to overcome caution. Gazing over the side he lost his balance.

"The sound of his head, etc., dashing successively upon the projecting masses of the chasm had such an effect upon the youth Liston that a serious sickness ensued, and even for many years after his recovery he was not once seen so much as to smile."

A month or so after this accident Liston's parents died, and the boy was thrown upon the charity of his great-aunt, a Mrs. Sittingbourne.

Ann Sittingbourne, who had the distinction of being painted by Hudson, was "stately, stiff and tall." She had a large estate in Kent, called Charnwood, and here young Liston wandered beneath the venerable trees, dreaming.

Mrs. Sittingbourne died from injuries sustained through burning a basin of charcoal in her bedroom, and Liston in his nineteenth year was left without resources.

The Charnwood regime had imposed upon Liston an ascetic mode of living. He ate no meat, drank no intoxicants. His food was little more than the nuts which grew in the woods.

His temperament, already affected by the tragedy of the mining shaft, had become as nervous as a rabbit's. He had illusions, saw ghosts and wildly gesticulating faces. He closed his eyes to shut them out ; but it was of no avail.

"The darker and more profound were his cogitations, the droller and more whimsical became the apparitions. They buzzed about him thick as flies, flapping at him, floating at him, hooting in his ear ; yet with such comic appendages that what at first was his bane became at length his solace, and he desired no better society than that of his merry phantasmata."

Liston now became a clerk in the office of Mr. Willoughby, a foreign merchant in Birchin Lane, London. He was treated more like a son than an employee. Congenial atmosphere made a change in Liston and he saw fewer visions. Two or three voyages to the Levant also improved his outlook.

Then Sally Parker came into his life.

Liston was spending a holiday in Norfolk when he visited a travelling vaudeville show. Sally was leading lady and belle of the cast. Liston was so struck with Sally, and the stage, that he applied for a part and was engaged.

In his twenty-second year he made his debut on the Norwich stage, and played tragic roles opposite Sally Parker.

At first he was successful. His commanding presence pleased the audience, and his popularity seemed assured. Then suddenly triumph turned to disgrace.

One evening, in the midst of one of the most pathetic passages in the piece—a parting with a dying friend—he burst out laughing. While the spectators sobbed with emotion Liston's laughter rang through the building.

A hasty apology was accepted. But when it occurred again on the following night, and was repeated time after time, no regrets would be tolerated by the audience.

The spectres had begun to haunt him again in such

absurd shapes that he could not act. He was no longer suitable for tragedy.

He determined to become a comedian.

That is the story told by Liston's anonymous biographer. His son-in-law has a different version of the actor's boyhood. According to him, Liston was born in 1776 and was educated at Dr. Barrow's Soho School, and later became second master in Archbishop Tenison's school.

The following anecdote of Liston appears to be authentic.

In the early days of his theatrical career he was given a part in a play at Newcastle. To save money he went to that city by ship which was beaten about by the winds for a fortnight. When he eventually appeared before Stephen Kemble, the manager, who was directing a rehearsal, the latter exclaimed : "Well, young man, you are come !"

Liston bowed. "Then you may go back again !" said Kemble, in a dreadful voice.

"It's very easy to say go back," replied Liston, "but here I am, and here I must stay, for I have not a farthing left in the world."

Kemble gave way to the actor's plea, and Liston remained in Newcastle until he made his debut in London.

His first comic part was Diggory in *She Stoops to Conquer*. He came on the stage in such an original garb that every actor on the stage broke out into laughter. Throughout the piece his antics were so funny that his fellow players had difficulty in finishing their parts.

Liston, when he had established himself in London, took liberties with his audiences.

On one occasion Hook, a friend of Liston, procured two tickets for the play for a young baronet and his fiancée, who have never before attended a London theatre.

When Liston came on his first words were greeted with laughter. He paused, pretended to be offended, and approached the footlights.

"I don't understand this conduct, ladies and gentlemen," he declared. "I am not accustomed to be laughed at. I cannot imagine what you can see ridiculous in me. Why, I declare, there's Harry B——, and his cousin, Martha J——." He pointed directly at the country couple. "What business have they to come here and laugh at me. I will go and tell his father and hear what he thinks of it."

The unfortunate couple squirmed; then jumped to their feet, and rushed out of the house.

A fellow performer was afflicted by a stutter. Nevertheless, he loved to tell long stories to Liston's annoyance.

Speaking of some individual who had gone abroad, the stutterer remarked. "He has gone to-to-let's see, it wasn't P-P-ennsylvania."

"Per-per-perhaps it was P-P-Pentonville," suggested Liston.

Liston's first engagement in London was at the Haymarket. He then obtained an engagement at Covent Garden, where he remained until 1823. When he was offered £40 by Elliston at Drury Lane he transferred his services to that theatre. He remained there until 1831, when the then enormous salary of £100 a week tempted him to join the Olympic Theatre Company. He performed there for six seasons and then retired.

When he first came to London he generally wore a peagreen coat, and was always accompanied by an ugly pug dog. The dog, like his master, was a universal favourite, and it is said that he could pull grotesque faces as well as his master.

Liston resided at the Orange Coffee House, Cockspur Street. At the height of his popularity on the stage he went into society. He died on March 22nd, 1846, leaving behind a fortune of £40,000.

The Death of Queen Elizabeth

There was lamentation and much weeping in the Palace of Richmond.

Elizabeth, who had ruled over England for forty-three years, was laying down the sceptre.

Her ladies flitted in and out of her chamber, or lingered fearfully whispering in adjoining rooms.

The indomitable old Queen had refused to take to her bed until she was physically unable to stand upon her feet. Now, as she lay helpless, occasionally wracked by convulsions or babbling foolishly in delirium, all but one or two of her Ministers and attendants were afraid of the consequences that might follow her death.

The question of her successor was a delicate one. James

VI of Scotland, son of Mary Queen of Scots, was heir-presumptive. There were others, however, some of them foreigners, whose claims, though weak, might find a backing in the country.

A rumour that she was already dead had stirred England and France. It had reached James in Scotland by means of his spies, and he, anxiously pacing day by day the corridors of his palace, awaited the official intimation.

Meanwhile there was something more sinister than sorrow and anxiety in Richmond Palace. The excitable and super-stitious women saw apparitions in the chambers and passages. Once Lady Guildford, the dying Queen's chief attendant in waiting, observing that her mistress was asleep, left the bed-chamber to go to her own apartments.

A few rooms away, she came face to face with Elizabeth !

Terrified of punishment for dereliction of duty, she began to stammer an apology.

At once the apparition vanished. Lady Guildford returned to the dying woman's room. Elizabeth was in a peaceful sleep.

Another rumour gained currency : Elizabeth was mad. Still another : she was dying of remorse for her part in the execution of her favourite, the Earl of Essex.

Undeniably the Queen exhibited some strange weaknesses in her dying hours. She refused to take medicine. "I wish not to live any longer, but desire to die," she said.

She hinted that her sleep at night had been disturbed by nightmare.

Another incident which added to the superstitious fears of the women was the discovery by two ladies-in-waiting of a queen of hearts nailed through the forehead and fastened to the bottom of the Queen's chair.

"They durst not pull it out," relates Lady Southwell, "remembering that the like thing was used to the old Countess of Sussex, and afterwards proved a witchcraft, for which certain persons were hanged as instruments of the same."

On the day before her death—she died on March 24th, 1603—Elizabeth signified that she wished a council to be called. When her Ministers had gathered round her bed she continually placed her hand on her head.

They took this to mean that she wanted the question of her successor settled. As monarchs of England were not chosen by their predecessors, the whole proceeding was a farce. Yet they carried it through, partly to humour her and partly for their own gratification, for there were various ideas on the subject.

They asked her to lift up her finger when they named the person she preferred.

"Was it the King of France ?" Elizabeth made no sign.

"Is it the Scottish king ?" The Queen did not stir.

They named Lord Beauchamp, the son of Lady Katherine Gray, who had minor claims to the throne.

"I will have no rascal's son in my seat, but one worthy to be a king," declared the invalid, finding her voice at last.

It was a sad scene. Elizabeth was now swinging her arms in her impotent endeavour to tell them what she wanted, for once more the pain in her throat was preventing speech.

During her last struggles she held her hands to her brow. They interpreted this as a desire that a ready-made King should sit on the throne.

Was it the King of France, or the King of Scotland ? The Ministers adjourned to discuss it among themselves.

The utter futility of it all ! James VI was the legitimate heir. He was already packing up to make the journey to England.

The Archbishop of Canterbury spent half an hour with the Queen. The others returned in time to hear him pray. "All that were by did answer him," records Sir Robert Carey, afterwards Earl of Monmouth, and a kinswoman of the Queen.

Carey has left behind a graphic story of Elizabeth's last moments. As a relative he was in her confidence. Yet he was a spy of James VI.

Lurking beneath the window of the death chamber in the early hours of the morning, he saw his sister, Lady Scrope, appear at the panes. She thrust out her hand and dropped a ring which Carey deftly caught.

This ring had been handed to Lady Scrope by James with instructions that it was to be returned to him immediately the great Queen had breathed her last.

Not a word passed between brother and sister. In an instant Carey rushed off to the palace stables, where he had a horse saddled and waiting.

Avoiding the vigilance of the guard, he galloped off.

G*

The pounding of hoofs was the only sound that broke the serene stillness of the surroundings of the Palace of Richmond.

Carey was miles on his journey to Edinburgh before others in the Palace awoke to the fact that the Queen was dead. Lady Scrope, who had been watching by the bedside, thought it unnecessary, and even injudicious, to arouse the other occupants.

History affords no riding feat the equal of Carey's. Turpin's fictitious ride to York was child's play compared with that of Carey.

In his autobiography Carey tells a different story. He asserts that he endeavoured to get an entrance to the castle to find out the truth. At first he was refused; but his persistence at last gained him admittance. He records that he found "all the ladies in the cofferers' chamber weeping bitterly." But it is natural that he should wish to conceal the little scheme which he and his sister had concocted.

The story that he tells of his ride to Edinburgh, however, may be taken as authentic.

"Very early on Saturday," he writes, "I took horse for the north, and rode to Norham about twelve at noon, so that I might have been with King James at supper time; but I got a great fall by the way, that made me shed much blood. I was forced to ride at a safe pace after, so that King James was newly gone to bed by the time I knocked at his gate. I was quickly let in and carried up to his chamber. I kneeled by him and saluted him by his titles of King of England, Scotland, France and Ireland."

Carey's account of his ride is somewhat ambiguous. It actually took him from three o'clock in the morning of March 24th to bedtime on March 26th to ride 400 miles.

James inquired about Elizabeth's death. Then asked if Carey had any message from the Privy Council. He admitted that he had not. But on his producing the ring, the King was satisfied.

Lady Day

In history, March 25th was once New Year's Day.

When an Act was passed in 1751 for the change of style of the calendar many people protested bitterly.

The Act provided that the legal year in England 1752 should commence on January 1st, instead of March 25th. It further laid down that after September 3rd in that year the next ensuing day should be called the 14th. Thus eleven days were dropped out of the calendar of 1752.

There were also regulations concerning the days for fairs and markets, and new tables for the movable feasts.

The loss of the eleven days caused an outcry. It was far worse than some people's prejudice against Daylight Saving.

Ministers responsible for the passing of the Act were waylaid in the street or tackled on the hustings and greeted with the cries : "Who stole the eleven days ?" "Give us back the eleven days !"

Some folk firmly believed that it meant cutting eleven days off their lives.

In adopting the new style England was two centuries behind the rest of Europe, except Russia. The change was well received by Catholic countries, for the alteration was made by Pope Gregory.

In England doubts had to be overcome. Near Malwood Castle, Hampshire, was an oak tree which appeared in bud regularly every Christmas Day. Hampshire folk declared that they would stand or fall by the oak.

On the new Christmas Day they went to the tree. There were no buds.

The sinfulness of the change was proved in the eyes of the opposition.

Their wrath was intensified when the oak began to bud on January 5th, the old Christmas Day.

At last the church had to make the remarkable admission that there were no sound historical grounds for the exact date of the birth of Jesus. Thus the new Christmas Day was just as likely to be right as the old one.

The alteration of the Julian calendar, which had been in operation since 46 B.C., was made at the instance of Pope Gregory XIII in the sixteenth century.

For centuries it had been recognized that the Julian calendar made the year eleven minutes fourteen seconds too long. Up to the time of Pope Gregory, it had fallen back ten days. It fell back at the rate of three days every four hundred years.

Gregory issued a Bill by which the ten days which represented the difference between the date of the vernal equinox in 325 and in 1582 were annulled, and October 5th was recognized as the 15th.

To prevent the discrepancy occurring again, a revision was made in the leap years.

The new style found immediate acceptance in Spain, Portugal, and parts of Italy. In the same year France fell into line, but the Protestant countries stood out.

Scotland adopted the change in 1600 and made January 1st the beginning of the year.

Most of the German States adopted the change at the end of the seventeenth century.

For a long time there was much confusion in England in the attempt to reconcile the dates in this country with those on the continent and in Scotland.

Lady Day was originally the name for all the days in the church calendar which marked events in the life of the Virgin Mary. It is now confined to the feast of the Annunciation, the day on which the Angel Gabriel appeared to her and announced that the Word was to become flesh.

Various versions of the Annunciation are given by painters. In some the Virgin is seated at a table reading ; in others she is shown kneeling.

Before the Reformation it was estimated that there were 2100 churches in England named after the Virgin Mary. In addition there were about 200 in which her name was associated with another saint.

Nearly every church had its Lady Chapel. Generally it was built eastward of the high altar and projected from the main building.

The earliest Lady Chapel ever built was constructed by Henry III at Westminster Abbey in 1220. It was thirty feet wide and extended along the site now occupied by Henry VII Chapel.

Cecil Rhodes

An eminent physician who examined Cecil Rhodes at the age of 20 wrote in his diary : "Only six months to live."

It was not the first time Rhodes had been given up by his medical advisers. He went back to South Africa, where he had recuperated his strength before, and found that the climate there was the only one which would keep him fit.

Backwards and forwards went Rhodes, studying at Oxford and spending his vacations in South Africa.

Rhodes was born at Bishop's Stortford in Hertfordshire, and was the son of a clergyman who held the living of that town.

He was educated at the Grammar School with the object of entering the Church, but at the age of 16 his health broke down, and in 1870 he was sent out to Natal to help his brother in farming.

In that year diamonds were discovered at Kimberley, and Rhodes and his brother set out for the diggings to try their luck.

Before Rhodes was 19 he was financially independent and strong in health.

He had a hankering to take a degree at Oxford, but before coming to England he carried out an eight months' trek through Bechuanaland and the Transvaal. This trip opened his eyes to the enormous possibilities of South Africa.

He became obsessed with the idea that this great stretch of territory should be made available for British enterprise and occupation by the British race.

In a will which he made two years later, he referred to this scheme of his and left all his money for this object. His second will, dated twenty years later, embodied the same principles.

He matriculated at Oriel College, and went back to South Africa each year. In the meantime his financial interests were becoming more important and his capital was increasing.

After taking his degree, Rhodes became a member of the Cape Ministry, and then gave his attention to the amalgamation of a large number of diamond mines at Kimberley with the De Beers Company.

In the meantime he was showing an ability for administration, so that his friends deplored the fact that he had his finger in the financial pie.

Rhodes, however, held other views. He maintained that money was essential to his other ideals, and although he had an immense fortune he spent little of it upon himself.

In 1881 Rhodes became a member of the Cape Assembly at a time when both South Africa and England were exercised over the Majuba affair. He began to expound his ideals, the chief of which was a South African Federation, with self-government within the Empire, which would gradually absorb adjoining native territories.

He was of the opinion that local self-government was the best system upon which the unity of an empire could be built.

In later years this attitude caused considerable suspicion in England, for he was given credit, erroneously, of being in favour of separation from the Motherland. This belief was strengthened by his gift of £10,000 to the Parnell Party of Ireland at a time when they were advocating a separatist policy.

When, however, the facts were disclosed by the publication of his correspondence with Parnell it was shown that his intentions had been the retention of the Irish members in the British House of Commons.

It was in 1881 that he began his project for the development of Bechuanaland. A convention signed in 1881 precluded the extension of the Transvaal outside its borders, but the Republicans were anxious for colonial expansion.

Rhodes forestalled the Transvaal by obtaining from the chief of half of Bechuanaland the cession of his territory to the Cape Government, but the Cape Government would not entertain the idea.

A second convention of 1884 further defined the western frontier of the Transvaal, Bechuanaland being left outside.

In the meantime the Germans were colonizing the west coast of Africa.

Following the execution of this convention Rhodes was appointed resident in Bechuanaland, where the Dutch of the Transvaal were gradually pushing their influence right into the "key of South Africa."

President Kruger declared that the Dutch colonials who

had crossed the border had done so without his knowledge or permission.

When a British force appeared on the frontier Kruger soon found a way of controlling the raiders, and Bechuanaland was declared a British protectorate.

Rhodes was bent on penetrating still farther northwards. Rumours had been received of Dutch and German emissaries having visited Lobengula with the object of persuading him to cede parts of his territory.

Other European nations were also seeking influence in the same area.

Rhodes conceived the idea of the British South Africa Company, its object being to trade as far as the Zambesi. Before the company received its charter, Rhodes had already visualized penetrating to the southern end of Lake Tanganyika.

In 1890 Rhodes became Prime Minister of the Cape. Strangely enough, he held office by virtue of the Dutch vote. During the six years he was in power he accomplished a great deal, but he was inclined to depend upon himself too much.

In 1896 he fell as a result of the Jameson Raid.

The Transvaal was now "housing" many aliens who were attracted by the fortunes to be made from mining. They considered themselves badly treated by the Transvaal Government, and determined upon a rising, asking Rhodes for his support.

Although one of them, he was also the Prime Minister of a British colony. He could not help knowing of the preparations that were going forward. Eventually he helped the movement with money and arms.

Rhodes was controller of the three great joint-stock companies, the British South Africa Company, the De Beers Consolidated Mines and the Gold Fields of South Africa.

Dr. Jameson was administrator of the British South Africa Company in Rhodesia. Jameson's idea was to make a raid with a force of 500 men with the object of overthrowing the Transvaal Government.

At this stage Rhodes drew back and refused to be a party to the movement.

The bomb burst. News was brought that Jameson was on the move. "Jameson has marched into the Transvaal," he gasped. "I have sent to stop him," he told Sir Graham

Bower, the Imperial Secretary, "and it may be all right yet."

Just before midnight, as Bower was about to depart, Rhodes in an outburst of despair cried :

"I know I shall have to go. I will resign to-morrow."

Rhodes took full responsibility for the raid. He resigned his premiership in January 1896, and turned his attention to Rhodesia.

A rebellion broke out in Matabeleland and a punitive force was sent into the country. The natives were driven into the hills, but there they stuck and nothing could dislodge them.

Rhodes believed that he could pacify the natives, and he went alone and undefended into the enemy country.

He met the chiefs, and after a discussion and the suggestion of certain concessions, he asked, "Now, for the future ; is it peace or is it war ?"

The chiefs put down their sticks as a symbol of surrender and replied : "We give you one word : it is peace."

For the rest of his life Rhodes contented himself with the development of the country which had been named after him. Railways were built, and Rhode's scheme of communications from Cairo to the Cape was in process of formation.

Then the Boer War broke out. Rhodes was in the Kimberley siege, and his health was already failing. He died on March 26th, 1902, before peace had been proclaimed.

In his will he left his fortune to the public service. The bulk of it went to Oxford for the foundation of Scholarships of £300 a year for students from every British colony, as well as the United States of America.

In a codicil executed shortly before his death he included scholarships for Germans.

Up to the time of his death, and even afterwards, his complicity in the Jameson Raid was freely believed. The Commission of Inquiry had declared that Rhodes was the controller of the three great companies "which rendered such a proceeding as the Jameson Raid possible."

When Rhodes's will was published, many of those who had been his keenest critics were converted. The will disclosed, at least, that he was not a self-centred man, and that he was actuated by desire for the expansion of the Empire entirely, with no thought of personal aggrandisement.

John Jacob Astor

In the year 1781, a lad of eighteen packed up his scanty wardrobe, left his native town of Waldrop, near Heidelberg, in the Duchy of Baden, and made for London.

His sole equipment consisted of coarse home-made clothes, a blue cap, and a pair of stout hob-nailed boots.

That boy was John Jacob Astor.

John went to his brother, a musical instrument maker, in London.

Three years passed away, and the worldly wealth of John Jacob Astor had increased to a sum sufficient to buy a steerage passage to New York.

America had just settled down after the War of Independence, and the youth of Europe were flocking to the new Eldorado.

By now John had learned the English language. In November 1784 he embarked in an emigrant ship, carrying with him several manufactured articles, including seven flutes.

Ice held up the ship in the Chesapeake, and the voyage was long and tedious.

Young Astor struck up an acquaintance with another German, a furrier by trade, who recommended him to enter the same kind of business.

In New York, John Jacob sold his flutes and other articles, and invested the small sum thus obtained in furs. He sold them for a good profit, and then apprenticed himself to the trade. He had been only a short time in it when he considered he knew enough about furs to begin for himself.

Meanwhile, however, Robert Bowne, an old Quaker, became interested in the lad and offered him employment as a clerk. Astor accepted the post, and soon made himself acquainted with the methods of buying and selling furs, a side of the business he had hitherto neglected.

At this time the traffic in furs had received a big set-back as a result of the revolutionary war. Traders had been driven away or drafted into the armies. The trappers, too, had joined up.

At the end of the struggle, the posts of Oswega, Detroit, and Niagara were in the hands of the British, who showed no inclination to restore the fur business. The Indians, too, were reluctant to begin trapping while they were able to obtain fire-water, rifles, and tomahawks from the British, who urged them to continue a guerilla warfare against the colonials.

After long negotiation, however, these posts were conceded to the United States, and Canada was reopened for the fur trade.

Astor had a brother who was a butcher in the Bowery. From him he obtained a loan of a few thousand dollars, and when the British retired from the west side of the St. Clair and thus opened up the fur trade to the west, John Jacob began buying furs.

It was clear to him that the posts would soon be thronged with Indians eager to dispose of a large quantity of furs accumulated by the tribes during the war. He established agencies, occasionally visiting the stations himself, but devoting himself chiefly to the New York business.

In six years Astor is said to have accumulated a capital of 250,000 dollars. He invested this money in stocks that seemed likely to yield the best returns.

At the beginning of the nineteenth century, the American fur dealers were subjected to competition from British fur companies. At almost every eligible site in the fur trapping area, block-forts were built, and it seemed that they would soon monopolize all the fur trade unless something were done to stop them.

In 1803, therefore, Astor established the American Fur Company, whose agents boldly pushed their outposts into unexplored country. The Indian tribes, who had never before seen white men, looked upon them as gods, and brought to them their skins instead of handing them to agents of their own race for delivery to the whites.

The American Fur Company had barely been established when Astor began to look about for additional means of making money. He proposed to the United States Government the establishment of forts along the shores of the Pacific Ocean and the Columbia River to stop the British trade west of the Rockies.

This was done, and a new settlement called Astoria, which gave its name afterwards to a large tract of country, came into being. It very soon became the trading emporium of the Northern Pacific.

During the war of 1812-14 the Astoria station nearly collapsed owing to the dislocation of business. But it revived and seemed to be on a fair way to success when one of Astor's partners, M'Dougal, a Scotsman, sold Astoria to the British North-West Fur Company, and thus cut the ground from beneath John Jacob's feet.

By this time Astor had a fleet of ships carrying furs to France, England, Germany and Russia, and even to China, from which country he received rich silks in exchange.

Astor's next move was to buy a large portion of the land lying round New York. The city grew rapidly, and the returns from his real estate multiplied. He speculated upon the settlement of Iowa, Missouri, Wisconsin and other parts of the West, purchasing immense tracts of country at the Government price.

Thus the German lad who had left his native country with hardly the means of subsistence soon acquired a fortune second only to that of the Rothschilds.

For many years he lived in a style of princely grandeur in Broadway, New York. It is estimated that his income was £400,000 a year.

His one aim was to make money. At the same time he spent large sums in good causes. The famous Astor House, then the largest and best-managed hotel in America or Europe, was built by him. He gave 350,000 dollars for the foundation of a library in New York.

Yet there was a streak of miserliness in Astor's character, as is shown by the following anecdote.

When Audubon published his great work on ornithology, the subscription price of which was 1,000 dollars a copy, Astor's name was on the subscription list. But when Audubon applied to him for payment Astor put him off time after time.

"Ah, M. Audubon," was the inevitable excuse of Astor, "you come at a bad time; money is very scarce; I have nothing in the bank. I have invested all my funds."

At last the attitude of the author was somewhat peremptory, for it was the sixth time he had called upon the great financier.

"Hard times, M. Audubon, hard times—money scarce," said Astor before the other could get in his plea. "However," added John Jacob, "we must contrive to let you have some of your money if possible.

"William," he said, turning to his son, "have we any money at all in the bank?"

"Yes, father," replied the son, who was in an adjoining room and was not aware of the identity of his father's visitor. "We have two hundred and twenty thousand dollars in the Bank of New York, seventy thousand in the City Bank, ninety thousand in the Merchants', ninety-eight thousand four hundred in the Mechanics', eighty-three thousand——"

"That will do! That will do!" exclaimed the old man. "William, it seems, can give you a cheque for your money."

John Jacob Astor died at his residence in New York on March 29th, 1848, in his 85th year.

William Backhouse Astor (1792-1875), a son of John Jacob, was sometimes known as the "Landlord of New York." Under his direction the building for the Astor Library was erected. His son, another John Jacob, was also a big American capitalist and philanthropist.

William Waldorf Astor, a son of William Backhouse, was a member of the United States Legislature from 1877 to 1881. From 1882 to 1885 he was United States Minister to Italy. In 1890 he came to England, and nine years later was naturalized. Meanwhile he became proprietor of the *Pall Mall Gazette*, and afterwards started the *Pall Mall Magazine*. He also owned the *Observer*.

In 1916 he was created a baron and took the title of Baron Astor of Hever Castle.

One of his outstanding activities was the restoration of Hever Castle, historically associated with Anne Boleyn. This castle was built by William de Hever in the reign of Edward III. In the time of Henry VI it came into the possession of Sir Geoffrey Boleyn, a wealthy mercer and Lord Mayor of London. He was great-grandfather of Henry VIII's ill-fated queen, Anne Boleyn.

On the death of Anne's father, Sir Thomas Boleyn, Henry seized the estate in right of his own wife. He afterwards enlarged it by purchases from other members of the family. The next owner was Anne of Cleves, who made the castle her general place of residence, and she died there in 1557.

Crown Commissioners then sold it to Sir Edward Waldegrave, who, during the reign of Elizabeth, was committed to the Tower, where he died in 1561. From his family the manors passed to the Humphrey family, and then to the Malleys.

On acquiring Hever Castle, Lord Astor restored it completely. Its battlements were patched up, the use of the drawbridge over the moat was revived.

About two thousand workmen were employed for several years on the restoration and changes, for not only the castle but the whole of the property was dealt with. A Tudor village was built and the course of the River Eden was diverted for the purpose. Everything had to be in keeping with the general Tudor atmosphere. Even the torture chamber was restored and appropriate instruments of torture placed inside.

Having made Hever Castle and its grounds perfect, Lord Astor gave the estate to his young son and went to live in seclusion in a detached house at Brighton.

Lord Astor died on October 18th, 1919, after having been made a Viscount in 1917. On his death the title descended to the present Lord Astor, who was born in New York in 1879.

He represented Plymouth as a Unionist from 1910 to 1918, and the Sutton division of Plymouth 1918-19, when he gave up his seat on succeeding to his father's peerage. His wife, Lady Astor, is Member of Parliament for Plymouth.

George Hanger, Lord Coleraine

George Hanger, Lord Coleraine, had queer sentiments. "I care not whether I am a nobleman or a gentleman; but one thing I know, and that is that I am a dead shot," he said.

Hanger's antecedents were obscure. He could not trace his family beyond his grandfather. This is not surprising, for it is believed that its earlier members could not agree among themselves about the correct spelling of the name. Thus at different times it was Ainger, Aunger, Aungre and Aungrier.

An old chronicler suggests that the "h" was prefixed by some of the family whose spelling and pronunciation were alike at fault.

Hanger was one of the bosom friends of George, Prince of Wales (George IV). It was said of him that he was not the constant Hanger but the constant Hanger-on.

His mode of living was such that few of his contemporaries lamented his death, and, adds his biographer : "The extinction of his title, which was caused by his death, could scarcely be said to have created in the Irish Peerage any gap or void which it was difficult to fill up."

Hanger has left behind a quaint autobiography. He speaks of his father thus :

"His sister, Miss Anne Hanger, was married to Hare, Lord Coleraine : but my father was not in the most distant degree related to his lordship or connected with him except by marriage. Lord Coleraine however happening to die at the very nick of time without issue or heir to his coronet, my father claimed it, with just as much right as the clerk or sexton of the parish."

Hanger was educated at Eton, and entered the Foot Guards as an ensign. He left the regiment in high dudgeon through a fancied slight in regard to advancement. He spent the next few years in dissipation, but as soon as the American War of Independence became a certainty, he joined up for the British service in America, and became a captain in the Landgrave of Hesse's corps of Jagers. Eventually he rose to the rank of major.

On the conclusion of peace Hanger had no prospects. There was every reason why he should not return to London for, at the time of his departure for America, sheriffs' officers were dancing attendance on him.

Richard Tattersall offered him a home in his house and promised to pay his debts. This act of kindness restored Hanger in the estimation of society, and he soon became one of the most jovial, hard-drinking associates of the Prince of Wales, who made him one of his equerries, with a salary of £300 a year.

Hanger also received an appointment to collect recruits for the East India Company. These two incomes were sufficient to enable him to live as a gentleman, but it was not long before the King's Bench prison claimed him for debt. There he spent ten months and lived like a gentleman on three shillings a day "in rural retirement."

On his release from prison he applied for a commission in the Army, but was refused. Whereupon he determined to enter a trade.

He had strange ideas. He began as a dealer in powder for the purpose of setting razors. He carried his samples in his pocket to show to "persons of quality," but there seems to have been more "quality" about the "persons" than about his powder, for the market in that particular commodity was not brisk.

He then started an agency in the coal business, but this did not flourish, and once more Hanger—who seems to have stepped up into the rank of colonel—had to accept the charity of a friend.

He was often to be found at the cock-pit, and at the boxing booths.

When his elder brother, William, died in 1814, George Hanger was averse from assuming the title of Lord Coleraine. In fact, he always signed his name as plain George Hanger.

He lived and died unmarried, but there was a romance in his life, as he states in his autobiography. He appears to have had an affair of some duration with a gipsy girl whom he described as the "lovely Egyptia."

"I used to listen with raptures to the melody of her voice," [he writes] . . . "I thought her the 'Pamela' of Norwood, the paragon of her race, the Hester of the nineteenth century. But alas! on my return after a short absence one day I found that she had gone off with a rambling tinker of a neighbouring tribe, who wandered about the country mending pots and kettles."

Hanger was the author of other works besides his autobiography. In 1795 he published a pamphlet entitled *Military Reflections on the Attack and Defence of the City of London, to which is added Reflections on the Loss of Plymouth or Harwich.* From this it is to be inferred that Hanger believed himself to be a military strategist. He followed this up with another entitled, *Reflections on the Menaced Invasions, and the Means of Protecting the Capital*; *with a letter on the proposed fortifications round London, and a defence of the volunteer system.*

Some years later he wrote a letter to Lord Castlereagh, attempting to prove that 15,000 men, well disciplined, could be obtained for the volunteers in two months. It contained a manual of instruction for the volunteers and a plan for the formation of a special corps of marksmen.

Hanger had no reverence for blue blood. He preferred a man who could fight with his fists or use a sword. He prefaces his autobiography with a picture of himself swinging on the gallows at Tyburn.

Tyburn, indeed, was a favourite resort of Hanger, and he would frequently ride on the tail of the cart which carried malefactors from Newgate along Holborn Hill and Oxford Street to their execution.

Occasionally, however, a trace of ancestral pride would be noticed in his character. It was a proud boast, for instance that his father was "an honest M.P., in favour of King and Constitution, and above a bribe."

He mixed with all classes. One night he would dine in Mayfair and on the next sleep in a cellar of St. Giles's.

A great deal of the responsibility for Hanger's mode of living was due to his father's neglect. On one occasion when George wanted to mend his ways and join the Russian Army fighting against the Turks, old Lord Coleraine refused the money for the necessary equipment. Hanger, who had got as far as Germany, had to remain there.

Yet there is some wisdom in Hanger's autobiography. It contains hints for the removal of vice from the theatres, and suggestions for the encouragement of street-preaching, and there are many quaint recommendations for putting down the very amusements in which he himself indulged.

He had a habit of visiting the cells at Newgate, and offering condolences to the prisoners, particularly those whom he believed to have been sentenced unjustly.

At last, in a periodical of 1824, appeared the following notice :

"March 31st.—Died of a convulsive fit, at his residence near the Regent's Park, aged 73, the Right Hon. George Hanger, fourth Lord Coleraine, of Coleraine, Co. Londonderry, in the peerage of Ireland, and a major-general in the Army; better known by the title of Colonel Hanger, or the familiar appellation of 'George Hanger.'"

The title became extinct at his death.

The Rev. Richard Napier

From the time of Queen Elizabeth to that of William and Mary, astrology was in high repute. Among the astrologers who flourished during that period were Drs. Dee, Lamb, Forman, Lily, Gadbury, Evans, and many others.

There was no law against telling fortunes. Thus every town and village had its so-called astrologer who professed to cast nativities, to restore stolen goods, and to forecast happy marriages—or otherwise.

In William Lily's *Memoirs*, many of the inferior quacks are exposed. He looked upon these people with horror, not because they claimed to be astrologers, but because they took fees for the recovery of stolen property. It can be said in favour of Lily that he never turned his reputed astrological knowledge to evil account.

In the time of James I, Charles I, and the Commonwealth, astrology was in vogue to such an extent that it was indulged in by people in all walks of life.

James I was particularly addicted to astrology as he was to demonism and superstition generally. He was unusually credulous, and was the author of works on demons and witchcraft.

In the next reign, and during the Protectorship of Cromwell, eminent people did not hesitate to consult astrologers. It was even said that Cromwell was seen, before one of his battles, conversing with the Devil in a secluded dell.

Lily, who wrote *An Introduction to Astrology*, went with another astrologer named Booker to the headquarters of the Parliamentary army at Windsor. They were well received by General Fairfax, who seemed interested in some of their predictions. He hoped that their "art was lawful and agreeable to God's word; but he did not understand it himself."

Lily declared that astrology was not against the Scriptures, and he prophesied that the Commonwealth army would overthrow the King.

The clergy in many instances sanctioned and even practised the art of astrology. One of the most enthusiastic of these clerics was the Rev. Richard Napier, a son of Sir Robert Napier, of Luton Hoo, in Bedfordshire. He became rector of Great Linford, Buckinghamshire, in 1589.

He received his instruction in astrology from the then famous Dr. Forman, who, however, expressed grave doubts about his ability to become proficient. Yet in course of time he "proved a singular astrologer and physician."

Eventually Forman thought so highly of his pupil that he left him "all his rarities and secret manuscripts of what sort soever."

Napier was a Master of Arts, but although he was styled "Doctor" it is doubtful whether he ever took a degree in divinity. "Whether doctored by degree or courtesy, because of his profession, I know not," says Aubrey. "He was a person of great abstinence, innocence and piety, and spent two hours every day in family prayer."

When a patient or anyone in search of an astrological forecast came to him he would retire into his closet, and, it is said, could be heard holding conversations with angels and spirits. He asked them questions about his patients, and by the answers they gave he was able to utilize his skill in medicine and astrology for the specific cases under review.

"He conversed with the Angel Raphael," records Aubrey. "The angel told him if the patient were curable or incurable."

The angel told him that Mr. Booth of Cheshire should have, three years hence, a son who should inherit. This was in 1619, and we are informed that in 1622 his son George was born, who eventually became Lord Delamere.

"At some times," adds Aubrey, "upon great occasions he had conference with Michael, but very rarely. He outwent Forman in physick and holiness of life : cured the falling sickness perfectly by constellated rings ; some diseases by amulets, etc."

A woman suffering from ague called on the doctor and was given a spell for its cure. Returning home, she injudiciously told her minister, who declared that it was the devil's work and advised her to burn it immediately. She did so, but the ague, which had already been relieved, returned in greater severity. She again applied to the doctor for the spell and was benefited.

Her minister soon learned what she was doing, and proceeded to frighten her with the consequences that would ensue if she persisted. Badly scared she once more destroyed the spell.

"Whereupon she fell extremely ill, and would have had the spell the third time, but the doctor refused, saying that she had contemned and slighted the power and goodness of the blessed spirits, and so she died."

About the year 1634 the Earl of Sunderland fell ill and placed himself under the care of Dr. Napier. The doctor was also patronized by the Earl of Bolingbroke and Lord Wentworth, and when there was a movement by magistrates to interfere with Napier's work these peers protected him and saved him from persecution. They even extended their patronage to his friends who practised the same art.

The doctor, it appears, instructed many other ministers in astrology and "lent them whole cloakbags full of books."

A certain William Marsh, of Dunstable, a minister and a recusant, who found himself in trouble on many occasions through his activities in astrology, was protected by Napier through his distinguished friends, and "by Dr. Napier's interest was still enabled to continue his practice, no justice of the peace being permitted to vex him."

"This man," says an old chronicler, "had only two books, Guido and Haly, bound together. He had so numbled and thumbled the leaves of both, that half one side of every leaf was torn even to the middle. He did seriously confess to a friend of mine that astrology was but the countenance, and that he did his business by the help of the blessed spirits, with whom only men of great piety, humility and charity could be acquainted."

An old biographer of Napier sarcastically suggests that Dr. Napier did not appear to have been assisted by Raphael in his clerical ministrations; for "miscarrying one day in the pulpit, he never after used it, but all his lifetime kept in his house some excellent scholar or other to officiate for him."

Finally, Aubrey declares: "'Tis certain he told his own death to a day and an hour, and died praying upon his knees, being of a very great age, on April 1st, 1634. His knees were horny with frequent praying."

His burial was entered in the register of his parish thus:

"April 15th, 1634. Buried Mr. Richard Napier, rector, the most renowned physician both of body and soul."

Dr. Napier's papers and manuscripts, including a diary of his practice over a period of fifty years, came into the possession of Elias Ashmole. He had them bound, and they were deposited in the Ashmolean Library at Oxford, where there is also a portrait of Napier. Among the manuscripts are many medical recipes which are marked as having been given to Napier by the Angel Raphael.

Richard Cobden

"It is not possible for the House to proceed to business without every member recalling to his mind the great loss which the House and country has sustained by the event which took place yesterday morning."

In these terms did Lord Palmerston draw the attention of the House of Commons to the death of Richard Cobden, apostle of Free Trade.

Whatever may have been the opinion of members on the merits of Free Trade, there was universal sorrow at the passing of a man whom Disraeli described as "an ornament to the House of Commons and an honour to England."

John Bright tried to speak, but was compelled to sit down, saying in a tremulous voice that he must leave to a calmer moment what he had to say on the manliest and gentlest spirit that ever quitted or tenanted a human form."

In the French parliament, too, the vice-president referred to the death of Cobden. "It is not alone a misfortune for England," he said, "but a cause of mourning for France and humanity."

The French Minister of Foreign Affairs sent a special dispatch to England expressing "the mournful sympathy and truly national regret which the death, as lamented as premature, of Richard Cobden had excited on that side of the Channel.

"He is above all," he added, "in our eyes the representative of those sentiments and those cosmopolitan principles before which national frontiers and rivalries disappear. Whilst essentially of his own country, he was more of his time. He knew what mutual relations could accomplish in our day for the prosperity of peoples. Cobden, if I may be permitted to say so, was an international man."

Richard Cobden was born in a farmhouse near Midhurst, Sussex, on June 3rd, 1804.

At an early age, Cobden was placed in a position in a London warehouse. Later he became a traveller for a Manchester cotton firm.

At 26 he was a master calico-printer in partnership with two other men in the neighbourhood of Blackburn. Later, with an elder brother, he engaged in the same kind of business at Chorley, Lancashire, under the name of Richard Cobden and Brothers.

Until 1835, the name of Richard Cobden was barely known in Lancashire, save in his ordinary business capacity. In that year, however, the editor of a Manchester paper received a number of anonymous letters from a "Manchester manufacturer" on political topics which were lucid and intelligent.

Then the editor received a copy of a pamphlet entitled, *England, Ireland and America, by a Manchester Manufacturer*.

The inscription on the flyleaf read : "From the author." The editor recognized the handwriting as that of the writer of the letters.

This pamphlet was Cobden's first literary work. It advocated the principles of non-intervention in the dispute between Russia and Turkey, retrenchment and Free Trade.

The pamphlet attracted considerable attention. Soon after its publication, Cobden went to America for a three months tour, and on his return to England began to write another publication for the Press.

It went further on the Russian question, and tried to oppose the wild outbursts against Russia which were then the vogue.

He was obliged to leave England for a time because of ill health, and travelled in Spain, Turkey, and Egypt.

On his return to Manchester he began to take a leading place in the politics of the city.

While attending a meeting at Rochdale he became acquainted with John Bright.

In 1837, the death of William IV and the accession of Queen Victoria caused a general election. Cobden stood for Stockport, but was defeated by a small majority.

The following year the Anti-Corn Law Association was formed in Manchester. It became national under the name of the Anti-Corn Law League. Of this Cobden was the directing genius. In 1840 the Free Trade Hall was built in Manchester on ground belonging to Cobden. It was actually on the scene of the famous Peterloo massacre of 1819.

At the General Election of 1841 Cobden was returned for Stockport.

Cobden's opponents predicted that he would be an utter failure in the House of Commons. He made his first speech during the course of the debate on the Address.

Jeers greeted some of his statements when he began to argue against the corn laws. But his mastery of the subject compelled attention, and he soon became recognized as one of the foremost debaters in the House.

On February 17th, 1843, a scene took place in the House. Cobden had described the suffering and distress which then existed in the country, and had blamed Sir Robert Peel, as the head of the Government.

Peel was not then in his best form. Instead of taking the statement for what it was worth—a legitimate attack on the Government—he declared that Cobden's statement was an incitement to violence against himself.

Peel later apologized for what he had insinuated, and when Cobden had won through with his Free Trade policy Peel gave Cobden the credit for the persistence which had brought it about.

"The name which ought to be, and will be associated with the success of these measures," said Peel, "is not mine, or that of the noble Lord (Russell), but the name of one who, active I believe from pure and disinterested motives, has, with untiring energy, made appeals to our reason, and has enforced those appeals with an eloquence the more to be admired because it was unaffected and unadorned. The name which ought to be chiefly associated with these measures is the name of Richard Cobden."

In October 1859, Cobden went to France as a private person with the object of concluding a commercial treaty. At first he was repudiated by the Government, but having settled the objections of the Protectionists of France, he was given power to negotiate.

At last he and Lord Cowley signed a treaty.

Commenting on this, Gladstone remarked : "Rare is the privilege of any man who, having fourteen years ago rendered to his country one signal and splendid service, now again within the same brief span of life, decorated by neither rank nor title, bearing no mark to distinguish him from the people whom he serves, has been permitted to perform a great and memorable service to his country."

Cobden died in London of bronchitis on April 2nd, 1865. His widow declined to accept a pension of £1,500 a year.

John Wilson

"Call not the life of Burns unhappy . . . Burns went to his own grave without having been commanded to look down into another's, where all was buried."

John Wilson, the Scottish poet, who wrote under the name of "Christopher North," bemoaned his fate because he was called upon to stand before two open graves. The first was that of his father, who died when Wilson was a youth. The second was that of his wife, whom he lost after twenty-six years of happy married life.

But many a person experiences greater bereavement in the course of a lifetime. Wilson's sorrows were not the equal of Burns's, and when, in his essay on the great Scottish bard, he endeavours to magnify his own troubles and belittle those of the other, he discloses a temperament susceptible to maudlin sentiments.

Confirmation of this is to be found in some of his poetry, particularly in the following :

> *When nature feels the solemn hour has come*
> *That parts the spirit from its mortal clay,*
> *May that hour find me in my weeping home,*
> *'Mid the blest stillness of a Sabbath day !*
> *May none I deeply love be then away !*

The Sabbath day had just passed as Wilson drew his last breath. The reverberations of the chimes of the grandfather's clock had not died away. Wilson's death occurred exactly as he had hoped.

Wilson was the eldest son of another John Wilson, a prosperous manufacturer.

H

There was a tradition in the family that the precocious child, then only four, used to lecture the goldfish on their parental obligations.

At the age of 6 or 7 Wilson left his home at Paisley and went to stay with the minister of the neighbouring parish of Mearns. His happy days at the Manse are recorded by himself in *Christopher in his Sporting Jacket*, *Our Parish*, and *May Day*.

His father died in 1797. John was then 12. As the heavy clay fell upon the coffin he fell in a swoon.

The orphan went to Glasgow College, where he carried off first prize in logic, then regarded as the highest honour to which a student could aspire.

While still at College he became attached to a young woman, his senior by several years. He wanted to marry her, but his mother objected. In later years John Wilson saw the value of his mother's advice. Letters written by him at the time, however, indicate how difficult it was for him to give up his first love.

About the same time he began a correspondence with Wordsworth. Wilson was one of the first members of the public to recognize the beauty of Wordsworth's lyrical ballads. "I fell down on my knees to him, when I was a boy," Wilson once said, "and I have never risen since."

Yet in his first letter to the poet Wilson had the temerity to criticize Wordsworth's "Idiot Boy," declaring that it was a subject unfit for poetry. Wordsworth replied defending the work. This did not satisfy Wilson, but he was more than gratified with other sentiments in the letter.

In 1803 Wilson went to Oxford, and entered Magdalen as a gentleman commoner. Here he was noted for his intellect as well as his prowess as a boxer, a runner, and a jumper.

Wilson won the Newdigate prize for poetry, and obtained his degree after an examination described as "the most illustrious within the memory of man."

The Rev. R. Dixon, one of the examiners, wrote : "I can never forget the very splendid examination which you passed in this university, an examination which afforded the strongest proofs of very great application and genius and scholarship, and which produced such an impression on the minds of the examiners as to call forth (a distinction very rarely conferred) the public expression of our approbation and thanks."

Soon after leaving Oxford Wilson bought a small estate near Windermere, where he was a neighbour of Wordsworth, Here he was able to give vent to his animal spirits in racing. leaping, wrestling, boxing, fishing, boating, and cock-fighting.

Then Wilson fell in love again. The girl was Miss Jane Penny, "the belle of the Lake District." They were married in 1811.

In 1815 he quitted the Lakes and was called to the Scottish Bar.

When Wilson's father died in 1797 he had settled upon his son an estate worth about £50,000. It was managed by a trustee, and so long as Wilson got his income regularly he took little interest in the way it was handled. He placed implicit confidence in the trustee, and never asked how his funds were invested.

Suddenly he found that his whole fortune was lost. He did not murmur. He could earn his living. He forgave the man who had betrayed his trust, and kept him for the remainder of his life.

Briefs came slowly to John Wilson at Edinburgh. Soon they ceased altogether, much to his relief. A surer living was literature.

In 1816 he published the *City of the Plague*, but the public were not impressed.

At last he secured a contract to write for *Blackwood's Magazine*.

In 1820 he secured the chair of Moral Philosophy at Edinburgh University, where he remained for thirty years. During the summer months he usually went to the Lakes. Once, as admiral of a regatta on Windermere, he headed in a ten-oared barge a beautiful pageant. His party included Canning, Sir Walter Scott, Wordsworth and Lockhart.

When his wife died in 1837 the shock was almost too great for him to bear.

At the Burns Festival in 1844 Wilson delivered an eloquent oration. Sometimes he was more eloquent when he said little. Such an occasion occurred when he was presiding at a Waterloo banquet and he was asked to say something about the Duke of Wellington's great victory.

He did it in one sentence : "The morning rose in clouds and tempest—and the sun set on the regenerated liberties of Europe, and the immortal fame of the victor of Waterloo."

Although Wilson was generally serene and inoffensive, he was sometimes known to lose his temper. One day, in an Edinburgh street, he saw a miserable horse being whipped by a carter. Wilson wrenched the whip from the man's hand, belaboured him with it, unharnessed the horse from the cart full of coal, upset the coal in the street, and took the animal to the police.

In 1851 his health began to fail, and he had to resign his academical chair. The Queen granted him a pension of £300 a year. He died on April 3rd, 1854.

Algernon Charles Swinburne

At Bonchurch, in the Isle of Wight, there is one of the most beautiful churchyards in the country. It nestles on the hillside overlooking the sea. In it is the grave of Algernon Charles Swinburne, one of the greatest of England's poets, the centenary of whose birth is being celebrated to-day.

Only a simple white stone with a metal nameplate beside it marks the spot where Swinburne is laid. It is as unostentatious as was Swinburne himself.

For many years he lived quietly on Putney Hill, pursuing literature in peace and leisure, basking in the friendship of Theodore Watts-Dunton.

Swinburne was born in London on April 5th, 1837, and was the son of Admiral Charles Henry Swinburne and of Lady Jane Henrietta, a daughter of George, third Earl of Ashburnham.

Soon after his birth he was taken away from London to the placid beauty of the Isle of Wight, where his father bought an estate between Ventnor and Niton, called East Dene.

Swinburne's uncle, Sir John Edward Swinburne, Bart., owned an estate in Northumberland. The two families spent six months of the year alternately at the Isle of Wight and in the north.

It was the Isle of Wight which seems to have influenced his poetry. He was a frequent visitor to the Orchard, owned by friends of his family, and some of his most beautiful pieces were written there.

For some years Swinburne was educated privately and

was then sent to Eton, where he remained for five years, afterwards going to Balliol College, Oxford, in 1857.

After three years at the University he left without taking a degree. His career, indeed, was without any outstanding success beyond winning the Taylorian prize for French and Italian.

He was, however, already writing poetry and contributing to the "Undergraduate Papers." Generally speaking Swinburne does not appear to have been a favourite of the tutors.

He left Oxford in 1860, and within a month or two published the two dramas, *The Queen Mother* and *Rosamond,* both extraordinary achievements for a young man. They are regarded as having more dramatic energy than much of his later work.

Swinburne went to Italy with his family. His mother had been educated in that country. There he met Walter Savage Landor, whom he greatly admired.

In 1865 Swinburne published his *Atalanta in Calydon,* and followed this up next year with the *Poems and Ballads.* It was the latter which made him popular with the public, and he enjoyed a vogue.

The *Poems and Ballads* were attacked by the critics, however. But when *Dolores and Faustine* appeared the approbation was universal.

Thus by the end of his thirtieth year Swinburne had succeeded in placing himself well among the leaders of the contemporary poets, and had a great following.

Meanwhile, there was gloom in his private life. A favourite sister died in the Isle of Wight and was buried in the cemetery at Bonchurch. This loss so overwhelmed Swinburne with grief that he was no longer content to live on the island.

In deference to his wishes the family moved to Holmwood, in the valley of the Thames, near Reading. This nearer approach to London caused Swinburne to pine for the literary circles in the metropolis.

At last he obtained rooms in North Crescent, off Oxford Street, and immediately plunged into the pleasures of London life. His health, which had never been of the best, was made worse by his unsteadiness. It was fortunate for him that in 1879 he paid a visit to his friend, Watts, who lived in a quiet and secluded house on Putney Hill.

Swinburne was fascinated with the place, and when Watts moved to a larger house on Putney Hill, he eagerly accepted his offer to find him accommodation.

The quietude of this household was soothing, and Swinburne's health gradually returned. It was arranged that he should continue to live with Watts, and he was allotted a sitting-room on the first floor, giving a view of the garden, and a bedroom on the floor above.

Swinburne lived in the house for thirty years. Each day he would walk across Putney Heath, which Mrs. Watts described as his "great event of the day." There was a book-shop at Wimbledon to which Swinburne generally went to buy volumes for the Watts's.

During his residence at Putney, Swinburne wrote a great deal of his poetry. At the same time Watts was also busy writing. In 1897 Watts changed his name to Watts-Dunton, the affix being his mother's maiden name, and in the same year he published his volume of poems called *The Coming of Love*, the theme of which was the wandering life of gipsies.

Besides the great deal of poetry produced by Swinburne, he was also an active critic. In 1877 he wrote his *Note on Charlotte Brontë*, and in 1880 a *Study of Shakespeare*, followed in 1909 by *The Age of Shakespeare*.

There has been a good deal of criticism of Swinburne's prose, but little about his poetry. Included in his prose work is an early novel entitled "Love's Cross-currents" which he wrote in the *Tatler*. In 1905 this novel was reproduced in book form.

"Swinburne was the greatest metrical inventor in English literature" [writes a biographer]. "Other poets have equalled him in melody, but none other has revealed the tunefulness and pliancy, the majesty and grace of the English speech in such a variety of lyrical forms.

"He can impart dignity and distinction to the simplest measures, and move with faultless ease in the most elaborate. He can give rapid and graceful movement to heavy-laden, long-drawn metres, which other artists in verse would fine unworkably cumbrous. He can stir the blood by the rush and resonance of a battle-chorus, or charm the ear by the music of a love-lyric as sweet as the songs of spring.

"His music is like no other man's, and whether the verses are running lightly, marching proudly, or swinging impetuously, the music is alike irresistible."

In personal appearance Swinburne was small and lightly built. But he had a large head covered with red hair. He had a peculiarly nervous temperament.

In 1903, Swinburne, then 66, contracted a chill which turned to pneumonia. Both lungs were affected, but he recovered.

In 1909 the whole of the Watts-Dunton household were laid low with pneumonia. Swinburne again developed pneumonia, and died within a few days.

Theodore Watts-Dunton survived his friend by six years.

Sanzio Raphael

Sanzio Raphael and Michelangelo were always at loggerheads. Pope Julius craftily set one against the other, and watched the effect with amusement.

Raphael always had a little following of hero-worshippers at his heels. Michelangelo went about sour-faced, boiling over with his wrongs.

One day Michelangelo met Raphael with his train. "You look like a sheriff and his bailiffs," he said.

"And you, my dear sir," retorted Raphael, "resemble a hangman walking to your gallows."

Raphael was born on April 6th, 1483. He died on his birthday, thirty-seven years later.

Raphael was the only son of Giovanni Santi. The Italian version of his name is Sanzio Raffaello. His father was a painter, and he intended the boy to follow in his footsteps.

Raphael's mother died when he was eight. His father married again, and his stepmother encouraged the boy in a career of art.

He went to study under the celebrated Pietro Vanucci at Perugia.

In 1502 he began to assist Pinturicchio, a pupil of Perugino, who executed the famous frescoes in the library at Siena.

Two years later Raphael went to Florence, where Michelangelo and Leonardo were established.

In 1508 he was invited to Rome by Pope Julius II, through the recommendation of his fellow-townsman Bramante.

In Florence he had painted his series of studies of the Madonna, including the "Ansidei Madonna," now in the National Gallery, the "Cowper Madonna," sold to America a few years ago, and the "Belle Jardiniere," now in the Louvre.

The great work of Raphael in Rome was the decoration of the dwelling-rooms of the Popes in the Vatican. They consist of four principal rooms, generally called after the most remarkable frescoes which they contain.

He painted a magnificent portrait of Pope Julius, which now hangs in the Pitti Palace.

Though Raphael despised Michelangelo, he was not above taking hints from him.

He would watch him at work on the vast series of frescoes on the ceiling of the Sistine Chapel, and profit from the brilliance of the older man.

Raphael's improvement of style is generally attributed to the example set by Michelangelo.

In 1514 Raphael was appointed architect to St. Peter's in succession to Bramante. A lot of the work he was executing at this time was done by pupils, Raphael himself sketching only the outlines.

In fact, Raphael had more than he could do. He overtaxed his energy, and his life was shortened.

Raphael might have married into a good family. His bride would have been a beautiful girl with a dowry of 3000 crowns, but he had a mistress for whom he had a great affection. She was "Bella Fornarina," daughter of a Siena baker, and was the model for the Sistine Madonna, now in the Dresden Gallery.

Raphael chose to remain with his mistress.

In 1514, however, he nearly got married. No doubt the ecclesiastics were behind the plot to marry him to Maria Bibbiena, the daughter of Cardinal Bernardo Divizio. The nuptials were arranged, when Raphael changed his mind, and broke off the engagement.

Maria died of a broken heart.

Though Raphael was a courtier and kept himself well in the limelight, there were occasions when he was inclined to give short shrift to the cardinals and others who attempted to interfere with his work.

Two cardinals once complained that he had painted the

cheeks of St. Peter and St. Paul with too much carmine. "My lords," Raphael retorted, "they blush for shame that their Church on earth should be governed by such men as you."

Commissions poured in for Raphael from all over Italy. He was able to pick and choose, and, naturally, he chose the more magnificent assignments.

The Pope made him superintendent of ceremonies, and afterwards he became inspector of antiquities.

All the while he was living in the most extravagant style. He had a palace in Rome, and entertained lavishly. The pomp of this painter was the talk of Rome.

In 1516 Raphael drew the cartoons for the tapestries to complete the Sistine Chapel. The work was carried out in Florence. Some of the tapestries are still preserved in the Vatican.

Some of them were found by Rubens in Flanders in the seventeenth century and bought by Charles I. They are now in the Victoria and Albert Museum.

In March 1520, Raphael was suddenly summoned to Leo X at the Vatican. Raphael hurried to carry out the order, became overheated, caught a chill, and died suddenly on April 6th.

His body lay in state, with his last work, the "Transfiguration," at his head.

He was buried with great pomp in the Pantheon or Santa Maria della Rotonda at Rome.

In the academy of St. Luke, for many years there rested a skull which was supposed to be that of Raphael. In 1833, however, his tomb was opened and the skeleton was found intact.

A mould was taken from the skull and the tomb reclosed.

Raphael was of sallow complexion, had brown eyes, and a small frame.

His estate was estimated at 16,000 ducats, an immense fortune at the time. He had two houses at Rome, a fine mansion in the city, and a small villa just outside the walls.

It was in this villa that the baker's daughter "Fornarina" lived. To her he left sufficient for a life's independence.

Raphael is credited with about nine hundred works and drawings.

H*

Robert Elliston

As a young man, Robert William Elliston, the actor, was not discreet in his love adventures. He was scarcely eighteen when he began to woo a tavern-keeper's wife in Wapping.

Their love-making was done behind the bar in the absence of the woman's husband, and while business was going on.

One night the cry of "Fire !" was raised. Robert William was preparing to decamp, but the woman, fearing that in the commotion their secret would be discovered, pushed him into a large chest and locked him in.

The woman hurried into the bar. Elliston, in the box, could hear the noise, the arrival of fire-fighters, people running to and fro.

He tried to raise the lid, without result.

Then came the sound of splashing water, the breaking of glass.

Elliston did not relish the idea of being burned alive. He kicked frantically in the restricted space.

Soon he was exhausted by his struggles and gave himself up for lost.

"I had nothing for it but patience and prayer," Elliston afterwards told a friend.

"Prayer," replied the friend, "under the circumstances that brought you there, should have been preceded by repentance."

"Sir," returned Elliston, "I did not pray directly for myself, but that those who were endeavouring to subdue the fire might be induced to take care of the furniture."

The fire, after all, was of little consequence, and was speedily extinguished.

But Elliston was never seen in that place again.

Elliston had a remarkably elegant figure and good features, with a sweet and mellow voice. He was an unusually versatile actor, but shone best in humorous parts.

Although careful of his general appearance, he often forgot to wash his hands.

One day he was playing cards with Charles Lamb. The latter regarded the actor for a few minutes and then remarked : "Elliston, if dirt were trumps, what a hand you would have !"

Elliston was as much an actor off the stage as on it. When he took the Surrey Theatre there was an acrimonious dispute between him and Davidge, of the Coburg Theatre, on the respective merits of their entertainments. The dispute was reflected in the bills which they posted.

While the argument was at its height, Davidge had occasion to send a message to Elliston.

"I come from Mr. Davidge of the Coburg Theatre," announced the messenger.

"Davidge—Coburg Theatre—I don't remember—" replied Elliston.

"Sir," said the messenger, "you know—Mr. Davidge of the Coburg, close by here."

"It may be as you say," said Elliston. "I'll take your word, young man. I suppose there is such a theatre as the Coburg, and such a man as Davidge, but this is the first time I have heard the name of either."

He then strode away, leaving the messenger in a state of bewilderment.

Elliston, who was born in London on April 7, 1774, was the son of a jeweller. His uncle was the master of Sidney Sussex College, Cambridge.

At first destined for the Church, young Elliston became a student at St. Paul's School. Later he was to go to Sidney Sussex.

But he early began to take part in amateur theatricals and, making a hit in the plays put on by the school, he began to turn his mind to the boards for a profession.

Ignoring the pleadings of his relatives, he one day left school and started out for Bath. Here he obtained an introduction to the manager of the theatre, secured an engagement, and made his first professional appearance on the stage in April 1792, in the character of Tressell in *Richard III*.

He was so successful that he was soon regarded as the leader of the circuit, and when he came up to London he had little difficulty in securing a part at the Haymarket Theatre in *The Mountaineers*.

His reception was enough to turn the head of any actor. Soon afterwards he became lessee and manager of Drury Lane Theatre, the interior of which was entirely rebuilt according to his own scheme. He held this theatre, together with several others in the country, for several consecutive seasons.

In 1796 Elliston married at Bath the beautiful and accomplished Miss Rundall.

Elliston was always a favourite with the women. Of him, Mrs. Matthews, the wife of the comedian, writes :

"He was a delightful companion, and it might have been said of him in homely phrase, with more point than of most people, that in conversation he was as good as a comedy, aye, and one of the best comedies, too. I remember few people who carried their professional charm more entirely into their private life.

"Mr. Elliston in manner was like that of many other actors : a distinct person behind the scenes and in society, that is, in and out of the theatre. In the former position, it always seemed to me that he felt it necessary to put an antic disposition on, especially when he became a manager, in order to cope with the oddity and variety of characters and tempers he then encountered; but at these times I am fully persuaded that, like Hamlet, he was only mad 'North-north-west.' "

One of Elliston's best parts was Falstaff.

"His tones, his look and carriage convinced you that on occasion he could rise above the mere bolter of capons and swallower of sherries. He proved what every other Falstaff has failed in, or, rather, what they never attempted, considering it no part of the character—that he could be a courtier."

Thus wrote a contemporary critic, who proceeds with even more enthusiasm :

"The Falstaff of other actors is the mere cookshop Falstaff— the Falstaff of Elliston might, if he pleased, have attended levees. We fear that few, very few, critics crossed the bridge to see the fat knight, which, it is our faith, was the highest triumph of Elliston as an actor, inasmuch as it combined, heightened, and enriched all the qualities which he severally displayed in other parts. . . ."

But the flattery of Charles Lamb outshines all the other critics :

"In green-rooms impervious to mortal eye, the Muse beholds thee wielding posthumous empire. Thin ghosts of *figurantes* (never plump on earth) circle thee endlessly, and still their song is, 'Fye on endless phantasy.' Magnificent were thy *capriccios* on this globe of earth, Robert William Elliston! for as yet we know not thy new name in heaven."

Elliston died ten years after his wife, on July 8, 1831, and was buried in St. John's Church, Waterloo Road, London, where a tablet to his memory was erected in the chancel.

The First Earl of Craven

In the latter half of the sixteenth century a poor peasant lad living at Wharfedale, Yorkshire, began to tramp to London. He arrived in the City, somewhat disappointed to find that the streets were not paved with gold.

During the latter part of the journey he had assisted to drive the pack-horses of a carrier. When the carrier arrived at a wholesale house in Watling Street and delivered his cargo of Yorkshire cloth the lad was about to disappear into one of the narrow streets when the driver called him back.

"Wait here," said he; "there may be a job for such a likely lad as you."

He went into the warehouse. In a few minutes he returned. "They want you inside," he announced curtly.

The boy went in and was engaged to run errands.

He quickly made good; was advanced to the position of apprentice.

In a few years he had learned all there was to know about the cloth business. He set up in business for himself in the Leadenhall district, became an illustrious citizen of London, and in 1611 sat in the civic chair as Sir William Craven.

The authentic—not the legendary—story of Whittington does not surpass in romance that of Craven.

Sir William was the father of an even greater member of the family. He was another William, whose fame was earned as a soldier.

At an early age he took service in the forces of Henry, Prince of Orange. Then, when Gustavus Adolphus enlisted Englishmen for his campaign to restore Count Palatine Frederick in the Palatinate, Craven volunteered and led the charge at the storming of Creutznach. The first assault was repulsed, but Craven, with apparently foolish bravery, returned to the attack and the position was carried.

Craven was severely wounded. Gustavus Adolphus knighted him as he lay on the ground.

The wife of Frederick, Elector Palatine of the Rhine, was Elizabeth, daughter of James I. She appears to have been a fascinating woman, so much so that every member of the staff of Gustavus was in love with her. She was conspicuous for bravery and presence of mind, and she had an extraordinarily graceful figure.

Among those who fell a victim to her charms was the daredevil Christian, Duke of Brunswick. Another was Sir William Craven.

There is a legend that Craven married this fascinating Queen of Bohemia on her widowhood. If he did, it was a private ceremony.

On the death of Gustavus, Craven entered the services of the States of Holland, and remained in their army until the restoration of Charles II.

He took no active part in the Civil War, but, having great wealth, he assisted the exiled Stuarts. It is said that he gave Charles II not less than £50,000 at one time.

For this the Commonwealth Parliament confiscated his estates, and, although Holland interceded on his behalf, he remained comparatively poor until the Restoration, when he regained his estates and was elevated to an earldom.

During the Great Plague, Craven is said to have taken horse and galloped westward until he reached an isolated farmhouse on the Berkshire Downs where he built Ashdown House. Four avenues led up the house from the four points of the compass. At the end of each lane there was a window in the mansion, the popular theory being that if the plague gained access through one window it could escape through another.

Another acquisition of Craven's was the old Drury House in Drury Lane. This stood on the site of what later became the Olympic Theatre and a public-house adjoining named the Craven Arms.

Elizabeth of Bohemia went to live there with Lord Craven. He was then fifty-three and the Princess sixty-five. It was said that they had been privately married on the Continent, and that the fifty thousand pounds given to Charles II was to secure his consent. All this, however, is talk that cannot be substantiated.

What is known is that the Princess died a year after leaving the Continent, and she never lived in the magnificent mansion which the Earl began to build on his estate of Hampstead Marshall.

This house, moreover, was burned to the ground before it was finished.

Lord Craven was one of the most active of plague-fighters. In Tuttle (Tothill) Fields, Westminster, were five plague-houses built by him.   Here hundreds of victims of the plague were buried.

Samuel Pepys on July 18th, 1665, wrote :

"I was much troubled this day to hear at Westminster how the officers do bury the dead in the open Tuttle Fields, pretending want of room elsewhere ; whereas the new Chapel churchyard was walled in at the publick charge in the last plague-time, merely for want of room, and now none but such as are able to pay dear for it can be buried there."

These five pest-houses were still in existence in 1832. According to a contemporary writer :

"With the moss and lichens growing on the roofs and walls, and their generally old-fashioned quaintness, a very small stretch of the imagination removed the buildings which had surrounded them even then, and brought them once more into the open ground. . . ."

Lord Craven was not satisfied with building these hospitals for plague victims.   Many of those who had no place to go to because they were turned out by their friends, were sheltered by him, "with the same coolness with which he had fought the battles of his mistress, the Queen of Bohemia."

The pest-houses consisted of a row of red-brick buildings, and were built at a cost of £250.   Some years after the plague they were made into alms-houses for twenty-four aged married people.

Lord Craven had an extraordinary knack of calming the fears of crowds.   Whenever a fire broke out he would be on the spot to render assistance and to stem panic and preserve order.   It became a saying that his horse could smell a fire before it happened.

He was, indeed, the most popular man in London.   His association with the Queen of Bohemia was regarded as only another of his acts of kindness, for Elizabeth was a rather pathetic figure, although of course, she was *persona grata* at Court and in society circles.

The Earl of Craven died on April 9th, 1697, at the age of 88.

Until the beginning of last century there was a fresco painting on the wall of Craven Buildings in Drury Lane of the Earl mounted on a white charger with a marshal's baton in his hand.   It was frequently repainted in oil until at last it was forgotten and became entirely obliterated.

Dick Turpin

As a hero of romance, Dick Turpin is a fraud. He had no horse called Black Bess. He did not make that epoch-making ride to York.

With all respect to Harrison Ainsworth, the real Richard Turpin had no redeeming feature in his character. He was a common horse-stealer, assaulter of women, and murderer.

When he was executed at York on April 10, 1739, he had well earned that fate.

Turpin was the son of a farmer at Thackstead, Essex. He was apprenticed to a butcher, and on the expiration of his indentures he married a young woman named Palmer, whose home was in West Ham.

Soon afterwards he began to steal the cattle of neighbours and cut them up for sale.

Two carcasses were traced to Turpin's home and a warrant was issued for his arrest. He escaped the law officers by getting through a back window of his house and hiding in Essex, where he joined a gang of smugglers.

The gang was broken up by Customs officers, and Turpin threw in his lot with deer-stealers in Epping Forest. But this business did not prosper and the gang turned to house-breaking.

They robbed a chandler at Watford and deprived him of all his money.

Their next exploit was at Loughton, where they forced their way into the home of an old widow and demanded to know where her reputed hoard of money was concealed. She refused to tell. Whereupon Turpin gagged her and her maid and threatened further violence.

She still refused to disclose the cache and Turpin placed her on the fire. Tormented with pain, the unfortunate woman at last gave them the information. They robbed her of £400.

At Barking they broke into the house of a farmer and secured £700.

On January 11th, 1735, Turpin and five others secured an entry to the home of a farmer named Saunders at Charlton, Kent, and found the family playing cards. They broke open escritoires and chests and obtained £100 and a quantity of plate. They then ransacked the larder and the wine cellar and sat down and regaled themselves with mince-pies and drink. Meanwhile the farmer and his family were in a state of terror.

The robbers retired to a public-house at Woolwich, where they further refreshed themselves and then broke open an empty house at Ratcliffe, where they deposited the stolen articles.

Following another successful robbery in Croydon, they committed an offence which led to the offer of a reward.

About seven o'clock in the evening of February 4th, they arrived outside the house of a Mr. Lawrence, near Stanmore, Middlesex. They left their horses at the gate, trussed up a shepherd lad, held up a man-servant, and entered the place. They bound Lawrence, rifled his pockets, and broke open a closet. Their haul was small and, in revenge, they threw a kettle of boiling water over him.

A maid-servant appearing on the scene was assaulted.

A proclamation was issued for the apprehension of the offenders, and a reward offered without effect.

A farmer near Marylebone was the next victim, and the reward was considerably increased. It led to the arrest and conviction of two of the gang, which was thus dispersed.

Turpin now decided to plough a lonely furrow. While jogging along the Cambridge Road, he met a man genteelly dressed. Scenting a good haul, Turpin presented a pistol at his head.

The man burst out into laughter. "What, dog eat dog?" he exclaimed. "Come, come, brother Turpin, if you don't know me I know you, and I shall be glad of your company." The man proved to be another "gentleman of the road" named King.

For some months they operated on the Cambridge Road and committed numerous robberies until they became so well known that they could never secure accommodation at a public-house.

Eventually they found a cave on the Loughton Road, in Epping Forest, that was large enough for themselves and their horses.

From this hiding-place they robbed everyone on the road. In time pedlars had to carry firearms to defend themselves.

Occasionally they wandered farther afield—into Suffolk and Cambridgeshire.

On May 4th, 1737, occurred the crime which brought Turpin to the gallows.

A reward of £900 had been offered for the capture of Turpin. The keeper of Epping Forest had received information about Turpin's hiding-place, and sent one of his men to take the highwayman into custody. The man was accompanied by a higgler (a travelling produce buyer).

They met Turpin in the forest.

"There are no hares in this thicket," said the rogue, desirous of getting them out of the way.

"No," replied Morris, the keeper's man, "but I have found a Turpin." Presenting his gun, he called upon Turpin to surrender.

The highwayman began coolly to temporize, at the same time backing to where he had hidden his gun.

The man was taken off his guard. Turpin seized his firearm and shot Morris dead. The higgler ran off in terror.

A few days later the following appeared on the hoardings and in public-houses :

"It having been represented to the King that Richard Turpin did, on Wednesday, the 4th of May last, barbarously murder Thomas Morris, servant to Henry Thompson, one of the keepers of Epping Forest, and commit other notorious felonies and robberies near London, his Majesty is pleased to promise his most gracious pardon to any of his accomplices, and a reward of two hundred pounds to any person or persons that shall discover him, so that he may be apprehended and convicted.

"Turpin was born at Thackstead, in Essex, is about 30, very much marked with the small-pox, his cheek-bones broad, his face thinner towards the bottom, his visage short, pretty upright, and broad about the shoulders."

During following weeks Turpin had a number of hair-breadth escapes, but still continued his robberies, again joining up with King.

One Saturday night the two men were at the Red Lion, in Whitechapel, when they were recognized. They tried to bolt, but were caught in a trap. Turpin, a little in advance, fired his pistol at their pursuers, but hit King.

"Dick, you have killed me !" the wounded man cried. But Turpin rode off at full speed in the diversion.

King lingered a week, giving information that Turpin could be found at a house near Hackney Marsh.

For some time Turpin skulked in the forest, several vain attempts being made to capture him. Soon he changed the scene of his operations to Lincolnshire ; then Yorkshire. Finally, he was caught in the latter county, lodged in York Castle, and was the sensation of the country people who came to see him behind bars.

He was speedily tried and executed. The corpse was buried in St. George's churchyard, York.

Richard Coleman

How many innocent men have been hanged for murders they did not commit ?

Such a question will seem absurd to people who believe that justice in England cannot err. Yet there have been in the past many instances of people being convicted of offences through mistaken identity, and there are known cases of innocent men being hanged.

In the days when highwaymen infested the roads near London, it was not an uncommon occurrence for an innocent party to suffer imprisonment through being identified as one of the "gentlemen of the road."

An extraordinary miscarriage of justice occurred at the little village of Chipping Camden, Gloucestershire. William Harrison, steward of the Campden estate, after collecting rents, suddenly disappeared. After a search a comb and hatband were found near a furze bush covered with blood. They belonged to Harrison.

Suspicion fell on John Perry, a tenant. When charged he told several different tales. In the end he, his mother, and brother were hanged.

Two years later William Harrison walked into the village, telling a tale of having been kidnapped by pirates and taken to the Barbary Coast.

Another case was that of Thomas Gedelley, who disappeared with a quantity of gold belonging to his mistress, the landlady of the Packhorse Inn, York.

Three years later a stable lad rushed into the inn crying: "I have seen him!" He swore he had seen Gedelley. The man was arrested, tried, and executed for robbery, although he had declared that his name was John Crow.

Some time later a York solicitor, visiting Dublin on business, saw a man in the dock at the criminal court who was the double of the hanged man. It proved to be the real Gedelley.

A more remarkable case than any of these was that of Richard Coleman, who was hanged at Kennington Common on April 12th, 1749, for the murder of a woman named Sarah Green.

On July 23rd in the previous year, Sarah Green was returning home from a party in Kennington Lane, late at night, when three men, described as brewers' servants, assaulted her. She was able with difficulty to get home to her lodgings about two o'clock in the morning. On the following day her condition was so serious that friends advised her removal to St. Thomas's Hospital.

While lying in hospital she declared that one of the men was a clerk in Taylor's brewhouse, and it was supposed from her description that he was Richard Coleman.

Two days after the assault, Coleman and a friend named Daniel Trotman called at the Queen's Head Alehouse, in Bandy-leg Walk, Southwark, the former being in a state of intoxication. They called for some rum and water, and Coleman was stirring it with a spoon when a stranger said to him: "What have you done with the pig?"

Coleman looked at him with surprise. "What pig?" he demanded.

The stranger then mentioned that a pig had been stolen in the neighbourhood. Upon which Coleman shouted: "Damn the pig, what is it to me?"

"Do you know Kennington Lane?" asked the man.

"Damn ye, yes," replied Coleman, "but what of it?"

"Did you know the woman assaulted in Kennington Lane?"

"Yes; but what of that?"

Coleman, intoxicated, could not see the drift of the questioning.

"You were one of the parties in that affair," accused the stranger.

"What the— ?" demanded Coleman, and taking up his liquor, he threw it into the other's face.

There followed a violent quarrel; but finally Coleman allowed himself to be led away.

About a month afterwards, Daniel Trotman and another man appeared before a borough magistrate and charged Coleman with having been concerned in the assault. At first the magistrate was not impressed. Nevertheless, he sent a man to conduct Coleman to the hospital where the injured woman still lay.

Sarah Green was asked if Coleman were one of the men who had attacked her; she replied that she believed he was. She declined, however, to swear positively, and Coleman was admitted to bail.

The accused man again appeared before the magistrate, who was inclined to release him. But when pressed by the girl's employer, he agreed to give Sarah Green another opportunity of identifying him.

On the following day the magistrate, Coleman, and others visited the girl, when she swore on oath that he was not one of the men.

It was now argued that the girl was not in her right senses. Again Coleman was released on bail. Next day the girl died.

A coroner's jury returned a verdict of murder, and a warrant was issued against Coleman.

Though conscious of his innocence, the accused man had such a dread of prison that he immediately absconded and hid at Pinner, Middlesex.

The case was set down to be heard at the Surrey Assizes, and a proclamation was issued by the Lords of the Regency— King George II then being at Hanover—offering a reward of £50 for the apprehension of Coleman. The parish of St. Saviour, Southwark, offered a further £20.

Coleman read the advertisement in the newspapers, and replied with the following:

"*I, Richard Coleman, seeing myself advertised in the* Gazette *as absconding on account of the murder of Sarah Green, knowing myself not any way culpable, do assert that I have not absconded from justice: but will willingly and readily appear at the next assizes, knowing that my innocence will acquit me.*"

Information was received that a man answering to Coleman's description had been seen at Pinner, and a strict search was carried out. On November 22nd he was arrested and lodged in Newgate, and then taken to the new gaol at Southwark to await the trial.

A verdict of Guilty was returned by the jury, principally on the first statement of the woman and Trotman's evidence of what occurred when Coleman was interrogated in the public-house.

Several people swore that he was elsewhere at the time of the assault; but their evidence was not credited by the jury. Three of these witnesses were actually the men who had committed the crime!

It was no doubt a guilty conscience that had induced them to give evidence on Coleman's behalf. Of course, their testimonies were false, for they could not swear truthfully where the accused man was at the time.

Coleman died on the gibbet on Kennington Common. He left a wife and two children.

He had been laid in an ignominious grave for two years before the truth came out.

Circumstances then proved that the murderers were James Welch, Thomas Jones, and John Nichols.

Welch while in a state of drunkenness, admitted to a companion that he and two others had assaulted Sarah Green. This companion, a man named Bush, paid no attention at the time, but later he mentioned the fact to his father.

How the truth finally came out is a long story. Suffice to say that Welch and Jones were hanged, Nichols having turned King's evidence against them.

Matthew Arnold

Still glides the stream, slow drops the boat
Under the rustling poplars' shade;
Silent the swans beside us float—
None speaks, none heeds; ah, turn thy head!

In his poem, "The River," of which the above is the first stanza, Matthew Arnold has pictured the Thames that he knew as a child.

The scene has changed. Though ivy-coloured Laleham church stands sentinel on the Middlesex bank as it did in the

20's, and the low tower of Chertsey Abbey is a conspicuous landmark on the Surrey side, it is doubtful if Arnold would now recognize the Chertsey that he describes in the following letter :

Yesterday I was at Chertsey, the poetic town of our childhood, as opposed to the practical, historical Staines; it is across the river, reached by no bridges and roads, but by primitive ferry, the meadow path, the Abbey river with its wooden bridge, and the narrow lane by the old walls; and, itself, the stillest of country towns backed by St. Ann's, leads nowhere but to the heaths and pines of Surrey.

Born at Laleham in 1822, Arnold lived there until he was 6. At the age of 8 he was back, and remained for six more years while he received instruction from his uncle, the Rev. John Buckland.

His father was the famous Dr. Thomas Arnold, the headmaster of Rugby School, who held the living of Laleham until he was appointed to Rugby in 1828.

Matthew went to Winchester for a year, and then in August 1837 entered Rugby School. He was there at the period around which the story *Tom Brown's Schooldays* was written. Thomas Arnold had a stern, puritanical character, but his son was gay and full of humour.

Matthew began to write verses at an early age. His first publication was a Rugby prize poem, "Alaric at Rome," in 1840. In the same year he won an open scholarship at Balliol, and in the following year he went to Oxford.

At that time the Tractarian Movement was in full swing. This movement was designed to revive within the Church of England the Catholic doctrines retained after the Elizabethan Church settlement, and advocated by High Churchmen in the seventeenth century. Matthew was thus thrown into a circle of which his father did not approve.

In 1843 Matthew produced his poem "Cromwell," which won the Newdigate Prize, and in 1844 he graduated with second-class honours.

His father had died two years before and when, having left Oxford, Matthew went to Rugby to teach classics in the fifth form, Dr. Tait was headmaster of the school.

In 1847 Arnold gave up his mastership at Rugby and

became private secretary to Lord Lansdowne, President of the Council in Lord John Russell's administration. It was through this that he finally obtained his appointment as Inspector of Schools, a post he retained until two years before his death.

His tutor at Oxford had been Mr. Ralph Lingen (afterwards Lord Lingen) who had become Secretary of the Education Department. He invited Arnold to join him in that Department, where one of his colleagues was Arthur Hugh Clough, whose friendship Arnold commemorates in the elegy "Thyrsis."

Arnold married in June 1851, Frances Lucy Wightman, daughter of Mr. Justice Wightman.

Meanwhile, in 1849, appeared the *Strayed Reveller and other Poems*. In 1852 he published *Empedocles on Etna and other Poems*. Both these were printed under the pseudonym "A." Next year appeared *Poems* under his own name, consisting partly of poems selected from the other two volumes.

In 1857 Arnold was elected Professor of Poetry at Oxford, and in this capacity gave a series of lectures, some of which he published under the title of *Essays on Criticism*, which established his position as a critic.

Arnold held the chair of Professor of Poetry for ten years.

After he left the chair, his activity as a poet almost ceased, and he spent his time investigating social and religious theories. He was several times sent by the Government to inquire into the state of education in France, Germany, Holland, and other countries. His reports on the foreign methods contrasted with those of the English, were of immense value.

His fame as a poet and critic has overshadowed his reputation in the educational field.

At the time of his appointment as education officer, the Church of England schools were inspected by clergymen, the Roman Catholic by ministers of that denomination, but the Nonconformist schools were inspected by laymen. Arnold was one of the latter, and as there were only two inspectors, the districts covered were necessarily very large.

Naturally Arnold came into contact with many Nonconformists, from whom he appears to have gathered considerable material for his somewhat sarcastic essays on religious sects. When the Education Act of 1870 was passed, the area of inspection was reduced, and Arnold was appointed to the district of Westminster, where he remained until his resignation.

From letters written at this time it is evident that some of his work was distasteful, and he employed an assistant to do the examination of the schools and prepare statistics.

Arnold's annual reports on the schools he examined—about twenty in all—were published in a volume by his official chief Sir Francis (afterwards Lord) Sandford. As a rule blue books are dull, but Arnold made them fresh and interesting.

The theme of his reports was that education was a Government matter, and should not be left to private individuals or organizations. "One thing is needful," he declared. "Organize your secondary education."

In 1883 a pension of £250 a year was conferred on Arnold for his literary work. In that year, too, he went to the United States on a lecture tour, and again in 1886. But Arnold had a poor delivery, and the success of these lectures was to a certain extent prejudiced.

In April 1888 he was waiting at Liverpool to meet his daughter on her way home from America when he suddenly felt ill. For days he had felt remarkably well, and although he had suffered with heart trouble, he had shown his good spirits by jumping over a railing. A few hours later he ran to catch a bus, collapsed and died at once.

Matthew Arnold was tall and powerfully built. He had a good presence, had black hair, and blue eyes ; but an eye-glass made him look rather supercilious. He was "witty, pointed, and irresistibly droll" in conversation, and was always full of gaiety and fun. Yet there was pathos in some of his poetry. An example is another verse from "The River" :

> *My pent-up tears oppress my brain,*
> *My heart is swoln with love unsaid.*
> *Ah, let me weep, and tell my pain,*
> *And on thy shoulder rest my head !*

Tragedy of Culloden

Vowing that he would either die or be crowned, Charles Edward Stuart, the Young Pretender, crossed the Channel in two ships, lost one of them to the British Navy, and eventually landed in Scotland.

British Ministers heard the news, laughed, and went on plotting among themselves.

But it was soon evident that Charles Edward meant business. His rapid progress caused consternation in London.

George II, who had been rusticating in Hanover, hurried back. The Highlanders, remembering Glencoe, thirsted for revenge and rallied round the Pretender.

The Forth was crossed. Colonel Gardiner's Dragoons, who had boasted that they would cut to pieces all the rebels, turned tail and ran away.

Edinburgh was entered without a struggle, and Charles Edward strutted proudly in Holyrood House, almost persuaded that the Crown was his.

The "tall and handsome youth" led his army against the Hanoverians near Preston-pans, and the latter retreated in confusion.

Charles Edward began a bold march on London.

Carlisle, beseiged, surrendered to the Duke of Perth. At Manchester Charles recruited three hundred men. At Preston the bells rang a merry peal.

Yet there was no general rising in favour of the Pretender, which was not encouraging.

On December 4th, 1745, the rebel army reached Derby. And here their courage seemed to desert them, for news was received that the King's son, the Duke of Cumberland was in the vicinity.

Charles Edward wanted to push on towards London, but on the advice of his officers, gave orders for the return to Scotland, to join up with another Scottish army.

The rebels, numbering 9,000, and the forces of George II, met at Falkirk, the Hanoverians being completely defeated.

But the Duke of Cumberland kept on doggedly, determined to get at the man who claimed his father's throne.

For several weeks the Jacobites were chased in and out of first one town and then another.

On April 15th, 1746, the rebel army decided to give battle.

They established themselves on Drummossie Moor, a mile and a half from Culloden House, and determined upon a night attack.

The Duke's army lay at Nairn. At eight o'clock in the evening the Highlanders began to move.

It was a pitch-black night, and progress was slow. By two o'clock the rebels were still two miles from Nairn. By this time they were tired and without enthusiasm.

Suddenly they heard the sound of a bugle. The Duke of Cumberland had been warned of their approach. The rebel army turned and tramped back to Culloden.

Weary, they lay down to rest. But not for long. At eight o'clock the Duke's army was in sight. By midday they had opened fire.

For weeks the rebels had shown no inclination to meet the Duke, who concluded that they would run again.

He was soon undeceived. "They came," records an English officer, "running forward in their furious wild way on our right, where his Royal Highness had placed himself to receive them. . . . They came down several times within a hundred yards of our men, firing their pistols and brandishing their swords. . . ."

Then from the centre of the rebel army emerged the Clan MacIntosh.

"Notwithstanding that the three files of the front line of English poured forth their incessant fire of musketry ; notwithstanding that the cannon, now filled with grapeshot, swept the field as with a hailstorm, onward went the headlong Highlanders, flinging themselves into, rather than, rushing upon, the lines of the enemy, which, indeed, they did not see for smoke until involved among their weapons.

"It was a moment of dreadful, agonizing suspense, but only for a moment, for the whirlwind does not sweep the forest with greater rapidity than the Highlanders cleared the line.

"They swept through and over that frail barrier almost as easily and instantaneously as the bounding cavalcade brushes through the morning labours of the gossamer which stretches across its path. Almost every man in their front rank, chief and gentleman, fell before the deadly weapons they had braved ; and although the enemy gave way, it was not until every bayonet was bent and bloody with the strife.

"When the first line had been completely swept aside the assailants continued their impetuous advance until they came near the second, when being almost annihilated by a profuse and well-directed fire, the shattered remains of what had been but an hour before a numerous and confident force, at last submitted to destiny, by giving way and flying.

"Still a few rushed on, resolved rather to die than to forfeit their well-acquired and dearly-estimated honour. They rushed on, but not a man ever came in contact with the enemy. The last survivor perished as he reached the points of the bayonets."

Other clans attempted to imitate the example of the Clan MacIntosh, but soon stopped short and retreated.

For a battle in which the armies were comparatively small the carnage was terrible.

Charles Edward hurried round with the intention of rallying his men, but an officer caught the bridle of his horse and led him from the field.

The Highlanders lost on that day 2500 men. Two-thirds of these were put to death after the battle by the "Butcher" Cumberland, who had twice as many men as Charles Edward.

This disaster to the Stuart cause gave rise to the pathetic ballad :

> *Drummossie Muir, Drummossie day,*
> *A waefu' day it was to me !*
> *For there I lost my father dear,*
> *My father dear, and brethren three.*

The wretched wanderings of Charles Edward Stuart, a price of £30,000 on his head, and his escape with the aid of Flora Macdonald, form one of the most tragic romances of British history.

In 1822, George IV paid a visit to Scotland, where he was presented by Sir Walter Scott with the pocket-knife, fork and spoon which Charles Edward was believed to have used during his campaign and wanderings.

This relic subsequently passed to the Marquess of Conyngham, and from him to his son, Albert, first Lord Londesborough. The articles were in a case, and for portability they were each made to screw on handles.

Sir Walter had been commissioned by Mary Lady Clerk to present it to the King. She had more than ordinary interest in Charles Edward Stuart, for she was born at a time when the Prince's army was in occupation of Carlisle.

Her mother was still confined to bed when a party of Highlanders came to the house. The commanding officer, on learning the circumstances, ordered his men to depart, and pinned a white rosette or cockade on the infant's breast.

The rosette was in the possession of Lady Clerk at the time of her death, several years after the visit of George IV. How the knife-case came into her possession is not certain.

Charles Darwin

At the school at Shrewsbury which Charles Darwin attended they had a very poor opinion of the lad who was destined to become one of the world's greatest scientists.

His master's considered verdict was: "The boy is entirely dull."

Darwin himself has little to say in favour of the school.

"Nothing could have been worse for the development of my mind," he comments, "as it was strictly classical, nothing else being taught except a little ancient geography and history. The school as a means of education to me was simply a blank. When I left the school I was for my age neither high nor low in it; and I believe that I was considered by all my masters, and by my father, as a very ordinary boy, rather below the common standards in intellect."

From this school he went to Edinburgh to study medicine, with but poor result. He had no stomach for dissection, and when once he was called upon to attend two operations, one on a child, he had to hurry away from the operating theatre before they were finished.

The truth was that Charles Darwin was too soft-hearted for the profession of a surgeon, and soon he agreed with his father that he should become a clergyman.

Thus he was sent to Cambridge, but, as he records, "My time was sadly wasted then, and worse than wasted."

He spent too much time in sport, "and we sometimes drank too much."

The only thing that interested Darwin in connection with

college life was the music at King's College Chapel, which, he declared, caused a cold shiver to run down his backbone.

Beetles and insects were his chief study, which made one of his friends remark jokingly that he would one day be a Fellow of the Royal Society.

The most important and pleasurable experience in Darwin's life was his voyage as a naturalist on board the *Beagle*.

In five years he gathered an immense amount of data, and when he returned home he found that he had his "first note-book of facts in relation to the *Origin of Species*, about which I had long reflected, and never ceased working for the next twenty years."

Sir Francis Darwin, in the life of his father, states that in forty years Charles Darwin never knew one day of the health of ordinary men. Nevertheless, before the *Origin* was given to the world, he had attained eminence, as the following comment by a biographer will show.

Writing of the scientist's career up to about 1855, he says :

"Mr. Darwin's labours in the cause of natural science have been prosecuted under the disadvantage of shattered health. He is unable to continue for a long period study or literary labour of any kind, and he is a remarkable example of what difficulties may be overcome by untiring zeal, great perseverance, and a remarkable amiability and kindness of disposition.

"Mr. Darwin is yet in the prime of life, and we may hope that, with improved health, he may yet add further contributions to the advancement of science and his own reputation."

The writer little knew that within four years Charles Darwin would make a "contribution" that would startle the world of science and the sphere of religion.

Yet it was an open secret that Darwin was working on an important theory. The *Origin*, in fact, had been growing in his mind for many years.

In January 1844 he wrote to his friend, Sir Joseph Hooker :
"*At last gleams of light have come, and I am almost convinced (quite contrary to the opinion I started with) that species are not (it is like confessing a murder) immutable.*"

On November 24th, 1859, the work appeared with the full title, *On the Origin of Species by Means of Natural Selection or the Preservation of Favoured Races in the Struggle for Life.* The whole edition of 1250 copies was sold out on the first day of issue.

It was a strange coincidence that the thesis of the *Origin* should have been formulated at the same time by Professor Alfred Russel Wallace, who actually sent his paper on the subject to Darwin for his opinion.

Darwin was astonished to find in the essay a complete summary of his own theory. Wallace's essay was sent to the Linnean Society, together with an abstract of Darwin's work. Thus both men got equal credit.

In 1871 Darwin published the *Descent of Man*, which excited as much attention as his earlier work, and in the following year appeared *The Expression of the Emotions in Man and Animals*.

It is well known that these works aroused a fierce controversy; but Darwin would never enter into controversy himself. He would have been the last to declare that finality had been reached in biological theory.

Charles Darwin was born on February 12th, 1809, and died on April 19th, 1882—eighty years almost to a day after the death of his famous grandfather Erasmus Darwin—and was buried in Westminster Abbey.

Erasmus Darwin was born at Elston Hall, near Newark, on December 12th, 1731. He was twice married, Charles Darwin being a grandson of the first marriage, while Francis Galton, the scientist and explorer, and authority on fingerprints, was a grandson of the second marriage.

Erasmus was better known as a poet, though his first efforts were not acknowledged by him. The *Botanic Garden* appeared in 1781. The second part of this was entitled "Loves of the Plants."

He practised as a physician at Lichfield, where he was a contemporary of Dr. Samuel Johnson. Each man was the head of a local circle entirely distinct in sympathies and politics.

Darwin led a temperate life, and is credited with having reformed the drinking habits of the people of Lichfield.

Having lost his first wife, Erasmus left Lichfield and went to live at Derby.

Elizabeth Canning

The extraordinary case of Elizabeth Canning created a sensation in London in the years 1753 and 1754. So much attention was focused on it that Press and society were split into sections for and against the girl.

The following is the story told by Elizabeth.

On January 1st, 1753, she visited her uncle and aunt, who lived near Moorfields, London. On her way home she was robbed of half a guinea by two men, who also took her gown, apron and hat.

She screamed, and to silence her cries, one of the men bound a handkerchief round her mouth, and tied her hands behind her. This caused her to go into a fit.

On her recovery she found that she was being dragged along the ground. Finally she was taken to a house occupied by a certain Susannah Wells, at Enfield, Middlesex. There she saw a domestic named Mary Squires, who proposed to her that she should adopt a career, which Elizabeth refused to entertain. Whereupon she was taken upstairs to a hay-loft and her clothes removed.

A quartern loaf and a pitcher of water was all the food and drink she had during her confinement, which lasted until January 29th.

On that day, according to her statement, she removed a board nailed on the inside of the window, scrambled through and dropped into a narrow lane.

She made her way to the main road, inquired the direction to London, and reached her home at 10 o'clock at night. She told the story to her mother, and a general warrant was issued for the arrest of Susannah Wells, Mary Squires, and anyone else who was in the house.

Elizabeth accompanied the officers and identified the people concerned. All were taken before a magistrate. One of them, a girl named Virtue Hall, denied all knowledge of what had taken place at the house, and she was discharged. Squires and Wells were committed to New Prison for robbing the girl.

Hall was again arrested and examined before the Bow Street magistrate, when she confessed that Canning had been at the house as she had declared.

Squires and Wells were tried at the Old Bailey and convicted of robbery. Three men, John Gibson, William Clark, and Thomas Grevil, who swore that Squires was in Dorset at the time of the assault, were committed to be tried for perjury.

Several distinguished people who had been present at the trial, however, were dissatisfied with the evidence. They began a campaign for the release of Squires, who, at length, secured a free pardon.

Meanwhile it was argued that the countrymen had spoken the truth. That meant that Canning had concocted the whole story. The matter was now in an inexplicable tangle.

The only way out was to charge Canning with perjury.

At the next session of the Old Bailey, held on April 20th, 1754, it was found that bills of indictment had been brought by interested parties against both Canning and the men.

The Grand Jury were in a dilemma. Finally they threw out all the bills. All charges were therefore wiped out.

But in the following sessions in June, bills of indictment were found against the men. An attempt was made to get the case heard at the Court of King's Bench, but that court refused to deal with it. The men were therefore hailed to come up at the September Sessions.

They duly appeared and were honourably acquitted, there being no evidence against them of perjury.

Someone, however, had sworn false evidence. Who were the offenders ?

London divided on the subject, and the Lord Mayor, Sir Crisp Gascoyne, determined to solve the mystery.

In May 1754, Elizabeth Canning was indicted at the Old Bailey for perjury. A large number of witnesses swore that Mary Squires was at Abbotsbury at the time of the alleged assault. Thirty people appeared for the other side and declared that Canning had a good character and was not the type to commit wilful perjury.

The arguments used by counsel on both sides were ingenious. After long deliberation the jury brought in a verdict of guilty, and Elizabeth was sentenced to be transported for seven years.

Newspapers and public men now intensified their championship of one side or the other.

For the girl appeared a pamphlet by Henry Fielding, the

magistrate who had examined and secured a confession from Virtue Hall. It is possible to give only a few extracts.

"The girl, after an absence of a month" [wrote Fielding], "returned in a dreadful condition. A very fair presumption follows that she was confined somewhere and by some person ; that she was almost starved to death ; that she was confined in a place whence it was difficult to make her escape. . . .

"What motive can be invented for her laying this heavy charge on those who are innocent ? . . .

"Before noblemen, and magistrates, and judges, persons who must have inspired the girl with the highest awe, she went through her evidence without hesitation, confusion, trembling, change of countenance, or other apparent emotion."

Fielding proceeded to argue that the girl could not have simulated the modesty and simplicity which she preserved throughout.

Elizabeth, too, was able to describe most minutely the room in which she had been confined. This she could not have done if she had not been there.

"Another improbability is, that this girl should fix on a place so far from home, and where it doth not appear she had even been before. In this point her evidence stands confirmed by the declaration of Wells herself. It is true, indeed, that as to her being confined there, Wells utterly denies it ; but she as positively affirms that Canning was never there at any other time, nor in any other manner.

"Hence arises an utter impossibility of the falsehood of her story . . ."

Dealing with the fact that the evidence had first been heard by him, he adds :

"If Elizabeth Canning be guilty of a false accusation, I own she hath been capable of imposing on me ; but I have the comfort to think the same imposition hath passed not only on two juries, but likewise on one of the best judges that ever sat on the bench of justice, and on two other very able judges, who were present at the trial."

A pamphlet in reply was published by Dr. Hill, who alleged that Virtue Hall had "confessed" for fear of being indicted as an accessory.

"Let me ask you, sir," he says, "were these circumstances of the confession, viz., that it should be free and voluntary, without fear and constraint ?

"I need not ask you ; your pamphlet contradicts it. She refused to confess any such thing ; you tell us so yourself, throughout six hours of strong solicitation, and she consented to do it at last. Why ? She says, and you say the same—it was because she was else to be prosecuted as a felon."

Hill then argued that the stories of the two girls were too much alike.

"Hall had heard Canning's story many times," he suggested. "She had heard it from Canning's own mouth at Enfield on February 1st. For eight days after this the story was published in the newspapers to raise subscriptions. Hall can read, or, if she could not, she had ears."

There was much more of the same kind of argument in Hill's pamphlet, but neither this nor that of Henry Fielding assisted in the elucidation of the mystery.

Elizabeth Canning was transported on July 31st, 1754, taking with her several hundred pounds collected by her partisans.

At the end of her term of transportation she went to America, where she was married and eventually died.

Legend of the Wandering Jew

The legend of the Wandering Jew has persisted in all countries of Europe, but appears to have had its genesis in England.

From time to time through the ages individuals claiming to be the Wandering Jew have appeared.

On April 22nd, 1774, the Wandering Jew reached Brussels. Giving the name of Isaac Laquedem, he told his story to the credulous citizens, and disappeared. Since that date nothing has been heard of anyone answering the description of Cartaphilus, porter of the Hall of Judgment where Pilate interrogated Jesus.

A quotation from the chronicler who wrote the history of the Abbey of St. Albans, copied by Matthew Paris, carries the details of the Jew's wanderings up to medieval times.

A certain archbishop of Armenia Major came on a pilgrimage to England so see the relics of the saints and visit the sacred places in this kingdom, as he had done in others. He also produced letters of recommendation from His Holiness the Pope to the religious men and prelates of the churches, in which they were enjoined to receive and entertain him with due reverence and honour.

On his arrival he came to St. Albans, where he was received with all respect by the abbot and monks. At this place, being fatigued with his journey, he remained some days to rest himself and his followers, and a conversation took place between him and the inhabitants of the convent by means of their interpreters, during which he made many inquiries relating to the religion and religious observances of this country, and told many strange things concerning the countries of the East.

In the course of conversation he was asked whether he had ever seen or heard anything of Joseph, a man of whom there was much talk in the world, who when our Lord suffered, was present and spoke to him, and who is still alive, in evidence of the Christian faith.

In reply to which a knight in his retinue who was his interpreter replied, speaking in French: "My lord well knows that man, and a little before he took his way to the western countries the said Joseph ate at the table of my lord the Archbishop in Armenia, and he has often seen and held converse with him."

He was then asked about what had passed between Christ and the said Joseph, to which he replied: "At the time of the suffering of Jesus Christ, he was seized by the Jews and led into the hall of judgment before Pilate, the Governor, that he might be judged by him on the accusation of the Jews.

"Pilate, finding no cause for adjudging him to death, told them to judge him according to their law.

"The shouts of the Jews, however, increasing, he at their request, released unto them Barrabas, and delivered Jesus to them to be crucified.

"When, therefore, the Jews were dragging Jesus forth, and had reached the door, Cartaphilus, a porter of the hall, in Pilate's service, as Jesus was going out of the door, impiously struck him on the back with his hand and said, in mockery, 'Go quicker, Jesus, go quicker. Why do you loiter?'

"And Jesus, looking back on him with a severe countenance, said to him 'I am going, and you will wait till I return.'

"And according as our Lord said, this Cartaphilus is still awaiting his return.

"At the time of our Lord's suffering he was 30 years old, and, when he attains the age of a hundred years, he always returns to the same age as he was when our Lord suffered.

"After Christ's death when the Catholic faith gained ground, this Cartaphilus was baptized by Ananias (who also baptized the Apostle Paul), and was called Joseph.

"He dwells in one or other division of Armenia, and in divers Eastern countries, passing his time amongst the bishops or other prelates of the Church.

"He is a man of holy conversation, and religious, a man of few words, and circumspect in his behaviour, for he does not speak at all unless when questioned by the bishops and religious men, and then he tells of the events of old times, and of those which occurred at the suffering and resurrection of our Lord, and of the witnesses of the resurrection, namely, those who rose with Christ and went into the Holy City and appeared unto men.

"He also tells of the creed of the Apostles, and of their separation and preaching.

"And all this he relates without smiling or levity of conversation, as one who is well practised in sorrow and the fear of God, always looking forward with fear to the coming of Jesus Christ, lest at the last judgment he should find him in anger, whom, when on his way to death, he had provoked to just vengeance.

"Numbers come to him from different parts of the world, enjoying his society and conversation, and to them, if they are men of authority, he explains all doubts on the matters on which he is questioned. He refuses all gifts that are offered to him, being content with slight food and clothing."

In the middle of the sixteenth century the Wandering Jew put in an appearance in Germany. His name was then Ahasuerus, and he attended a sermon preached by a bishop at Hamburg, listening with peculiar devotion.

Questioned, he said that he was a Jew, that he had originally been a shoemaker, that he had been present at the Crucifixion, and had since wandered from country to country.

This story is told on the authority of the Bishop who preached the sermon.

The man was described as being tall, about 50 years of age, with long hair hanging down upon his shoulders. He wore no shoes and wore sailor's trousers, a petticoat and a mantle, all reaching to his feet.

He never took money unless he gave it to charity. He spoke good German in a Saxon dialect.

A few years later the Wandering Jew arrived at Strassburg

and told the magistrates that he had visited the town 200 years before. According to the registers, it is said, this proved to be true.

The subsequent wanderings of the Jew appear to have included the West Indies and France, where he appeared in 1604. In that year terrible storms visited France, and it was believed that they were due to the presence of the wanderer.

To this day in Brittany and Picardy, when a severe storm comes on, the peasants are in the habit of crying, "It is the Wandering Jew who passes."

There was an English ballad which related to the appearance of the Jew in Germany and Flanders in the sixteenth century.

Coronation of Charles II

When Charles II was crowned on St. George's Day, 1661, there was an unseemly brawl at the afternoon banquet in Westminster Hall.

The King was about to mount the stairs leading to his throne, and the barons and others were making their way to their seats, when the King's footmen attempted to wrest the canopy from the Barons of the Cinque Ports who, from time immemorial, had been granted that favour at Coronations.

The Barons made a valiant defence of their rights, but the footmen, stronger in number, gradually dragged them to the end of the Hall. Nevertheless they were able to maintain their hold of the silver staves, and the fight would have been renewed but for the York Herald, who shut the door and thus frustrated the object of the footmen, which was to carry the canopy away.

In the meantime Charles II was advised of what was going on, and one of his equerries was sent with instructions to imprison the footmen, and dismiss them from his service.

The footmen were afterwards ordered to make their submission to the Court of Claims, and this they did a week after the Coronation.

While this disturbance was going on, bishops and judges promptly seized the seats which had been allocated to the Barons of the Cinque Ports. These unfortunate peers were thus forced to take what seats they could at the bottom of the second table below the Masters in Chancery.

The Coronation of Charles was a most elaborate affair. On the day before his crowning he made a progress through the City of London, from the Tower to Westminster. The arches that were erected for the occasion remained in the thoroughfares for a year.

Samuel Pepys records that he rose at four on Coronation Day, and by the good offices of Sir J. Denham, the Abbey surveyor, secured a position on top of a "great scaffold" across the North end of the building. Here he remained "with a great deal of patience from past four till eleven before the King came in."

Pepys records what a great pleasure it was to see "the Abbey raised in the middle, all covered with red, and a throne (that is, a chaire) and footstoole on the top of it; and all the officers of all kinds, so much as the very fiddlers, in red vests."

According to an official account published a year after the Coronation, King Charles arrived by river at Parliament Stairs, and then went to the room behind the Lords' House, called the Prince's Lodgings. Here he rested for a while and was then arrayed in the royal robes of crimson velvet "furred" with ermine. The Peers robed themselves in the Lords' House and the Painted Chamber.

"After some space," the report proceeds, "the King's heralds and pursuivants began to set the proceeding in order, each of them taking his share assigned in chapter (held at the Heralds' Office the evening before), and then directed all the before-mentioned degrees (except the nobility) down into Westminster Hall, where the rest of the proceeding attended, and from whence the march began."

About half-past nine the "nobility" formed into procession according to rank and dignity, in their robes and coronets. Passing through the Court of Requests they entered Westminster Hall and ascended the state platform.

The King took his seat in the chair under a cloth of state and was handed the Sword of State by Sir Gilbert Talbot, Master of the Jewel House. The Lord High Constable, the Earl of Northumberland, received two swords from Talbot and handed them to the Lord High Chamberlain, and he placed them on the table before the King. The Master of the Jewel House then handed the Spurs to the Lord High Constable, who delivered them similarly to the Lord High Chamberlain.

The Dean and Prebends of Westminster formed in procession and carried the Regalia to the King, placing the various articles on the table before him.

The King now handed these out as follows: To the Earl of Sandwich, St. Edwards staff; to the Earl of Pembroke and Montgomery, the Spurs; to the Earl of Bedford, the Sceptre with the Cross; to the Earl of Derby, one pointed sword; to the Earl of Shrewsbury, the other; to the Earl of Oxford, the Curtana; to the Earl of Manchester, the Sword of State; to the Duke of Albemarle, the Sceptre with the Dove; to the Duke of Buckingham, the Orb with the Cross; to the Duke of Ormond, St. Edward's Crown; and to the Bishop of London, the Chalice. The Ampulla and the Spoon had been brought in mistake to Westminster Hall. They were, therefore, sent back to the Abbey and were not carried in procession.

At ten o'clock the procession began to file out of Westminster Hall, treading on blue cloth leading from the Hall to the Abbey.

Pepys gives details of the ceremony, or what he assumed to have been the ceremony, for he records that his view was obstructed.

"The King in his robes, bare-headed, which was very fine," says Pepys.

"And after all had placed themselves, there was a sermon and the service; and then in the Quire at the High Altar the King passed through all the ceremonies.

"The crowne being put upon his head, a great shout begun, and he came forth to the throne, and there passed through more ceremonies: as taking the oath, and having things read to him by the Bishop.

"And three times the King at Armes (Sir Edward Walker, Garter King of Arms) went to the three open places (south, west, and north) on the scaffold, and proclaimed, that if anyone could show any reason why Charles Stuart should not be King of England, that now he should come and speak.

"And a Generall Pardon also was read by the Lord Chancellor, and medalls flung up and down by my Lord Cornwallis, of silver, but I could not come by any."

The King was crowned by Gilbert Sheldon, Bishop of London, in the absence of the aged Juxon, Archbishop of Canterbury, who had been on the scaffold when Charles I was executed.

Pepys records that he got out of the Abbey as quickly as possible and went into Westminster Hall for the banquet. The King arrived wearing his crown beneath the canopy supported by the Barons of the Cinque Ports. It was at this point that the fight occurred between the Barons and the King's footmen.

During the feast, Sir Edward Dymock (or Dymoke), the King's Champion, appeared on horseback "with his speare and targett carried before him," and a herald cried: "If any dare deny Charles Stuart to be lawful King of England, here is a champion that will fight him."

The Champion flung down his gauntlet three times. The King drank his health from a gold cup, which he afterwards handed to the Champion, who departed with the trophy.

The banquet was barely over when there was a terrific storm of thunder and lightning, which reminded people of the earthquake that had occurred on the day of the crowning of the King's father, Charles I.

At night London went mad with excitement. Pepys sent his wife to bed and went out to enjoy himself. He found a great many "gallants, men and women," and they continued to drink the health of the King, until many were drunk.

"I wondered to see how the ladies did tipple," says Pepys.

He confesses that when he got to bed that night his head began to turn.

The Coronation festivities continued all night and well into the next day, for when Pepys woke with his head "in a sad taking through the last night's drink" the guns were booming.

On the evening of the 24th the King watched the fireworks on the Thames.

Louis IX

The woman who had attended Louis IX during his illness placed a cloth over the thin white face with its halo of dark hair and walked quietly out of the chamber.

It seemed an end to a promising reign, for it was said of Louis that in all his twenty-seven years he had never committed a mean action. He had, moreover, proved himself a competent military strategist, for two years before he had fought and gained the battle of Taillebourg against the English.

The news which the woman conveyed to the other members of the Court was not unexpected. Louis had been sinking for days and the question of his successor had already been discussed.

Courtiers hurried to the room to confirm the news of the King's death.

To their great astonishment Louis was still breathing, and he had apparently moved, for the cloth no longer covered his features.

On that very day information had been received at the French court of the Mogul invasion which, like a great flood, had swept westwards and now threatened to overwhelm Jerusalem, destroying both Saracens and Christians.

French kings had always been enthusiastic for the Crusades. That France should fail the Christians at this time was deplorable.

Would Louis IX recover?

The King answered that question himself by speaking to those by his bedside. His mother, Queen Blanche, ordered the others out.

In a few days Louis had recovered enough to take an interest in national affairs. Then he was told of what was going on in the East.

He immediately ordered the Cross to be fixed to his vestments, thus indicating that he was bent on a crusade.

His mother tried vainly to dissuade him. Calling the Archbishop of Paris, he said: "Now that I am in possession of all my faculties, I will take up the Cross again."

" 'Tis the finger of God," said the Archbishop. From that time no opposition was raised to the King's intentions.

Biographers are unanimous that there are few more virtuous monarchs in history than Louis IX. Born at Poissy on April 25th, 1215, he was only eleven at the death of his father. During his minority the regency was held by his mother, Blanche of Castile, despite attempts by the lad's uncle to seize the reins of Government.

Blanche was a resolute woman, of extraordinary talent and virtue.

Louis was given the best masters that could be obtained, and instructed in religion. His mother remarked: "I love you; but I would rather see you in your grave than guilty of mortal sin."

At the age of nineteen Louis married Marguerite of Provence, who was then thirteen. Blanche kept them separate for six years. She seems always to have been jealous of the young queen.

In 1242 Louis won the battle of Taillebourg. Then he suddenly fell ill, but made the remarkable recovery already related.

In August 1248 Louis sailed on his first crusade from the port of Aigues-Mortes. He took a large army in ships borrowed from the Venetians and Genoese, and carried the pilgrim's staff and the oriflamme of St. Denis.

He spent a short time in Cyprus and then sailed for Egypt, which seemed to him the best point of disembarkation. He occupied Damietta, and remained there several months.

This was a great mistake and contributed to the ultimate failure of this crusade, for when Mansourah was attacked by Louis's army the Saracens had gathered in great force. They inflicted on the crusaders a heavy defeat and caused their retirement.

In their retreat along the Nile they found their passage blocked by the galleys of the Saracens. A further attack by the latter resulted in Louis being taken prisoner.

Fortunately, Queen Marguerite, who had accompanied her husband, was at Damietta, which she still held with a garrison of Crusaders.

She ransomed Louis for eight thousand besants of gold, part of which came from the treasure chest of the Templars. Louis then went to Palestine, and for four years he organized the fortification of the coast towns which still remained in the hands of the Christians.

In 1253 Queen Blanche died, and Louis returned to his country to govern with extraordinary sagacity.

His various ordinances were collected into a code of laws known as the "Etablissements de St. Louis." He established a law known as the "quaranteen of the king," which provided that no recourse to arms must be taken until the elapse of 40 days from the commission of the offence. Thus, in many cases, there was no fighting or duelling, the suspension of hostilities resulting in an adjustment of grievances.

He published what was called the "pragmatic sanction," which was the foundation of the French Church, for it prevented the raising of money in France for Rome without the sanction of the king.

Louis was a great patron of learning. He established a public library, and in 1252—during his reign—Robert de Sorbon founded the college of the Sorbonne.

Louis, too had a great reputation as an arbitrator. When Henry III of England quarrelled with his barons, Louis was called in to adjudicate, and he decided in favour of Henry, which led to the repeal of the famous "Provisions of Oxford."

When the Latin empire of Constantinople fell in 1261, Louis again turned his eyes to the East. The Christians in the Holy Land were in a parlous condition. Unable to agree among themselves, there was no real and concerted defence against the Saracens, who overwhelmed the crusaders in battle after battle.

The Sultan of Egypt had captured Antioch and massacred 100,000 Christians within the walls. The terrible news reached western Europe, and Louis determined to head another crusade.

Once more taking the Cross, he sailed in 1270 for Tunis with 60,000 men, well armed.

But Louis was not destined to take a great part in the campaign. His army was smitten with the plague. His eldest son Louis, fell a victim and died, and soon afterwards he himself lay on a sick bed suffering with the terrible disease.

He quickly grew worse, and calling before him his second son, Philip the Bold, he gave him instructions for the management of France.

He then ordered that he should be carried from his bed and placed on a heap of ashes. There he prayed earnestly for his people, beseeching God to protect them from harm.

He became pitiably weak towards the end and, babbling about the crusade, he muttered frequently, "Oh, Jerusalem ! Oh, Jerusalem !" These words were the last he spoke.

He died on August 25th, 1270, and was succeeded by Philip the Bold.

By Marguerite he had eleven children, the fifth of whom, Robert of Clermont, took the name of Bourbon, a line which succeeded to the throne three hundred years later in the person of Henry IV.

Daniel Defoe

"Whereas Daniel De Foe, alias De Fooe, is charged with writing a scandalous and seditious pamphlet, entitled *The Shortest Way with the Dissenters*. He is a middle-sized, spare man, about forty years old ; of a brown complexion and dark brown-coloured hair, but wears a wig ; a hooked nose, a sharp chin, grey eyes, and a large mole near his mouth ; was born in London, and for many years was a hose-factor in Freeman's yard, in Cornhill, and now is owner of the brick and pantile works near Tilbury Fort, in Essex. Whoever shall discover the said Daniel De Foe to one of her Majesty's principal Secretaries of State, or any of her Majesty's Justices of Peace, so as he may be apprehended, shall have a reward of £50, which her Majesty had ordered immediately to be paid upon such discovery."

This advertisement for the apprehension of Daniel Defoe was posted for some months before anything could be heard of the fugitive. Then he appeared suddenly one day and gave himself up.

The pamphlet referred to must have afforded to the author much amusement and satisfaction in its preparation. It purported to be an attack on the Dissenters, but was really a carefully worded defence.

Defoe might have escaped punishment, the pamphlet being regarded merely as an interesting satire, but for the fact that he had obtained the names of several well-known High Churchmen as an endorsement to the pamphlet.

Defoe's defence was badly conducted. He was fined 200 marks, condemned to be pilloried three times, to be imprisoned indefinitely, and to find sureties for his good behaviour for seven years.

No man had an easier time in the pillory. Not one brick-bat was thrown at him, and the sympathetic populace brought him food and drink. This inspired him to write one of his best works : *Hymn to the Pillory*.

The practice of cutting off the ears of those exposed in the pillory had been discontinued for some years, so that Defoe was little the worse for his experience.

Alexander Pope described Defoe in the pillory, but could not resist introducing a little colour with the line :

"Earless on high stands unabash'd Defoe."

Defoe was in prison for nearly a year. Some of his best works were written while under restraint, although he had an occasional thrust in writing at the various political parties.

At last Robert Harley, Secretary of State, secured his release. Both he and Queen Anne recognized the author's genius, and Anne actually paid his prison fine and sent money to Defoe's wife.

Defoe was born in London in 1661. His father was a Dissenter, and the boy was educated at an academy for sons of Nonconformists. He soon acquired, in an even greater degree than his father, anti-High Church views, and he held them all through life.

He was intended for the ministry, but when at the age of nineteen he published a political pamphlet, which was successful, he decided that his pen would prove more useful than sermons.

The average person remembers Defoe as the author of *Robinson Crusoe* rather than a man who was almost fanatical on the question of religion.

Crusoe discloses a vivid imagination, for there is no evidence that Defoe ever went farther from home than Spain.

This work and his other fiction were published during the last fifteen years of his life. Had he begun his career with this type of publication, instead of spending years on political pamphlets, his output of readable novels would have been enormous.

But for the persecution to which he was subjected on account of his pamphlets, and the consequent ill-health and poverty, he would never have written *Robinson Crusoe*.

The misgovernment of James II and the treatment of the

Dissenters, drove Defoe to fury. When the Duke of Monmouth rebelled, he was one of the first to join the duke's troops.

How he escaped being convicted and executed for his part in that outbreak is a mystery.

Defoe was a restless individual with an active brain. As a new excitement he decided to enter business, and became a dealer in wool.

After several voyages to Spain in pursuit of this new line of activity he became bankrupt.

In 1695 he appears to have made a favourable impression at Court, for he was appointed accountant to the commissioners for managing the duties on glass. He held this post for four years, when it was decided to remove the duties, and he was out of a job.

Once more he began to write religious pamphlets. One entitled *Occasional Conformity of Dissenters* caused a storm of indignation, but had no pecuniary value.

Defoe turned to business again and produced a plan for the manufacture of pantiles with the object of capturing the export trade of the Dutch manufacturers. This venture was already going badly when he was arrested for the pamphlet, *The Shortest Way with the Dissenters.*

Through this reverse he lost his capital of £3,000.

During the next two years his productions were numerous. In 1706 he went to Scotland at the instance of the Court to carry on negotiations connected with the Union with Scotland.

He remained in Edinburgh for sixteen months, and received a regular salary from the Government. The sequel was his *History of the Union,* which appeared in 1709.

He was indicted for libel in 1715 for declaring that Lord Annesley was preparing an army in Ireland to join a Jacobite rebellion.

He was convicted, and imprisoned, but liberated a few months afterwards. The circumstances of his release were not known until the middle of last century, when certain letters were discovered in the Record Office from Defoe to a Government official which put a different complexion on the whole affair.

It was shown by these communications that he was acting in the interests of the Government when he was sub-editing a Jacobite paper called *Mist's Journal.*

It was his duty to make the "copy" as innocuous as possible by omitting objectionable items and toning down others.

He had agreed to act as a Government agent in return for his release. It was disclosed, moreover, that he had done the same work in connection with two other journals.

The *Life and Strange Surprising Adventures of Robinson Crusoe* was published on April 25th, 1719. It ran through four editions in a few months, and in August the second volume appeared. A year later appeared the sequel, *Serious Reflections*, new editions of which cannot be obtained nowadays.

The book was founded firstly on Dampier's voyage round the world, and secondly on the adventures of Alexander Selkirk, who communicated the story to Defoe.

It is clear that at this period Defoe was not in financial difficulty. In 1724 he built a large house at Stoke Newington, with extensive stables and grounds. When he negotiated for the marriage of his daughter Sophia, he disclosed the fact that he had property in many places.

Before his death in 1731 he settled an estate at Colchester on his unmarried daughter, while his widow and remaining children each received considerable possessions.

There has always been some mystery regarding the circumstances of his death. It cannot be true that he died in poverty, but for three years he may have been in considerable pain for an incurable complaint.

It is a fact that on his leaving no will, letters of administration were taken out by a creditor. He did not die in his own house, and thereby the mystery is increased.

There is a suggestion that he may have gone into hiding to escape the revenge of the Jacobites for his activities as a Government agent.

He died in Ropemaker's Alley, Moorfields, and was buried in Bunhill Fields. His death is variously stated to have occurred on April 24th and 26th, 1731.

The second date is probably correct.

Ferdinand Magellan

Portugal might have had the credit for organizing the first voyage round the world if King Manuel had treated Ferdinand Magellan as he deserved.

It has never been understood why Manuel took a sudden dislike to Magellan, and refused to employ him after he had served the King faithfully on more than one expedition.

The treatment drove Magellan out of Portugal. He went to Spain and there he was provided with a fleet of ships, one of which made the complete tour of the earth.

Magellan has never received sufficient recognition in history for what he achieved. His exploits are equal to those of Marco Polo or Columbus.

Magellan was a native of Portugal and was born at Sabrosa, in the Traz-os-Montes province, about the year 1480.

That he belonged to a noble Portuguese family is shown by the fact that he was employed for a time as a page in the court of Queen Leonor, wife of King John II, known as "The Perfect."

He was about 15 when he entered the service of the new King, Manuel "the Fortunate." Six years later he became a volunteer for an expedition to India. He was wounded in March 1506, at Cannonmore, and again in February 1509, at the Battle of Diu.

He distinguished himself in various voyages, and about October 1510 was rewarded with the rank of captain. He was present at the taking of Malacca by Albuquerque in August 1511, and was then sent to explore the Spice Islands (Moluccas).

Magellan commanded an expedition which set out from Malacca in December 1511, and returned with its ships laden with spices.

He returned to Portugal in 1512, and filled various offices about the Court. A year later he accompanied another expedition sent against Azamor in Morocco.

The city was taken in August 1513, but soon afterwards Magellan was wounded and lamed for life.

At this time Magellan was accused of trading with the Moors, and although he appears to have been able to clear himself, Manuel decided to get rid of him.

The King declared that no further employment would be given to Magellan after May 15th, 1514, and the discontented adventurer said good-bye to his native country for ever.

He renounced his nationality and set off for the court of Spain.

Magellan was well received by Charles V, who was always ready to take into his service men of reputation, irrespective of their nationality.

Magellan gained the ear of Charles with the aid of Juan de Aranda, a chief official at the India House at Seville, and Diogo Barbosa, a Portuguese who had become a naturalized Spaniard, and whose daughter Magellan married.

Magellan proposed a scheme for an expedition to the Spice Islands of the East Indies by a western route. He argued that there was a strait at the most southern point of South America. In this theory he was supported by Ruy Faleiro, another Portuguese exile, who helped him to prepare his plans.

He had numerous interviews with the ministers of Charles V, and it was finally arranged for the equipment of five ships carrying over 230 men.

On March 22nd, 1518, Magellan signed an agreement with Charles V, by which one-twentieth of the profit from the spices would fall to him and Faleiro, as joint-captains.

On September 20th, 1519, the expedition put to sea from the harbour of San Lucar on the coast of Andalusia.

The flagship of the fleet was the *Trinidad*. The crews of the ships were a mixed lot, and included Portuguese, Spaniards, French, English, and Germans.

The history of this celebrated voyage is told by Antonio Pigafetta, of Vicenza, an Italian, who went as a volunteer in Magellan's suite.

After a brief stay at Rio de Janeiro, Magellan made his way southward along the shores of the American continent, and reaching Port San Julian, he passed the winter months there from May to September.

The expedition left Port St. Julian in the middle of October, and on the 21st of that month entered the strait now known by the name of the great voyager.

His fleet was now reduced to three ships, for one had deserted and another had been lost. Exactly a month later a council was held to decide whether to continue the voyage;.

seven days later the three ships rounded the western end of the strait.

The expedition entered what was known as the "Great South Sea," but, owing to the steady and peaceful winds that assisted the ships across the great expanse, Magellan named it the Pacific.

It took 98 days to cross, during which time Magellan discovered only two islands, both without a sign of life. He called them St. Paul's and Shark Island, and these are believed to be those now known as Puka Puka, in the Tuamotu Archipelago, and Flint Island, in the Manihiki group.

During the voyage across the Pacific the expedition lacked water and fresh provisions. Scurvy attacked the ships' crews. The survivors were compelled to eat oxhides, sawdust, and rats.

On March 6th, 1521, Magellan came in sight of what he called the Ladrones, and the fleet rested at Guam and refitted and revictualled. Three days later they started westward and on the 16th sighted the southern point of Samar Island in the archipelago now called the Philippines.

In the Philippines Magellan was befriended by the native King of Zebu, who declared himself a willing vassal of the King of Spain.

Magellan was now induced to undertake an expedition against a neighbouring chief. He was surrounded by an overwhelming force, and, though he put up a stout defence, he was killed during a fusillade of stones.

The King of Zebu now changed his attitude, and soon afterwards massacred all the Spaniards he could find on shore. The men not on land burned one of the ships and set out in search of the Moluccas. Reaching the island of Tidore, they remained to refit. One of the two vessels tried to recross the Pacific, but was captured by Portuguese and taken to the Moluccas as a prize.

The remaining vessel, the *Vittoria*, under the command of Sebastian de Cano, crossed the Indian seas, doubled the Cape of Good Hope, and ultimately returned to Europe, having completely circled the globe in three years, fourteen days.

Only thirty-one men returned to Seville.

Catholic Peers Took their Seats in the House of Lords

One of the most dramatic incidents which followed the passing of the Catholic Emancipation Bill in 1829 was the appearance of John Henry Newman at a dinner in grey trousers.

To the lay observer this might mean nothing, but to his friends, who knew how punctilious he was in regard to wearing his clericals, it indicated much.

For years Newman had been examining his position in relation to the Church of England. For months he had said nothing to his friends, although they knew he was gradually drifting towards Rome. Many times they had discussed whether he would ultimately go a little further than his already advanced Anglo-Catholicism and take the plunge.

Bernard Smith, Fellow of Magdalen, and Vicar of Leadenham, had submitted to Dr. Nicholas Wiseman, the Pope's English representative, and afterwards Archbishop of Westminster. Many other Anglo-Catholics were wavering and showing a disposition to do the same when Wiseman suggested that Smith should call upon Newman and get him to make the declaration.

Strangely enough, Newman had already been charged by the Bishop of Lincoln with inducing Smith to change his creed. Actually there was no truth in this, for Newman had all along adopted a passive attitude, and pleaded with Smith to go and see him before he made a decision.

Smith had given no heed, but when he went to Newman's house at the suggestion of Wiseman, he was received very cordially. Newman and a number of his friends who held the same views were living in cottages at Littlemore, Oxford, living on two meals a day and preserving a complete silence for half a day.

To this community Smith went. In the evening Newman invited Smith to dinner with himself and his friends, and it was then that Newman appeared in grey trousers.

Smith, who had been Newman's curate at Littlemore, could not fail to understand the sign.

Denis Gwynn records, in *A Hundred Years of Catholic Emancipation*, that "Smith hurried back in jubilation with the news to Wiseman, who was utterly perplexed by such a manner of proclaiming truth."

How could Smith be so confident, the Cardinal argued, for Smith had to admit that he and Newman had barely referred to the matter.

He had no further information to give them than that Newman had appeared in grey trousers at dinner !

"But I know the man," he declared, "and I know what it means."

For two months nothing occurred. Then several Anglo-Catholics made their vows, including some of Newman's friends, J. B. Dalgairns, W. G. Ward, the acknowledged leader of the party in Oxford, and Ambrose St. John.

Edward Stanton, another friend, wrote to Newman, of his intention to join the Catholic Church; Newman replied, quickly: "Why should we not both be received together ? Father Dominic, the Passionist, comes here on the eighth to receive me. Come back on that day."

On October 9th, 1845, Newman was received into the Roman Catholic Church by Father Dominic.

A fortnight later he was confirmed, and in October of the following year he went to Rome, was ordained priest and given the degree of D.D. by the Pope.

In 1847 he returned to England as an oratorian. He established the London Oratory with Father Faber as its superior.

The Catholic Emancipation Act was passed in April 1829, and on the 28th of that month the Catholic Peers took their seats in the House of Lords.

But matters did not go smoothly. There was considerable opposition to the Act in the country.

It was not, however, until an attempt was made to establish a hierarchy in England that active opposition really became serious.

Then came the dramatic announcement that Wiseman was to return to England as the head of the new Roman Catholic hierarchy with the title of Archbishop of Westminster.

On October 7th, 1850, Wiseman sent out his famous pastoral letter. Immediately there was an outcry in the Press. An editorial in one newspaper went so far as to say:

"It is no concern of ours whether Dr. Wiseman chooses in Rome to be ranked with the monsignori of the capital. He is simply at Rome in the position of an English subject who has thought fit to enter the service of a foreign Power and accept its spurious dignities. . . .

"We are informed by the *Official Gazette* of Rome that the Pope having been pleased to erect the city of Westminster into an archbishopric, and to appoint Dr. Wiseman to that See, it is on this newfangled Archbishop of Westminster, so appointed, that the rank of cardinal is so conferred.

"It may be that the elevation of Dr. Wiseman signified no more than if the Pope had been pleased to confer on the editor of the *Tablet* the rank and title of the Duke of Smithfield. But if this appointment be not intended as a clumsy joke, we confess we can only regard it as one of the grossest acts of folly and impertinence which the Court of Rome has ventured to commit since the Crown and people of England threw off its yoke."

On Sunday, October 27th, Wiseman's pastoral was read in the Catholic churches. In the meantime the Press campaign was proceeding apace.

The storm was breaking, everyone began to anticipate a recurrence of the Gordon riots ; Lord John Russell, the Prime Minister, replied to a letter by the Bishop of London in which he considered the "late aggression of the Pope upon our Protestantism" as "insolent and insidious," and shortly afterwards confirmed his views in a public speech at Guildhall.

But when the Chancellor of the Exchequer, at the Mansion House dinner, quoted the lines :

> *Under our feet we'll stamp thy cardinal's hat,*
> *In spite of Pope or dignities of Church:*

it was a signal for general denunciation.

Coincident with Guy Fawkes Day, there was a gorgeous display of bonfires in which the Pope was burnt in effigy. At Salisbury they made the celebrations complete by including Wiseman and the twelve new Catholic bishops. The streets were crowded and there were great scenes of enthusiasm when the effigies went up in flames and smoke. Any moment riots were expected.

Wiseman, still in Rome, knew nothing of what was going on, but when he was apprised of the opposition, he decided to come to London at once. He arrived on November 11th and made a public appearance outside St. George's, Southwark. He was booed.

Then he wrote a manifesto to the English people. It appeared on November 19th, and on the following day was reproduced in full in the newspapers. In a few days 30,000 copies were sold, and the newspaper which had first opened the attack congratulated him "on his recovery of the use of the English language."

The next incident was the conversion of Archdeacon Manning of Chichester, and the consequent storm of indignation in that See.

It was a long time before matters settled down.

Cowper Thornhill

One evening near the end of April 1745, half a dozen sportsmen sat in the bar of the Bell Inn, Stilton, Huntingdonshire, discussing the endurance of horses and riders.

The argument became animated. Challenges were made and accepted, each man offering to go one better than another.

Finally, Cowper Thornhill, the landlord of the inn, undertook to do what the others believed to be impossible.

He offered to ride from Stilton to London and back, and again to London, in 15 hours.

The distance was about 213 miles, altogether, necessitating an average speed of over 14 miles an hour.

The challenge was accepted, and several thousands of pounds were wagered on the result.

On April 29th Thornhill set out from his house at Stilton at four o'clock in the morning. Despite the early hour, hundreds were present to see him start.

According to a contemporary print, Thornhill arrived at the Queen's Arms near Shoreditch Church, London, after three hours and fifty-two minutes in the saddle. The return journey to Stilton took four hours and twelve minutes, and the second outward run to London was accomplished in four hours and thirteen minutes. Thus he had covered the 213 miles in twelve hours seventeen minutes.

At this time this was regarded as the greatest feat of riding ever known, and it is doubtful whether it has even now been surpassed, assuming, as is to be understood from the print, that he did not change horses.

Cowper Thornhill is said to have had a large business as

corn factor in Stilton, and was "much respected for his gentle-manly manners." Thus, there is good reason to believe the genuineness of the feat.

Another remarkable ride on horseback was achieved by Nicks, the highwayman, who, having held up a party at Gad's Hill in 1676, was anxious to establish an alibi.

He is reputed to have crossed the Thames by the Graves-end-Tilbury ferry and, taking the Chelmsford Road, gone on to Cambridge and Huntingdon. He joined the Great North Road and continued to York, which city he reached about 8 p.m.

He changed his clothes and appeared on a bowling green a few minutes afterwards.

The distance was reckoned at about 240 miles, and as the robbery had taken place at 4 A.M. he had accomplished the journey in 16 hours at an average speed of 15 miles an hour. Thornhill's speed was over 17 miles an hour.

Nicks is said to have used one animal, a bay mare. He was ultimately arrested for the Gad's Hill robbery, but the jury had to give him the benefit of the doubt, it being held that it was impossible for him to have been at Gad's Hill and York on the same day.

Another version of this ride gives the starting-point at Barnet, which would cut down the distance by some 50 miles. Charles II appears to have some doubt about the highway-man's alibi, for he afterwards referred to him as "Swift Nicks."

Nicks is probably the hero of the famous "ride to York," and not Turpin, for there is no evidence in the official history of this horse-stealer and murderer to prove that he ever rode such a distance at one time, although it is known that under the name of Palmer he was lodged in York Castle before his trial.

.   .   .   .   .

In July 1621, Bernard Calvert, of Andover, left Shore-ditch at three o'clock in the morning, rode to Dover, crossed over to Calais in a barge, returned to Dover, and rode back again to Shoreditch, reaching St George's Church at eight in the evening The riding part of this journey, London to Dover and back, was about 142 miles

There is no evidence to show how long Calvert took to

cross the Channel each time, so his riding time is doubtful. Nevertheless, it was a good performance

. . . . .

One of the most famous equestrian feats on record was that of Robert Cary, who rode from London to Edinburgh to tell King James VI of Scotland that Queen Elizabeth was dead and that he was now King of England.

He set out from Whitehall between nine and ten o'clock on Thursday morning. By night he reached Doncaster, 155 miles away. Next day he arrived at his house at Witherington, where he halted to attend to some of his own business.

On Saturday he set out early for Edinburgh, and would certainly have reached the end of his journey before noon if he had not been thrown and kicked by his horse.

He arrived at Holyrood Castle, however, on the same night, and was able to give James the news soon after he had retired to rest. Cary had thus ridden 400 miles in three days.

. . . . .

The ill-fated Cardinal Wolsey is credited with a fast ride. About the year 1507, while chaplain to Henry VII, he was recommended by the Bishop of Winchester for a mission to the Emperor Maximilian, who was then in Holland.

Wolsey left London at four o'clock one afternoon by boat for Gravesend. There he took post-horses, and arrived at Dover next morning. He took boat for Calais, and on his arrival engaged horses which took him to his destination by night-time.

Next morning he rode back to Calais and reached Dover at ten next morning. By the evening he was in Richmond Palace, having done the journey in little more than two days.

It was this remarkable performance which started Wolsey on his rise to fame.

. . . . .

The performance of Matthew Milton, coach proprietor of Windsor, and his son, created much interest among sportsmen in the years 1810 and 1828.

In the former year Milton senior took a bet of £500 to £300 that he would ride from the end of Dover Street, Piccadilly, to Stamford, Lincolnshire, a distance of more than 90 miles, in five hours. The ride took place on Thursday, December 27th.

Milton started at eight o'clock in the morning, in a heavy shower of rain. At the end of the first hour he had covered 23 miles.

He arrived at Stamford at 12.25, having covered the distance in 4 hours 25 minutes, thus winning the wager with 35 minutes to spare. He averaged a speed of over 20 miles an hour. In this instance, however, the horses were changed at various points on the way.

．　　　．　　　．　　　．　　　．

In 1828 Matthew Milton, his son, left London at 2 o'clock on Wednesday afternoon to take the result of Tuesday's St. Leger to the King, who was at the Royal Lodge, Windsor. He arrived there at five minutes after three, having performed the journey, a distance of 23 .miles, in one hour and five minutes.

A report of this feat in a publication of the time adds :

"His Majesty expressed his gratification at the performance. . . . Mr. Milton rode a beautiful blood horse."

St. Catherine of Siena

St. Catherine of Siena was one of the most practical saints in the Roman calendar.

Her memory is not sustained by doubtful miracles, either during or after life. She is remembered rather for her efforts to prevent schism, and to rescue the Papacy from "Babylonian captivity" at Avignon.

She is described as one of the most heroic and remarkable women who ever lived.

Catherine was the youngest of twenty-five children of Giacomo de Benincasa, a dyer of Siena, and was born on March 25th, 1347. A twin sister did not survive birth.

If there is any part of her life surrounded with tradition rather than fact, it concerns her activities as a child. It is said that she was highly sensitive and imaginative, and was given to seeing visions.

The dyer's large family continued to live together until

his death in 1368. Their home is now a shrine at Siena.

A boisterous house, never free from the crying and shrieking of children, was a strange school for a saint, and hardly an environment for a visionary trying to spend her time in self-discipline and meditation.

But Catherine seems to have overcome all these difficulties. At the age of 7 she is said to have dedicated herself to the Church.

At an early age she became fascinated by the mode of living of the desert authorities, and at last persuaded her parents to allow her to take the habit of the Dominicans. Although she continued to live at home, she kept herself as much as possible from the other members of the family and lived the life of a recluse.

For a long period she spoke to nobody but her confessor. It was said that "within" her own house she found the "desert and a solitude in the midst of people."

She left her home only to go to and fro to the church of St. Domenico, where, it is said, she saw visions. On the occasion of the Siena carnival, when she herself stayed away from the festivities, she is said to have had a vision of a mystical marriage between Christ and herself.

Once, she said, she held the Holy Child in her arms, and was told to place the Crown of Thorns upon her own head.

After three years of seclusion, she began gradually to return to her place in the family circle.

Her father died and she had to look after her mother.

Her benevolence became widely known, but her peculiarities excited suspicion. She was called to account by the Dominicans, and had to go to Florence to answer certain charges, which she disposed of satisfactorily.

On her return to Siena she found the city ravished by the plague. She nursed the stricken and actually buried the dead with her own hands.

"Never did she appear more admirable than at this time," wrote one of her friends.

She went into the plague districts and deliberately sought out the sick.

Her attitude to life may be summed up in her own words :

"Could you but know the beauty of *one* immortal soul you would think it little to give your life a hundred times over for its salvation.

"The rule of the saints has always been to come forward in times of necessity and misfortune, but not in times of prosperity, for they fly such times.

"There is no occasion to fly now, in the fear that too much prosperity would cause our hearts to be carried away with vainglory and pride : no one can find anything wherein to glory just now except suffering."

Among the many stories told of her, one concerns the morning when she stood beside a man about to be executed.

He was a young nobleman who had refused to see a priest while in prison. Catherine had visited him and induced him to repent. She had promised that she would stand by him to the last.

"*In the morning before the bell tolled,*" Catherine afterwards wrote, "*I went to him and he received great consolation. I took him to hear Mass, and he received the Holy Communion, which he had never received since his first Communion.*"

She knelt down beside the block, and laying her own head on it, prayed that the victim might have peace and a joyful resurrection.

"*Then he came, like a meek lamb, and when he saw me he began to smile, and he would have me make the sign of the Cross over him. When he had received the sign I said, "Up to the nuptials, sweet brother of mine, for soon thou shalt be in eternal life.'*"

The axe fell, and the head rolled into her hands, staining her white robe with crimson.

The influence of this girl saint spread over the whole of Siena. She was induced to intercede in the disputes in the Church.

On the invitation of Peiro Gambacorti, the head of the Republic of Pisa, she visited that city, and tried to influence the people from joining the Tuscan League against the Pope.

It was in the church of Santa Cristina in Pisa, on the fourth Sunday in Lent, that, it is said, she attained her greatest glory.

Following the communion, she received the stigmata or impressions on her hands, feet and heart of the wounds received by Christ at his crucifixion.

The stigmata was the crowning triumph of the saint, and something which hitherto had been the monopoly of the Franciscans.

It led to a rivalry between the two orders until Pope

Sixtus IV intervened—he himself was a Franciscan—and made it a punishable offence to represent that St. Catherine had received the stigmata.

At that time it was the great wish of Italians that the papal court should return to Italy from Avignon, where it had been for seventy-three years.

Many popes had been urged to return, but all had refused. Catherine was 29 when she determined to use her powers to persuade Gregory to live in Italy.

She began by reconciling Gregory and the Florentines, who had been placed under an interdict. Then, as the representative of the latter, she went to Avignon and besought Gregory to visit Italy, even if he did not remain there.

Gregory went to Rome, but soon found himself in difficulties. There was perpetual strife with his enemies, while it was not an easy task always to raise mercenaries.

Catherine was blamed as the author of the trouble, and she reproved the Pope for paying attention more to temporal than spiritual things.

Then the Pope died and there was rioting. Catherine herself hoped for a martyr's death, but it was denied her. Eventually peace was signed with the new Pope, Urban VI, through her influence. She returned to Siena, but was recalled to Rome on the outbreak of more schism. The Eternal City was in revolt, and the Pope was threatened. Catherine threw herself again into the fray and, restraining the Pope's temper on the one hand, and remonstrating with the people on the other, the dangerous situation was overcome.

Catherine died on April 29th, 1380, at the age of 33. She was canonized by Pope Pius II in 1461, her day being celebrated on April 30th.

To the Bull of Canonization Pope Pius added:

"We should contemplate in any case with joy, the virtues, genius, greatness of soul, the strength and fortitude of this blessed Catherine, but we do so all the more because she, like ourselves, first saw light in the City of Siena."

Queen Matilda (Maud) of England

Henry I of England was lucky in the choice of his wives. He had two, the first, Matilda of Scotland, and the second, Adelicia of Louvaine.

History has nothing but praise for both, though, by reason of her direct descent from Alfred the Great, and her wider munificence, Matilda was the better remembered.

All the old chroniclers sing her virtues. One, writing after her death, adds : "Nothing happened to trouble the King save the death of his Queen Matilda, the very mirror of piety, humility, and princely bounty."

That Henry I married again less than three years after he had lost his Saxon Queen is no reflection on his regard for her memory. The second marriage took place at the bidding of his ministers, who hoped that the beautiful Adelicia would dissipate his melancholy, and produce an heir.

Matilda was the daughter of Malcolm Canmore and Margaret (afterwards canonized) of Scotland, who claimed descent from Edmund Ironside.

Malcolm Canmore was killed while raiding Northumberland. The news of his death killed his wife, Margaret, and Matilda and her sister, Mary, and their younger brothers, were orphaned.

When the illegitimate brother of Malcolm Canmore usurped the Scottish throne and exiled all the English, Edgar Atheling, Matilda's uncle, took his sister's family to England.

The two princesses were placed in the nunnery of Rumsey, of which Edgar's sister was abbess. The sons were received honourably at the Court of William Rufus.

Matilda wore the black veil of a votaress, a cumbrous article of dress, which she would throw off whenever the abbess was not in sight.

She lived in the nunnery for seven years, during which time she received two offers of marriage. The first suitor died, and as an excuse for declining the second, William Warren, Earl of Surrey, and grandson of the Conqueror, she pleaded that she intended to devote herself wholly to a religious life.

But when Henry Beauclerc, now King of England, came forward with his offer, it was different.

Matilda was called before a Synod at Lambeth to be interrogated by Archbishop Anselm about the real extent of her devotion to a monastic existence.

The Archbishop pointed out that there were objections to her marriage to Henry on the grounds that she had taken vows. He wanted to know whether she had made any binding engagement, herself, or whether her parents had done so for her.

She denied having committed herself.

Asked why she had worn the black veil of the votaress at her father's court and at the nunnery, she replied:

"I do not deny having worn the veil in my father's court; for, when I was a child, my aunt Christina put a piece of black cloth over my head. But when my father saw me with it, he snatched it off in a great rage, and execrated the person who had put it on me. I afterwards made a pretence of wearing it, to excuse myself from unsuitable marriages; and, on one of these occasions, my father tore the veil and threw it on the ground, observing to Alan, Earl of Bretagne, who stood by, that it was his intention to give me in marriage, not to devote me to the church."

She declared also that she had worn the veil in the nunnery to save herself from the advances of Norman nobles. When she had continued to wear it, she had done so at the express desire of the abbess, Christina.

The Lambeth council were satisfied. Moreover, they complimented Matilda for assuming the veil to save her honour.

It is said by some historians that Matilda was reluctant to marry Henry. Her modesty revolted against the thought that he had already acknowledged twenty illegitimate children.

But the fact remained that she could have acknowledged vows of chastity to escape the marriage, and did not.

She consented to share the throne when the Norman Henry promised to restore to the English nation the ancient laws and privileges established by Alfred the Great, and ratified by Edward the Confessor.

Her marriage and coronation took place on St. Martin's Day, November 11th.

"There was a prodigious concourse of nobility," writes a contemporary, who relates further that Anselm went into the pulpit to dispose of the prevailing impression that Matilda was a nun.

Concluding his address, he asked the congregation whether anyone objected to the marriage. All answered with a great shout "that the matter was rightly settled."

As a result of this union, Henry I obtained an allegiance from the country which neither the Conqueror nor William Rufus had ever achieved.

The Palace of Westminster was now ruled over once more by a Queen of the blood of Alfred the Great.

She earned the title of "Matilda the Good" by her great benevolence.

Every day in Lent she went to Westminster Abbey barefoot and clothed in a hair garment. She made it a practice to wash and kiss the feet of poor people, and when reproved by one of the courtiers replied that she was following the example of Our Lord.

Once, while fording the River Lea, near Stratford, she was in danger of being swept away by the flood. To obviate the danger at this spot, she built the first arched bridge ever known in England, known as Bow Bridge.

She built Channel's Bridge over a tributary of the Lea, and gave for the endowment of the bridges certain manors and a mill called Wiggin Mill.

She founded the hospital of St. Giles-in-the-Fields. She made new roads, repaired the old highways, and was responsible for the establishment of good laws.

She succeeded in negotiating a peace between Henry and Duke Robert, his eldest brother. But there was animosity between them again, when, in a drunken carousal, Robert resigned to Matilda the pension he had been receiving from Henry.

He charged Henry with having employed the Queen to beguile him out of his income. This led to a war between them, which ended in the success of the English King against Robert in Normandy.

Meanwhile Matilda was superintending the building of Windsor Castle and the completion of the royal apartments at the Tower of London.

She induced the Norman families to learn the peaceful

pursuits of the Anglo-Saxons, and it was not considered beneath the dignity of ladies of high rank to look after the poultry yard and dairy.

Matilda died on May 1st, 1118. The King was not present at her funeral, as he was then fighting in Normandy.

It is not known definitely where Matilda was buried. Some say in Westminster Abbey, others in old St. Paul's, and the monks of Reading declare that she was interred in their abbey.

No stone remains to mark her grave.

She had been married eighteen years, and she was 41 when she died. The two princes, her sons, were in Normandy fighting with their father.

William, the elder, was drowned in the *White Ship* on the way to England.

Sir William Stanhope

With the death of Sir William Stanhope on May 7th, 1772, the organization known as the Monks of St. Francis lost one of its leading members.

Alternatively known as the Medmenham Club, its headquarters were at Medmenham Abbey on the banks of the Thames. The secrecy with which the meetings of the fraternity were held led to the circulation of all sorts of wild stories.

It was said that orgies of an outrageous type were practised there. This was never proved; the last surviving member of the club denied it, but Lipscomb, the Buckinghamshire historian, who wrote about 1847, seems to have credited the stories.

No doubt the motto *"Fais ce que tu voudras"*, which appeared above the door of the Abbey, which was once a Cistercian monastery, gave the impression that the activities of the club had no moral limit.

Included among the members were John Wilkes, Charles Churchill, the two poets Lloyd and Paul Whitehead, Francis, Lord le Despencer, Bubb Dodington, and Dr. Benjamin Bates. Some of them were rich and they spent their money freely in connection with the society.

The originator and president of the club was Lord le Despencer, formerly Sir Francis Dashwood. The members wore monkish garb, and in addition to meeting at Medmenham, it is said that they used mysterious caves in the side of the hill below the Church of St. Lawrence at West Wycombe, Bucks.

This church, and the curious mausoleum adjacent, were built by Sir Francis about the time he was elevated to the peerage. The original church was demolished, and the other strange-looking structure erected in its stead, a part of the old building being utilized.

The buildings, which stand upon a hill, form a landmark that can be seen over several counties. At the top of the tower is a golden ball which is said to have been another rendezvous of the club.

But the mausoleum is an even better example of the eccentricity of the peer. It was here that the heart of Paul Whitehead was buried with remarkable ceremony.

Whitehead was the son of a London tradesman, and was apprenticed as a woollen-draper, but gave up business at the end of his apprenticeship, and published several poems.

They were generally satirical, on the lines of those of Alexander Pope, but were not highly appreciated. His writings of a political character, however, were successful, and his talents were recognized by Sir Francis Dashwood, who obtained for him an appointment valued at £800 a year. His wife had a fortune of £10,000, so that in later life he was able to live at Twickenham in affluent circumstances.

Whitehead was the secretary of the Medmenham Club. He appears to have been of a benevolent and hospitable disposition.

When he died on December 30th, 1774, two years after Stanhope, he left his heart "to his noble friend and patron, Lord le Despencer, to be deposited in his mausoleum at West Wycombe, a village two miles from the town of High Wycombe and adjoining Wycombe Park, his lordship's place of residence."

The mausoleum was built with money left by George Bubb Dodington (Lord Melcombe Regis). It stands at the east end of the churchyard and has the appearance to-day of the ruin of some bygone civilization. It is a large, roofless, hexagonal building in which tennis could be played with ease.

By order of Lord le Despencer, the heart of Whitehead was wrapped in lead and placed in a marble urn which cost

£50, and eight months after Whitehead's death was carried from London to West Wycombe for interment.

Arriving within easy walking distance of the church and mausoleum, a strange procession was formed. It included, in order: a grenadier officer in his uniform, nine grenadiers rank and file, two German flute-players, two choristers in surplices, two German flute-players, eleven singing men in surplices, two French horn-players, two bassoon-players, six fifers, four muffled drums, the urn containing the heart resting on a bier ornamented with black crepe and borne by six soldiers, with three others on each side to relieve them ; Lord le Despencer, in his regimentals as Colonel of the Bucks Militia, Major Skottowe, Captain Lloyd, seven other militia officers in uniform, two fifers, two drummers, and twenty soldiers with firelocks reversed.

By the side of the procession walked Dr. Arnold, Mr. Atterbury, and another friend, having in their hands scrolls of paper. They beat time as the *Dead March in Saul* was played all along the route successively by the flutes, horns and bassoons, fifes and drums.

Guns were discharged every three and a half minutes, while the bell of the church tolled. The hill was crowded with spectators, and the procession, compelled to climb the hill by a winding defile, took an hour to reach the mausoleum.

Round and round the building the procession marched, while the choristers sang funeral dirges. It was nearly three hours after the formation of the procession when the urn was carried ceremonially into the mausoleum, and placed in one of the niches on the walls.

Three volleys were fired, and then the military marched away to a merry tune on the drums and fifes. On the following day a new oratorio, composed by Atterbury, was performed in the church.

To-day several urns stand in the recesses, but that containing the heart of Whitehead was stolen in 1829, despite the warning of the epitaph, which ran :

PAUL WHITEHEAD OF TWICKENHAM, ESQR.
Ob. 1775.
Unhallowed hands, this urn forbear,
No gems, nor orient spoil
Lie here concealed ; but what's more rare,
A heart that knew no guile.

Half-way down the hill from the church of St. Lawrence is a tunnel or a cave hundreds of yards long, running under the church, which is also said to have been built by Lord le Despencer. It is more likely, however, to have been built at an earlier date, and may even be a relic of Norman times.

At the entrance to the tunnel is an old ruin with a powerfully made door. The tunnel connects a series of caverns, and terminates in one, larger than the rest, with a vaulted roof. A suspended hook suggests that it was once used for a lamp, and whether the "monks" of Medmenham ever met there or not, it is clear that it was a meeting-place of some kind during the history of West Wycombe church.

Whatever may have been the character of the Society of the Monks of St. Francis, there were, at that time, many others of a reprehensible character. They were called Hell Fire Clubs, and the Medmenham organization has, in later years, been given a similar designation, though most probably it did not warrant the name.

In 1721 an Order in Council denounced clubs of the Hell Fire type. It was believed that the meetings were held to bring all kinds of religion into disrepute. A Bill was therefore introduced in the House of Lords to prohibit blasphemy, but many of the Lords, believing that it would lead to persecution, there was eventually a majority against the Bill.

There were many rich young men, who had made their money by gambling, who had nothing else to do but indulge in a life of profligacy. It was this type of person who originated or joined a Hell Fire club. Generally the headquarters of these clubs were in London, but they had tentacles reaching as far as Dublin.

Mysterious rites were performed, and the members were known by symbolical names. Women were admitted to membership and indulged in the orgies.

As the name implies, the interior of these clubs was decorated in representation of hell, and fire and brimstone were a common accompaniment of the proceedings.

In Dublin there was a club about which sensational stories were told. The Irish peasants believed that it was quite a common occurrence for members to burn themselves to death. The smell of brimstone pervaded the district, and biblical episodes were parodied.

This particular club, it is said, was dissolved by a black

cat. A country curate visiting Dublin expressed a desire to visit the club. He was invited, and despite the opposition of the members he said grace. The cat was served first, according to custom. The curate inquired the reason.

One of the members replied that it was believed the cat was the oldest present, and as one of the rules of the club was to respect age, the cat was always served first. The curate replied that the cat was the devil, whereupon the club decided to put the clergyman to death. He was given five minutes to say a prayer. During the recital the cat howled, and no wonder, for the curate was saying an exorcism.

The cat assumed its fiendish form and flew off, carrying the roof of the club with him.

Antoine Laurent Lavoisier

When it was thought necessary to get rid of an aristocrat during the Reign of Terror in Paris, the victim was brought to the guillotine often on the most extraordinary charge.

Antoine Laurent Lavoisier, one of the world's most famous chemical philosophers, was executed in accordance with the following sentence :

"Condemned to death, as convicted of being author of, or accomplice in, a plot which has existed against the French nation, tending to favour the success of the enemies of France ; especially by exercising every kind of exaction and concussion (i.e., plunder of public money) against the said French nation, to wit, by adding to tobacco water and ingredients hurtful to the health of the citizens who made use thereof."

Lavoisier dealt with the disposal of tobacco in an official capacity.

There is no need to emphasize the fact that a certain amount of water is necessary in tobacco, but no evidence was brought against Lavoisier to prove that he had exceeded the normal quantity, or, if he had, that it was harmful to the citizens.

The truth was that Lavoisier belonged to the aristocratic section of the community, and the persecutors were indifferent about the nature of the charge so long as it was sufficient to sway the mob against him.

Thus, in this ignominious way, died a man who had contributed much to science.

Moreover, he died ticketed without a name. He was judged as "*fermier-general*, No. 5," and it is probable that only a few among the crowd who saw the tragedy in the Place de la Revolution knew the victim as Lavoisier.

Lavoisier, who was born in August 1743, was the son of a rich man. He was never called upon to work for his living, but in his youth Lavoisier was not idle. He studied mathematics and astronomy, botany, chemistry, and, later, geology.

When he was 22 the Academy offered, on behalf of the French Government, a prize for the best essay on lighting the streets of Paris.

Determined to enter and gain a good place in the competition, Lavoisier shut himself up in a dark room for six weeks. At the end of this time his sight had become extremely sensitive, and he was able to compare the respective intensity of flames, an acquirement that he considered necessary in order to write a satisfactory essay.

This devotion to science resulted in his winning the gold medal.

Two or three years later Lavoisier found that his health, and particularly his digestion, had been impaired by close study. He therefore gradually restricted himself to a milk diet for several months. This appears to have restored his health.

In 1771 Lavoisier resolved to confine himself to chemistry. It would appear at this time that his pecuniary circumstances were not as good as they had been, and in order to prosecute his chemical researches, which would involve a heavy expense, he applied for and obtained the post of a *fermier-general* (farmer-general).

Soon after he married Marie Anna Pierrette Paulz, the daughter of one of his scientific friends.

His mornings and evenings were now devoted to chemistry, and the middle of the day was spent in official business, in which he acquitted himself satisfactorily.

The yearly expenses of his laboratory amounted to nearly 10,000 francs.

It is impossible to go fully into Lavoisier's researches or his controversies with other chemists, but it may be said that he made many discoveries relating to the nature of the

K*

atmosphere. He also discovered the composition of water independently of Cavendish and Watt.

In 1776 Lavoisier became the head of the French Government saltpetre works, where he increased the production fourfold. He also improved the gunpowder used in the French army and navy, increasing its power by nearly one-half.

Among his other activities was a report on the sanitary state of prisons, a method for separating gold and silver, and an investigation of a process for disinfecting sewers.

He produced over sixty essays and reports, which appeared in the *Transactions of the Academy* and other journals.

Meanwhile, he carried out his official duties to the satisfaction of everyone.

In connection with his post as *fermier-general*, which was really a financial one, he urged the reduction of certain taxes, maintaining that it would lead ultimately to an increase instead of a reduction in revenue.

In 1790 he was nominated to the Commission of Weights and Measures, and in the following year he was asked by the Constituent Assembly to draw up a plan for simplifying the collection of taxes.

Up to this time the career of Lavoisier had been prosperous, and he was as popular with the leaders of the revolution as he had been with the Royalist Administration.

But evil days were coming. The revolution took on a new aspect ; Robespierre came into power, and the guillotine began its deadly work.

Lavoisier appears to have had some foreboding of trouble. One day he remarked to a friend that if he were stripped of his fortune he would open a business as an apothecary.

Meanwhile, however, he continued his researches, examining, among other things, the phenomena of perspiration. He found that the average weight of matter expelled by perspiration in twenty-four hours was 52.89 ounces.

He was preparing to collect all his papers into an edition when the blow fell.

On May 2nd, 1794, a member of the Convention, named Dupin, brought before the Assembly a charge against all the *fermiers-generaux*, including Lavoisier.

A form of accusation was soon laid before the revolutionary tribunal.

Lavoisier went into hiding, and was concealed by a friend

in the offices formerly occupied by the Academy of Sciences.

Here he remained a day or two, but on learning that his colleagues and his father-in-law had already been arrested, he left his retreat and surrendered of his own accord.

It is believed that Lavoisier could have escaped. All he did by giving himself up was to seal his doom.

On May 6th he was brought to trial, and with all his colleagues was condemned to death.

It is said that Lavoisier asked for a short respite to complete certain researches, but this request was refused.

Some of his friends were horrified to hear of his conviction, and hastily drew up a memorandum pleading for his release. Other petitions were proffered, all of which were treated with contempt.

On May 8th he was led to the scaffold, few among the crowd knowing who he was.

Lavoisier, who was 51 at his death, has been described as "the noblest victim of the guillotine—King Louis and his Queen not excepted."

Count Zinzendorf

When John Wesley saw the courage of the Moravian emigrants as the ship plugged its way across the Atlantic through one gale after another, he marvelled that they should be more self-possessed than he.

It convinced him that he did not own the faith which casts out fear.

The emigrants had left Germany and were on their way to the new settlement of their brethren in North Carolina, and Wesley and his brother Charles struck up an acquaintance with them.

In America, John Wesley sought out the leaders of the community, and learned how they had been persecuted before seeking a new home in another land.

Although the Wesleys were leading lights of Methodism, as revivalists, something still was wanting.

When Wesley returned to England after his visit to America in an attempt to open a mission to the Indians, he met Peter Bohler, who had been ordained by Nicolas Lewis Zinzendorf, the leader of the Brethren, for work in Carolina.

It was following some heart-to-heart talks together that Wesley was induced to go to a meeting of the Moravians in Aldersgate Street.

Wesley himself records : "About a quarter before nine . . . I felt my heart strangely warmed. . . . An assurance was given me that He had taken away my sins."

Zinzendorf was the man who had, therefore, been indirectly responsible for the conversion of one of England's greatest religious reformers. He was the founder of the renewed church of the Brethren.

The Moravian Church had its origin in the fifteenth century, its leader being John Huss, the martyr. After his death the communion was split into factions. The Hussite wars made further inroads, and the character of the sect in the sixteenth century had changed to an almost Presbyterian constitution. At the head of the Church was a body of ten elders, elected by the synod consisting of all the ministers. The synod acted as the supreme legislative authority, the bishops ruling in their dioceses and having a seat in the synod.

The Thirty Years War broke out in 1618. The Brethren were driven from their homes, and many fled, some to England, some to Saxony, and some to Texas.

The Brethren thus dispersed, the sect was almost extinct for a century. There was, however, a small flock which held together until the early part of the eighteenth century.

How the communion was revived and extended to almost every country is one of the romances of religious progress. The revival had its origin in Germany.

In 1722 a small number of Moravian emigrants, after suffering persecution on account of their faith, left their native country, and arrived in the neighbourhood of Great Hennersdorf. They applied for permission to live on the the estate of Count Zinzendorf, and this was granted. The settlement was afterwards called Herrnhut.

Two years later five more emigrants arrived at the settlement. In a short time further emigrants brought their number to 200. By this time they were attracting the attention of the people living in the country of their adoption, and their numbers gradually increased by conversions.

But a religious community without sufficient control cannot exist for long without discord. There were dissensions on matters of doctrine, and at last the Count stepped in and took charge of the community.

As he was living at Dresden, where he held an official position, he obtained leave of absence, and took up his residence in the manor house at Berthelsdorf.

Zinzendorf was descended from a noble family in Austria, whose origin could be traced back to the days of the Crusaders, and although one branch of the family had embraced the Reformation doctrines in the days of Luther, they were held in such high esteem that they continued to hold offices at the Emperor's court.

The Count's father was a Cabinet Minister in Dresden, and he died a few months after the birth of his son. On the marriage of his widow, shortly afterwards, young Nicholas Lewis was placed in the hands of his grandmother.

At the age of 11 he was placed in a seminary at Halle, where he studied theology. In 1719, when he was not yet 20, he went to Holland, to study the Reformed Church there, while in France he learned the teaching of the Church of Rome, and became acquainted with the Archbishop of Paris Cardinal de Noailles. To the Cardinal he frankly acknowledged his protestant beliefs.

In 1722 he married Erdmuth Dorothy, the sister of Henry Count Reuss of Ebersdorf. Soon afterwards he accepted an office at Dresden with the title of Counsellor of Justice. While there he held religious meetings in his house, and issued a religious periodical in which he condemned the vices of the age.

Having given up his post in Dresden, the Count gave the whole of his attention to consolidating the views of the newly formed congregation. The form of worship and the control was based upon that of the old Brethren of the ancient Church in Bohemia and Moravia.

Then he conceived the idea of missionary propaganda. In 1731 he was sent to Copenhagen to attend the coronation of Christian VI of Denmark, and it was here that he met a negro from St. Thomas, in the West Indies, who was a valet to one of the officers of the household.

Through him he heard of the dreadful condition of the negro slaves. On his return to Herrnhut, he told the congregation what he had learned, with the result that certain of the members offered to go to the West Indies as missioners.

On August 21st, 1732, the first missionary pioneers left Germany. They were Leonard Dober and David Nitschman, and they began a work which has extended under the name of the Moravians to all heathen countries.

Meanwhile trouble was brewing at the Court of Saxony. Complaints were made as to the Count's spiritual activities, and attention drawn to the fact that Protestants were emigrating from Moravia.

The Saxon Government instituted a committee of inquiry, which met at Herrnhut. Although the subsequent report was a favourable one, the enemies of the Count persisted in charging him with various offences.

They obtained an order requesting that he should sell his estates. His property, however, had already been sold to his wife by a legal contract.

In 1733 the Count decided to examine the situation with a view to joining the Lutheran Church. A commission was held by the Lutherans and a judgment given that the tenets of the Brethren were in accord with Protestantism.

A year later he was ordained, and then went to Switzerland and Holland, when he formed branches of the Brethren.

In 1736 an order was issued from the Court of Saxony decreeing his banishment from the country. For some months he travelled Europe, visited Livonia, where he opened another branch of the Brethren, received an invitation from King Frederick William I of Prussia to an audience, and was assured of that monarch's protection.

Another branch was begun in Prussia, and in the following year the Count was consecrated bishop of the Church of the Brethren by D. E. Jablonsky, the court Chaplain, who was himself a grandson of the celebrated Moravian bishop L. Amos Comenius.

In 1737 the Count came to England, and the question then arose whether the Church of England should recognize the functions of the Moravian Church. Dr. John Potter, Archbishop of Canterbury, acknowledged that there was no doubt that the church of the Bohemian Brethren was apostolic and episcopal.

While in England the Count became acquainted with the founders of Methodism and lived with them for some time until there was a cleavage of opinion on certain doctrines.

Back in Berlin the following year, he spoke at meetings

all over Prussia and excited much jealousy. Only the protection of the Emperor saved him from persecution. In October 1738, he visited the mission at St. Thomas. He found his missioners in prison, but obtained their release, represented their case to Copenhagen, and secured them from further interference.

In 1741 he went to North America, took charge of the German Lutherans of Pennsylvania, and inspected the work of the missionaries to the Indians.

On his return to Europe he was arrested at Riga, imprisoned in a citadel, and was later requested to leave Russia. In the meantime a flood of libellous writings appeared against him. They were a retaliation for some of his published works.

Ten years after his banishment from Saxony, Herrnhut was a flourishing town, with an unmistakable voice in the affairs of the country, and there was no reason, therefore, why the Count should not return. The banishment was rescinded, and he arrived at Herrnhut to the great delight of the congregation. Two years later a royal decree was issued which secured full rights to the Herrnhut Brethren.

At the instance of the Count, the British House of Lords passed an act formally acknowledging the Church of the United Brethren of the Episcopalian. As a result many churches were opened in this country, and for three years Zinzendorf remained, visiting the congregations and preaching in their chapels, one of which was established in a turning off Fetter Lane, E.C.

He negotiated for the purchase of 100,000 acres of land in North Carolina, and about the same time a hymnbook of the Brethren was published. The church was in debt, but by his giving up all his possessions it was freed.

On June 19th, 1756, his wife died. During the next four years he travelled all over Europe, but on his return to Herrnhut he was suddenly seized with an illness and died on May 9th, 1760, at the age of 60.

Joseph Ady

For nearly twenty years during the first half of the nineteenth century Jospeh Ady reaped a rich income in a simple way. His victims had no remedy at law.

He was frequently exposed in the newspapers. But there was always somebody who had not heard of him.

Ady was a pleasant individual, serene and courteous. He was a Quaker.

He had access to liets of unclaimed dividends, bank balances, estates with lost heirs, and the like. He took a note of the names, and sent letters to people who, he thought, might be interested.

He told them that if they sent a guinea they would hear "something to their advantage."

When one complied, he sent a second note saying that his correspondent's name appeared in a list of unclaimed money or estates, and advising him to have an investigation.

This information might in some cases prove an "advantage," and Ady, if challenged, had good grounds for declaring that he had been of assistance.

It was debatable whether he were breaking the law, but under no statute could it be proved that he was carrying on a dishonest business.

Thus Joseph went on from year to year, frequently prosecuted but never convicted. At intervals of a few months he appeared at Bow Street Police Court—and was discharged.

On May 10th, 1830, he made one of his appearances there.

On that occasion there was reason to believe that they had caught him on the wrong side of the law at last.

A London solicitor named Blamire, acting for a Mr. Salkeld, had prosecuted Benjamin Ridgeway for defrauding him of a sovereign.

Salkeld, who was also a solicitor practising in Cumberland, had received one of Ady's letters.

A trap was set for Ady, and Ridgeway, who was one of Ady's clerks, was given a sovereign.

Salkeld received the usual letter from Ady stating that his name appeared in a list of persons having unclaimed money in Government securities.

Blamire then proceeded to catch Ady by declaring that there was no connection between the two Salkelds and demanded the sovereign back. Unable to get a refund, Blamire gave Ridgeway into custody.

Ady appeared in court to support his clerk.

Sir Richard Birnie, the magistrate, began to question Ady. "You are the Mr. Ady to whom so many persons, myself among the number, have been indebted for such valuable information, are you not ?" he inquired.

"I have come forward on behalf of my servant," replied Ady. "If you have any charge against *me*, here I am."

Sir Richard took the challenge, and Ady's name was added to the charge.

"Now," said the magistrate, "you are charged in conjunction with your servant, with having swindled Mr. Blamire out of a sovereign, under the pretence of furnishing a Mr. Salkeld with information which turns out to be false. What have you to say ?"

Ady replied : "I have lived for upwards of twenty-five years in Houndsditch and, if I were a swindler I could not have preserved my character so long."

Sir Richard smiled. He was about to score a point.

"You admit having empowered your agent to receive the money in your name ?" he said.

"I do," declared the prisoner, candidly. "I have carried on transactions of a similar description for years. It is true that some persons have been so ungrateful as to demand their money back ; but I maintain that I have always given value for their fees. If this gentleman has a grievance against me he knows my address, and the law is open to him. This is not the right place to try the question."

"Oh," retorted the magistrate, "we will see about that presently."

He then ordered the police constable who had taken Ridgeway into custody to stand forward, and produce the money found on him.

The officer produced two sovereigns and some coppers. At the magistrate's request, he handed one of the sovereigns to Mr. Blamire, who declared that he knew it by a private mark.

"I have not the least objection to my servant stating where and from whom he got the other," interposed Ady.

Ridgeway looked nervously at his master, and then said that he had forgotten from whom he had received the coin.

Pressed by the magistrate, he gave the address as Suffolk Place.

Sir Richard Birnie directed that a constable should be sent at once to ask the occupant of the house to come forward and explain under what pretence Ridgeway had obtained the sovereign.

Meanwhile the colloquy between the magistrate and Ady was resumed.

"There is no doubt whatever that Ady has been carrying on a system of fraud for years," said Sir Richard. "I have received more than 50 letters from people complaining that they have been swindled out of their money."

"There are laws in England," retorted Ady, "designed to reach every kind of offence. If I had done wrong, I should have been punished long ago."

"You are a clever fellow, and manage to keep within the law. But take care, Mr. Ady, for I am determined to have my eye on you."

"I have no objection to that," said Ady, "but you have never lost a sovereign by me yet."

"No; but you tried hard for it, by sending me one of your swindling letters."

"If I did, I have no doubt that I could have told you something to your advantage."

"Not you," replied the magistrate with heat. "I will go further and say that I never had a relation so rich as I am myself; therefore it would be quite useless to throw away your information on me."

"If that is the case, Sir Richard," said Ady with a bow, "I will remove your name from my books when I get home."

At that moment the constable returned from his mission, and whispered a name to the magistrate.

"What !" exclaimed Sir Richard, "Mr. Doherty, Solicitor-General for Ireland ! Why, you pitch your game high indeed ! So you got the other sovereign from the Irish Solicitor-General ?"

"I did," replied Ady. "And that proves that my transactions are fair and above-board. I should be a fool to attempt to impose on a Solicitor-General."

This disclosure appears to have overcome the magistrate. The conversation ended, and so did the case.

Ady left the court unconvicted—and resumed business.

Isaac D'Israeli

In the year 1748, Benjamin D'Israeli, a lad of eighteen, left Venice, where his family were prosperous merchants, and came to England.

D'Israeli belonged to a Jewish family, driven out of Spain by the Inquisition at the end of the fifteenth century, in common with a large number of others.

He built up an important business, and when he died in 1816 he left a considerable fortune to his son, Isaac. During his sojourn in England Benjamin had belonged to the London congregation of Spanish and Portuguese Jews.

To understand the difficulties which beset the Jews in those early days, it is necessary to give a brief history of their treatment in Britain.

There were Jews in England certainly as early as the Norman Conquest. At the Coronation of Richard I many were massacred. In the early part of the thirteenth century they were required to wear badges. At that time they were the country's bankers and supplied the Royal treasury.

In 1275 they were permitted to hold property, but this was a left-handed concession, for they were not allowed to engage in finance. In 1290 they were completely expelled from England.

The ban against the Jews lasted for nearly 400 years. Then Cromwell announced that there was no legal opposition to their return. Charles II adopted a still more tolerant policy and many hundreds of Jews came to England though, as yet, they had no rights of citizenship.

In 1753 the Naturalisation Act was passed, but quickly repealed. It was at that period that Benjamin D'Israeli, despite prejudice against his religionists, laid the foundations of a business.

A century passed before Jews obtained full Parliamentary rights. By that time the D'Israelis and many other Jewish families had deserted the synagogue.

In 1835 the office of City of London Sheriff was made available to Jews, and Moses Montefiore was elected. He afterwards became Lord Mayor and was knighted. Sir I. L. Goldsmid became a baronet in 1841 ; Baron Lionel de Rothschild was elected to Parliament seven years later, but was unable to take his seat until the Emancipation Bill was passed. Alderman David Salomons became Lord Mayor in 1855, and was knighted.

Following the legislation of 1860 there was no bar to the Jews, and many soon rose to high positions. Lord Rothschild, the first Jewish peer, took his seat in the House of Lords in 1886.

Isaac D'Israeli was the first of the family to break away from the business tradition. He was born on May 11th, 1766, and was educated at Amsterdam, where he imbibed the principles of Rousseau, and when his father intimated that he was to be placed in a commercial house at Bordeaux Isaac promptly wrote a poem condemning commerce.

There is an interesting story concerning this poem which Isaac D'Israeli used to tell his friends in later years.

He sent it to Dr. Samuel Johnson for his criticism, and waited impatiently for the reply that never came. One day in December 1784 he resolved to beard the literary lion in his Bolt Court den.

There was something about Johnson's house, and particularly the knocker on the door, which was calculated to increase the nervousness of a nervous individual. Samuel Rogers, the poet, had experienced the same fears when, years before, he had gone to Johnson's house on a similar mission.

When the heavy knocker had fallen upon the massive door and echoed throughout the dismal passages Rogers had run away. The knocker was just as vibrant when D'Israeli called, but he did not run. The door was opened by Frank Barker, Johnson's coloured servant, who informed the lad in a whisper that his master had just breathed his last.

The packet containing the poem was returned unopened.

Isaac now addressed a letter to Dr. Vicesimus Knox, principal of Tonbridge Grammar School, asking to be taken into his family to benefit by his learning and experience. It is not known what answer D'Israeli received.

But Isaac's determination not to enter business was recognized by his parents, and he was sent to travel in France, with permission to do as he pleased. He naturally sought out the literary people and learned a great deal.

He returned to London in 1788, and a year later attacked Peter Pindar (John Wolcot) in a poem that appeared in the *Gentleman's Magazine.* It was published anonymously, and caused much speculation. Some, like Wolcot, attributed it to William Hayley, and the latter was subjected to a vindictive attack by "Peter."

On learning the name of the real author, however, Wolcot sought out his young attacker, and they became friends for life.

Isaac's parents were now reconciled to their son's revolt. D'Israeli wrote his first book, *A Defence of Poetry*, and dedicated it to Henry James Pye.

In 1802 he married Maria Basevi, by whom he had five children. Benjamin, afterwards Lord Beaconsfield, was the second. In 1817 Isaac broke with the synagogue and had his children baptised.

Isaac D'Israeli's chief work was *Curiosities of Literature*, published in 1791. This was followed in 1796 by *Miscellanies, or Literary Recreations*, in 1812 by *Calamities of Authors*, and in 1814 by the *Quarrels of Authors*.

Towards the end of his life he conceived the idea of a history of English literature. Three volumes appeared in 1841 under the title of *Amenities of Literature*. The most delightful of his works, however, is *Essay on the Literary Character*, which appeared in 1795.

In 1797 he published three novels. His last, called *Despotism, or the Fall of the Jesuits*, appeared in 1811, but none of his romantic books was popular. He also published a Jewish history in 1833.

In a historical work, D'Israeli sought to defend the character of James I, and he also wrote a commentary on the life and reign of King Charles I, for which he received the degree of D.C.L. from the University of Oxford.

Until he was 72, D'Israeli studied incessantly. Then his eyes became affected, and he retired to his seat at Bradenham House, Buckinghamshire, where he lived for a further ten years, and died on January 19th, 1848.

D'Israeli led a placid life. A charming and interesting picture of his father was written by Lord Beaconsfield, and prefixed to the 1849 edition of *Curiosities of Literature*.

Thomas Wentworth, Earl of Strafford

"Put not your trust in princes, nor in the sons of men, for in them there is no salvation."

When Thomas Wentworth, Earl of Strafford, uttered these words he had just been told that three days thence he was to suffer death at Tower Hill.

Like Wolsey, he had found that a life spent in the service of a fickle king goes unrewarded in the end, particularly if the king himself be unpopular.

Strafford has never been so popular with dramatic historians as Wolsey. Yet his was an even more tragic case than the Cardinal's.

He alternated between disgrace and favour, but there was no mercy for him when the people secured the upper hand of Charles I, for in the words of one biographer, "He was the ablest instrument of tyranny that England has ever produced."

He had much courage, sagacity, and eloquence; he was persevering but ambitious, cruel, licentious and overbearing. In his early days as one of the favourites of James I, he used much diplomacy in keeping out of the disputes between king and people. When Charles I succeeded he appears to have lost all discretion.

Strafford was the eldest of twelve children of Sir William Wentworth, of ancient and wealthy family, which had been located at Wentworth Woodhouse since the days of the Conqueror.

Among his ancestors were John of Gaunt, Lancaster, and many of the famous barons. He was educated at St. John's College, which was founded by the grandmother of Henry VII, whom he claimed as an ancestor.

Before he was eighteen he married Frances, the eldest daughter of the Earl of Cumberland. He toured the Continent, and on his return was elected knight of Yorkshire, in the second Parliament of James.

When this Parliament was dissolved after two months, Wentworth was merely an interested spectator, and at the end of the trouble received as reward an office in the Customs for the West Riding.

Throughout the next six years of government by the King,

Wentworth kept friendly with the Court, and was again elected for Yorkshire.

Again there was a dispute between King and Parliament, and once more Wentworth succeeded in remaining neutral.

An attack of fever which he caught, and which carried off his wife, sent him into seclusion for two years. In 1624 he was returned for Yorkshire, but this was contested and declared void through the activities of Sir John Eliot.

Ever afterwards these two were bitter enemies.

The resultant poll brought him back to Parliament, when he again fell ill, and on returning to office he found Charles I on the throne and Buckingham practically in charge of affairs of State.

In some way not disclosed, Wentworth had incurred the dislike of Buckingham, and when the new Parliament was summoned in 1626 he discovered that he had been pricked a sheriff and was ineligible.

Wentworth submitted to the insult without protest. This was the last time in his career that he appeared willing to give way to any indignity.

There followed the trouble between the King and Commons on the question of levying tonnage and poundage with the impeachment of Buckingham. Although Wentworth did not take sides in this quarrel his office of the Keeper of the Records was taken from him and given to his rival, Sir John Saville.

This was the last straw, and he decided to take sides with the opponents of the Government.

When Charles dissolved his second Parliament, and the King enforced loans from the nobility, Wentworth was called upon to furnish some money. On his refusal he was summoned to appear before the Council, and committed to the Marshalsea Prison, where he remained six weeks. He was then taken to Dartford, in Kent, where he was allowed the company of his second wife, Lady Arabella, daughter of Lord Clare.

Wentworth was allowed to take his seat in the third Parliament summoned by Charles in 1628, and it was at the session that the famous Petition of Right was wrested from the King.

Wentworth was one of the leaders of the opposition to the King, and was now regarded a supporter of the popular cause. In his newly found capacity as one of the leaders of the people, he took every opportunity of condemning the exactions of the King.

Gradually the King realized the mistake he had made in slighting a man with the accomplishments of Wentworth. Accordingly, negotiations were opened with him, and before the end of the session he was created a baron and became a member of the Privy Council.

When Buckingham died, the last obstacle to Wentworth's advancement was removed, and he was created a Viscount and Lord President of the Council of the North.

He adopted a most arrogant attitude, imposing fines upon those who did not give him the respect due to a representative of the King. He obtained a severe sentence against Sir David Fowler and his son, who had not treated him with sufficient courtesy.

About this time his wife died. This did not interfere with his ambitious projects, and at last Charles offered him the post of Lord-Deputy of Ireland, where, at the time, there was a lot of strife.

Immediately on taking office, Wentworth began to initiate a regime with the object of making the royal power absolute in Ireland.

He obtained an order from the King that "none of those that has either office or estate here" should leave Ireland without the permission of the Lord-Deputy.

But as soon as Parliament met Strafford was impeached of high treason.

Strafford was found guilty on two charges, and Charles, who had promised to preserve him from harm, gave his assent to the Bill.

On hearing of Charles's treachery, Strafford placed his hand upon his heart and spoke the words quoted above.

He was allowed three days to prepare for death, and on the day of his execution, May 12th, 1641, there were, on Tower Hill, the largest crowd that had ever attended an execution.

A few words to those standing round, and Strafford's head was severed by the axe at one blow.

Charles, Marquess of Rockingham

Edmund Burke has left behind a glowing tribute to Charles Watson Wentworth, Marquess of Rockingham.

"A man worthy to be held in esteem, because he did not live for himself," says Burke. "He far exceeded all other statesmen in the art of drawing together, without the seduction of self-interest, the concurrence and co-operation of various dispositions and abilities of men, whom he assimilated to his character and associated in his labours."

One might question whether this were the private opinion of Burke, for if a man is not a hero to his valet, it is difficult to see how he can be a hero to his secretary.

Burke is referring to a period of distinguished men—Pitt, Grenville, Lord Shelburne, Fox, Lord North, and many others. Is Burke's epitaph a testimony to the fact that Rockingham gave him a place in his administration?

Rockingham, as Prime Minister, was a compromise to satisfy the prejudices of George III. The King would not have Grenville. "I would sooner see the devil in my closet," he said.

Pitt would not form a government without certain of his friends. As they were not disposed to accept office, Pitt declined.

At length Rockingham was approached by the Duke of Cumberland. He had no outstanding qualifications. He had never been tried as a statesman, was not a good speaker, and had not been educated in politics. His only claim to fame at that time was his success in the first St. Leger race.

He had great wealth and was a big land-owner, which suited some of the malcontent politicians.

He formed his government from "worn-out veterans and raw recruits." In experience it was weak, and it had no debaters of note. "A jumble of youth and caducity which could not be efficient," was Lord Chesterfield's estimate. Charles Townshend called it "a mere lutestring, pretty summer wear," and prophesied that it would not stand the winter.

The acquisition of Edmund Burke, however, increased the fighting abilities of the Government.

Rockingham accepted office at a time when the zephyr of

discontent in America was becoming a breeze. Grenville's Stamp Act was bringing the colonists to the brink of rebellion. Rockingham resolved to repeal the Stamp Act, and did. At the same time, he threw a bone to the Opposition by declaring that the power of Parliament over the Colonies was supreme.

The latter measure was carried, but the repeal of the Stamp Act was opposed by a faction that sought to curry favour with the King.

The Ministry, however, scored a victory, though it did not add to their strength and stability. Their patron, the Duke of Cumberland, had died, and Pitt, asked time after time to join them, refused.

The King disliked them, and he had considerable support in both houses.

At last George III induced Pitt once more to come forward, and soon after the close of the 1766 session, Rockingham was dismissed, Pitt taking his place.

The Marquess had been in power one year and twenty days, but during that time his Ministry had achieved a lot. The Colonists were more amenable, the cider tax was repealed. The issue of general warrants was condemned, as well as the seizure of papers in cases of libel.

But the greatest honour of the Rockingham administration was the absence of bribery of Members of Parliament. Burke says : "They practised no corruption, nor were they ever suspected of it. They sold no offices. They obtained no reversions or pensions, either coming in or going out, for themselves, their families, or their dependents."

During the next sixteen years Rockingham remained out of office. They were fateful years. It is a matter of speculation whether he would have been able to overcome the King's determination to harass the Colonists, but he could not have done worse than Lord North.

To his credit Lord North had made many attempts to retire from an awkward position, but unfortunately for his own reputation and for the country, he was induced to retain office by entreaties of the King.

After the American War of Independence the people clamoured for a change of Government. The King fought against the return of the Whigs, and even threatened to go to Hanover. In a letter to Lord North he declared : "His sentiments of honour would not permit him to send for any of the leaders of the Opposition, and personally treat with them."

At length even George III had to give way—ten days after he had written the letter to Lord North—and the Marquess of Rockingham became first Minister of the Crown.

The new administration created in March 1782 was composed partly of Whigs and partly of Tories, and included Lord Shelburne and Lord Thurlow.

They lost no time in passing measures of reform, and entered into negotiations for the conclusion of a peace with France and the recognition of the new independent American Colonies.

In the midst of this work, however, Rockingham died on July 1st, in the fifty-second year of his age, three months after he had become Premier.

Born on May 13th 1730, Charles Watson Wentworth was the son of the first Marquess of Rockingham, formerly Baron Malton.

He himself was created Earl of Malton in the Irish peerage in 1750, and a few months later succeeded to the higher title on the death of his father. Though only twenty he soon began to take part in the debates in the House of Lords, but, according to Horace Walpole, he was no orator.

His great wealth and his conspicuously upright and honourable character, together with moderation in his political opinions, made him an influential man both in Parliament and in the country.

His attachment to the Whigs was well known. George III disliked him for this, but was anxious to conciliate so important a nobleman whom his party regarded as one of their leaders.

In 1760 Rockingham was made Knight of the Garter, and shortly afterwards was appointed to office in the Royal Household.

He became dissatisfied with the Bute administration and particularly with the Peace of Paris, and he resigned his appointment in 1762.

George III retaliated by depriving him of his lord-lieutenancy.

Grenville is said to have lectured the King for hours at a stretch for his treatment of Rockingham, and Rockingham was eventually asked to form his Ministry.

The Marquess had sound common sense and judgment. He was entirely disinterested in honours, but knew how to choose his friends.

He left no heir, and his large estates descended to Lord Fitzwilliam, his sister's son.

Monk Lewis

In the days of his celebrity, Matthew Gregory Lewis, affectionately known as "Monk," was staying one night in a country town when he went to visit a performance given by strolling players.

"Monk," himself a playwright and no mean critic, was not impressed. On return to his hotel he found a young woman waiting to see him.

She proved to be one of the actresses. Hearing that the great Monk Lewis was in the town, she had hurried to him immediately the show was over to plead for an original play from his pen for her benefit, which was due to take place shortly.

Lewis had a short unpublished play called *The Hindoo Bride*, the central scene of which was the burning of a widow on the funeral pile of her husband. It was ideally suited to the melodramatic taste of a country audience.

The actress departed overjoyed on a promise from Lewis that he would give her the play on the following day.

But the *Bride* could nowhere be found. He searched his trunk, his pockets and other likely places without result. He went out to think the matter over, and had to seek shelter from the rain in a huckster's shop.

Two voices were in conversation in an adjoining compartment.

"There now, mother—always that old story—when I have brought such good news, too. I called on Mr. Monk Lewis and found him so different from what I expected. He was so good-humoured, so affable and willing to help me. I did not say a word about you, mother. In some respects it might have done good; but it would seem like a begging affair. He promised to give me an original drama which he had with him for my benefit. I hope he did not think me too bold."

"I hope not, Jane," an old querulous voice replied. "But don't do these things again without consulting me ; for you don't know the world, and it may be thought . . ."

"Monk" did not hear what the world might have thought. The rain having stopped he left the shop, disliking his position as eavesdropper.

At his hotel he wrote the following letter :

Madam, I am truly sorry to acquaint you that my Hindoo Bride has behaved most improperly—in fact, whether the lady has eloped or not, it seems that she does not choose to make her appearance either for your benefit or mine. To say the truth, I don't at this moment know where to find her. I take the liberty to jest upon the subject because I really do not think you will have any cause to regret her non-appearance, having had an opportunity of witnessing your very admirable performance of a far superior character, in a style true to nature, and which reflects on you the highest credit. . . .

Trusting you will permit the enclosed (£50) in some measure to discharge the debt which I owe you for the gratification received.

This act was typical of the benevolence of Monk Lewis, who, being well supplied with money, seldom refused to assist a player down on his luck. His father held a high place in the War Office, and owned extensive West Indian estates.

He got his nickname of "Monk" from his chief literary production, a novel *The Monk*, which he wrote in ten days at the age of nineteen at The Hague, where he was living as an attaché. It was published in 1795, and caused a storm of protest, for it told of a monk who, fettered by his religious vows, was influenced by passion.

The Society for the the Suppression of Vice endeavoured to force the Attorney-General to institute proceedings against the author. Instead Lewis found himself a literary lion on his return to England, and he retained an important position in literature until the rise of Scott and Byron.

He was friendly with Byron and was a favourite in society. Among his fictions are : *Tales of Terror*, *Romantic Tales*, *The Bravo*, and his dramatic pieces include *Castle Spectre*, *East Indian*, and *Timur the Tartar*. The death of his father left him a handsome fortune and the estates in Jamaica, which he visited towards the close of 1815 and again in 1817.

He describes how the negroes received him.

As soon as the carriage entered the gates the uproar and confusion which ensued set all description at defiance. The works were instantly all abandoned; everything that had life came flocking to the house from all quarters, and not only the men, and the women, and the children, but the hogs, and the dogs and the geese, and the fowls and the turkeys, all came hurrying along by instinct, to see what could possibly be the matter, and seemed to be afraid of arriving too late.

Whether the pleasure of the negroes was sincere may be doubted, but certainly it was the loudest that I ever witnessed. . . . One woman held up her little naked black child to me, grinning from ear to ear : "Look, massa ! him nice lily neger for massa !" . . .

Nothing could be more odd or more novel than the whole scene ; yet there was something in it truly affecting.

The Castle Spectre was "Monk's" greatest dramatic success. It was a piece that stirred the emotions of Drury Lane, and even affected the players, so that they were perpetually in a condition of goose-flesh.

"Oh, this ghost, this ghost ! Heavens, how it torments me !" exclaimed Mrs. Powell, who played the part of Evelina, as she threw herself upon a divan in her drawing-room after the play.

"Madam !" said a weak voice from the other end of the room.

Mrs. Powell jumped up trembling with fear.

It was a diminutive man, wearing a dark mantle with a dagger peeping from its folds, and a dark lantern in his hand ; a typical villain.

"Sir !" she exclaimed, recovering her wits. "What are you doing in my room !"

"Madam, the room is mine, and I will thank you to explain——"

"Surely this is No. 1 ?"

"No, indeed, madam, this is No. 2," was the reply.

Mrs. Powell was now conscious that the furniture in room was not familiar. "Ten thousand pardons !" she said. "The coachman must have mistaken the house. I am Mrs. Powell, of Drury Lane, and have just come from performing the *Castle Spectre*. Fatigue and absence of mind have made me an unconscious intruder. I lodge next door, and I hope you will excuse the unintentional alarm I have occasioned you."

"Permit me to introduce myself," said the man. "I am Monk Lewis, the *author* of the *Castle Spectre*. I hope you will excuse the unintentional alarm I have occasioned *you*."

One of Lewis's great hits was the ballad of "Crazy Jane." This was found among his papers and was set to music by several composers. The original and most popular melody was by Miss Abrams, who sang it herself at parties and otherwise in public. It was a favourite tune on the barrel organs and it set the fashion for a "Crazy Jane" hat.

Lewis died at sea on his return from his second journey to the West Indies on May 14th, 1818.

In his early days Lewis represented Hindon, Wiltshire, in the House of Commons, but made no headway in politics.

Daniel O'Connell

Benjamin Haydon, the painter, who was called upon to convey to canvas the face of Daniel O'Connell, the "Liberator," was not impressed either by the manner or appearance of the Irish hero.

"At 12 o'clock," says Haydon, "I went to O'Connell's, and certainly his appearance was very different from what it is in the House of Commons. It was, on the whole, hilarious and good-natured. But there was a cunning look. He has an eye like a weasel.

"I was shown into his private room. A shirt was hanging by the fire, a hand-glass tied to the window-bolt, papers, hats, brushes, wet towels, and dirty shoes, gave intimation of 'Dear Ireland.'"

"Mr. Haydon," said O'Connell, "you and I must understand each other about this picture. They say I must pay for this likeness?"

"Not at all, sir," replied Haydon, who afterwards records that this was the "only thing of the sort that has happened to me."

Writing of another sitting, Haydon reiterates: "O'Connell came in his best wig, and looking in great health and vigour. He has a head of great sentiment and power, but yet cunning."

They discussed the Irish question, and Haydon hazarded

the opinion that the Irish were barbarous, which shocked
O'Connell, who attempted to explain why they were not.
"He did not succeed," comments the painter in his diary.

On the debit side of O'Connell's account there is also the
trenchant comment of Lecky, who declares that the "Liberator"
failed to accomplish the chief object of his life—the separation
of Ireland from Britain.   Says Lecky :

"By a singular fatality the great advocate of repeal (of the Act
of Union) did more than anyone else to make the Union a necessity. . . . He destroyed the sympathy between the people and their
natural leaders, and he threw the former into the hands of men who
have subordinated all national to ecclesiastical considerations or
into the hands of reckless, ignorant, and dishonest adventurers."

O'Connell's implacable hostility to England was no doubt
induced by his illustrious Celtic descent.   He sprang from a
race of Celtic chiefs who had lost their lands in the Irish wars
and had suffered from the persecution which ground down
the Catholics.   His forbears had been compelled to work as
tenants on the very estates which had belonged to them, or to
obtain an illegitimate livelihood by smuggling.

It is not surprising, therefore, that he inherited the traditional antipathy for British rule.   While a boy he was adopted
by his uncle, Maurice O'Connell, of Derrynane, and sent to
school at Queenstown, one of the first Catholic schools.   He
became a student in the English colleges of Douai and St.
Omer in France, and he witnessed on several occasions the
excesses of the French revolutionaries.

These scenes made a great impression on him and instilled
a dread for anarchy and communism.

In 1798 he was called to the Irish Bar and soon rose to
eminence.

It was in the field of Irish politics, however, that O'Connell's name was to become a household word.   From his very
early days he had been moved by the condition of the mass of
people in Ireland.   Although the worst effects of the penal
code had been removed the Catholics had been unable to
make any headway towards emancipation.   Even the efforts
of a few influential Protestants, including Grattan, had been
unavailing.

O'Connell initiated a new policy which ultimately brought
victory.   He conceived the idea of combining all the Irish

Catholics into a huge league which maintained a permanent agitation against whatever party was in power. Attempts were made by the Government to suppress it piecemeal, but nothing could be done against an all-Ireland clamouring for its rights.

O'Connell was at the head of this great national movement. In 1828 he was elected for Clare, and next year the Catholic claims were granted. Emancipation would have come in time, but he hastened it many years.

On entering Parliament O'Connell sided with the Whigs and was prominent in matters of reform.

But events were moving towards more trouble for Ireland. The agitation on the Catholic question had sharpened the wits of the people. Before long there was an agitation against tithes and the Established Church, and O'Connell found himself in the midst of this campaign willy-nilly. Certainly it passed beyond his control, and for many months Ireland was at war with itself. Appalling crimes occurred and the country was in a state of anarchy.

When Lord Grey proposed repressive measures they were resolutely opposed by O'Connell. Hitherto, he had been opposed to anarchy and bloodshed; now, however, he was condoning it. It caused a breach between him and his Parliamentary party, and it was not until the Government abolished Irish tithes that he gradually returned to his allegiance.

O'Connell was in the first rank of debaters, and was an accomplished orator, albeit sometimes scurrilous and coarse. He was a strong supporter of Lord Melbourne's Government, and a powerful advocate of the emancipation of the slaves. At the same time, from a strictly political point of view, he was inconsistent.

For instance, he opposed the Irish Poor Law because it seemed to him to have a Communist flavour. A movement against payment of rent, he declared to be a crime.

When Peel advanced to power in 1841, O'Connell began an agitation for the repeal of the Act of Union. It has been suggested that he did this to embarrass Peel, whom he disliked. But it is clear that he had been in favour of repeal for many years because it was an obstacle to the Catholics.

He was by no means a separatist, for on more than one occasion he declared that self-government would not weaken the ties between Ireland and England. What would have been his attitude to the republican movement of later years, however, is a matter of speculation.

The League once more functioned on behalf of repeal. Meetings were convened by the priests and addressed by O'Connell. He believed success was certain. But the issue now was different from Catholic Emancipation. Opinion that had been in favour of the latter now rallied against repeal.

In October 1843, one of O'Connell's projected meetings was declared illegal. He and twelve of his followers were arrested. O'Connell was convicted and sentenced to a year's imprisonment and a fine of £2000. But he and his colleagues were freed by the House of Lords.

Ireland was now in further trouble. Famine visited the country and the agitation for repeal was temporarily forgotten.

On May 15th, 1847, O'Connell died at Genoa, while on his way to Rome. His body was brought back to Ireland and buried in Glasnevin cemetery, Dublin.

Nathaniel Hawthorne

Nathaniel Hawthorne wrote home to his mother :

I do not want to be a doctor and live by men's diseases ; nor a minister, to live by their sins ; nor a lawyer, and live by their quarrels. So I don't see that there is anything left for me but to be an author. How would you like some day to see a whole shelf full of books written by your son, with "Hawthorne's Works" printed on their backs ?

Nathaniel might have been more candid and admitted that he could not be a doctor because he was too sensitive ; that a career in the law would be hopeless because he was shy of society ; that the profession of a parson did not appeal to him because he was silent and retiring.

At school he was shrinking and modest. When he stood up to give his recitations he was afraid of his own voice. Construing a Greek or Latin sentence, or replying to a difficult question with the eyes of his classmates upon him, was agony.

The widowed Mrs. Hawthorne gave way to her boy. It was a relief to Hawthorne when he graduated from Bowdoin College, Brunswick, Maine, and was able to steal back to the retirement of his home at Salem, Massachusetts.

We now have a picture of the lad, completely isolated from society, venturing out only at night like a frightened rabbit, seldom seen by anyone.

In the forenoon he studied; in the afternoon he wrote. His family saw very little more of him than did the towns-people, for his meals were left before his locked door.

Day after day he produced manuscripts which he promptly tore up. He could not please himself.

At length, when he had the courage to print one of his compositions, it appeared anonymously when he was 24.

It is surprising that Hawthorne should have chosen such a crude, melodramatic story as *Fanshawe* to test the pulse of the public, for he must have written and destroyed far better efforts.

If it pleased the author, it certainly did not meet with the approval of others. It died an early death.

For years Hawthorne was the least known of America's novelists. He wrote for a holiday magazine called *The Token*, to which many of his more fortunate contemporaries contributed. In course of time his name became known.

But it was England that gave him his first public recognition.

In 1835, Henry F. Chorley, one of the editors of the *Athenæum*, reprinted three of Hawthorne's articles from *The Token*. America still lagged behind in the appreciation of a genius.

Goodrich, the editor of *The Token*, gave Nathaniel little or no encouragement, and paid him poorly.

At length the avaricious Goodrich was induced to bring out a collection of Hawthorne's contributions under the title of *Twice-told Tales*. A small edition was sold, but the greater part of the reading public ignored the book.

It was the first time, however, that Hawthorne had got into the reviews. Longfellow, then a critic for the *North American Review*, declared that the work was that of a genius. "As clear as running waters," was the poet's description. This generous tribute was inspired by the fact that he and Hawthorne had been chums at college.

More than ten years of weary plodding had brought Hawthorne no nearer fame, and when he was offered an appointment as weigher in the Custom house at Boston he gratefully accepted the £250 a year. His duties consisted in measuring coal, salt, and other bulky commodities on incoming foreign vessels.

It was heavy and irksome employment, but Hawthorne stuck it for two years until there came a change in the administration. Once more Nathaniel returned to his writing. But recognition was not yet.

In the spring of 1841 he wrote a collection of children's stories, called *Grandfather's Chair*, and joined an association at West Roxbury, Massachusetts, composed of a number of advanced thinkers. It was a scheme on Socialistic lines, whereby its members endeavoured to do the manual labour of the establishment and still have time for intellectual culture.

In theory it was a good scheme; in practice it was a failure. Nathaniel once more returned to Salem.

Then came Miss Sophia Peabody.

She was a young woman of Salem who seems to have changed the course of his career. He married her in the summer of 1842, and made his home in an old manse at Concord.

Here, on the site of the old revolutionary battlefield, he seems to have worked with renewed energy. He wrote for the *Democratic Review*, published more children's stories and more *Twice-told Tales*. In 1845 he edited the *African Journals* of Horatio Bridge, a naval officer, who had been a college friend. In the following year he brought out two volumes of a collection of his more recent writings, entitled *Mosses from an Old Manse*.

After four years he returned to Salem to take up another appointment as Customs officer. Once again a change of administration caused his retirement.

He now began to write his *Scarlet Letter*. It was published in 1850, and, at the age of 46, Hawthorne had at last proved his genius.

In quick succession appeared *The House of the Seven Gables*, *The Wonder-Book*, *The Blithedale Romance*, and *The Snow Image*. Back at Concord, where he bought an old house which he called 'The Wayside,' he wrote a *Life of Franklin Pierce* and *Tanglewood Tales*.

Pierce was the Democratic candidate for the presidency, and when he was elected Hawthorne reluctantly accepted the post of American consul at Liverpool. He sailed for Europe in the summer of 1853 and remained until 1860.

When Hawthorne returned to 'The Wayside' he was hardly any richer than before, and it was with a heavy heart that he recommenced writing.

His energy was gone, his health declined; his hair became white.

On the night of May 18th, 1864, America lost one of its greatest novelists.

Tom Spratt, Bishop of Rochester

Tom Spratt, Bishop of Rochester, "condescended to the times" with a facility equal to that of the Vicar of Bray.

For "in good King Charles's golden days" he was a zealous high churchman. When "Royal James possessed the crown" he was a good papist; when "William was our king" he steered with the new wind; and when Anne acceded he was seen in the Tory camp.

Thus, by the clever manipulation of his conscience, he retained his preferments.

But there was much to be said in favour of Tom Spratt, as we shall see hereafter.

Thomas Spratt—the name is spelled both with one and two "t's"—was born in 1636 at Tallaton in Devonshire, where his father was incumbent of the parish. He entered Wadham College, Oxford, took his degrees and became a Fellow in 1657. He took orders after the Restoration, and became chaplain to the Duke of Buckingham.

He became a royal chaplain and was elected a Fellow of the Royal Society, of which in 1667 he published the history. After the failure of the notorious Rye House Plot, Spratt published *A True Account and Declaration of the Horrid Conspiracy against the late King, his present Majesty, and the present Government.*

Spratt declares that he wrote this expressly at the command of James II, an excuse which served to divert suspicion from the cleric's mobile politics, after this Stuart had left the country.

That he was in great favour with James, however, is shown by the fact that he was appointed a member of the Ecclesiastical Commission created by the King for the coercion of disobedient parsons in defiance of two Acts of Parliament.

Commenting on Spratt's willingness to serve on this Commission, Macaulay says:

"He was a man to whose talents posterity has scarcely done justice. . . . He was indeed a great master of our language and possessed at once the eloquence of the preacher, of the controversialist, and of the historian. His moral character might have passed with little censure had he belonged to a less sacred profession; for the worst than can be said of him is that he was indolent, luxurious and worldly; but such failings, though not commonly regarded as very heinous in men of secular callings, are scandalous in a prelate."

The truth was that the Bishop had his eye on the Archbishopric of York when he accepted a place on the Commission. His activities on that body were lukewarm. He tried to do little mischief and to make as few enemies as possible, fearing to be called to account by a future Government.

At length he resigned his seat on the Commission. This proved the death-blow to this unconstitutional body, for if a man of Spratt's type could see its illegality, it was not good enough for others whose principles were sounder.

On the abdication of James, Spratt proposed a Regency, but afterwards took the oaths to the new Government and assisted at the coronation of William and Mary.

In 1692 an attempt was made to implicate Spratt in an alleged plot to restore James to the throne.

The Bishop had a sumptuous mansion at Bromley, in Kent. He had magnificent quarters in the cloisters of Westminster. The Government did not look upon him with much favour, for he detested puritanism. This dislike, however, did not arise from a religious bigotry. He could not stand their austerity, their phraseology or their lack of appreciation of the good things of life, particularly rich food.

Although he loathed the Nonconformists, who regarded themselves as specially protected by King William, he was not the kind of man to prejudice himself by taking part in a scheme to bring back the exiled monarch.

A certain Robert Young, with a long criminal record, decided to emulate Titus Oates, the author of the so-called Popish plot. He declared that there was a conspiracy to restore James.

There were, in 1692, a good many people in the country

who wanted the ex-King back, and the Government were not surprised to learn that some scheme of the kind was afoot.

Young swore on oath that a peer, several gentlemen and ten Presbyterian ministers were parties to the plot. Some of the accused were brought to trial, but the story told by Young in the witness-box was discredited by overwhelming evidence and the prosecution was dropped. Soon afterwards Young found himself in prison for forgery.

As he lay in confinement he conceived another "plot." This time he intended to accuse Jacobites rather than Presbyterians.

There was a conspiracy, said he, "as deep as hell." Some of the first men in England were implicated. King William, however, treated it lightly. "I will have nobody disturbed on such grounds," was his reply.

Rebuffed, Young remained quiet for a time. Soon, however, he was at it again. He forged a document which purported to be an "Association for the restoration of the banished King."

The names were among the most illustrious in the country. Among them was that of Spratt, Bishop of Rochester and Dean of Westminster.

Young, who was still in Newgate, got a confederate to hide the document in Spratt's house. The man dropped it into a flower-pot in the Bishop's study.

Young now implored to be heard, and informed the Government of the document. Officials went to Bromley, searched the house, but found nothing. They failed to look in the room in which it had been secreted.

Nevertheless, Spratt was arrested and brought before the Council, and then taken to his deanery and confined for ten days. He denied everything.

Blackhead, Young's confederate, was questioned, and broke down under cross-examination. At length he confessed.

Young was questioned again. He knew nothing about the flower-pots, he declared.

"This business," he maintained, "is a trick got up between the Bishop and Blackhead. The Bishop has let Blackhead off, and they are both trying to stifle the plot."

Members of the Commission who examined him laughed.

"Man," cried one of them, "wouldst thou have us believe

that the Bishop contrived to have this paper put where it was ten to one our messengers had found it, and where, if they had found it, it might have hanged him ?"

Young and Blackhead were removed in custody.

The bishop visited Young in prison. "Young," said he, "your conscience must tell you that you have cruelly wronged me. For your own sake I am sorry that you persist in denying what your associate has confessed."

"Confessed," he exclaimed. "No; all is not confessed yet; and that you shall find to your sorrow. There is such a thing as impeachment, my lord. When Parliament sits you shall hear more of me."

"God give you repentance," answered the Bishop. "For depend upon it, you are in much more danger of being damned than I of being impeached."

Back in prison Young contrived another "plot." But the Government had had enough of him. He was finally convicted of perjury and executed.

Spratt was a poet and author. Among his works are *Plague of Athens, The Rehearsal,* which he wrote in collaboration with the Duke of Buckingham; the *History of the Royal Society, The Life of Cowley, The Answer to Sorbière,* the *History of the Rye House Plot,* and a volume of sermons. He also told the story of his own apprehension and examination for treason.

He lived to his seventy-ninth year, and died at Bromley, Kent, on May 20th, 1713.

Francis Egerton, Duke of Bridgewater

A broken romance led to the construction of the first canal in England.

The young Duke of Bridgewater—he had just attained his majority—fell in love with one of the celebrated Irish sisters, daughters of a squire named Gunning.

These two girls, having taken Dublin by storm, and afterwards London, married into the peerage. One married Lord Coventry and the other the Duke of Hamilton.

The Duchess of Hamilton was soon widowed, and again eligible to contract marriage. The wealthy and jolly Duke of Bridgewater seemed to fill the bill nicely. As he was head over heels in love with the beautiful widow, he offered her his hand and coronet and was accepted.

Unfortunately, rumour had been busy with the name of Lady Coventry, the Duchess's sister. It was at this stage that the Duke of Bridgewater began to make conditions. Before the marriage could take place, said he, the Duchess must give up her intimacy with her sister.

Said the Duchess : "I will do nothing of the kind."

Replied the Duke : "Then the wedding is off."

The Duchess sought solace with Colonel Campbell, and with his elevation to the peerage became the Duchess of Argyll.

The Duke of Bridgewater deserted London and Newmarket, gave up racing, forswore the fair sex, and retired to his Lancashire estates, where he remained, feeling very sorry for himself.

To appreciate the Duke's subsequent achievements it is necessary to recall his upbringing and boyhood. He was born Francis Egerton, on May 21st, 1736, and was the eighth child of Scroop, fourth Earl and first Duke of Bridgewater.

Francis succeeded to the Dukedom in his twelfth year on the death of his elder brother, John. His father had died three years before, and his mother the Duchess had married, within twelve months, Sir Richard Lyttelton, a brother of the literary Lord Lyttelton.

Francis was not strong, and it had seemed unlikely that he would survive the four brothers who stood between him and the title.

It is said that the Duchess, after her second marriage, ill-treated Francis. She neglected his education, and, according to the family tradition, it was at one time contemplated placing the boy under restraint as an imbecile.

If this were true it was strange that he should have been sent to Europe in his eighteenth year by his guardians, the Duke of Bedford and Lord Trentham, ostensibly to acquire a knowledge of classics and art.

His companion on his travels was Robert Wood, the Irish scholar and archæologist. The pair were ill-suited as companions, and Wood had much difficulty with his pupil, who insisted on buying huge Egyptian marbles and tables and, having done so, leaving them in their packing-cases and taking no further notice of them. Many of them, in fact, were found exactly as they had been packed after the Duke died.

Returning to England, he bought horses and raced. He often rode them himself, for he was a feather-weight, though in later years he became corpulent.

That, briefly, is the career of the Duke of Bridgewater to the time when he broke off his engagement with the pretty widow.

Bridgewater changed completely. The reckless, eccentric man about town became a serious and intelligent individual, anxious to do something for the benefit of the country and industry.

He conceived the idea of building a canal from Horsley to Manchester, a distance of seven miles. He enlisted the aid of his steward, John Gilbert, and James Brindley. The Duke possessed at Horsley a rich and extensive coalfield which could not be developed to its greatest extent as there was no means of conveyance of the coal to a suitable market.

He conjectured that if he could get the commodity to Manchester he would make a fortune. He consulted Brindley, who produced the necessary plans, and then applied to Government for powers to construct a canal.

Bridgewater could not get his bill through Parliament without much difficulty. He was inexperienced in the wiles of politicians, while Brindley was handicapped by his want of education. Neither could explain lucidly to others the advantages of the canal.

Limiting his expenses to £400 a year, Bridgewater placed the remainder of his income at the disposal of Brindley for the building of the canal.

At length prejudice was overcome and the canal was completed in 1761.

Great additional expense was occasioned in earthwork and masonry because there were no locks. These were dispensed with as they were an impediment to navigation. An aqueduct across the River Irwell made another big hole in Bridgewater's budget. The latter was a huge undertaking which caused the most criticism.

Between 1761 and 1766 Brindley planned and executed for the Duke an extension of his canal, twenty-nine miles in length, ending at a junction with the estuary of the Mersey.

As the first part of the scheme had reduced the price of

coal at Manchester by 50 per cent, the promoters proceeded with the utmost confidence with the second part, which linked Manchester with Liverpool.

The opposition to the extension of the canal was even greater than to the first project. Bridgewater found himself up against the vested interests, and the landowners. The proprietors of the old Mersey and Irwell Navigation, who used these streams as waterways, fought the scheme tooth and nail.

Before the whole scheme was complete the Duke found himself in financial difficulties. But so great was the faith of his tenants that many of them lent him £5 or £10 to help him through.

When it was found that goods could be carried by canal at half the cost of the "Navigation" the new waterway also became a popular passenger route between Liverpool and Manchester. Fast fly-boats were utilized and were equipped with "refreshments saloons" or "coffee-houses," and one could even obtain a good glass of wine.

The Duke and Brindley argued that what was beneficial for Lancashire would be good for the rest of England. A scheme was therefore conceived of connecting the Mersey with the Severn and the Trent, and was carried into effect.

Investing in canals became a mania. All sorts of schemes were projected ; and all kinds of opposition raised by townships which would not have an artificial waterway within miles.

Canals, however, multiplied. Shares leapt up to prodigious heights. There is record of shares selling at £400 premium even before the first sod had been cut.

Bridgewater's income rose to £110,000 a year, as was shown by his income tax return. He was able, too, to subscribe £100,000 to the loyalty loan.

Although Brindley was the engineer in the Duke's projects, he did not have it all his own way. The "uneducated" Duke insisted upon his own ideas in the matter of detail.

The Duke died of influenza on March 8th, 1803, in his sixty-eighth year, at his mansion in London.

Towards the end of his life he became so corpulent that he resembled Dr. Johnson.

Maria Edgeworth

Maria Edgeworth was the inspiration of Scott's *Waverley Novels*.

This is not an extravagant statement. Scott himself has remarked that he was prompted to do for Scotland what she did for Ireland.

Says Scott: "Without being so presumptuous as to hope to emulate the rich humour, pathetic tenderness, and admirable tact which pervades the works of my accomplished friend, I felt that something might be attempted for my own country of the same kind with that which Miss Edgeworth so fortunately achieved for Ireland—something which might introduce her natives to those of the sister kingdom in a more favourable light than they had been placed hitherto, and tend to procure sympathy for their virtues and indulgence for their foibles."

To understand clearly what Maria Edgeworth did for Ireland it is necessary to recall the condition of that country in the latter part of the eighteenth century.

A statute of William III, called "An Act to Prevent the Growth of Popery," was still in operation. By this Catholics who had been educated abroad were deprived of their inheritance, their estates being confiscated to the next Protestant heir. Papists could not acquire property by purchase, and a Catholic priest who carried out his ordinary religious ministrations was liable to life imprisonment.

Some of these enactments were no longer enforced, but many Catholics were fearful that they might be produced against them at any time, for the Act was a weapon in the hands of informers.

The position between landlord and tenant was deplorable. It was generally a hopeless task for magistrates to judge fairly in the interminable squabbles brought before the Courts. The tenant was ground beneath the heels of the middle-man landlord, who demanded uneconomical rent.

In 1782 Richard Lovell Edgeworth, father of Maria, became a resident Irish landlord and a magistrate. He administered justice in a way that was not understood either by the rich or the poor. He insisted upon the fullest evidence before giving a judgment, an example that was followed at first reluctantly and afterwards agreeably by his brother magistrates.

Edgeworth's views were in advance of his time. His daughter Maria adopted them herself, and while she wrote her novels, her father was the inspiring genius until the time of his death.

She was brought into contact with his numerous tenantry, saw their mode of living, understood their wit and their good qualities. At the same time she was not blind to their vices.

The gentry living in the neighbourhood of Edgeworthtown, as the home of the Edgeworths was called, despised Richard Lovell because he was not a hard-drinker and was indifferent to field sports. Thus Maria was not often invited out. This did not worry her, for she was of a retiring disposition, was shy and reserved.

When about the age of 25 she wrote the *Letters for Literary Ladies*, but they were not published for several years. She then began the delightful set of stories which opened with the *Parent's Assistant*. This was followed by *Early Lessons*. The set concluded with *Harry and Lucy*.

These works were intended for children, but proved equally attractive to grown-ups. They were the joint works of herself and her father, though Edgeworth senior did not put pen to paper.

The next book they published "in partnership" was the *Essay on Irish Bulls*, full of factual anecdotes. The novel *Patronage* was invented by the father, and he conceived the leading characters.

At the beginning of the nineteenth century, Maria wrote *Castle Rackrent*, which appeared without her name. Like Scott's *Waverley*, it was history rather than fiction. It had the immediate effect of reforming the miserable state of society which it exposed. Her subsequent novels, chief among them being *Belinda* and *Helen*, maintained her reputation.

In 1817 Richard Lovell Edgeworth died, and she felt his loss intensely. During the next few years she found it difficult to continue her work. She passed those years in the society of friends in England, Scotland, and France, visiting Scott, Joanna Baillie, Rogers, Thomas Moore, and the scientists Davy, Wollaston, Herschel, and Cuvier.

In 1823 she resumed her literary labours, but in the course of a few years they were again interrupted by domestic cares.

The Edgeworths were a large family, for Richard Lovell had married four times. After her father's death, Maria became the mother of the establishment. She continued to write, however.

At the time of their appearance, and indeed since, her novels have been criticized because of the so-called improbable incidents which Maria introduced into them. Strangely, however, those incidents had a real existence.

Maria Edgeworth died on May 22nd, 1849. She expressed a wish that no life of her should be published. "My only remains shall be in the church at Edgeworthtown." All her correspondence was returned to its authors, for she regarded as a breach of trust the publishing of letters written in confidence.

She always suffered from feeble health and this trouble gradually increased as she got older.

Yet she would sit for hours writing on a little table in the corner of the Edgeworth library. On that small table Richard Lovell Edgeworth placed the following inscription :

"On this humble desk were written all the numerous works of my daughter, Maria Edgeworth. In these works, which were written to please me, she has never attacked the personal character of any human being, or interfered with the opinions of any sect of party, religious or political ; while endeavouring to inform and instruct others, she improved and amused her own mind and gratified her heart ; which I do believe is better than her head."

Trinity House

About the end of the twelfth century Stephen Langton, Archbishop of Canterbury, established a society of "Godly disposed men in the love of our Lord Christ, in the name of the Master and Fellows of Trinity Guild" to look after the English sea coast.

There were no lights to guide seafarers ; robbers descended on the towns and hamlets and pillaged to their hearts' content. There was no organization—and little disposition—to assist shipwrecked mariners.

There is little record of the early activities of this body, but it is known that two bands of such workers were in existence in the sixteenth century, one at Deptford and the other at Leigh, Essex.

In the reign of Henry VIII, Sir Thomas Spert, Comptroller of the Navy, and commander of the battleship *Henri Grace a Dieu*, founded a guild known as "The Master, Wardens, and Assistants of the Guild, or Fraternity, or Brotherhood of the Most Glorious and Undividable Trinity, and of St. Clement, in the Parish of Deptford Strond, in the county of Kent."

It was incorporated in 1529 and its headquarters were at Deptford.

It became known as Trinity House, and through the centuries has provided pilots, moved dangerous wrecks, erected and maintained lighthouses, lightships and other devices to simplify navigation.

During the reign of James I and Charles I, the brethren had a busy time suppressing the pirates who infested the English coasts. They had the disagreeable task of impressing seamen for the King's ships. In fact, until the end of the Stuarts, Trinity House did a great deal of the work that the Admiralty do to-day.

Pepys, the gossiper, was a Master of the Corporation in 1676, and again in 1685. Another important individual of the time—Andrew Marvell—was a younger warden of Trinity House in 1678.

The Corporation received a grant of arms from Queen Elizabeth in 1573, together with the right of erecting beacons and other marks for the guidance of seamen, and to collect tolls for their upkeep.

In 1604 a select class, called Elder Brethren, was established, the other members being called Younger Brethren. Five years later the Elder Brethren became responsible for the whole direction of affairs.

From its earliest days, Trinity House has been associated with charitable work. It is known that even before 1514 almshouses belonging to the Brethren were in existence at Deptford. These, of course, have been long since demolished, but others have taken their places in the East End of London for occupation by aged mariners.

When the Corporation's naval responsibilities were taken over by the Admiralty in the seventeenth century, the Brethren retained their right to light navigation and to examine and license pilots.

Until the year 1680 lighthouses around the coast were built by private individuals under a patent from the Crown, but in that year Trinity House erected the first of its own. Private rights in light dues existed until 1854, when they were abolished, and the exclusive right of lighting and placing buoys around the coast handed over to Trinity House.

The Corporation were also empowered to bind and enroll apprentices to the sea and examine mathematical masters for the Navy. They once ballasted ships leaving the Thames, and gave permission to old and maimed mariners to row "upon the river of Thames" without the usual licence from the Watermen's Company.

Foreigners serving in English ships had to obtain a licence from Trinity House. The Corporation, too, heard complaints between officers and men in the merchant service, and had power to punish for desertion and mutiny.

The Corporation had some quaint by-laws in early times. In the reign of James II every captain of a ship was required to "unshot" his guns at Gravesend. The penalty for disobedience was 20 nobles.

Every mariner who swore, cursed, or used blasphemous words was compelled to pay 1s. to the ship's poor-box. The penalty for drunkenness was 1s. ; a seaman who was absent from prayers without good excuse paid 6d.

The activities of the Brethren are carried out in an unpretentious building on Tower Hill. This building replaced an earlier one destroyed by fire at Deptford in 1714, and was built in 1793-95 from the designs of Samuel Wyatt. In 1795 the headquarters of the Brethren were transferred to it from temporary offices in Water Lane, Lower Thames Street. The earliest records of the Corporation were lost when the old building was burned.

Every Trinity Monday, in accordance with ancient custom, the Court of the Brotherhood of Trinity House meet for the election of the Master and Wardens for the next twelve months. Afterwards they attend a service in St. Olave's Church, Hart-Street, E.C.

The Office of Master has always been held by a distinguished individual. In the nineteenth century it was held in succession by Lord Liverpool, the Marquess Camden, the Duke of Clarence (afterwards William IV), the Duke of Wellington, the Prince Consort, Viscount Palmerston, the Duke of Edinburgh, and the Duke of York.

The present master is the Duke of Connaught.

The Corporation is now responsible for keeping 2400 miles of coast safe for seamen. It has over 60 lighthouses, more than 40 lightships, and a fleet of about ten steamers. About a thousand men are employed by them in safeguarding life at sea.

The Trinity Brethren wear a uniform that is similar to naval uniform. The buttons, however, bear the arms of the House, and there are three bars of gold lace on the outside of the cuff, placed lengthwise instead of across. The arms are a cross, between four ships under sail.

It was once the custom every Trinity Monday for the Corporation to embark from Tower Wharf, and proceed in state barges down the river to Deptford Green, where they were received by the vicar and parish officers. There was also a procession to Trinity Hospital, and the Corporation's almshouses, where the floor was strewn with green rushes according to tradition.

After the election of Master and Wardens, the procession re-formed and made its way to St. Nicholas Church, led by two maidens in white who cast flowers along the route. When the Duke of Wellington died in 1852, the Trinity Monday visits to Deptford were discontinued, and since then the Brethren have met at Trinity House for the purpose of the election.

The Church of St. Olave, where the service is held, is one of the most ancient in London. It survived the Great Fire. In this church Samuel Pepys and his wife are buried in a vault by the Communion Table.

In *The Uncommercial Traveller* Dickens refers to the gateway of St. Olave's as the entrance to "one of my best-beloved churchyards. I call it the churchyard of Ghastly Grim."

There are many things of interest to the visitor at Trinity. There are busts and portraits of many of the great people in the history of Britain. There is a candle sconce, in which stand twelve old wax candles similar to those which lit the Eddystone Lighthouse until 1810. This was Smeaton's Eddystone Lighthouse, long since passed away.

Samuel Wyatt, who designed Trinity House, was thought to have transferred his own vein of humour to the building, for some years ago it was found that the angle of the front and right-hand side walls were wider than a right-angle.

But Wyatt was neither careless nor humorous so far as the design was concerned. He intended that the building should stand square with the side street and with Tower Hill. The strange corners inside the building are noticeable, but are hidden by specially made tables.

Gregory VII

Through the slotted windows of his castle of Canossa, Pope Gregory VII regarded the shivering man who stood by the gate.

There was a gleam of triumph in the eyes of the Pontiff. The man's forlorn condition, his bare feet covered by inches of snow, the common sackcloth around his loins, evoked no pity in the stony heart.

How many times had the great Emperor Henry IV knocked for admittance? Neither the guards of the gate, who had surreptitiously given him bread, Henry himself, nor the Pope had kept count.

For three days the Emperor had renewed his entreaties for forgiveness, but Gregory had refused to give audience to his excommunicated enemy. Meanwhile the winter drifts had piled up on the ground, and the sombre walls of the fortress had become a silhouette of white.

Pope Gregory VII, formerly Hildebrand, the son of a carpenter, had reached the pinnacle of his power. Henry, who had been his most determined foe, was at his mercy. For four years there had been bitter strife for supremacy between Church and State. The Church had won, and the chief instigator of the revolt against papal power was now humbled and repentant—or so it seemed.

It was on the fourth morning that Gregory relented. By that time the Emperor was willing to grovel at the feet of his tormentor.

He passed into the palace, received absolution, and departed, his ears tingling with the scathing words of the Pope.

But Henry IV, Emperor of Germany, was only chastened; he was not beaten.

A ruthless Pope would have removed his enemy from his

path for ever. Gregory was content to believe that the contrition of the Emperor was genuine. In that he erred, for the final blow came from Henry. It knocked the Pope from his pedestal to die in exile.

Gregory was one of the greatest of Popes, but there has always been diversity of opinion about his character and conduct. He was the first to establish the doctrine of papal supremacy in temporal as well as spiritual matters, and if he himself did not live to see the consummation of that principle, about a century afterwards Innocent III was able to celebrate such a victory.

Hildebrand was born about the year 1013 in Tuscany, though he is said to have been of German origin. He was educated at Rome and became a member of the Benedictine order.

It was a dark time for Europe. Rulers warred against each other, and there were popes and anti-popes striving for power.

In 1046 Gregory VI was forced into exile by two anti-popes. He took with him his friend Hildebrand. They went to the monastery of Cluny in France, and there they remained, Hildebrand passing some years in retirement.

About 1049 Leo IX called Hildebrand to Rome and made him cardinal. He proved a worthy lieutenant to the Pope, co-operating in his schemes for reform and the aggrandizement of the Church.

On April 22, 1073, Hildebrand was chosen Pope, adopted the name Gregory, and immediately began to show proof of his vigour. His ambition was to build a theocracy that would rule over the whole of Europe.

He argued the system of papal omnipotence in twenty-seven theses in his *Dictatus*. The eleventh of these maxims declared that "the Pope's name is the chief name in the world"; the twelfth affirmed that "it is lawful for him to depose emperors"; the eighteenth that "his decision is to be withstood by none, but he alone may annul those of all men."

Thus the Pope vested in himself the power to depose and restore bishops and to annul the allegiance of subjects.

The power of appointing bishops and clergy generally was in the hands of the emperors, and for many years they had sought to retain that right against the growing power of Rome.

There was a great deal to admire in Gregory VII. He did his utmost to clean up the abuses in the Church, to purify the altar and to brand simony. There may be differences of opinion, however, on his vast project to treat Catholic kingdoms as if they were fiefs of the Church. But—other days, other manners.

Gregory's attempt to turn monarchs into puppets was naturally resisted. War began between the mitre and the empire.

The young Henry IV had other troubles besides Gregory VII. A Saxon rebellion induced him to come to terms with the Pope at any cost. Therefore, in May 1074, the Emperor appeared before the papal legates at Nuremburg to do penance and to take an oath of obedience to Gregory. He promised further to help the Pope to reform the Church.

Having gained the upper hand of the Saxons at the battle of Hohenburg in June 1075, he began to reassert his rights in Upper Italy. Reprimands from Gregory upset Henry and his court. He pronounced the deposition of the Pope, and called upon the Romans to choose a new candidate for the Papal chair. The bishops renounced their allegiance to Gregory, and an envoy was sent to inform Gregory of that fact.

In Germany itself, however, there was a revulsion in favour of Gregory, and the princes met to elect a new German king. Henry was saved through their inability to agree on a successor. They decided that if Henry—who had been excommunicated—remained a year under the Pope's ban, the throne was to be considered vacant.

Although Gregory sustained occasional reverses, in the long run he gained steadily upon the empire. Discord was spread through Europe. "From Denmark even to Apulia, from Carlingen to Hungary, have the arms of the empire been turned against its own vitals."

Spiritual and temporal principles had hitherto acted in collaboration. Now everything was confusion.

"*The rulers of holy Church—archbishops, bishops and priests to wit—these thou hast trodden beneath thy feet as were they slaves,*" wrote Henry IV to Gregory. "*In trampling on whom, thou hast gained applause from the mouths of the populace.*"

It was at a low state of his fortunes that Henry went to Canossa and was at length allowed to do penance. The reconciliation was not definitely effected until after long negotiation and pledges by the Emperor.

The absolution of Henry had no immediate effect upon his recalcitrant nobles. They set up a rival king of Germany in the person of Duke Rudolph of Swabia, in March 1077. Gregory tried to remain neutral, but eventually had to side with Rudolph.

Again Gregory pronounced the excommunication and deposition of Henry. The frequent deposition of each other has its humorous side, despite the tragedy involved.

Rudolph died in October 1080, and in the following year a new claimant to the throne was put forward—Hermann of Luxemburg.

Henry now called a council and induced them to pronounce the deposition of Gregory, and in 1081 began hostilities against the Pope.

Thirteen cardinals deserted Gregory. Henry strengthened his party, and gathered more adherents around him. He raised up the anti-pope Clement III.

Henry marched on Rome and attacked the city. It withstood a two-years' siege, and then capitulated.

Though the Pope had many faithful friends, including the Countess Matilda, who ruled extensive territories in Italy, he found himself no longer a match for the growing power of the Emperor.

Gregory was compelled to call to his aid the Normans of the north of Italy, whom he had actually excommunicated not long since. They came forward and gave him valuable assistance.

But the star of Gregory VII was in the descendant. Robert Guiscard, Duke of Apulia and Sicily, and Gregory had to escape hurriedly from Rome. They took refuge at Salerno, where, on May 25th, 1085, Gregory VII died.

"I have loved justice, and hated iniquity, and therefore I die in exile," he muttered on his death-bed.

Captain Forrest

It was surely the shortest council of war in history.

"Gentlemen, you see the force of the enemy," said Captain Arthur Forrest, of H.M.S. *Augusta*, "is it your resolution to fight them or not ?"

"It is," came the prompt reply.

That was all that was said. The commanders of the *Dreadnought* and the *Edinburgh* returned to their ships. The council of war had lasted half a minute !

Within an hour or two the three British vessels went into action against a French squadron of four ships of the line and three frigates.

It was the year 1757. Britain was at war with France. The scenes of action changed rapidly from the Mediterranean and the Channel to the West Indies. Victories were won on both sides. Many gallant fights, small compared with the major actions, are not to be found in general histories of the period. The battle off Cape François is one.

The circumstances which led to Captain Forrests's command of the three ships are interesting.

He belonged to an impoverished Scottish family and went to sea early. He served as lieutenant in a ship under the command of Admiral Vernon in the unsuccessful expedition against Carthagena, and in other actions, in which he distinguished himself in the years 1741 and 1742.

In March 1745 he was promoted to the rank of post captain, and appointed to the *Wager*. A year later he was with this ship on the Jamaica station, and here he captured a large Spanish privateer of 36 guns and over 200 men, which had been doing considerable damage to British shipping in the Windward Passage.

For several years Forrest appears to have had a period of inactivity. There was nothing unusual in such an experience, for an officer with a fine record would often find himself dropped temporarily for no apparent reason.

In 1755 Forrest was appointed to the *Rye*, and soon afterwards removed to the *Augusta* and ordered to the West Indies.

In October 1757 the *Augusta* was detached by the Commander-in-Chief, Rear-Admiral Cotes, with the *Edinburgh* and

Dreadnought, to cruise off Cape François. The French were preparing to leave that port with a large convoy for Europe under the command of De Kersaint.

On October 21st the French commodore left the harbour with his seven ships, hoping that this superiority would induce Forrest to quit his station. The names of the vessels were : *L'Intrepide, Le Sceptre, L'Opiniatre, Greenwich, L'Outarde. La Sauvage*, and *La Licorne*, the whole having a complement of 3880 men and an armament of 300 guns.

In addition to the seamen, the ships had a large number of soldiers on board.

Of Forrest's ships, the *Augusta* and *Edinburgh* badly needed reconditioning. The enemy's superiority, however, failed to frighten him.

A furious battle raged for two hours and a half. At the end of that time De Kersaint's ship was in such a disabled condition that he had to signal a frigate to tow him out of the line.

The following is the unromantic official report of Admiral Cotes :

On the 25th of last month, Captain Forrest in the *Augusta*, with the *Dreadnought* and *Edinburgh* under his command, returned from the cruise off Cape François. On the 21st they fell in with seven French ships of war. At seven in the morning the *Dreadnought* made the signal for seeing the enemy's fleet coming out of Cape François, and at noon discovered with certainty they were four ships of the line and three frigates.

Captain Forrest then made the signal for the captains, Suckling and Langdon, who agreed with him to engage them. Accordingly they all bore down, and about twenty minutes after three the action began with great briskness on both sides. It continued for about two hours and a half, when the French commodore making a signal, one of the frigates immediately came to tow him out of the line, and the rest of the French ships followed him. . . .

The French on this occasion had put on board the *Sceptre* her full complement of guns, either from the shore or out of the India ships, and had also mounted the *Outarde* store ship with her full proportion of guns, and had taken not only the men out of the merchant ships, but soldiers from the garrison, in hopes their appearance would frighten our small squadron, and oblige them to leave the coast clear for them to carry out their large convoy of merchant ships ; but our captains were too gallant to be terrified at their formidable appearance. . . . I hope their good behaviour will be approved by their lordships.

The French squadron made for Cape François. The *Opiniatre* had no masts; the *Greenwich* leaked. About 600 French were killed and wounded. The British losses were about 120 killed and wounded.

Although this action did not stop the sailing of the French convoy, it delayed it for so long that it struck bad weather and several of the ships were wrecked.

In December of the same year Captain Forrest had a further opportunity of distinguishing himself.

It was learned that a large French convoy was preparing to sail from Port au Prince to Europe, and Forrest was ordered to cruise in the vicinity. On the following day Forrest's ship, the *Augusta*, sailed into the bay between the islands of Gonaives and St. Domingo. There the captain saw two sloops and hoisted Dutch colours as a disguise.

At five o'clock in the evening seven more ships appeared and sailed westward. Forrest made no move until dark. Then he set off in pursuit.

At ten o'clock he came up with two, one of which opened fire. At the same time eight more ships were seen to leeward.

Coming up to the ship that had fired the gun, Forrest ordered her commander to strike. The Frenchman submitted, and a lieutenant and 35 men were put on board as a prize crew.

At daylight the *Augusta* found herself in the middle of the convoy. There were 10 ships, who made a feeble show of opposition. After firing a few guns they struck.

It was found that these prizes carried cargoes of sugar, indigo, coffee and cotton. the value of which was £170,000. They were conducted to Jamaica and sold.

Forrest soon afterwards came to England, but in January 1760 again sailed for Jamaica with a convoy, and he continued to serve on that station until the end of the war.

On the death of Rear-Admiral Holmes in November 1761, Forrest became commander, but had no further opportunities for increasing his reputation.

In 1769 he was appointed commodore and retained the Jamaica command. He died on the 26th of May in the following year.

There is still in existence a copy of the standing orders to the fleet issued "By Arthur Forrest Esq." Some of the regulations make quaint reading in these days.

One has a flavour of espionage.   It reads :

"When you are in any foreign port, you are to make particular observations of its strength, fortifications, yards, docks, ships, advantages and disadvantages in point of defence, and how it may be most advantageously attacked in case of a rupture ; likewise ships of war, trade, and such other observations as may occur to you, and tend to the honour of his Majesty's arms.   All which you are, at your return, to deliver to me in writing, signed by yourself, together with a journal of your proceedings during your cruise."

Margaret Plantagenet, Countess of Salisbury

In Christchurch Priory, Hampshire, there is a memorial to the everlasting disgrace of Henry VIII.

It commemorates a brave woman, a victim of the King's personal malice, who died on the gallows innocent of any crime.

She was Margaret Plantagenet, Countess of Salisbury, a daughter of the famous Earl of Warwick, the "King-maker." Because her son, Cardinal Reginald Pole, had espoused the cause of the Pope against Henry, the King took the drastic step of exterminating the family.

The Countess's grey hairs evoked no pity in the heart of the monarch.   Nor was Henry stirred by the fact that she was the only remaining Plantagenet of unblemished descent.

In the Priory is a chapel erected by Margaret, Countess of Salisbury, for her own burial-place when in course of time she was destined to need it.   The noble family of the Montacutes, Earls of Salisbury, were the chief individual patrons of the priory church.   The tower at the west end was built by them in the fifteenth century, and the chantries in the north transept were raised by them.

Margaret Plantagenet had a tragic life as well as death. Her only brother, to her great sorrow, was unjustly executed by Henry VII.   After this she married Sir Richard Pole, a supporter and relative of the King.

When she was widowed with three sons, one of whom was Reginald, afterwards the Cardinal, Henry VII appears to have taken pity on her and created her Countess of Salisbury in her own right.

Reginald Pole was educated at the Carthusian monastery at Sheen, and at Magdalen College. According to Froude all this was carried out "under the king's eye and at the king's expense."

He took deacon's orders and soon received valuable preferments from Henry VIII. When the question of Queen Catherine's divorce arose, Pole was to be found on the side of those who opposed the measure, despite the fact that he was almost certain to get the Archbishopric of York on the death or retirement of Wolsey.

But Henry was not yet offended with Pole. It was not until the latter declared open war, and deliberately supported the Pope against Henry's claim to be head of the church, that the King struck.

The chief result of Pole's activity was to procure his own attainder, and eventually to bring his brother, Lord Montacute, and his mother to the block.

Thus, in 1538, Lord Montacute and Sir Geoffrey Pole, Reginald's brothers, were suddenly arrested, with the Marquess of Exeter and others.

A vague charge was made against them that they had supported Pole—who, in the meantime, had become a Cardinal—and they must be adjudged enemies of the King.

The youngest son, Geoffrey, pleaded guilty and made a confession which involved all the others, on being promised a pardon. Lord Montacute and the Marquess of Exeter were beheaded on Tower Hill.

A month afterwards a French vessel was wrecked on the English coast. When an examination was made of the wreckage, it was asserted that certain papers were found which implicated others in the alleged plot against the King. Further arrests took place, and Parliament were now instructed to issue bills of attainder against the relatives of those who had been apprehended.

They included the Countess of Salisbury, her grandson the child of Lord Montacute, and the widow of the Marquess of Exeter. Two knights were also attainted.

The Countess, then seventy years old, with grey hair and a dignified yet pathetic mien, was ordered to appear for examination before the Earl of Southampton and the Bishop of Ely. She proved an enigma to her accusers. She answered all their questions satisfactorily, and when they were called upon to report to the King, they had to confess that she had disclosed nothing to her detriment.

They declared that she was more like a powerful man than a woman. She denied all the charges, and it seemed to them that either she was not privy to the activities of her sons, or she was an accomplished actress and "the most arrant traitress that ever lived."

Some of the Countess's servants were now examined and, it is suggested, given money or threatened with punishment if they did not implicate their mistress.

But this did not bring any material evidence against the accused and certainly not sufficient for a criminal trial.

Henry, however, now proceeded to obtain a bill of attainder without trial. Parliament granted the bill and thus showed itself once more the tool of the King.

The two knights met their deaths on the scaffold; the Marchioness of Exeter received a pardon some months later. History is silent about what became of the young son of Lord Montacute.

As to the Countess, she remained in doubt about her fate for two years. Then, when everyone believed that the whole affair was settled, the people of England were horrified to hear that the aged woman had been dragged to the block.

Pole, who had escaped abroad, was continuing his activities and giving further provocation to Henry. Thus the innocent had to suffer for the guilty.

The execution of Margaret, Countess of Salisbury, which took place on May 27th, 1541, was one of the most degrading scenes in the history of England. The deaths of Mary, Queen of Scots, and Lady Jane Grey were made less revolting because of their passive attitude to the headsman's axe.

On the other hand, the spirited Countess fought with all the strength that her seventy years could muster.

She refused to put her head on the block at the behest of the executioner, exclaiming: "No! My head never committed treason. If you will have it, you must take it as you can."

She darted round the stage, the man in pursuit. A second executioner was called in to help.

The Countess tossed her head from side to side so that it was impossible for them to get in a direct blow. Her hair fell in disorder over her throat.

At length the headsmen forced her to the block and completed their task.

One would have thought that Henry VIII would have been satisfied with this awful picture which his genius had conjured up to "encourage the others."

But no. His vengeance was carried to greater lengths. At the time of the Dissolution his agents, with great glee, reported on their visit to Christchurch Priory :

In the church we found a chapel and monument made of Caen stone, prepared by the late mother of Reginald Pole for her burial, which we have caused to be defaced, and all the arms and badges clearly to be deleted.

Jane Lewson

There is not a more striking example of the saying that death is a great leveller than Bunhill Fields Cemetery, which seems to intrude itself into London's City Road, a relic of another age and entirely out of keeping with the commerce of this busy thoroughfare.

It is the last resting-place of great and small, rich and pauper. Here are the ashes of John Bunyan, Daniel Defoe, John Horne Tooke, Isaac Watts, William Blake, Susannah Wesley (mother of John), and many others.

An Act of 1867 has preserved the graveyard as an open space, so that a disturbance of these vaults is unlikely. People can sit on the benches and look round the thousands of grey stones, many of which bear inscriptions denoting the character of the persons there buried.

But there is one grave that would be difficult to find, although it is little more than a hundred years old. It is that of an eccentric old woman named Jane Lewson, who died at the age of 116 and whose funeral was attended by a large concourse of curious sightseers.

Jane Lewson was a rich woman, who had lived in Cold Bath Square, Clerkenwell, for ninety years, a widow. Her eccentric conduct and mode of living had made her notorious if not popular, while her extravagant dress, which was an incongruous accompaniment to her unwashed face and hands, caused her to be called "Lady" Lewson.

She is said to have been born in the year 1700, during the

reign of William and Mary, in Essex Street, Strand. Her maiden name was Vaughan, but little is known of her parents except that they were honest and industrious.

She married at the age of 16 a man named Lewson, who was wealthy and had a comparatively sumptuous house in Cold Bath Square. When she was 26 her husband died, leaving her with a daughter.

Having plenty of money, she remained single, though many suitors came to offer their hands.

Jane Lewson's daughter married and the mother became a recluse, rarely venturing out or allowing anyone to visit her.

During the last thirty years of her life she kept an old woman servant, who, when she died, was succeeded by her granddaughter. The latter remained with "Lady" Lewson only a short time and then married.

The old woman then took into her service an old man. He did duty as butler, cook and housemaid. The only other occupants of the house were two lap-dogs and a cat.

The house was lavishly, even gaily, furnished. There were many bedrooms, each of which had its bed, ready, if necessary, for a visitor, but guests were never encouraged.

Though the beds were constantly made, none of the rooms was ever cleaned. Her own apartment was occasionally swept, but never washed. Very little light came through the dirt-encrusted windows.

The old woman argued that if the rooms were washed, she would catch cold, and she refused to have the windows cleaned as many accidents occurred through that "ridiculous practice," and she would be responsible if such did happen.

A large garden at the back of the house was always kept in order, and here she sat and read, or talked to acquaintances over the wall.

She went out only to a grocer's, and having no relatives she indulged her odd tastes without interference.

But the quaintest thing about "Lady" Lewson was her dress. She always wore fashions that were popular in her youth, and she never changed from the mode that prevailed at the time of George I.

Thus, when she was seen in the street, which was not often, spectators had a vision of a woman dressed like pictures of Queen Anne, and carrying a long, gold-topped walking-stick, tottering slowly along.

Her dress was generally of silk, with a long train, a deep flounce all round, and a very long waist. Her gown was tightly laced up to her neck, round which was a ruff or frill. Her headgear was a flat bonnet, and she affected high-heeled shoes and a large black silk coat, trimmed round with lace.

This was her everyday costume for over eighty years, and in this she would walk round her square.

"Lady" Lewson was never known to wash herself. Those people who did so, she declared, caught cold. She would smear her face and neck all over with hog's lard. She found this was most "soft and lubricating." But, to add a little colour to her cheeks, she would daub them with rose pink.

Almost at her door was the Coldbath, after which her square was named. This was fed by a spring, discovered in 1697, and reputed to have healing properties.

According to the advertisement of the owner, the cold bath from this spring "prevents and cures cold, creates appetite, helps digestion, and makes hardy the tenderest constitution."

The bathing hours were from five a.m. to one, the charge being two shillings unless the visitor was so infirm as to make it necessary for him to be let down into the pool.

In her younger days "Lady" Lewson would stand and watch the patients arriving, a smile of disdain on her face, for she had an antipathy both for baths and medical treatment. She always enjoyed good health and despised those who did not.

At the age of 83 "Lady" Lewson cut two new teeth. She always boasted that she had never suffered with toothache.

She had a vivid memory and could, when she felt disposed, discuss the great events that occurred during four reigns. Her pet subject was the strife between the Hanoverians and the Jacobites, and she could recall the Rebellion of 1715.

At the age of 116 she decided that her time had come. On May 28th, 1816, therefore, she lay down and passed away. She had never been attended by a doctor.

A Clerkenwell historian writes :

At her death I went over the house, and was struck with astonishment at the number of bars, bolts, etc., to the whole of the doors and windows ; the ceilings of the upper floor were completely lined with strong boards, braced together with iron bars, to prevent anyone getting into the house from the roof,

The ashes had not been removed for many years; they were neatly piled up, as if formed into beds for some particular purpose, around the yard. Her furniture, etc., was sold by auction, and persons were admitted to view by producing a catalogue, which was sold at sixpence, and would permit any number of persons at one time.

Restoration of Charles II, 1660

As soon as Charles II was safely established on the throne, hundreds of petitions began to pour in.

Those who were responsible for dispensing patronage found themselves inundated with applications.

Parsons wanted their pulpits back; noblemen their honours; landed proprietors their estates. Others requested rewards for loyalty to the ill-fated Charles I; office-bearers who had been kicked out by "Noll" emphasized their distress, expressed pleasure at the King's restoration, and, in effect, said: "What about it?"

In fact, it would seem that half the educated people of the country were busy writing: "May it please Your Majesty."

So Secretary Nicholas floundered in a heap of wordy pleas from early morning till late at night, destroying some and recommending a few to the clemency of his master.

In the Calendar of State Papers for 1660, some of these petitions are preserved.

One, from a score of officers of the troop of the Marquess of Hertford, asked for pensions; for the "late King" had promised that they should receive "the same pay as long as they lived." These gallant gentlemen had lost no time in making their application, for it was dated May 29th, the official date of Charles's restoration.

A "quartermaster of artillery" requested the position of King's painter on the ground that Charles I "had promised him the office on seeing a cannon painted by him when he came with artillery after the taking of Hawksby House."

A Colonel Dudley, of the Artillery, asked for reward because he had lost an estate valued at £200 a year, £2000 in money, had had his sick wife turned out of doors and his men taken.

One of his officers had been "miserably burned with matches, and himself stripped and carried in scorn to

Worcester, which he had fortified as general of artillery, where he was kept under double guard; but escaped, and being pursued, he took to the trees in the day-time, and travelled in the night till he got to London; was retaken, brought before the Committee of Insurrection, sent to the gatehouse, and sentenced to be shot; but escaped with Sir H. Bates and ten others during sermon-time; lived three weeks in an enemy's hay-mow, went on crutches to Bristol, and escaped."

Many soldiers asked for compensation. One wanted a place in the King's barge, because he had been often imprisoned; had been twice tried for his life, and three times turned off the river. Another, who sustained fifteen wounds at the Battle of Edgehill, asked for a palliative in hard cash. A comrade who declared that the "barbarous soldiers of the grand rebel, Cromwell, hung him on a tree till they thought him dead," pleaded to be included.

An officer requested the return of thirty of his men who, after being taken prisoner at Salisbury, were "sold as slaves in Barbadoes."

John Fowler, who fought at Worcester, recorded in his petition that he was sent to Barbadoes, and underwent the penalty "with satisfaction and content."

It is generally thought that Oliver Cromwell did not encourage gambling, but we have the authority of one petitioner that this was not the case, for he declared that he was compelled to throw dice for his life and having won was banished the country.

Harrowing tales were told by some of the suppliants. A clergyman said his mother was beaten to death, his servant killed, and he was deprived of property worth £300 a year. Another gentleman of the cloth recorded that he was imprisoned for three years and twice flogged for preaching against rebellion and using the Book of Common Prayer.

One Abraham Dowsett claimed compensation for supplying the late King with pen and ink at the risk of losing his life, carried letters between him and Henrietta Maria, and helped to scheme Charles's escape from Carisbrooke Castle. For this he was imprisoned and his property was confiscated.

Two brothers named Samburne deserved the gratitude of Charles II if their claims were correct. According to their statement they spent £25,000 in supplying war material to their armies, transmitted letters for the Royal family "when no one else would sail," and when Charles II sought refuge at Rouen after his defeat at Worcester, James Samburne was the only person who was in the secret of the Prince's identity. In return for all these good offices they asked for the commissionership of excise.

There were many women among the petitioners. Katherine de Luke was anxious to obtain the lease of certain waste lands near Yarmouth for suffering torture in the Royal cause. For carrying letters she was sent to prison, whipped every other day, and burned with matches.

For carrying the King's proclamation from Oxford to London, Elizabeth Cary was imprisoned successively in Windsor Castle, Newgate, Bridewell, the house of the Bishop of London, and finally in the Royal Mews. But this was not all. The Roundhead soldiers broke her back at Henley-on-Thames while trying to hang her on a gibbet. Charles II rewarded this loyalty with a pension of £40 a year.

A certain Mary Graves had as good a claim as anyone. When Charles II made his last bid for the throne she lent him twelve horses and ten men and money. On one of the animals Charles escaped after the battle of Worcester. The woman lost an estate of £600 a year and property worth £2,000.

These misfortunes did not deter the loyal Mary Graves. She induced her husband to send provisions from Ireland to Chester to assist the rising of Sir George Booth. Again she was imprisoned and the remainder of her property confiscated.

Mary Graves supplemented her first petition with another. In this she said that she sent one of her men, Francis Yates, to assist Charles's escape from Worcester to Whitehaven. For this the man had been hanged and she had had to support his widow and children. These particulars were certified by Richard Penderel, who conducted Charles to the safety of Boscobel House after his defeat.

Many quaint claims are listed. An old man of 95 asked to be given back his office of cormorant-keeper ; another who, in his early days, was keeper of the king's tennis shoes and socks, also wanted his job back.

Of course, Charles II was unable to grant all the petitions, genuine or otherwise. Some of the worst cases had their claims allowed ; but it can be seen from the large number of complaints that many were unsuccessful.

James Gillray

An agent for a printseller had been instructed to get a satirical design etched by James Gillray. He had called repeatedly at the artist's house only to find him out each time.

On the day before the work was due to be finished the agent called again. This time Gillray was at home.

"You have lost a good job and a useful patron, Gillray," said he.

"Oh," replied the artist, "how's that ?"

"I wanted this subject drawn and etched, but it is now too late."

"When is it wanted ?"

"To-morrow."

"It shall be done."

"Impossible, Gillray."

It was then 11 o'clock in the morning.

"I'll bet you a bowl of punch," said Gillray, "that it will be completed, etched and bitten in, and in proof before four o'clock."

"Done !" said the other.

The agent went about his other business. Returning at four, he was surprised to find everything ready. Gillray had achieved an extraordinary feat, for there were many figures on the plate.

Forthwith they both adjourned to the Gray's Inn Coffee-House and got drunk.

Gillray was not only a distinguished engraver, but was one of the best caricaturists. The facility with which he drew his pictures and the rapidity with which he etched them astonished eye-witnesses.

In the works of Gillray there is a pictorial record of English history during the greater part of the reign of George III. Gillray had all the assets of the good caricaturist—a keen sense of the ludicrous, a knowledge of human nature, the ability to reason and argue, and an appreciation of the follies of others.

Little is known of his early life. He is said to have been born at Chelsea in 1757; was apprenticed to Ashby, the well-known engraver, and was afterwards a pupil or assistant with the famous Francis Bartolozzi.

Gillray first appeared as a caricaturist in 1782, and for more than twenty-five years he produced his satirical drawings in extraordinary numbers. They are said to total more than twelve hundred. He attacked every party and every individual in the public eye.

He lampooned the King and his Tory Ministers, but the Prince Regent (George IV) was the particular object of Gillray's pen. The Whigs, as supporters of the French Revolution, met with little mercy. His caricatures of Edmund Burke, Charles James Fox, and Pitt are among his best, if somewhat brutal.

Before Gillray's time it was usual for these satires to be published anonymously, but he boldly put his name to his productions.

Gillray had periods of insanity. During these times he was carefully watched by Miss Humphrey, a printseller who lived in St. James's Street, Piccadilly. He lived in her house and kept her business going with his caricatures.

It is said that they once determined on matrimony. Arm-in-arm, they were on their way to church when they both suddenly stopped in the street. They looked at each other, read each other's thoughts, and then turned round and walked home again.

Some writers charge Gillray with blackmail. One biographer writes :

He would, by his publications, either divulge family secrets which ought to have been ever at rest, or expect favours for the plates which he destroyed. This talent, by which he made many worthy persons so uneasy, was inimitable ; and his works, though time may destroy every point of their sting, will remain specimens of a rare power, both for character and composition.

Often Gillray was threatened with violence. Fox was once disposed to prosecute him because he had portrayed him as a sensualist. Burke usually appeared as a half-starved Jesuit, and Sheridan as a portly individual with a large red nose.

These three politicians, after considering what could be done with Gillray, finally contented themselves with laughing at the caricatures of each other.

In Miss Humphrey's house he had every opportunity for obtaining all the news of the day, for his unconscious victims passed frequently up and down St. James's Street. Gillray sat behind a window and sketched them rapidly as they appeared.

At last his over-taxed imagination, the feverish working, the etching and printing, told upon his mind. His mental powers failed completely, and his caricatures which had upset the politicians gradually ceased. Now and again his sanity returned, but in 1811 his pen finally stopped working.

During the last four years of his life he was poverty-stricken and was supported by Miss Humphrey.

One morning Gillray was found insensible on the pavement below his window. He had thrown himself out. He died on June 1st, 1815.

General Sir Redvers Buller

In October 1899, General Sir Redvers Buller went to South Africa to command the field forces, supported by the goodwill and the high hopes of the whole nation.

Exactly a year later he returned to England to face adverse criticism on his conduct of the Boer War campaign. If, however, officialdom was critical, Buller remained in the eyes of the public one of the most picturesque of figures, his fame as a soldier untarnished.

Indeed, it is doubtful whether complete success would have brought him a greater measure of popularity. People felt that he was a great man with whom fate had dealt unkindly. And, as subsequent events proved, the public were right, for it was shown that his failure was due to the lack of understanding by others of the big task in hand.

But the cheering of the mob cannot console a great man who is under a cloud, and Sir Redvers Buller died disappointed and chagrined.

Buller arrived in South Africa to find Ladysmith invested, and a grave situation in Natal. Pessimistic dispatches began to arrive in England. In December his first attempt to cross the Tugela River was repulsed with heavy loss. The Government became alarmed and sent out Lord Roberts to supersede Buller in the chief command, the latter being left in the subordinate command of the Natal forces.

A second attempt to relieve Ladysmith in the following January achieved no better result, the Spion Kop operations causing further alarm at home. Following a third unsuccessful attempt in February, the Natal army accomplished its task in the series of actions which culminated in the Pieter's Hill victory, and Ladysmith was relieved on February 27th.

Sir Redvers Buller remained in command of the Natal army until October 1900. He then returned to England and was created G.C.M.G. Meanwhile he had done a great deal of work driving the Boers from the Biggarsberg in May, and forcing Lang's Nek in June. These actions, together with the occupation of Lydenberg which was effected just before Buller left for home, helped to re-establish his reputation as a dogged fighter, although it did not dispel the doubt about his capacity to command important and delicate operations.

Thus, when it was decided to continue his appointment to the Aldershot command, there was vigorous Press criticism in which it was recalled that Buller had seriously contemplated the surrender of Ladysmith.

On October 10th, 1901, Sir Redvers, at a luncheon in London, made a speech in answer to the criticisms. The language he used was regarded as a breach of discipline, and a few days later he was placed on half-pay. In his retirement as a country gentleman he was still subjected to pin-pricks in connection with his alleged failures in South Africa.

Buller was immensely popular among his men, the great secret of which was his bravery. The most outstanding incident in his career was the way in which he gained the Victoria Cross.

In the Zulu War of 1879, Buller, then a major, was the first to ascend the Inhlobane Mountain in the grey dawn. He was the last to descend when his forces were compelled to retreat before a body of 23,000 Zulus. The retirement was down dangerous slopes which he and seven men held against the savage enemy while the rest sought safety. In that terrible retreat Buller personally saved the lives of our men.

The following is a testimony by a contemporary of Buller's services in the Zulu War.

"Here was a man with £6,000 a year, a beautiful house in fair Devon waiting for his occupation, a seat in Parliament all but secure, and yet for the patriotic love of leading that strange medley of reckless adventurers, he was living squalidly in the South African veldt, sleeping in the open for three nights out of the six with a single blanket thrown over his body, his hands so disfigured by cattle sores, the curse of the veldt, that I never saw them not bandaged up.

"With his intrepid heroism he had saved the lives of so many of his men that in talking to them it seemed almost that he had saved all their lives.

"A strange, stern, strong-tempered man, whose pride it seemed to be to repress all his own emotion and to smother its display to others. He would order a man peremptorily back to his duty who came into his tent to ask him to read a letter in which a mother thanked him for saving the life of her son.

"When the officer who was the Prince Imperial's sole companion on that fatal day when the heir of the Napoleons lost his life came to Buller to tell the story of the Prince's death, Buller turned square upon him and asked in stern tones, 'But how is it that you are alive?'"

Redvers Henry Buller was the son of James Wentworth Buller, M.P., of Crediton, Devonshire. He was descended from an old Cornish family which traced its ancestry back to the days of Edward I. Born in 1839, he was educated at Eton, and entered the Army in 1858. In the China campaign of 1860 he served in the 60th (King's Royal Rifles).

He was made a captain in 1870 and went on the Red River Expedition. Three years later he accompanied Wolseley in the Ashanti campaign as head of the Intelligence Department, and received a slight wound at the battle of Ordabai. He was mentioned in dispatches, made a C.B., and elevated to the rank of major.

As chief of Wolseley's Intelligence Department, he took Graham's Brigade across the desert in the famous night march from Kassassin to Tel-el-Kebir which resulted in the final defeat of Arabi. Later he served with great distinction at El-Teb. In the great fight at Tamai he saved the situation.

Charles Lowe in *Our Greatest Living Soldiers* says:

Buller's square, composed of the "Gay Gordons," the Royal Irish and the 60th Rifles, amongst the ranks of whom he had first

M*

won his spurs, had been assailed in the same furious manner as that of Davis, but had blown away all opposition to its advance, about five hundred yards on the right rear of its fellow brigade, to whose support it now moved up, steady and machine-like, as if on parade. Encouraged by the splendid steadfastness of Buller's embattled men, Davis's disrupted square was quick to rally, and then the two brigades began to rain such an infernal fire of bullets on their savage foe, that the latter was forced to break, and the day was won.

Buller was again successful in the Sudan campaign. He conducted the dangerous retreat from Metemmeh to Korti.

From that time until the South African War he had no service in the field, but held several important positions at home, including the post of Under-Secretary for Ireland, which he filled for a short time.

Buller's death followed a lingering illness from an incurable complaint. He died on June 2nd, 1908.

Saint Kevin

Kevin, the fair born, scion of the noble house of Leinster, awoke suddenly from a brief sleep.

Throughout the night something had continually disturbed his slumbers. It was not the animals who howled on the slopes of the Wicklow Hills, for Kevin had long since become used to them. Nor was it the screeching birds whose cries echoed across the lake to his fastness in the rock. It was rather a feeling of an impending shock; an emotional disturbance that kept him rolling restlessly in his blanket of sackcloth.

Kevin crawled slowly out of his cave to the rocky ledge that overhung the limpid waters of the lake.

Then suddenly he saw, balanced almost on the edge of the rock, a beautiful maiden. Water dripped from her naked body and golden hair. She had apparently swum across the wide lake from the distant shore and clambered up the face of the cliff.

Kevin looked at her with horror. For many months he had sought to evade this lovely daughter of an Irish chieftain. He had taken refuge in one likely place after another, but she had always turned up to disturb his seclusion.

She had made a vow that she would follow him wherever

he went. Kevin, on the other hand, had taken vows of fidelity to his church, and here in this quiet spot among the mountains he had felt secure.

There was a smile of triumph on the maiden's face. There was only one way of escape for Kevin, and that was by diving into the lake and swimming across. As she was as good a swimmer as he, this method of avoiding her was by no means a certain one.

At length Kevin rose to his feet and advanced towards her. She misinterpreted the gesture; nor could she see the anger in the monk's eyes.

She realized his intentions when it was too late. Grasping the girl round the body, he lifted her in his arms and, with a mighty heave, threw her into the water of the lake.

The noise of the splash echoed and re-echoed along the cliffs, disturbing the wild fowl.

Kevin crawled to the edge of the rock and watched with fascination the ever-extending ripples. Soon the surface of the lake returned to its normal calm. He had expected the golden head to reappear, but when several minutes had passed and nothing arose out of the depths he realized that the maiden had sunk like a stone.

The sun now broke through a mountain crevice and turned the surface into silver.

Kevin returned into the cave and began his frugal meal of fruit and berries.

That is the legend told of St. Kevin, the founder of Glendalough of the Seven Churches so famous in the history of Irish Christianity.

The visitor to Glendalough, which is in the county of Wicklow, can still see the remains of the great religious establishment begun by Kevin, or Coemgen, the Irish saint, who is said to have been born in 498, though some historians declare his birth to have been at a later period.

His parents were Christian and of high birth. Great care was spent on his education, and he was tutored by Petrocus, "a learned and holy Briton," with whom he remained five years.

He was ordained a priest by Lugidus and lived a life of great piety. Retiring to the secluded valley of Glendalough, he founded a religious establishment there which extended a long way down the valley.

On first taking up his abode between the mountains he had a few followers. Soon the establishment became famous all over Ireland and the brotherhood increased in numbers. Kevin, as the leader, always lived in his cave over the lake, away from the others, and issued forth only at certain times to superintend the building of the churches or to carry out administrative duties.

In Kevin's day, and for many years afterwards, Glendalough was a centre of learning.

Kevin began the building of his great religious establishment with a little church on the south bank of what is known as the upper lake, some time in the sixth century. Towards the end of his life he moved to the entrance of the valley where other buildings were put up. His disciples built a monastery that flourished until the eleventh century, when it became the prey of the Danes, who ruthlessly destroyed the religious buildings.

Succeeding centuries wrought further ravages, and by the middle of the sixteenth the establishment had become a ruin.

Nowadays, as one enters the valley of Glendalough, one sees the remains of a magnificent gateway containing two arches and a tower between. There are the ruins of a cathedral, the building of which was begun in the eighth century, but it was probably completed many years afterwards, for the chancel is less stoutly constructed than the nave.

The chancel arch has been partly restored, and some notable features are the Norman doorway, the ornamental east window made of a stone foreign to the district, and the stone slabs used to cover graves.

A little distance from the cathedral is what is known as St. Kevin's Cross, eleven feet high and made of granite, and nearby is the Priest's House, which has been reconstructed within recent years.

Adam Smith

When Adam Smith, ex-Professor of Moral Philosophy, returned from a tour on the Continent, it was expected that he would resume association with his former friends. But Smith had other ideas. He retired to his house at Kirkcaldy, and there he remained for ten years in close seclusion.

His many admirers urged him to come out into the open. He refused, and everyone began to wonder what Adam Smith was up to.

"My business here is study," wrote Smith to David Hume. *"My amusements are long and solitary walks by the seashore. I feel myself, however, extremely happy, comfortable and contented. I never was, perhaps, more so in my life. You will give me great comfort by writing to me now and then, and letting me know what is passing among my friends in London."*

With that they had to be content.

They had given him up entirely when suddenly the mystery of his seclusion was solved by the appearance of Smith's *Inquiry into the Nature and Causes of the Wealth of Nations.*

It was published in 1776, and was immediately pronounced as the most important work of the eighteenth century.

Yet it had a mixed reception. Pitt, extreme Tory though he was, embraced Smith's doctrines, among which were the principle and practice of free trade. Charles James Fox, on the other hand, would have nothing of the *Wealth of Nations,* despite his Liberal politics.

Before the days of Smith two theories of wealth prevailed. One called the "mercantile system" held the notion that money was the true wealth of nations. In other words, the extent of the prosperity of a country was estimated on the amount of precious metals—gold and silver—that it possessed.

The fallacy of this theory, however, was proved in the case of Spain. When America was discovered the coffers of Spain were filled with precious metals. Then, one of the most powerful nations in the world, she began to decline, despite her accumulated treasures.

Although this system had already begun to lose ground before Smith's time, he was the first to show that industry and not mere gold and silver was the basis of a country's prosperity.

Smith also exploded the second theory, known as the "agricultural system," which was propounded by Quesnay and the French economists.

According to this system, the only truly productive labour was on the soil. The supporters of the theory argued that all other industry, such as manufacturing, was unproductive.

With the appearance of the *Wealth of Nations* Smith returned

to his friends and made many others.   He spent the next two
years of his life in London, where he frequently met Pitt,
Addington, Dundas (afterwards Lord Melville), and Lord
Grenville, who hailed him as their master in political science.

Smith's father, who died just before the birth of his son,
who was born on the 8th day of June, 1723, was a controller
of the Customs.

In early life young Smith was delicate and infirm.   When
three years old he was stolen by a party of itinerant tinkers.
There was a hue and cry, and Smith's uncle, a Mr. Douglas,
obtained assistance, eventually overtook the tinkers, and
rescued the child.

Smith was educated at the grammar School of Kirkcaldy
until he was 15, and was then sent to Glasgow University.
Having obtained a scholarship, he entered Balliol College,
Oxford, in 1741.

In his *Wealth of Nations* he speaks disparagingly of the
system of education at Oxford, and this is believed to be due
to a reprimand he received for reading Hume's *Treatise on
Human Nature*, then recently published.

Despite his dislike for Oxford, however, he remained for
the unusually long period of seven years.

His first intention was to enter the Church of England, but
he abandoned this design and determined to attain an academical chair in Scotland.

He left Oxford in 1747 and returned to Kirkcaldy, where
he lived with his mother for two years.   In the winter of 1748
he delivered a course of lectures on rhetoric in Edinburgh,
which introduced him to the notice and friendship of Hume,
Blair, Lord Kames, and other literary men in Glasgow.
Through their influence he was appointed in 1751 to the
professorship of Logic in the University of Glasgow.   In
the following year he changed this chair for that of moral
philosophy.

He held this professorship for thirteen years, during which
time his reputation as a lecturer was high.   Multitudes of
students went to Glasgow merely to hear him, and Smith's
opinions were often the chief topics of discussion in clubs and
literary societies.

In 1763, Smith received an invitation from Mr. Townshend, the husband of the Countess of Dalkeith, to accompany
her son, the young Duke of Buccleuch on a tour of the

Continent. He could not resist the liberal terms offered, which included an annuity of £300 for life.

While in Paris, Smith made the acquaintance of Turgot, D'Alembert, Buffon, and Quesnay, and many other prominent Frenchmen.

In 1778, after the publication of the *Wealth of Nations*, Smith secured an appointment as commissioner of customs for Scotland. The duties of this office required his residence at Edinburgh, and here he spent the remainder of his days. This employment could have been filled by a man of far inferior intellect, and no doubt Smith himself would have preferred a university chair. As, however, the appointment had been secured for him by his patron the Duke of Buccleuch, Smith could not well refuse.

In 1787 Smith was elected Lord-Rector of his own University. In his acknowledgement of this honour Smith referred to his regret at having left his academical occupations.

Among other writings which Smith left behind were some *Essays on Philosophical Subjects*, later published in a volume.

Smith died on July 17th, 1790, aged 67.

Shah Nadir

Often when the fortunes of a country have been at a low ebb, a patriot has come forward and saved the situation.

Such was the case of Persia in the first half of the eighteenth century. That country had been dismembered by the Russians and the Turks. Tahmasp, titular king of a non-existent country, had given up the struggle.

Suddenly there came a dramatic turn with the appearance of Nadir Kuli, leader of a robber band, who joined forces with Tahmasp, bringing with him about 5,000 Afshar tribesmen. The two men were able to put into the field about 8,000 soldiers.

They first turned their attention to the Afghans who were endeavouring to occupy provinces uncaptured by the Russians and Turks. A few initial successes were obtained by the Persians, whose armies gradually increased as a result.

By 1730, six years after the dismemberment of Persia, Nadir Kuli was in a position to face the strongest army that the Afghans could put in the field.

Nadir, who was destined to restore the power and prestige of Persia, was born in a tent at a village near Meshed, the capital of Khorassan. His father died when Nadir was 18, and he and his mother were carried off by a band of Uzbegs and sold as slaves. Four years later he escaped, returned to Persia, and entered the service of the Governor of Darragaz, whose daughter he married.

Next he became a soldier in the service of the Governor of Meshed, and distinguished himself in the wars against the Uzbegs. Frustrated in his desire for promotion, he maintained himself as the head of a band of robbers. Aiming at higher things, he took the town of Nishapur and held it in the name of Shah Tahmasp.

Nadir soon obtained complete power over the weak shah, and by his energy and military talents he conquered the Afghans. Soon afterwards he fought three campaigns against the invading Turks, finally beating them and recapturing the western provinces of Persia.

After the death of Peter the Great the Russian Government became alarmed at the growing power of Nadir, decided to withdraw from Persia, and actually restored to her in 1732 her Caspian provinces.

In 1735 war broke out between Russia and Turkey. This was Nadir's advantage. He threatened to join Turkey unless Russia evacuated the fortresses of Baku and Derbent. Russia had no option but to yield.

This diplomatic success increased Nadir's prestige, and the Persian nation was ready to give him anything he asked. Suggesting the dethronement of Tahmasp, Nadir proceeded to put himself forward as king. He had freed Persia from the Afghans, Turks and Russians, and his election seemed merely a matter of course. At an assembly of the leading men of Persia, therefore, he was unanimously chosen Shah.

Nadir now thirsted for conquest, and with the approval of the people decided upon a campaign against the Afghans, whose country formed part of the Persian Empire in the days of Shah Abbas a century before.

About a year after his coronation, Nadir raised a force of 80,000 men and began a march on Kandahar. The assault and defence of this city is one of the most dramatic episodes in Oriental history. Husayn, ruler of Afghanistan, possessed insufficient forces to resist Nadir in a field battle. He retired behind the walls of the city and prepared to defend it at all costs.

Nadir had no artillery and was thus forced to blockade Kandahar. He built a wall, fortified with towers, all round the city, and awaited results. For over a year nothing happened. So far as Nadir could ascertain, the Afghans were able to hold out indefinitely.

He then made preparations for an assault. He captured some of the outworks, and guns having arrived he dragged them up. After a short bombardment Kandahar capitulated.

Having in mind the conquest of India, Nadir treated the Afghans leniently and thus enlisted thousands of them in his army.

While awaiting the collapse of Kandahar, Nadir had gradually perfected a plan for an Indian campaign. The moment for an attack on India was propitious. The declining Moghul dynasty had for its representative Mohammed Shah, a man of whom it was said "he was never without a mistress in his arms or a bottle in his hand."

Corruption was rife in the land, and many nobles had already been in communication with Nadir. Thus the Persian king was well informed about the state of things in India. Moreover, the ruler at Delhi, certain that Kandahar would hold up the march of the Persians, had taken no steps to protect himself.

Nadir took the route followed by Alexander the Great, occupied Kabul, the key to the Khyber Pass, and obtained a large sum of money with which to pay his troops, whose morale increased in consequence.

By this time Mohammed Shah was in a state of distraction. A hurried concentration of troops was decided upon, but before any definite move could be made, the eighteenth century Alexander had captured Peshawar and had successfully crossed the Indus.

In 1738 an historic battle was fought at Karnal, on the Jumna.

At this point Mohammed had established an entrenched camp. His position was a strong one, and Nadir hesitated to attack, as his troops were not used to attacking fortifications. A diversion was created by the appearance of Saadat Khan, who had brought reinforcements for Mohammed. Nadir attacked him in the open and inflicted a heavy defeat, 20,000 being killed. The Persians captured much heavy artillery as well as other rich spoils.

Nadir now surrounded the Indian camp and brought up his artillery. Mohammed Shah, however, had had enough and he surrendered.

Marching forward to Delhi, Nadir had no further difficulty. The capital was entered and the loot which fell into the hands of the Persians is estimated at nearly £100,000,000.

Nadir stayed two months in India and then returned to Persia with a reputation equal to that of the great Tamerlane.

In 1740 Nadir decided upon a conquest of the Uzbeg states, who finally capitulated.

Persia was now greater than she had been for many years.

But Nadir had no administrative capacity. Moreover, a sudden change came over his character. He was possessed by avarice, jealousy, and cruelty. He lived in continual fear of assassination, and even charged his own son, Riza, with conspiring against his life. Despite that gallant prince's protestations, Nadir ordered his eyes to be put out.

"It is not my eyes you have put out, but those of Persia," was Riza's reply to this.

It was true. Nadir's star was rapidly descending. The glory of his country and the pride of his soldiers became the object of universal hate.

Nadir conspired against his generals, and they retaliated by plotting to kill him.

The years passed; the situation did not improve. Nadir became possessed with the idea of destroying sectarianism among the Mohammedans. It led to an attack by the Turks, who, however, were repulsed. Nadir finally agreed to drop his religious ideals in face of a growing insubordination among his officers.

The end came on the 8th of June, 1747.

A number of his generals crept stealthily to his tent at Fethabad. A desperate struggle occurred.

Fighting to the end, Nadir was at length overcome.

They killed him and cut off his head,

Jeanne of Navarre

La Noue, Huguenot general, and "the bravest soldier in the world," preferred death to the loss of a limb.

He refused to submit to the amputation of a mortifying arm, caused by a wound at the battle of Sainte Gemme. Compelled to relinquish his command, he retired to La Rochelle.

"You must lose your arm to save your life," said his physicians.

"I will not submit," was the general's curt reply.

His obstinacy was told to Jeanne D'Albret, Queen of Navarre.

She immediately hurried to his bedside, trembling with emotion. With extraordinary eloquence she impressed upon him that even yet his services were necessary for the welfare of Navarre.

She drew the bedclothes from the blackened arm. His eyes were wet with sympathy as she earnestly urged him to undergo the operation.

There was no anæsthetic in those days and an operation for the removal of a limb was an experience at which the bravest man might quail.

A half-consent from La Noue was enough for the Queen of Navarre. She signalled her physicians to approach, and, taking the injured arm in her own hands, she held it while the saw bit through the flesh and bone. At the same time she whispered words of encouragement and solace. Ever afterwards La Noue recalled that trial with tears of gratitude.

The operation was successful, and Jeanne immediately ordered an artificial limb to be made of metal so that La Noue could guide his horse. From that time he was known as "Bras de Fer."

Jeanne (or Joan) of Navarre, the mother of the great Henry IV of France, was one of France's greatest daughters, as great, perhaps, as her namesake, Joan of Arc.

As a girl it is said that her beautiful face was marred by the abundance of her tears ; "her hair floated negligently on her shoulders, and her lips remained without smiles."

They were fateful days for France. Huguenot and Catholic strove for supremacy. The sinister figure of Philip

II of Spain obtruded itself into the affairs of France as it did into the affairs of England. Jeanne, the daughter of Henry, King of Navarre, and niece of Francis I of France, feared that they might decide to wed her to him.

But French politics changed and Francis I was no longer enamoured with his southern neighbour.

Then came the young handsome Duke of Cleves. But he was almost as distasteful to her as had been Philip. The 13-year-old girl refused to have anything to do with him. "I deem it no advantage to leave France," said she, "to espouse a Duke of Cleves. I shall die if the project is persisted in."

She wrote a long protest, beginning :

"I, Jeanne de Navarre, persisting in the protestations I have already made, do hereby again affirm and protest by these presents, that the marriage which it is desired to contract between the Duke of Cleves and myself is against my will ; that I have never consented to it, nor will consent. . . ."

It was a long document and was signed before witnesses. What could have been her objection to the Duke of Cleves ? Nothing could have been said against him. He was a Protestant, and although Jeanne had been brought up in the Catholic faith, she was already tending towards the reformed religion.

The King of France insisted on her marriage to the Duke. This brought another document from Jeanne in which she declared that one day—if the marriage took place—she would set aside the nuptials.

Nevertheless the marriage took place. Jeanne refused voluntarily to walk to the altar. She complained of indisposition, of the weight of her ornaments, to the annoyance of Francis I.

"The bride," says Brantome, the French historian, "being led to church, covered with gold and jewels, sunk under the weight of her robes. Francis, observing her unable to proceed, commanded the constable of Montmorenci to bear her in his arms." It was in this way that Jeanne D'Albret went to the altar.

There was a grand ball in the evening and jousts for the remainder of the week. Then the Duke resigned his wife to the care of her mother and went off to fight against the Emperor.

When the French king learned that the Duke had made heavy concessions to the Emperor of Germany, he was so disgusted that he declared that "no vassal of the empire should receive investiture of a fief appertaining to the French crown."

Thus the marriage was annulled. Soon afterwards Francis I died and Henry II ascended the throne with Catherine de Medici.

Philip of Spain, having lost his first consort, now made another attempt to secure the hand of Jeanne, but received no encouragement from Henry II.

In October 1548, Jeanne was married to Antoine de Bourbon, Duke of Vendome, a gay, luxurious, unstable, passionate prince without conscience. While the Duke lived a life of gaiety, Jeanne took an interest in the religious questions of the day, and drifted more and more towards the reformed faith.

Dissipated though he was, the duchess was attached to her husband.

Jeanne became the mother of two sons, both of whom died in infancy. Her father, Henry of Navarre, now threatened to marry again if she did not produce an heir. He blamed her with neglecting her children and insisted that when she was again expecting to become a mother she should place herself entirely under his care.

The following are the extraordinary circumstances of the birth of her third son, who was destined to become the great Henry IV of France.

Jeanne had often attempted to obtain the secret of her father's will. One day she asked him what his intentions were assuming that she had a son. Henry of Navarre went to a cabinet and took out a small gold box. "My daughter," said he, "this shall be your own with my last will which it contains, provided that, when the pains of labour assail you you will sing me a Gascon or Bearnois song. I do not want a peevish girl or a drivelling boy!"

The Duchess accepted the proposal, and when on the morning of December 13th, between the hours of one and two o'clock, she expected her child to be born she sent her attendant, Cotin, to her father. The King rose in haste and went to visit his daughter. Immediately she heard her father's step she began to sing a famous Bearnois song with numberless verses, which she bravely struggled through.

Two years after the birth of this infant, the King of Navarre died, and Jeanne became Queen.

Jeanne now definitely turned to Protestantism, and her husband became a Romanist and was appointed lieutenant-general of the kingdom. He died at the siege of Rouen, and Jeanne became the object of persecution of the King of France and Catherine de Medici. They threatened her, and she agreed to the reintroduction of the mass in her states. In 1567, however, on the demand of her people, she established Calvinism.

In the wars that followed between the crowns of France and Navarre she harangued the Huguenots. She took an oath and called on them to swear "on soul, honour and life" never to abandon the cause.

The last years of her life were full of trouble and stress. She died on June 9th, 1572. It was said that she was poisoned by means of a pair of gloves at the instance of Catherine de Medici.

A large number of nobles attended her burial in the cathedral of Lescar, near Pau.

She missed by two months the massacre of St. Bartholomew.

Thomas Hearne

They called him Old Tom Hearne, but he was not really old. He was fifty-seven when he died, the illusion of age having surrounded him for twenty years.

Tom held the keys of the Bodleian Library at Oxford, a humble but, to him, a congenial post, for he was profoundly learned in books, though ignorant of the ways of the world.

He was eccentric, the butt and jest of the ignorant and an easy prey to the thoughtless. A predilection for "the King across the water" did not improve his popularity, although he never disguised his opinions.

In Tom's time there was an inn in Oxford known as "Whittington and his Cat." One night he was induced to go there to see a "Roman mosaic pavement" recently discovered in the kitchen of the house.

This pavement had been faked with the bones of sheeps' trotters, artistically laid and flattened.

Tom's first reaction to the "mosaic pavement" was not encouraging. He showed no enthusiasm, and it was not until he had been taken to the bar and plied with plenty of liquor that he showed signs of providing sport.

Led back to the kitchen completely intoxicated, however, Tom got to his knees to make a closer inspection. He lost his equilibrium and rolled on the floor, where he lay unable to rise.

The wags had to carry him home and put him to bed.

On many other occasions Tom investigated reputed antiques only to find that they were bogus and "planted" for his especial benefit. But he had spent enough time among ancient things to become one of the most eminent authorities in the country, and he could soon detect a fraud.

Thomas was born in 1678 at Littlefield Green in the parish of White Waltham, Berkshire, of which his father was clerk and schoolmaster.

By the kindness of a neighbouring squire he was sent to school at Bray, near Maidenhead. When the boy was 17 the squire took him into his own house for a time and then sent him to Oxford, where he was entered at St. Edmund Hall. Tom never left Oxford, despite inducements offered him from outside.

He attracted the attention of Dr. John Mill, principal of St. Edmund Hall, the editor of the Greek Testament, who gave the lad some work in comparing manuscripts and in other directions.

The friendly squire who had been responsible for Tom's education was Francis Cherry, of Shottesbrook, who was a notorious Jacobite, and through him Hearne acquired a distaste for the new reign.

Hearne took the degree of B.A. in 1699, and immediately afterwards was offered an appointment as a missionary in one of the colonies, which he refused.

He was fully determined not to take holy orders, and was equally determined not to leave Oxford. His chief delight in the city was the Bodleian Library, where he spent as much of his time as University regulations would permit. His one object was to get a post in the library.

His diligence and knowledge attracted the notice of Mr. Hudson, principal librarian, who resolved to give him work as soon as ever the opportunity occurred. The post of janitor fell vacant in 1701, and Hearne was content to take this humble situation and thus be more closely connected with the Bodleian. In this capacity he held the keys of the great storehouse of books.

He assisted in the arrangement of the books, and helped to catalogue them. A new orderliness was soon apparent on the bookshelves.

In 1703 Hearne took his M.A. degree, and although many attractive employments were now offered him, he still refused to leave the University city.

Nine years later he was promoted to the office of second keeper of the library. In accepting this he made it a condition that he should still retain the keys. Hudson opposed this arrangement and suddenly developed a dislike for Hearne, making an attempt to get him ejected. The reason for this is not known, but it is supposed to have had its basis in Hearne's Jacobite views.

Hearne knew little of the world and its ways, and was no politician. But he was stubborn, and no amount of argument would cause him to change his opinions.

In 1716 an Act was passed requiring all office-holders to take an oath of allegiance to George I. A year before he had been elected archetypographus and esquire bedel in civil law in the university, but had resigned this because objections had been taken to his holding this office together with that of second librarian. Although the Act required that anyone refusing to take the oath would have to pay a penalty of £500, he refused to conform, and was deprived of his librarianship.

He now received many other offers to leave Oxford. Though he had no regular employment, however, he firmly refused them all. Nothing would draw him away from Oxford, and he continued to occupy himself in editing the English chroniclers.

A few years afterwards he was actually offered the office of chief librarian of the Bodleian, but as this would necessitate his taking the oath, he reluctantly refused.

Hearne naturally made many enemies because he felt himself bound to introduce his extreme religious and political sentiments at every opportunity. He was unpolished in manners and careless in dress.

His chief mission in life was to recover ancient manuscripts, and when he made any discovery of this kind he would go down on his knees and return thanks.

Hearne died after a short illness on June 10th, 1735. His manuscripts, including his diaries, which alone make one hundred and forty-five small volumes, were left to William Bedford, who sold them to Dr. Richard Rawlinson, who in his turn bequeathed them to the Bodleian. Two volumes of extracts from his diary were published by Philip Bliss (Oxford 1857), and later an enlarged edition in three volumes appeared through a London publisher. His autobiography is published in W. Huddesford's *Lives of Leland, Hearne and Wood*.

Among the most important works of Hearne were those done as editor of many of the English chroniclers, and, for a time, his editions were the only ones obtainable. They were most carefully prepared and are still of great value to history students.

Four years before his death an attempt was made to discredit Hearne by the publication of a pamphlet entitled *A Vindication of those who take the Oath of Allegiance*. He had written this as an essay in his early days before he came under the influence of Cherry.

It was found among Cherry's papers at the time of his death, and it demonstrated clearly that at one time Hearne entertained opinions diametrically opposite from those he expressed during the remainder of his life.

The Rev. Alexander Forsyth

In the Tower of London there are two tablets bearing the motto *Per Aspera Tenax*. They commemorate the work of a man—a Highland parson—who issued forth from his manse for a brief period, caused a flutter in the sporting world, frightened Napoleon Bonaparte, and then retired disgusted with Government·departments to look after his little flock.

There is little in the ordinary encyclopædias about the Rev. Alexander Forsyth, beyond a passing reference to the fact that he was the inventor of the percussion lock for guns.

It seems strange that a parson should have interested himself in a death-dealing invention, but Forsyth was a scientist as well as a minister of the Gospel. Although he lived and worked in the little parish of Belhelvie in Aberdeenshire, he kept himself well informed about the latest discoveries and inventions.

Thus when Jenner began his vaccination for small-pox, Forsyth himself inoculated all his parishioners.

Forsyth and Jenner were on friendly terms and frequently corresponded.

The village preacher knew all there was to be known about the experiments connected with coal gas and steam, and was often consulted on the subject. He was particularly interested in the work of Galvani and Volta and even visualized the introduction of the telegraph.

But the invention with which the name of Forsyth is linked is the use of detonators or fulminates in connection with firearms of all kinds.

Forsyth was a sportsman and a good shot. While out with his flint-lock gun he saw the necessity for an improvement in its construction. The flint-lock did not preserve the priming from damp; the flint sparks sometimes failed to ignite the charge or the flash of the pan would scare a bird before the slow-burning powder in the gun exploded.

In a little workshop attached to the manse Forsyth set about righting the defect.

Experiments had been going on in France, but many experimenters had been killed by premature explosions and trials were suspended.

At last Forsyth produced a crude percussion gun. Scottish sportsmen began to talk. By degrees the bigwigs in London became acquainted with the activities of the Aberdeen parson. Lord Moira, Master General of Ordnance, heard of them.

To the credit of Moira, he immediately invited Forsyth to London to display his invention. He arranged for a *locum tenens* for the parson's parish, and in 1805, the year of the Battle of Trafalgar, when England was engaged in the great struggle with France, the Tower of London was the scene of experiments with a gun by a minister of the Established Church.

Forsyth was forced to work alone, for no one would risk his life testing detonating mercury and chlorate of potash. At length Forsyth produced percussion locks for muskets and three-pounder guns.

Then his work came abruptly to an end. The Govern

ment crashed—as it was wont to do in those days—and Moira and his Board of Ordnance were overturned.

The new Master General of Ordnance, Lord Chatham, knew nothing of Forsyth and cared less. The village preacher was ordered out of the Tower of London and instructed to "remove all his rubbish."

Disappointed but not disheartened, Forsyth continued his experiments without the blessing of a Government department, and in 1807 he patented his percussion locks, and returned to his manse without money or thanks.

Though the Government refused to have anything to do with Forsyth, sporting interests took up the new invention. It gradually spread over Europe, manufacturers considering it legitimate to pirate his work.

Then Napoleon Bonaparte stepped in and offered £20,000 for Forsyth's detonators. To the annoyance of the French dictator, Forsyth would not sell to a foreign Power.

What Wellington thought of the invention is not known. His army were still using the "Brown Bess," a flint-lock smooth-bore musket with shortened barrel, browned instead of bright, perfected as a result of experience gained in the American Revolution. In any case, it would have been utterly useless for him to advocate the re-arming of the British Army with the new weapon in face of vested interests at home.

Thus for seventeen years the percussion lock was shelved by the British Government. Meanwhile, however, it was being gradually developed abroad. In America, Thomas Shaw, of Philadelphia, first used fulminate in a steel cap in 1814, changing it to a copper cap in 1816.

At length, in 1834, Forsyth's invention was tested at Woolwich by firing 6,000 rounds from six flint-lock muskets, and a similar number from six percussion muskets. Remarkable results were obtained in all weathers, and the advantage of the percussion lock was fully established.

In 1836-7 the new musket was issued to the 3rd Grenadier and 1st Coldstream Guards. Two years later the lock was fitted to the Brunswick rifle of the 1st Battalion Rifle Brigade, and gradually the percussion lock was fitted to all muskets.

The conversion was effected by replacing the hammer and pan by a nipple with a hole through its centre to the vent or touch-hole, and by replacing the cock which held the flint with a hollow to fit on the nipple when released by the trigger.

The copper cap was placed on the nipple. The cap contained a detonating composition which is now made of three parts of chlorate of potash, two of fulminate of mercury, and one of powdered glass.

The copper cap was a simplification of Forsyth's invention, but without his experiments it might never have come into existence.

In 1840 an agitation was begun on behalf of Forsyth. Supported by Lord Brougham and Mr. Bannerman, M.P. for Aberdeen, it was soon taken up by the Press, and finally a petition, accompanied by some of Forsyth's pistols, was laid before Parliament.

The Government had the cheek to suggest a reward of £200. Members argued, Government departments wrangled among themselves for a long period without result. No doubt Forsyth knew what was going on, but he appears to have given up hope of any acknowledgment of his work. He gave no further interest to his percussion lock and went on saving souls instead of seeking means for destroying lives.

On the morning of June 11th, 1843, Forsyth sat at breakfast, at his manse at Belhelvie.

In London, Government departments still haggled over the sum, if any, they would pay the inventor.

Forsyth had long since lost faith in officialdom.

For fifty years he had been a pastor. He was contemplating his long career in the "cloth" when he slid from his chair. They picked him up dead.

Three months later the Treasury grudgingly gave way and paid £1,000 to Forsyth's surviving relatives.

At his old university of Aberdeen Forsyth's memory still lives, a degree of LL.D. being recorded against his name.

Some of Forsyth's experimental pieces can be seen in the Tower of London, and a medal in his honour is awarded at Bisley.

Magnetic Telegraph Patented

But for a lucky break Charles Wheatstone and William Cooke might have waited many years before obtaining recognition of their great invention, the electric telegraph.

In 1844 a woman was foully murdered at Slough, Bucks. The murderer, a man named Tawell, escaping from the scene of his crime, boarded a train for Paddington, and no doubt congratulated himself that he would soon be safely hidden away in London.

But on arrival at the terminus, he was astounded to find detectives awaiting him with a full description of his appearance.

The electric telegraph had been inaugurated between Paddington and Slough by the Great Western Railway, and by this means a description of Tawell had been flashed over the wire.

In the message he was described as a "kwaker," there being at that time no "q" on the dial of the instrument.

Hitherto railway authorities had doubted the value of the invention, and it had been installed reluctantly for experimental purposes. The publicity gained for it by the apprehension of the Slough murderer, however, finally overcame criticism.

The practical use of the telegraph dates from 1837. It was on June 12th that Wheatstone and Cooke patented the magnetic needle telegraph.

Charles Wheatstone was an assistant in the shop of a music-seller, and William Fothergill Cooke was a doctor. Neither man was a professional scientist or mechanic.

Wheatstone became a professor at King's College, and while he was carrying out experiments in the cellars of that institution, Cooke was also working independently. Later the men became acquainted; they collaborated, and in 1837 patented instruments with two, three, four, and five needles, and their respective codes.

Their system was the practical outcome of the theories of Johann Gauss and Wilhelm Weber, who had invented a code of signals for each letter of the alphabet, and a method of signalling with a mirror which threw a beam of light to right or left.

Wheatstone and Cooke's telegraph lines were not at first carried overhead. They were laid in wooden grooves, which held the wet and thus caused rot and the final destruction of the insulation.

In the same year (1837) Samuel Morse, an American painter and sculptor, also successfully finished a series of experiments and produced an electric instrument for conveying messages.

A few years before he had visited England, and during the return voyage had met in the ship an electrical expert named Professor Jackson, who entertained the American with some experiments.

Morse knew nothing of electricity, but could see the possibilities, and when he arrived home he obtained the assistance of experts. The outcome was the appearance of an instrument in which lead type, bearing certain projections in combination, was set up in a carrier which was passed by rollers under a rocking arm connected to a battery and line. This instrument was successfully used on September 4th, 1837. By this time Morse had spent almost all his money.

He went into partnership with a young American engineer named Vail. He brought his invention to England, but was ignored, and in 1840 was on the verge of starvation. At last he erected his first telegraph line between Washington and Baltimore, about forty miles. Morse was then fifty-three.

Wheatstone afterwards invented many improvements in electric telegraphy. In 1858 he produced the printing telegraph, capable of transmitting signals at the rate of 600 letters a minute.

He was also the inventor of the magneto-alphabetical telegraph, later used extensively through the United Kingdom for the purpose of private telegraphic communication, and in 1862 he completed a self-acting magneto-letter-printing telegraph. He also invented the concertina and harmonium.

He received the honour of knighthood in 1868 and died in 1875.

Until the year 1899 the number of telegrams dealt with by the Post Office increased yearly. In that year about 90,000,000 messages were handled. From that date, however, there has been a decline due to trade depression, the Great War and the competition of the telephone. The traffic is now less than 50,000,000 messages a year.

Some indication of the newspaper traffic of early years may be gathered from the fact that on April 8th, 1886, one and a half million words were handed in to post offices concerning Gladstone's Home Rule speech. On November 27th, 1911, Grey's announcement on the Moroccan crisis gave rise to nearly one and a quarter million words.

The telegraph services of this country passed under the control of the Post Office in 1870, but it was not until 1885 that there were any signs that it would eventually pay its way.

The introduction of the sixpenny telegram which was passed by Parliament against the advice of the Government finally dissipated any idea of making a profit. The introduction of the shilling telegram in 1920 did not make up the deficit and merely served to reduce traffic.

The actual annual loss before the War was one and a quarter million pounds.

For hundreds of years men have been able, by some means or other, to send messages over long distances, and many curious devices have been put in operation. Smoke, bells, musical instruments, and guns, were among the most successful. Wooden clapper, whistling, yodelling, were methods employed in Europe and, in the African bush, the tom-tom.

Signalling by flags from ships was known as early as the thirteenth century.

In 1774, Richard Lovell Edgeworth invented what is known as the semaphore, which consisted of six shutters fixed in pairs in a large frame. This was eminently successful and was used by the Admiralty for years after the invention of the electric telegraph.

Edgeworth's device jumped into prominence when he was able to give the result of a race at Newmarket at 5 o'clock on the evening of the same day to sportsmen in London. But it was many years before it was accepted officially.

The heliograph was another form of telegraph. It transmitted signals by the sun's rays, but, of course, was useless when the sun was not shining. In dull weather and at night signalling lamps were later used.

Harriet Beecher Stowe

In the preface to her work, *Uncle Tom's Cabin*, Mrs. Harriet Beecher Stowe makes the following comment on the slavery question : ·

The hand of benevolence is everywhere stretched out, searching into abuses, righting wrongs, alleviating distresses, and bringing to the knowledge and sympathies of the world the lowly, the oppressed, and the forgotten.

In this general movement, unhappy Africa at last is remembered ; Africa who began the race of civilization and human progress in the dim, grey dawn of early time, but who, for centuries, has lain bound and bleeding at the foot of civilized and Christianised humanity, imploring compassion in vain.

But the heart of the dominant race, who have been her conquerors, her hard masters, has at length been turned to her in mercy ; and it has been seen how far nobler it is in nations to protect the feeble than to oppress them. Thanks be to God, the world has at last outlived the slave-trade.

When she wrote the book the author could never have foreseen what effect it would have in America. The world had outlived the slave-trade in theory, but there were elements in her own country who were determined to keep it in practice at all costs.

In March 1852, when *Uncle Tom* was published, many countries had abolished the traffic. The Danes had been the first. A Royal order, dated May 1792, prohibited slavery after the end of 1802. In 1794, the United States had forbidden American subjects to participate in the slave trade to foreign countries, and in 1807 they prohibited the importation of slaves from Africa into their dominions.

At the Congress of Vienna in 1814, the principle of abolition was acknowledged. Within a few years, the United States, Britain, Sweden, Holland and France passed legislation to that effect. Portugal followed in 1830.

Meanwhile, however, an even more drastic reform was contemplated, namely, the abolition of slavery itself in the foreign possessions of the various States of Europe. This agitation was brought about by the deliberate evasion of the laws.

Slave-running was rife, and it is estimated that three times as many negroes were exported from Africa, two-thirds of them being murdered on the high seas to escape discovery by cruisers.

In 1821 the question of the emancipation of the slaves was raised in the British Parliament. In 1838 freedom was given to negroes in the British possessions. Other European countries followed, and some American states had already taken action.

Three important slave areas remained—the Southern United States, Cuba, and Brazil.

In America the pros and the antis were gradually working themselves into a frenzy. In the legislature the slave owners of the south more than held their own, and even the Christian churches in the Southern States used their influence in the maintenance of slavery.

It was at this juncture that public opinion in the north was stirred by the disclosures in *Uncle Tom's Cabin*, which, although a novel, was in addition a pamphlet against slavery.

Harriet Elizabeth Stowe was the seventh child of Lyman and Roxana Beecher, and was born at Litchfield, Connecticut, on June 14th, 1811.

Her father, formerly a blacksmith, had risen to be a Presbyterian minister of high repute. In 1832 he was made principal of the Lane Seminary, established for Presbyterian students in Cincinnati.

Harriet had been a teacher in a school at Hartford. She accompanied her father to Cincinnati and, in course of time, married the Rev. Calvin E. Stowe, Professor of Biblical Literature at the academy.

She began to write religious stories for various charitable organizations. At the age of 32 she published *The Mayflower, or Sketches of Scenes and Characters among the Descendants of the Pilgrims*.

Her interest in the abolition of slavery was quickened by her father and her husband, both of whom were advocates of anti-slavery.

The seminary became a centre of the anti-slavery agitation, and on many occasions was in danger of attack by the mob. Threats were made to burn down the professor's houses unless the college were dissolved. At length it was

N

broken up, and Stowe and his wife removed to the theological seminary at Andover, Massachusetts.

About this time Mrs. Stowe began to write *Uncle Tom's Cabin*. It was published chapter by chapter in a weekly periodical entitled the *Washington National Era*. After a few instalments, the anti-slavery ranks were reinforced. When the story was completed it was reprinted, and went rapidly through several editions. It is said that 200,000 copies were sold in the United States in the early days of its appearance.

The sale was so extraordinary that an English publisher decided to bring out an edition, ignoring all claims to copyright.

In England the book was not well received. It was declared to be an exaggeration, was regarded as repulsive and a melodramatic outburst of a misguided woman.

But it was not long before the quaintness of Topsy, the negro maid, and the suffering of Uncle Tom gripped the people of this country as well as of America.

One of the numerous editions published in England in 1852 was edited by Lord Carlisle. In the following year Mrs. Stowe came to England, and at the house of Lord Carlisle's sister, the Duchess of Sutherland, she received an address from the women of England, expressing their appreciation of the book, which was afterwards translated into twenty-three languages.

Her reputation having been established, Mrs. Stowe used her influence to the utmost on behalf of the emancipation of the slaves. For the benefit of those who questioned the truth of the details in *Uncle Tom*, she wrote a *Key to Uncle Tom's Cabin* which contained a statement of facts on which she had based her narrative. They were supported by numerous documents and testimonies against the great evil.

In 1856 Mrs. Stowe published *Dred : a Tale of the Dismal Swamp*, in which she argued the deterioration of a society based on slavery. She also published *Sunny Memories of Foreign Lands*, which recorded her travels in England, Scotland, and other parts of Europe.

A year later the *Atlantic Monthly* was first published, and she was invited to become a regular contributor. She wrote also for *The Independent* of New York and, later, *The Christian Union*. Her brother, Henry Ward Beecher, was successively editor of all three publications.

In 1869 Mrs. Stowe created a sensation with her article in *Macmillan's Magazine*, entitled "The True Story of Lord Byron's Life," in which she charged the poet with a serious crime. The charge was open to question and could not be substantiated. There was a storm of indignation which culminated in the publication in 1870 of "Lady Byron Vindicated."

After the war between the North and South, which she had done so much to bring about by the publication of *Uncle Tom*, Mrs. Stowe bought an estate in Florida in the hope of restoring the health of her son, Captain Frederick Beecher Stowe, who had been wounded in the war, and here she spent many winters.

Her husband died in 1886, and she passed the rest of her life at her home at Hartford, where she died on July 1st, 1896. She was buried in the cemetery at Andover, Massachusetts.

Harrow School

In the year 1571 plain yeoman John Lyon, of Preston, Middlesex, obtained a charter from Queen Elizabeth to found a "Free Grammar School" at Harrow, and to draw up rules for its management.

It was not until twenty years afterwards that Lyon drew up and circulated the document entitled : "Orders, Statutes and Rules for the Government of the School."

In it he ordered that £300 should be spent on building the school with residences for the master and usher, the former "to be on no account below the degree of Master of Arts," nor the latter "under that of Bachelor of Arts."

Lyon directed that the work should be begun after his death, and he expressed his desire thus :

"And I, the said John Lyon, doe purpose, by ye Grace of God, to build wth some pte of my lands lying within the towne of Harrow uppon ye Hill meete and convenient Roomes for the said Schoole Master and Usher to inhabite and dwell in : as alsoe a large and convenient Schoole house, with a chimney in it. And, alsoe, a cellar under the said Roomes, or Schoole house, to lay in wood and coales, which said Cellar shall be divided into three several Roomes, ye one for ye Mr., the second for the Usher, and ye third for ye schollers."

Included in the bequest was the property at Harrow and lands in Marylebone and Paddington.

Lyon further directed that a certain number of children of "inhabitants within the parish" should receive free education. But the schoolmaster was also empowered to receive so many "foreigners" as the place would contain in the judgment of the governors.

"And of the foreigners," Lyon continued, *"he may take such stipends and wages as he can get, except they be of the kindred of John Lyon, the founder, so that he take pains with all indifferently, as well of the parish of foreigners, as well of poor as of rich; but the discretion of the governors shall be looked to that he do."*

Lyons original school is now, of course, only a modest part of the great educational establishment.

In his will John Lyon specified the salaries of the masters, the numbers of the "forms" in the school, the school hours, recreations and vacations. And, in case there should be any doubt about the nature of the recreations, he made it lawful that the following games should be played : "Driving a top," "tossing a hand-ball," and "running and shooting."

Shooting was insisted upon, and parents were required to supply their children with "bow-strings, shafts, and bracers, to exercise shooting."

Thus archery became one of the most important recreations. To encourage it Lyon instituted a prize of a silver arrow to be shot for annually on August 4th. The date was later changed to July.

The competitors originally numbered six. In later years they were increased to twelve. All were dressed in fancy costume of spangled satin, usually white and green with silk sashes and caps.

The last contest for the silver arrow took place in 1771. An arrow had been prepared for the 1772 contest, but on the abolition of the shooting it came into the possession of an assistant master. In the middle of last century the Rev. Henry Drury, the then owner, presented it to the school library.

It is said that the headmaster decided to stop the archery contests because of a serious accident which befell one of the competitors. But there were, no doubt, other reasons, one being the interruption of studies caused by the shooters claiming time off for the purpose of practice.

There is a tradition that one of the boys shot so wide of the mark—intentionally or otherwise—that the arrow entered the eye of the village barber, who was acting the part of a Peeping Tom.

When the archery contests were discontinued public "speeches" were introduced. These took place on the first Thursdays in May, June, and July, and were attended by many old Harrovians and friends of the boys. In 1829 the number of speech-days was reduced to two, and in 1844 one.

The number of boys in the school has fluctuated at various times. During the eighteenth century there were rarely more than 100, and in the nineteenth the number was between 300 and 580.

In 1871 the tercentery of the foundation of the school was celebrated. To commemorate it a subscription among old Harrovians resulted in the building of a new "speech-room," school-rooms, a museum, laboratory, gymnasium, and lecture-rooms. The first stone of the new buildings was laid by the Duke of Abercorn on Speech-day, July 2nd, 1874.

Until 1840, the boys of Harrow School attended the parish church. A chapel was then built for them in High Street. In 1854 that was pulled down and a new chapel built to the design of Sir Gilbert Scott.

Distinguished clergymen have been headmasters of Harrow School. In 1660 the office was taken by the Rev. W. Howe, Fellow of King's College, Cambridge.

During Dr. Sumner's headmastership the number of pupils rose to 250. His predecessor was Dr. Thackeray, a personal friend of the Prince of Wales.

Dr. Sumner was followed by Dr. Heath. On the latter's election the famous Dr. Parr was the defeated candidate. He had been an assistant master under Dr. Sumner and, in view of his popularity with the boys, fully expected to take his place.

When Dr. Heath was chosen, the boys registered their disapproval by rebellion. Among those who took part in this insubordination was Richard Wellesley, afterwards Marquess Wellesley, who was removed to Eton by his guardian. With him went his younger brother, Arthur

Wellesley (the Iron Duke). Thus it was that the Battle of Waterloo was won on the playing fields of Eton, and not those of Harrow.

Dr. Parr felt his rejection keenly. He resigned his post as assistant master and founded a school at Stanmore. That venture failed, and he was later appointed to the living of Hatton, Warwickshire, and subsequently to a prebendal stall in St. Paul's Cathedral.

During the headmastership of Dr. Drury, who followed Dr. Heath, the number of pupils rose to 350. Included among them were Lord Byron and Sir Robert Peel. Dr. Drury was succeeded in 1805 by Dr. Butler, afterwards Dean of Peterborough.

Theodore Hook, the eminent dramatist and novelist, was a pupil at Harrow. Notorious as a practical joker, he began his tricks on his first day at school. On the night of his arrival he threw a stone at a window where an elderly lady was dressing. It is said that he was induced to do this by Byron. The window was smashed, but the woman escaped unhurt.

A pretty story is told of Byron at Harrow. Peel was being severely thrashed when a small boy ran up and asked how many strokes Peel was going to get.

"What is that to you, you little rascal?" he was asked.

"Because I would take half myself," was the boy's reply. That boy was Lord Byron.

Battles of Quatre Bras and Ligny

Napoleon's crown was at stake. He knew that as early as the morning of June 15th. Yet he tried to console himself with a number of "ifs."

If he could throw himself on the junction-point of the two armies—Prussian and Anglo-Dutch—before they expected his approach; if the British and Prussians were crushed he could hasten down the Rhine, meet the Austrians, and beat them before the Russians began to arrive.

If he could hold out until September, new levies would bring him a reinforcement of 500,000 men. If he could beat Wellington the British Ministry would fall.

These were some of the possibilities that ran through the mind of Napoleon three days before Waterloo.

In the new campaign against Belgium on which he had embarked he had about 125,000 men, all veterans of the regular army. The eastern and southern frontiers of France were guarded by irregular forces.

A three days' start over the Allies in the concentration of troops was necessary to give the Emperor a sporting chance against 210,000 of the enemy which were strung over a hundred miles.

Napoleon had started for the front on June 12th. The fifth army corps were concentrated successfully, unknown to the Allies, on a front of about thirty-five miles at the point where the frontier then projected into Belgium.

The Allied commanders, Wellington and Blücher, learned nothing of what was going on. "We have reports of Bonaparte joining the army and attacking us," wrote Wellington. "But I judge from his speech to the Legislature that his departure is not likely to be immediate, and I think we are now too strong for him here."

At the very moment Wellington was writing these lines, Napoleon was on his way to the Belgian frontier.

At sun-up on the morning of the 15th the French army crossed the Belgian frontier. Napoleon had gained the three days he desired. The outposts of the Allies were contacted, and an attack was made on the Prussian army's right near Charleroi. On the side of the Allies the only corps engaged was Ziethen's. Unable to concentrate in time it was forced northward and eastward with considerable casualties.

At night Napoleon was in Charleroi, had occupied the Sambre bridges, and had driven Ziethen well back behind Fleurus.

Blücher appears to have heard of this assault first, and begun a march westward. By noon on the following day he had concentrated three corps, those of Ziethen, Pirch and Thielmann, having at his disposal 90,000 men.

A fourth army, commanded by Bulow, had yet to arrive.

Blücher determined to fight without Bulow, and deployed his forces on the hill-sides behind Ligny and St. Amand. It was an unsatisfactory position, but it was better than that held by Wellington, for the latter had not heard of the enemy's movements until long after Blücher had been informed.

It was at 4 p.m. on the 15th that Wellington heard that the French were attacking, but was not certain whether the whole of Napoleon's army was engaged in the movement, or whether a second force might be expected on the Mons road. Thus a delayed concentration, at the same time misjudging the speed at which the Emperor was advancing.

That night Wellington remained at Brussels and, as is well known, was present at the Duchess of Richmond's ball. In the morning he rode out to his outposts and later conferred with Blücher.

Napoleon had instructed Marshal Ney to attack the flank of the Prussians at Ligny, after disposing of what Allied forces might be at Quatre Bras. The French commander was confident that there could be only one corps at Ligny. Later he discovered his mistake, and delayed action.

At noon, therefore, everything was more or less quiet on both the Ligny and Quatre Bras fronts.

Between two and three o'clock in the afternoon Napoleon had massed his troops in front of Blücher's position at Ligny, unaware that his army was numerically inferior.

He began a furious attack, repeatedly storming Ligny and St. Amand. Using his reserves, Blücher won the positions back, but his troops suffered heavily from the artillery fire of the French.

The battle continued, with Napoleon continually expecting to see Ney appear on the Prussian right. But Ney had more than he could handle at Quatre Bras, Wellington's army being stronger than either he or his Emperor had anticipated.

Napoleon now sent orders to d'Erlon, the commander of Ney's reserve corps, to come to his assistance at Ligny. D'Erlon obeyed and eventually found himself on the Emperor's left. But he had barely taken up his position when an urgent message was received from Ney ordering him back. Ney was being badly pressed by Wellington's superior numbers.

The Emperor continued the Ligny battle without this support, and at length brought it to a successful conclusion as darkness came on. Blücher had been unable to withstand the veteran French troops. Both sides suffered heavily; Blücher lost 20,000 men and Napoleon 10,000.

What of Quatre Bras?

Ney attacked Wellington at 2 p.m. with a whole corps. The Allies fell back, and were about to give way when there arrived a British division under Picton, which had been hurried from Brussels. Soon afterwards the Duke of Brunswick and his army corps arrived.

Wellington was able to deploy the new troops in the nick of time. There was a renewal of the struggle and the Duke of Brunswick fell.

Both sides now received reinforcements, Kellerman's cuirassiers arriving in support of Ney, and another British division under Alten reinforcing Wellington.

In another fierce attack by Ney the cuirassiers succeeded in gaining a foothold in Quatre Bras. At length they were driven off and the badly dented Allied line was able to re-form.

It was about this time that Ney learned that Napoleon had called for d'Erlon. He was furious, and ordered him back.

The battle of Ligny was nominally a success for Napoleon, but what would have been the effect if the Emperor had had the help of d'Erlon is not difficult to estimate. It would most certainly have resulted in the decisive defeat of Blücher. Actually d'Erlon had been unable to help either Napoleon or Ney, for he was engaged going backwards and forwards.

Long before d'Erlon got back to Ney Wellington had assumed the offensive. A further reinforcement of British guards had enabled him to press the attack, and he was markedly superior in numbers, having 32,000 to Ney's 22,000.

The French fought fiercely, but nothing could now stop Wellington, and the enemy were forced back to their original positions just as darkness brought an end to the fighting. Thus neither side could claim a victory, and as their losses were about equal—4,000 each—the battle of Quatre Bras may be considered as drawn.

But there was another aspect to the matter. Napoleon had not achieved what he had intended, for Quatre Bras had resulted in a check to Ney. On the other hand, had Wellington been able to defeat Ney earlier in the day, he could have sent reinforcements to Blücher, and the battle of Ligny might well have been the final defeat of the Emperor.

Wellington's reinforcements had been tardy in arriving. During the night of the 16th other troops arrived from Ghent, Oudenarde and Ath. Details of the battle of Ligny had arrived, and it was now seen that Napoleon and Ney would effect a junction before evening. Wellington therefore decided to withdraw from his positions and join Blücher.

N*

Despite the defeat of Blücher at Ligny and the doubtful fight of Quatre Bras, taken as a whole June 16th was a bad day for Napoleon, for events had not gone according to plan. Two days later he was defeated at Waterloo.

John Sobieski

A victorious general is not necessarily a good administrator. The truth of this has no better illustration than in the case of Poland.

For well over a century she had a series of illustrious fighters who rose to power, even to the dominant position of head of the State, but none seemed capable of successfully handling internal politics.

Such a one was John Sobieski, who gained the crown under the title of John III.

Like many others, he had to admit that the pacification of Poland was beyond him. He died a bitter, disillusioned man, exclaiming : "I am powerless to save her. I can do no more than leave the future of my beloved land, not to destiny, for I am a Christian, but to God the High and Mighty."

Onwards from the latter part of the sixteenth century the Poles had a quaint way of choosing their kings. The crown was offered literally to the highest bidder. In 1575, and again in 1587, it was put up for public auction, and secured first by a Hungarian and then a Swede. It is true that the best candidates usually obtained the prize, but the election left the country in a turmoil for years afterwards, for the defeated candidates had to be driven out by force of arms if they did not retire gracefully.

In 1669 Poland elected one of her own countrymen, and all might have been well but for John Sobieski, commander-in-chief of the army, who formed a series of conspiracies for dethroning the sovereign and eventually succeeded.

John Sobieski was born either in Galicia or Austrian Poland in 1629. He came of a long line of illustrious ancestors, his father, James Sobieski, being castellan of Cracow and governor of Poland. As a youth he was trained in the body-guard of Louis XIV of France, and then travelled with his brother Mark through Italy and Turkey.

They were living at Constantinople when tidings of an

insurrection by the Cossacks and Polish serfs were received, and they prepared to return home at all speed.

They took up arms to assist in suppressing the revolt, and John was present at the battles of Beresteczko (1651), and Batoka (1652). Mark Sobieski was killed in battle.

When the Swedes invaded Poland in 1654, John actually deserted his country, fought with the invaders and helped them to conquer the Prussian provinces in 1655. What impelled him to do this is not known, but he appears to have regretted his treachery and, in the following year, he helped to expel Charles X of Sweden from the central Polish provinces.

In 1665 he became acting commander-in-chief of the army, and in 1668 he received the grand baton of the Crown as permanent commander.

So far so good. He had shown himself to be a great military strategist. He had defeated the Muscovite general Sheremetoff, and had carried out a succession of brilliant exploits against the Muscovite and Tartars. His most signal success had been his victory over an army of Cossacks and Tartars amounting to 120,000, whom he defeated with only 20,000 and thus saved his country from destruction.

Sobieski now showed himself to be typical of the Polish nobility, who were ready to sell their own country to line their pockets. At the election diet of 1669 he accepted a bribe from Louis XIV to support one of the French candidates for the Crown. But soon after the election of Michael Wisniowiecki he again conspired in the French interest, for the downfall of the king.

At that time the Turks were attacking the southern frontier of Poland and, seizing the opportunity, Sobieski emphasized the utter weakness of Michael and endeavoured deliberately to make any form of government impossible.

He and the primate, Prazmowski, formed a league with the object of dethroning the king. The plot was discovered; Louis XIV was charged with being the chief instigator. He repudiated all knowledge of the conspiracy, but this did not satisfy the loyal Poles, who threatened Sobieski, so that he and his confederates were compelled to enlist the services of the Elector of Brandenburg on their behalf.

For two years internal matters remained in abeyance; meanwhile, however, the Turks were still raving the southern

borders of Poland. Sobieski was secretly gratified at the
defeats of the Polish army now that he was no longer commander-in-chief. The Turks had already occupied the key
fortress to south-east Poland, and Lemberg had been saved
only temporarily.

The distracted king did what he could in the circumstances to arouse the country. But it was too late, and he
had to sign the ignominious peace which gave the Turks the
whole of Ukraine, Podolia, and Kamieniec.

At this juncture Sobieski appears to have had another fit
of remorse. He hurried to the frontier, routed the army of
Sultan Mahomet IV, consisting of 300,000 men, out of which
only 15,000 escaped. He afterwards took the fortress of
Kotzin, which till then had been considered impregnable,
with a loss to the enemy of 20,000. He could not, however,
recover Kamieniec.

King Michael called the national armed assembly and
ordered an inquiry into the conduct of Sobieski and his confederates. John retaliated by calling a counter confederation.

Sobieski's victories against the Turks had now made him
popular, and the King and his ministers were powerless to
oppose a rebel who carried with him a majority of the country.
At length a compromise was reached whereby the King
agreed to repudiate the peace he had made with the Turks,
and Sobieski was given a chance to show what he could do
to save the situation.

On November 10th, 1673, he defeated a large Turkish
force at Khotin. On the same day Michael died.

Determined to secure the throne for himself, Sobieski
hurried to the capital, despite the fact that many thousands
of Tartars were swarming over the border.

The elective Diet was held in 1674, and Sobieski appeared
with 6,000 veteran soldiers to support his candidature. Every
other candidate was overawed, and he was elected, notwithstanding considerable opposition from the Lithuanians.

Trouble now broke out in the Ukraine, and Sobieski had
to hurry to the front. His energy and valour temporarily
retrieved the fortunes of the kingdom, which were then at
the lowest ebb. A formidable Ottoman force besieged him
in Lemberg, but, under cover of a snowstorm, he sallied out
with a small force and put the enemy to rout.

In 1676 another army of 200,000 men invaded Poland

under the Pasha of Damascus, the Turks' most famous general. With only 10,000 men Sobieski advanced to meet him. But his reputation threw terror in the ranks of the Turks, and they refused to fight, their leader being glad to escape with honourable terms of peace.

For a few years Poland was immune from the attacks of invaders, and Sobieski was now anxious to establish absolute monarchy with himself as King. But Louis XIV would not hear of it, and the relations between Poland and France were strained to breaking-point.

Sobieski did his best to redress the grievances of the people and to restore order and security internally. All his efforts, however, were of no avail, the nobles refusing to subordinate their interests for the benefit of the country.

Meanwhile the Turks were assembling for another attack on Poland and a general inroad into Europe. Their main attack was against Austria and, in this, they were encouraged by Louis XIV. In 1683 Hungary was overrun, and Kara Mustapha led an army of 300,000 men against Vienna.

Sobieski now achieved the greatest feat of his career.

Vienna seemed certain to fall; Europe was in a state of consternation.

Although Sobieski had no reason to trust Austria, he came at the earnest request of Christian Europe, and, assembling an army of 16,000 he marched to the seat of war. On the way he gathered auxiliaries which increased his force to 70,000. He crossed the Danube, and on September 11th, 1683, he occupied the ridge of the Kalemberg, overlooking Vienna.

Next day he rushed down on the enemy, and after a desperate struggle, drove them from their camp, and captured all their artillery and supplies. He continued the pursuit into Hungary and finally expelled them from the country.

The tide of Turkish invasion had been stemmed, and all Europe sang the praises of Sobieski.

But Poland profited little from this success, for after he had saved Austria, the Empire would not help him to regenerate his own kingdom. Evil fate followed him, and his last campaign in 1690 was a failure. He died on June 17th, 1696, a broken-hearted old man.

Edward the Martyr

When miracles occurred before the tombs of holy persons, it was customary, in the Middle Ages, to transfer the bodies to more elaborate resting-places. This was done in the case of Edward, King of England, known as "The Martyr."

Edward, the "unwaxen child" of the Saxon Chronicle, began to reign at the age of 12. Five years later he was either poisoned or stabbed at the gate of Corfe Castle, some say by his stepmother, Alfreda the Beautiful.

He was buried at Wareham, Dorset, in A.D. 979. Two years later his canonized relics were conveyed to Shaftesbury Abbey for interment.

It must have been an impressive cavalcade that made its way over the Dorset Hills. Behind the coffin was the great St. Dunstan, Archbishop of Canterbury, and Alfwold, Bishop of Sherborne. In the *cortège*, too, were Wulfrith, Abbess of Wilton, followed by her nuns, a large number of Saxon thanes and earls, and many lower orders of clergy.

And so to the majestic Convent on the Hill, founded by Alfred the Great, where they laid Edward to rest with appropriate ceremony in the wall on the north side of the High Altar of the convent church.

The Abbey now received an additional dedication. To St. Mary the Virgin the name of St. Edward the Martyr was added. So many miracles were reputed to have been wrought at the saint's shrine that the religious establishment was known more frequently as the Abbey of St. Edward, while the town itself was referred to as Edwardstow.

Two or three years after the transference of the relics Alfreda became patroness of the Abbey, and her son, King Ethelred, half-brother to Edward, also appears to have taken a great interest in it.

Twenty years later St. Edward himself appeared in a vision to a certain holy man, who was instructed to go to the abbess and tell her that his bones could no longer be allowed to remain in the tomb. In confirmation of this, the cover of the tomb raised itself and remained standing on edge.

Thus in 1001 a second translation was decided upon. On

June 20th of that year the Bishop of Sherborne and others removed the relics and deposited most of the bones in a magnificent shrine in the Abbey. The remainder of the bones were sent to the abbey of Abingdon, Berkshire, and to a small nunnery belonging to Shaftesbury Abbey at Leominster, Hereford.

It was before the shrine of St. Edward that the great King Canute made his last confession and laid down his sceptre, his body being taken to Winchester Cathedral.

For half a millennium Shaftesbury Abbey was one of the most important religious foundations in the country. As a result of endowments and bequests the abbey estates grew into gigantic proportions. Indeed, it was an old saying that "If the Abbess of Shaftesbury could have married the Abbot of Glastonbury their heir would have held more land than the King of England."

At length, in 1539, came John Tregonwell, William Petre and John Smith, commissioners of Henry VIII, and demanded the surrender of the Abbey and estates. The interior of the Abbey church was looted and despoiled.

During subsequent years the church gradually disappeared, its stones being used for building houses in Shaftesbury. Two castles were actually built out of the remains. Finally nothing was left of the magnificent buildings that had stood on an area of eleven acres. The site became a wilderness of grass and weeds.

In 1861 excavations were undertaken by the then owner, the Marquess of Westminster. A portion of the site was cleared and many interesting discoveries were made, including seven tombs inside the church and four nuns' graves outside. The tomb of St. Edward was found, but, of course, it was empty.

Later the excavation was filled in and the site of the Abbey became a garden.

In 1901 another decision was made to excavate on the site. Many objects of interest were found. Graves were opened. A tiled floor, regarded as the best in any church in England, was disclosed. Gold rings, a lead bulla (seal) of Pope Martin V, and some beautiful statuettes were discovered. Many valuable articles were looted by souvenir hunters.

At the end of these excavations the site was neglected

until 1930, when it was offered to the Shaftesbury Corporation, but not acquired.

It then came into the possession of the present owner, who immediately began systematic excavations.

The result of the exploration is given in detail in a booklet by Mr. J. Wilson Claridge, the honorary director of excavations.

The whole site has been cleared and the foundations preserved.

What of the relics of St. Edward ?

On January 22nd, 1931, while work was proceeding on the north transept, a large bedding stone was found at a depth of ten inches. When the covering was removed a small vault was disclosed, filled with a lead casket. The latter contained the bones of a young man. They were nearly all broken, and appeared to have been fractured during life or immediately after death.

This was a remarkable fact, as it is known that King Edward was dragged with one foot in the stirrup, and was actually bruised to death, after he had been either poisoned or stabbed.

The position in which the relics were found suggested that it was a hastily-contrived hiding-place at the time of the visit of Henry VIII's commissioners. The rough casket of lead is further evidence of a hurried reinterment.

Mr. J. Wilson Claridge comments : "Taking all these and other less prominent facts into account, I have no hesitation in concluding that these are actually the sacred remains of St. Edward, King and Martyr, hidden at the Dissolution by the nuns."

The bones have now been placed in a shrine at the north end of the church.

Several other graves were found with their skeleton occupants intact. One is believed to be that of the abbess Agnes Farrar, 1247-1267.

The first pilgrimage to the shrine of St. Edward the Martyr for five hundred years was held last year.

The End of the Pillory

On June 22nd, 1830, the pillory tormented its last victim. Seven years later—June 30th, 1837—an Act of Parliament abolished this barbarous method of punishment.

It is easier to date the end than the beginning of the pillory. A form of it certainly existed before the Conquest, when it was known as the stretch-neck. A statute of Edward I confirmed its use, and recommended that the device should be strongly constructed to avoid damage to the bodies of offenders !

A wooden frame, supported by a post resting on a stool, was the earliest form of the pillory. A much more elaborate affair was a large round contrivance which was capable of holding a dozen. According to an old chronicler, this was used for mountebanks and quacks "that, having gotten upon banks and forms to abuse the people, were exalted in the same kind."

It was, however, used for other offenders, for, in 1287, it is recorded that Robert Basset, Mayor of London, "did sharpe correction upon bakers for making bread of light weight ; he caused divers of them to be put in the pillory, as also one Agnes Daintie, for selling of mingled butter."

The records of pillory punishments disclose some curious offences. Counterfeiting papal bulls and forestalling the markets are two such.

One man suffered punishment for pretending to be a sheriff's officer and arresting some bakers of Stratford for alleged breaches of the city regulations. Another, probably a practical joker, represented himself to be an official of the Archbishop of Canterbury, and summoned the prioress of Clerkenwell to attend before a council.

Until the beginning of the seventeenth century no political or religious offenders appear to have been subjected to the pillory. In the days of Laud and the Star Chamber, however, the victims were almost wholly of this type.

In 1637 the Star Chamber passed a decree prohibiting the printing of any book or pamphlet without a licence from the Archbishop of Canterbury, the Bishop of London, or the two universities. All printers not having licences were set in the pillory and also whipped through the City of London.

One of the earliest "rebels" was Leighton, the father of the Archbishop of that name, who published *Zion's Plea Against Prelacy*, and was fined £10,000, unfrocked, pilloried, branded, whipped, his ear cut off and his nose slit.

On April 18th, 1638, Warton and Lilburn were sentenced to pay £500 and were whipped from the Fleet Prison to the pillory at Westminster for publishing seditious works.

While in the pillory Lilburn courageously distributed copies of the offending publications, and opened his mouth to such good purpose that the authorities found it necessary to gag him.

In 1637 William Prynne suffered the pillory for denouncing plays. This was regarded as an attack on the Queen, Henrietta Maria, who herself took part in amateur theatricals. Prynne eventually lost both ears.

A fellow victim was Dr. Bastwick, whose offence was a pamphlet in which he concluded with the phrase : "From plague, pestilence and famine, from bishops, priests and deacons, good Lord deliver us !"

They stood two hours in the pillory. When Bastwick's ears were removed his wife got on a stool and kissed him, placed the ears in a clean handkerchief and took them away with her.

One of the most infamous of pillory victims was Titus Oates, the author of the so-called Popish Plot. In 1685 he was found guilty of perjury and condemned to be exposed on three separate days.

In 1703 a reward of £50 was offered for the apprehension of a man who was described as "a spare, brown-complexioned hose-factor," who had written a pamphlet entitled *The Shortest Way With the Dissenters*. He was Daniel Defoe, author of *Robinson Crusoe*. He gave himself up and was pilloried three times.

The sympathetic crowd threw flowers instead of rotten eggs and vegetables, and freely circulated his *Hymn to the Pillory*, at the same time singing the lines :

> "*Tell them the men that placed him here*
> *Are scandals to the times ;*
> *Are at a loss to find his guilt,*
> *And can't commit his crimes.*"

Very often a man condemned to the pillory received more punishment than the law intended. It depended upon the temper of the crowd. Rotten eggs were permissible as missiles, and no objection was raised to ordinary street refuse which, before the days of cleanliness, included dead cats, dogs, and rats.

Smithfield was not a good place in which to stand in the pillory, for the market drovers were ready on the target. In 1756 two notorious agents of the police, convicted of perjury, were so roughly treated by the market men that one of them died of his injuries. In 1763 another was killed similarly at Bow, and in 1780 a coachman, named Harry Read, was stoned to death by a mob at Southwark.

There was humour as well as tragedy connected with "pillorings." In 1758 when Dr. Shebbeare was placed in the pillory, a servant stood beside him to protect him from the two kinds of rain that descended upon him. In connection with Shebbeare's punishment, the Sheriff of Middlesex was fined £50 for not conforming to the regulations.

It was laid down that an offender should be set "in and upon the pillory." The sheriff, out of consideration for the Doctor, did not put his neck and arms in the contraption. In allowing the umbrella, he committed a further breach of the law.

An amusing law case was settled in favour of a pillory victim in the days of Elizabeth. The device in which he was confined was so rotten that the footboard collapsed, leaving the unfortunate man hanging by his neck. On his liberation he sued the town for damages caused by an inefficient pillory and won his case.

George Miller, "the man with thirty wives," had a rough time from his "spouses" when he paid the penalty for his indiscretions.

George was one of the fastest wooers on record. He is said to have married thirty times in as many weeks. His sympathetic nature made a great appeal to lonesome domestics.

He began by addressing a love-letter to his intended victim declaring that he had fallen in love with her at first sight and pleading for an interview. A good percentage of the numerous letters he sent to women proved successful. He struck an "I can't live without you!" attitude at the interviews, and one after another of the women fell to his blandishments.

George's next move was to marry, or go through a form of marriage, and finally, to secure his victim's money.

At length George met his Waterloo at the hands of a determined woman.

The sequel was his appearance in the pillory, the target of his thirty "wives."

Women are not good throwers. In this case it was hardly necessary, for, armed with whatever they could find in the street, they walked close up to George and plastered his face.

A pamphlet dated about 1790, entitled *A Warning to the Fair Sex, or the Matrimonial Deceiver, being the History of the noted George Miller, who was married to upwards of thirty different women on purpose to plunder them*, illustrates the scene.

Women are seen scooping up mud from the gutter, and George, his face covered with filth, is shrieking for mercy.

Lady Hester Stanhope

"Stanhope, remember me to your sister."

These last words of Sir John Moore as he lay dying at the Battle of Corunna, were addressed to one of his aides-de-camp, the Hon. Captain Stanhope, son of the Earl of Stanhope, and the person to whom he referred was Lady Hester Stanhope.

That there was an attachment between Moore and Lady Hester seems certain in view of her subsequent eccentric behaviour. Within a year she left England and ultimately took up her residence among the barbarous tribes near Lebanon, adopting their dress and manners, and acquiring an extraordinary power over them.

Lady Hester was the eldest daughter of Charles, third Earl Stanhope, and niece of William Pitt, and was born on March 12th, 1776.

She was noted for her great beauty and accomplishments, her resolute and eccentric character. During Pitt's tenure of office she presided over his establishment and acted as his secretary.

Pitt's death was the first blow to her morbid temperament, and her sorrow was not allayed by the £1,200 a year pension which was granted to her by George III.

A useful woman in a political sense, she could have gone over to the party of Charles James Fox, who offered her a maintenance more in keeping with her previous position, but her pride revolted at the thought of taking anything from him.

Then came the news of the death of her brother and Sir John Moore. Reviling fate, she went to Wales, but after a short residence there she finally went abroad.

In Syria she was often visited by European travellers, who returned with extraordinary stories about her. Her solitary life appears to have increased her eccentricity. It also brought a power of penetration that was the marvel of all. She was able to tell the character of a person by the shape of the head, body and limbs.

Some individuals, she noticed, resembled certain animals, and she inferred from this that they had dispositions peculiar to those animals.

In addition, she believed implicitly in astrology.

As to Lady Hester's own star, we have the authority of her physician, who tells the following story :

What Lady Hester's own star was may be gathered from what she said one day, when, having dwelt a long time on this her favourite subject, she got up from the sofa, and approaching the window, she called me. "Look," said she, "at the pupil of my eyes ; there ! my star is the sun—all sun—it is in my eyes. When a sun is a person's star it attracts everything."

I looked and I replied that I saw a rim of yellow round the pupil.

"A rim," cried she, "it isn't a rim—it's a sun. There is a disc, and from it go rays all round : 'tis no more of a rim than you are. Nobody has got eyes like mine."

Prophecies of all kinds interested Lady Hester, including those of Richard Brothers, who declared that the Jews would one day reoccupy the promised land of Palestine. When he was arrested and committed to prison in the time of Pitt, he asked to see her.

Out of curiosity she complied with his request, and Brothers told her that "she would one day go to Jerusalem and lead back the chosen people ; that on her arrival in the Holy Land, mighty changes would take place in the world, and she would pass seven years in the desert."

So far as is known Lady Hester had not contemplated leaving England at that time. There was no occasion for it, for at that time she was a society hostess and a popular woman. She may have remembered Brothers's prophecy in later years, and deliberately fulfilled a part of it by going to Syria.

At Mount Lebanon she became acquainted with a village doctor, named Metta, who seems to have been impressed with her occult powers. *For some years he was in her service as a kind of steward. He was old, and in common with all Syrians believed in astrology, spirits and prophecy.

In conversation one day he said that he knew of a book on prophecy with references in it which he thought applied to her. Fate, he said, had ordained that he should be the instrument with which she would become acquainted with her great destiny. He requested the loan of a good horse and promised to bring the book if she would promise to ask no questions about it. Lady Hester was intrigued. The mystery appealed to her.

Metta got the horse, and a short while afterwards returned with the book.

It was written in Arabic, and only he could read and explain the text. It contained a phrase which, translated into unromantic English, explained that a European woman would come and live on Mount Lebanon at a certain epoch, would build a house there, and would obtain power and influence greater than a sultan's ; that a boy without a father would join her ; that the coming of the Mahedi would follow, but be preceded by war, pestilence, famine, and other calamities. Furthermore, the Mahedi would ride a horse born saddled, and that a woman would come from a far country to assist in the mission.

There were many other prophecies which interested Lady Hester Stanhope.

She at once began to look round for the "boy without a father," and came to the conclusion that he was the Duke of Reichstadt. Unfortunately, he died before anything could be accomplished ; but Lady Hester was not a wit abashed, and immediately fixed on someone else.

In 1835 another part of the prophecy seemed to be fulfilled when a certain Baroness de Deriat, living in the United States, asked if she might come and live with her.

She awaited the appearance of the Mahedi, and, determining not to be caught unawares, she kept two mares called Laila and Lulu. The former was "born saddled," or, to be more explicit, belonged to a hollow-backed breed. This was for the Mahedi ; the other for herself.

But the Mahedi never came.

Lady Hester formed a new religious creed, and gave away enough of her income to keep herself in serious straits continually.

The closing years of her life were spent in great misery. When she died on June 23rd, 1839, she was buried in her own garden.

Queen Eleanor

Many poems and romances have been written round the ball of silk that led to the exposure of Henry II's intrigue with "his adored charmer," Rosamond.

One day Queen Eleanor saw her husband walking in the garden of Woodstock Palace, a thread of silk attached to his spur.

An accomplished schemer herself, Eleanor was quick to see the significance of this. The fire of Henry's ardour for his Queen had long since extinguished itself ; now, it seemed, it had blazed up somewhere else.

So the suspicious woman followed the thread to its source. It led her to a thicket in the middle of the park. There she found the ball of silk, gradually unwinding itself as it rolled.

The mystery was not solved, and Eleanor determined to keep her secret until she had ascertained in what company he could meet with balls of silk.

A few days afterwards the King left Woodstock for a long journey. He was barely out of sight before Eleanor began to search the thicket.

At length she discovered a low door cunningly concealed by undergrowth. She forced the door and found that it gave entrance to a tortuous subterranean path. Following this she eventually found herself again in the daylight outside a beautiful bower in a particularly lonely part of the adjacent forest.

There followed a terrible scene in which the Queen vented her spite on the fair Rosamond and caused her death.

A loathsome story of the Queen's revenge is told in the French Chronicle of London. The more harrowing details are omitted here. But it is said that the Queen had Rosamond stripped naked and placed between two fires. Then she was put in a bath and beaten with a staff by an old hag until the blood flowed from her body.

She was subjected to other atrocities until she was dead. Her body was thrown into a filthy ditch.

When the King heard how the Queen had treated Rosamond "he made great lamentation." Consulting one of his sorceresses, he ascertained that the Queen had had the body taken from the ditch and was about to bury it at Godstow.

Henry hurried along the road, overtook the modest procession, opened the coffin, gazed at the dead Rosamond, and fell in a swoon.

Recovering, he vowed vengeance for this "most horrid felony," and, according to the legend, prayed : "May the sweet God, who abides in Trinity, on the soul of the sweet Rosamond have mercy, and may He pardon all her misdeeds ; very God Almighty, Thou Who art the end and the beginning, suffer that this soul shall never perish, and grant unto her true remission for all her sins, for Thy great mercy's sake."

He then commanded his attendants to ride on with the body of his beloved, and ordered a funeral service to be held at the "house of nunnes" beside Oxford, known as the Godstow Nunnery.

The legend proceeds that the King "appointed thirteen chaplains to sing for the soul of the said Rosamond as long as the world shall last. And this was according done."

Somehow this story does not ring true. That Henry was capable of carrying on an intrigue with a mistress admits of no doubt ; they all did in those days. But his alleged piety is in conflict with his actions. He is said, for instance, to have instigated the murder of Archbishop Thomas Becket before the altar of Canterbury Cathedral.

One version of the death of Rosamond charges the Queen with poisoning her. Thus did she die :

> *"And casting up her eyes to heaven,*
> *She did for mercye calle ;*
> *And drinking up the poyson stronge,*
> *Her life she lost withalle."*

On the banks of the Isis, about two miles from Oxford, are the remains of the Benedictine Nunnery of Saint Mary and John the Baptist. This religious establishment, founded by Editha of Winchester, was undoubtedly the burial-place of Rosamond.

One legend states that she was an inmate of the nunnery, and that she left the cloister to become his mistress. Another story has it that she was not killed by the Queen, but that she retired to the nunnery with a broken heart through the defection of her royal admirer, and lived there for twenty years before her death.

This version seems the most likely.

Rosamond's remains were originally placed in front of the high altar of the nunnery church. An elaborate hearse was provided which was covered with white silk, and adorned with burning tapers and waving banners.

The tomb remained with wax-lights burning around it until the year 1191, when Hugh, Bishop of Lincoln, had it removed, declaring that it was unfit for the sight of the chaste sisters of the nunnery.

The nuns, however, highly esteemed their companion, and they re-buried her bones in the chapter house and preserved them until their establishment was dissolved in the days of Henry VIII.

Rosamond was the second daughter of Walter, Lord Clifford. She had two sons by Henry—William Longspe, afterwards Earl of Sarum, and Geoffrey, Archbishop of York.

Queen Eleanor was a daughter of William V, Duke of Aquitaine. She was first married to Louis le Gros of France, the wedding being solemnized with great pomp at Bordeaux. She and her husband were crowned Duke and Duchess of Aquitaine in August 1137.

Eleanor was beautiful and she had been reared in all the accomplishments of the south. She was a fine musician and singer.

On her husband's accession to the crown of France she instigated a war with the Count of Champagne, in the course of which the cathedral of Vitry was burned to the ground and thirteen hundred people who had taken refuge therein perished.

Later, when Louis took a crusading army to Palestine, she persuaded him to give her the direction of the army. She directed the campaign so badly that seven thousand French knights lost their lives.

At length Eleanor and Louis were on bad terms and the marriage was dissolved. In the same year she married Henry of Anjou, who became King of England in 1154. She was the mother of eight children by Henry, including the brothers who afterwards became kings, Richard I and John.

Henry had to put up with the mutiny of his sons, probably instigated by Eleanor. He had always been an indulgent father, and had made every provision for them. In addition to revolting against him they quarrelled among themselves. The King's favourite, John, caused the most trouble towards the end of Henry's reign, and this eventually broke his heart.

Tired of the squabbles and his virago wife, he turned his face to the wall, exclaiming : "Let everything go as it will, I have no longer care for myself or the world."

Eleanor lived thirteen years after the death of Henry. She died on June 26th, 1202.

The Martyrdom of John Southworth

The eyes of Sergeant Steel, Recorder of London, were filled with tears.

There was nothing woebegone about the appearance of the aged man who stood before him. With quiet dignity he had listened to the evidence and impressed everyone with his fortitude.

John Southworth had confessed to being a priest, and thus, according to statute, a mortal enemy of the Commonwealth Government. But his judges had little desire to enforce the law. They did their utmost to save his life, even to withholding his confession.

If he would only plead not guilty, they would give him the benefit of the doubt, and thus save their own consciences.

The trial went on for many hours. The judges played for time, rehearing the evidence, hoping that Southworth would relent and plead not guilty.

At length Steel had to pronounce the sentence of the law. He did so in a halting speech, the tears coursing down his cheeks.

Laws had been passed against the Catholics during the

reigns of Elizabeth and James I still remained on the Statute Book at the time of the Commonwealth. When Charles I became King, it was thought that a measure of toleration would be given to the co-religionists of his wife, Henrietta Maria. But Parliament refused to relax the persecution. Thus in 1626 there were many convictions of Catholics throughout England.

Subsequently the influence of Henrietta Maria increased, and a number of Catholic priests were released from prison. In 1627 Southworth, then 35, was tried in Lancaster and found guilty of discharging the office of Catholic priest in England, and sentenced to death. Later he was reprieved and kept prisoner in Lancaster Castle.

There he remained for nearly three years, and then was brought to London and released from the Clink, with several others.

In 1636 London was visited by plague. It was not so virulent as in 1665, but the City and Westminster were deserted by all those who could afford to seek asylum elsewhere. The poorer classes thus suffered most.

Plague houses were closed and no inmate was allowed to leave. Warning notices were placed on the doors. Parishes discriminated and gave relief only to those of the established religion. About 400 Catholic families are known to have been stricken.

Southworth administered Extreme Unction to the dying with other priests. Finally he was the only one who did not contract the disease.

In March 1636-7 information was laid before the Privy Council that Southworth had been seducing people to the Roman Catholic religion. He was arrested and committed to the Gatehouse.

A petition to the Queen eventually secured his release.

In November 1637, Southworth was again detained, this time on the information of a priest-catcher. Again he secured his freedom.

Within three years Southworth was again in trouble and was brought before the Court of High Commission. He was formally committed to the Clink, but on a warrant by Windebank, Secretary of State, was allowed to go.

At the end of 1640 the priest was again in the Gatehouse. The Long Parliament had got the upper hand of the King and determined to enforce the law against recusants and the Popish priests. It would seem, however, that once again Southworth was successful in gaining his freedom.

Little is known of his movements during the next ten or more years. Presumably he was unmolested during the Civil War, and it was not until the Commonwealth was firmly established that efforts were made to get him apprehended.

In 1654, on the information of a man named Jeffries, a priest-taker, he was taken out of bed at night. He confessed that he had exercised his religious functions since his last release.

A record of his trial has been left by a Protestant or a Dissenter.

Attempts were made by the ambassadors of the Roman Catholic countries to get Cromwell to spare Southworth's life.

Cromwell, it appears, replied: "God forbid my hand should be consenting to the death of any for religion," and, presumably, promised a reprieve. Next day, however, according to Richard Symonds, the diarist, Cromwell intimated that he could not carry out his promise as "his Council had advised him that the laws should be executed, to which he had sworn. And he (Southworth) was hanged and quartered, and the quarters the Spanish Ambassador bought of the hangman for 40s."

Southworth's execution took place on June 28th, 1654, "being the eve of the feast of the Prince of Apostles."

It was a stormy day, yet thousands of people crowded round the gibbet at Tyburn.

Says the French Ambassador in his official report:

He was attended to the place of execution by 200 coaches and a great many people on horseback, who admired his constancy.

He made a speech at the gallows, which I send you with these, according to a copy I had from one of the same profession (a priest) who stood under the gallows. . . . There were four coiners hanged, drawn and quartered with Mr. Southworth. He was clothed in a priest's gown, and had a four-cornered cap.

The body was embalmed and sent to the English College at Douai, where Southworth had studied. The remains were buried in the chapel of the College.

Within three months a number of cures, attributed by

people to the intercession of the martyr, were reported. Later the body was laid near St. Augustine's altar in the new chapel that was built.

In 1793, during the French Revolution, all English establishments were suppressed and the Douai College was seized. The students succeeded in saving some of the College treasures, including the relics of John Southworth, which were reinterred beneath the building. There they remained for 134 years.

Meanwhile the college buildings were used as a spinning factory, and later as a cavalry barracks.

In 1863 the hidden college plate was discovered, but the relics were not found.

In 1926 a movement was made for the beatification of John Southworth.

The English College buildings were bought by the town of Douai, and pulled down to make way for a new road.

On July 15th, 1927, a workman engaged on excavation discovered a leaden coffin, moulded to the shape of a human body. It was opened and its occupant was seen swathed in brown linen bands.

St. Edmund's College, Ware, Hertfordshire, whence a part of the Douai College had migrated, was advised, and efforts were made to establish the identity of the relics. X-ray photographs established the fact that the body had been quartered. Other evidence satisfied the examiners that it was the body of Southworth.

The relics were brought to England and deposited at St. Edmund's College. On April 30th, 1930, they were removed to Westminster Cathedral, and translated to the Chapel of St. George and the English Martyrs.

Southworth was a member of a well-known Lancashire family, and the son of Sir John Southworth, of the Manor of Salmesbury.

Admiral Sir John Lawson

A curious story is told about the cause of the outbreak of the war with the Dutch during the reign of Charles II.

The English and Dutch navies were operating against the pirates of Algiers. The port was blockaded by Sir John Lawson, who expected to make an attack as soon as the Dutch admiral appeared on the scene.

De Ruyter arrived with his reinforcements, and saluted Lawson. The latter did not deign to reply; whereupon the Dutchman turned his ships about and sailed for Guinea.

It was not lack of courtesy on the part of Lawson. He was acting under instructions from England.

The Dutch were under treaty to salute British ships in their own waters. It was an indignity which they resented, and, in order to minimize or evade it, they struck their flags whenever they met them, so that it appeared more as a compliment to an ally than a mark of submission to a superior.

The English court knew what the Dutch were doing, and when Lawson went on the voyage to the Mediterranean he received orders not to strike his flag to the ships of any prince or state whatever.

Soon after this incident, Lawson returned to England to find that fighting had already begun between the two countries..

The King sent for him and gave him a command under his brother, the Duke of York, as rear-admiral of the Red. Lawson suitably acknowledged the honour, and suggested a new method of attack against the Dutch.

Lawson had noticed that in the last Dutch war the enemy had been more concerned at the captures of merchant ships made by the British than they had at the destruction of their war vessels. Lawson argued that the Dutch could build ships quicker and cheaper than King Charles could, and that the Dutch Government were heavily subsidized by their traders.

He suggested an attack on Dutch commerce in general, so that the traders might "become beggars through these misfortunes."

The advice was rejected, and King Charles decided to send the whole fleet to sea to engage the enemy's men-of-war, for, aid he, it would not be consistent with his honour to stand n the defensive and avoid fighting them.

After the death of Lawson, circumstances caused the King to remember the advice. The expense of the war had been burdensome. But when he would have put Lawson's ideas into operation there was no Lawson to carry out the scheme, and his designs miscarried.

The failure of the scheme is blamed on Lawson by some historians; but it was too late, in any case, when Charles decided to adopt it, for his ships were badly manned and managed.

Clarendon described Lawson as an "extraordinary person."
He could not understand how a man belonging to a family in
such low circumstances as Lawson's could rise to one of the
highest positions in the Navy.

Little is known of Lawson's early days, but he is said to
have served under the Parliament with fidelity and distinction.
He went to sea at an early age and in course of time obtained
a ship, being made a captain.

In 1653 he commanded a fleet of forty-four ships which
were sent over to the coast of Holland. In this expedition he
captured so many prizes that it brought an end to this war
with the Dutch.

When Cromwell assumed full autocratic power, Lawson's
allegiance to the Commonwealth became lukewarm. He was
an Anabaptist in religion and a republican in politics. He
disliked the Protector's government, but did not resist it.
Cromwell knew his opinions, yet for all this Lawson was
employed to command a fleet for the Channel service in 1655.

Lawson, however, had no belief in the justice of the Spanish
war. Cromwell, he thought, had acted arbitrarily in attacking
the Spaniards, for Spain had made more advances to the
Parliament than any other foreign power.

About this time a conspiracy was hatched against Cromwell.
The conspirators were known as Fifth Monarchy Men, and
Lawson was one of those who joined them.

The plot was discovered and several of the plotters, including Lawson, were arrested and imprisoned.

When he was released, Lawson considered it proper to
retire, imagining that he would never again get a command.
But, strangely enough, on the promotion of Admiral Montagu,
afterwards the Earl of Sandwich, Lawson was called in, given
command of a few frigates, and instructed to take charge of
the whole fleet on its arrival from the Baltic.

Matters were gradually drifting towards a restoration of
the monarchy, and Lawson had many conferences with
cavaliers. When General Monk marched on London, many
wondered what Lawson would do. He made the cryptic
remark to General Ludlow "that, since the Levite and the
priest had passed by without helping them, he hoped they had
now found a Samaritan who would."

Lawson was soon found on the side of the Restoration.
He was appointed vice-admiral, and received the honour of

knighthood.   He became a member of the Navy Board, and was entrusted to conduct Queen Catherine from Portugal.

Then followed the incident in which he did not return the Dutch salute.

During the second Dutch War, Lawson was daily consulted by the Duke of York, who was in supreme command.

On April 21st, 1665, the Duke of York sailed with the grand fleet to the coast of Holland.   On June 3rd an important engagement occurred off Lowestoft.

Lawson was hurt in the knee by a musket ball, and was disabled.   He died on June 29th following gangrene of his leg.

The historian, Lord Clarendon, remarks of his contemporary :

There was another almost irreparable loss this day in Sir John Lawson, who was admiral of a squadron, and of so eminent skill and conduct in all maritime occasions, that his counsel was most considered in all debates, and the greatest seamen were ready to receive advice from him.

In the middle of the battle he received a shot with a musket bullet upon his knee, with which he fell ; and finding that he could no more stand, and was in great torment, he sent to the Duke to desire him to send another man to command his ship, which he presently did.

The wound was not considered to be mortal and they made haste to send him on shore as far as Deptford or Greenwich, where for some days there was hope of his recovery ; but shortly his wound gangrened, and so he died on June 29th, 1665, with very great courage, and profession of an entire duty and fidelity to the King.

Clarendon describes him as the "modestest and wisest man." According to him, Lawson had served in all the actions carried out by Blake, "some of which were very stupendous."

Raymond Lulli

One of the queerest characters of the thirteenth century was Raymond Lulli, the alchemist.

In visions he heard a voice which told him to go and convert the Mohammedans.   He put his affairs in order and went into a mountain solitude, where he learned Arabic, studied science and the works of the Eastern writers.

Raymond believed that he would suffer martyrdom in the cause he had espoused. He even prayed that he might.

His youthful Arabian servant heard his master's fervent appeal, and resolved to facilitate his martyrdom.

One day as Raymond sat at table, therefore, the youth aimed a blow at him with a knife. But the alchemist's instinct of self-preservation was stronger than his desire to become a martyr.

There was a struggle. The Arab was overpowered and handed over to the authorities. He eventually died in prison.

There was another occasion when Lulli might have gratified his wish to die for the cause. But he didn't.

He had gone to Tunis and was preaching Christianity in one of the bazaars. He was arrested and thrown into prison, brought to trial and sentenced to death.

Here was an admirable opportunity for Raymond to show his pluck. But no !

When they offered him a pardon on condition that he quitted Tunis for ever, Raymond left the city in a cloud of dust.

That was the end of his missionary enthusiasm.

But there were other things which made Lulli notorious. His whole history was romantic.

He is said to have belonged to an illustrious family of Majorca, and was born in the year 1235. He married at an early age, left the solitude of his native isle, and took his bride to Spain.

Made Grand Seneschal at the court of the King, he led a luxurious life for several years. He tired of his wife and became enamoured of Ambrosia de Castello, but that lady did not reciprocate his affections.

He wrote passionate appeals in verse, lingered under her window at night, and attempted to attract her attention. All to no purpose ; the chaste wife would have nothing to do with him.

She would not even reply to his letters, until one day she received one which was unbecoming to a gentleman. She responded by telling him that she could never listen to his suit, and advised him to mend his ways and devote himself to some Christian cause.

But Lulli still followed her about. One day she stopped him and made an earnest appeal to him to accept her good advice.

It had the desired effect. Lulli went home, threw up his valuable appointment at court, left his wife and children dividing half of his possessions between them.

He vowed that he would henceforth devote himself to a Christian life. It was then he had the vision in which a voice ordered him to go and convert the Mussulmans.

As we have seen, this proved a farce, and Raymond finally established himself at Milan, where he practised alchemy with success.

It is said by some writers that Lulli received letters from Edward, King of England, inviting him to his country. It is asserted that he gladly accepted the invitation, and was given apartments in the Tower of London, where he "refined much gold." He superintended the coinage and issue of "rose-nobles," made gold out of iron, quicksilver, lead and pewter to the amount of six millions !

Others deny that Lulli was ever in England, and that all the stories of his wonderful powers are to be attributed to another Raymond, a Tarragona Jew.

A work, reputed to be by Lulli himself, but written probably by his admirers, declares that he was in England "at the intercession of the King," but it is not clear whether it was Edward I or Edward II.

As the date of his journey was about 1312, they make it appear that it was Edward II.

Edmond Dickenson, in the *Quintessence of the Philosophers*, declares that Lulli was engaged on work in Westminster Abbey. Years after his departure it is said that much gold dust was found in the cell which he inhabited. This was sold by the architects to their good profit.

In Lenglet's biography of John Cremer, Abbot of Westminster, the latter is given the credit for inviting Raymond to England. Cremer himself had searched fruitlessly for the philosopher's stone for thirty years, when he met the alchemist accidentally in Italy.

Cremer tried to induce Lulli to disclose his secret, but the scientist replied that the Abbot must search for himself.

On his return to England the Abbott urged Edward to invite Lulli to this country.

According to Robert Constantius (1515), Raymond resided for some time in London, and changed base metals to gold in the Tower. He states that he himself had seen the coins made by the alchemist, which were called in England the nobles of Raymond, or rose nobles.

In his own *Testamentum* Lulli claims to have converted fifty thousand pounds weight of quicksilver, lead and pewter into gold.

There is good reason to believe that Raymond came to England and was engaged in refining gold and coining. The historian Camden supports this view, and suggests that the alchemist may have encouraged the belief that he had discovered the philosopher's stone. The alchemist was then 77 and a little childish.

After a short stay in England, Raymond went to Rome, where he tried to carry out some ideals that he had cherished for years.

He had proposed to several Popes that Oriental languages should be introduced into the monasteries of Europe. These suggestions had met with little favour. Other proposals were that all the military orders should be included in one order, so that the united body might more effectively deal with the Saracens and that works written by anyone favourable to the Mohammedans should be excluded from the schools.

On reaching Rome he made a further attempt to lay his ideas before the reigning Pope, but got no encouragement.

The old man then left for Africa, alone and unprotected, to preach the Gospel. Landing at Bona in 1314, he cursed the Prophet before the Mohammedans and so irritated the faithful that they stoned him and left him for dead on the seashore.

Some hours later he was found by a party of Genoese traders, who took him on board one of their vessels bound for Majorca.

Lulli was unconscious. He lingered for several days and then died on June 30th, 1315, as the ship came in sight of his native isle.

James (*Admirable*) Crichton

The academic bigwigs of Paris were astonished one morning when they found attached to the gates of the schools, halls and colleges of the university, and on the pillars and posts of the houses of the literary people of the city, a challenge to anyone to come forward and dispute on any subject at the College of Navarre.

The challenger was James Crichton, a Scotsman, who declared that he would answer any of their questions in any art or science, and in any of the twelve languages, Hebrew, Syriac, Arabic, Greek, Latin, Spanish, French, Italian, English, Dutch, Flemish and Slavonian.

When inquiries were made about the type of person who had made this boastful challenge, they found that he was a frequenter of the worst resorts in the city. They therefore wrote underneath the notices : "If you would meet with this monster of perfection, the readiest way to find him is to inquire for him at the tavern, or the houses of ill fame."

Nevertheless, there were many who were ready to take Crichton seriously, and a day was appointed for the disputation in the certainty that the young braggart would be easily discomfited.

Meanwhile Crichton spent the whole of the intermediate time in hunting, hawking, tilting, vaulting, riding, tossing the pike, handling the musket, and other military feats. He attended concerts, balls, played cards, dice, tennis, and took part in every possible diversion.

In view of this the authorities of the university began to wonder whether they had been victimized by a practical joker.

But, on the day appointed, Crichton was there. The fun began early and continued until six in the evening. The whole learned fraternity of Paris pitted their brains against him without shaking his confidence. He answered all their questions satisfactorily, and, at length, the president became tired of the affair, and had to admit that Crichton was the most extraordinary young man he had ever met.

The president praised Crichton highly for "the many rare and excellent endowments which God and nature had bestowed upon him," and, rising from his chair, advanced with four of the most eminent professors of the university, to offer the congratulations of Paris.

Crichton was presented with a diamond ring and a purse full of gold as a testimony of their respect and admiration.

The Scotsman was given a tremendous ovation, and accorded the title of "Admirable Crichton."

Crichton was not in the least affected by the ordeal, and next day he was to be found at the Louvre, engaging in a tilting match in the presence of a large number of ladies, and the French princes and court.

He won fifteen contests in succession, to the amazement of everyone and the admiration of the women.

Who was this extraordinary person, known as the "Admirable Crichton?"

He is said by most writers to have been born in 1551, but the Earl of Buchan, in a paper read before the Society of Antiquaries at Edinburgh, stated that Crichton was born in August 1560. His father was Lord Advocate of Scotland during the reign of Queen Mary, that is, during the years 1561 to 1573. His mother was the daughter of Sir James Stuart, a member of the family which then occupied the throne of Scotland.

James Crichton is said to have been educated at Perth and to have studied subsequently at St. Andrews. His tutor at that university was John Rutherford, a professor famous for his learning, who wrote four books on Aristotle.

At the age of 20 Crichton had studied all the sciences and could speak and write perfectly ten languages. He was a good rider, dancer, singer, and player on all sorts of instruments.

He began a tour of the Continent, visiting all the great cities.

Two years after his amazing success in Paris he was in Rome throwing out a similar challenge. He affixed a placard on all the conspicuous places of the city as follows: "We, James Crichton of Scotland, will answer extempore any question that may be proposed."

Rome flattered itself on its wit. They treated Crichton as a buffoon. He was ridiculed and satirized, but allowed to appear before the great ones of the Eternal City.

There were present the Pope, several cardinals, bishops, doctors of divinity, and professors of all the sciences, and it is said that he exhibited such wonderful knowledge that he amazed Rome as he had amazed Paris.

A different account of this matter is given by an Italian writer, who declared that Crichton was treated with such disdain, being put on a level with jugglers and mountebanks, that he left the city in disgust before the disputation could take place.

He went on to Venice, and there he met people from all quarters who came to hear him give demonstrations of his ability. After an illness of four months he went to Padua, a university then enjoying a high reputation.

Crichton produced an extempore poem praising the city and university, debated the errors of Aristotle, and excited universal admiration. This exhibition of his talents took place on March 14th, 1581, when, according to the Earl of Buchan, he was only 21.

There were at Padua, however, people who tried to detract from Crichton's merit. In reply to these critics he caused a notice to be fixed on the gate of St. John and St. Paul's Church offering to dispute in all sciences, to turn down certain mathematical professors, to disprove Aristotle, either in figures or in verse, to suit the pleasure of his opponents.

The challenge was accepted, and the contest lasted for three days without in any way exhausting the youthful paragon. Finally he received a great ovation from thousands of people.

Crichton set out for Mantua, where a different kind of fight was awaiting him.

The Duke of Mantua had sponsored a gladiator who had killed three men who had entered the lists with him. Fearful of further danger from this murderer of his own creating, the Duke was anxious to get rid of him. But there was no one who could beat him.

Crichton offered his services, promising to drive the man not only from Mantua but from Italy for a stake of 1,500 pistoles.

The fight took place before the Court. Crichton stood on his defence, parrying the furious blows of the gladiator until the latter became exhausted. Then Crichton ran him through in three places, and the "unbeaten" ogre died amidst the acclamation of the crowds.

The Duke of Mantua now engaged Crichton to reform his son Vincentio de Gonzaga, a young rake who had caused his father much anxiety. Crichton proceeded in a subtle way by writing a comedy, satirizing youths of Vincentio's type.

But the extraordinary part of this story is that he himself played fifteen separate parts in his own play. He acted as clergyman, lawyer, mathematician, soldier and physician with such ability that he seemed to be an entirely different person on each occasion.

The end of Crichton came in a dramatic manner.

On the night of July 1st, 1582, during a carnival, he was walking through the streets of Mantua, playing a guitar, when he was set upon by six masked men.

There was a furious fight which ended in Crichton disarming the leader of the band. The man pulled off his mask, and to Crichton's consternation disclosed the features of Vincentio.

Crichton fell upon his knees and expressed his concern, saying what he had done was only in his own defence. Taking his own sword by the point he handed it to Vincentio, and bid him do what he would with it.

The irritated prince, annoyed that he should have been humbled before his attendants, ran Crichton through the heart.

The reason for this attack on Crichton is not known. It is suggested that the "Admirable" supplanted the other in the affections of a young lady.

The whole court of Mantua went in mourning for Crichton for nine months. Many epitaphs and elegies were composed upon his death, and for a long time afterwards his picture was to be seen in most of the houses of the Italian nobility.

Was Crichton a fabulous person? For centuries his existence or otherwise has been the subject of argument. The problem will probably never be solved.

Samuel Richardson

Many stories are told of the vanity of Samuel Richardson, the novelist.

On one occasion a large party were present at his house in North End Lane, Fulham. One of the men who had recently returned from a visit to Paris, desirous of paying a compliment to Richardson, remarked that he had seen a copy of his *Clarissa* on the table of the French King's brother.

There was a hubbub of conversation at the time and the author affected not to hear the intended tribute.

When there came a general pause, however, Richardson said: "Sir, I think you were saying something about . . ."

He paused, expecting the other to repeat his story. But, to his mortification, his guest replied: "A mere trifle, sir—not worth repeating."

Richardson's vanity annoyed Samuel Johnson. "You think I love flattery," he once said to Mrs. Piozzi, "and so I do. But a little too much always disgusts me. That fellow Richardson, on the contrary, could not be contented to sail quietly down the stream of reputation without longing to taste the froth from every stroke of the oar."

Clarissa Harlowe is generally considered Richardson's masterpiece, but the furore with which *Pamela* was received eight years earlier was enough to make any author vain.

One literary critic remarked that if all other books were to be burned, *Pamela* and the Bible should be preserved.

When it first appeared in 1740, it was received with great applause. It was recommended in the pulpit by well-known clergymen. Alexander Pope said that it would do more good than volumes of sermons. At Ranelagh the ladies held up the book to one another to show that they were in the fashion.

The novelty of the work made it popular. Before *Pamela* was published the romances in existence were mainly according to the French model, melodramatic descriptions of adventure in the days of chivalry. Richardson's novel dealt with contemporary English life, imanners and character.

It thus formed a definte era in English literature, and antedated the first of Fielding's novels by two years. Indeed, Fielding's *Joseph Andrews* was intended as a caricature of *Pamela*.

There was nothing outstanding in the private life of Samuel Richardson.

He was born in 1689 in Derbyshire, but he never referred to his birthplace. His father had been a joiner in London. It would appear that the family were in comparatively poor circumstances, for a design to make Samuel a parson was dropped for lack of funds.

He was educated at a village school, and knew no language but his own.

He was a bashful boy, never taking part in the school sports. He had, however, an extraordinary talent as a story-teller.

In his seventeenth year Richardson was apprenticed to a London printer, whose daughter he afterwards married. Six years after the end of his apprenticeship he began business for himself. He printed newspapers, compiled indexes, and through Lord Onslow was entrusted with the printing of the journals of the Houses of Parliament.

Richardson was over fifty before he made his first notable appearance as an author. How he came to write *Pamela* has already been explained.

Eight years after the appearance of *Pamela* appeared the first instalment of *Clarissa Harlowe*. In this work he portrayed the villain, Lovelace, as a fascinating rogue—too fascinating, Richardson himself believed. Thus in *Sir Charles Grandison*, which appeared in 1753, he made the hero a model of virtue.

In 1754 Richardson was elected master of the Stationers' Company. He was wealthy, and had a country villa first at North End, Fulham, and afterwards at Parson's Green, where, as usual, he lived "in a flower-garden of ladies," happy in their flatteries.

His private life, however, was exemplary. He was hos-pitable, friendly, and generous.

He was married twice. By his first wife he had five sons and one daughter, and by his second five girls and one boy. He lost all six sons and two of the daughters.

In a letter to Lady Bradshaigh he tells of his bereavements.

Thus I have lost six sons and two daughters, every one of which I parted with with the utmost regret. Other heavy deprivations of friends, very near and very dear, have I also suffered. I am very susceptible, I will venture to say, of impressions of this nature. A father, an honest worthy father, I lost by the accident of a broken thigh, snapped by a sudden jerk, endeavouring to recover a slip passing through his own yard.

My father, whom I attended in every stage of his last illness, I long mourned for. Two brothers, very dear to me, I lost abroad. A friend, more valuable than most brothers, was taken from me. No less than eleven affecting deaths in two years!

My nerves were so affected by these repeated blows, that I have been forced, after trying the whole materia medica, *and consulting many physicians, as the only palliative (not a remedy to be expected), to go into a regimen; and, for seven years past, have I forborne wine and flesh and fish; and, at this time, I and all my family are in mourning for a good-sister, with whom neither I would have parted, could I have had my choice.*

From these affecting dispensations, will you not allow me, madam, to remind an unthinking world, immersed in pleasures, what a life there is that they are so fond of, and to arm them against the affecting changes of it ?"

Richardson died on July 4th, 1761.

Sir Stamford Raffles

"In Raffles, England had one of her greatest sons."
So spake Sir Frederick Weld, Lieutenant-Governor at Singapore, when he unveiled the statue of Sir Stamford Raffles in 1887.

Seventy years had passed since Raffles had planted the British flag on the little island in the Malay States. It was then uninhabited save for a few fisherfolk who lived along its shores. It was swampy and unhealthy, and the Government under Castlereagh and Canning thought nothing of it as a British possession.

It was not until half a century later that the importance of Singapore dawned upon the great men in Whitehall. The little colony grew. It became an important export and import centre. It attracted many thousands of orientals, but only a few whites.

Now, however, it has become a strong naval base in the Middle East, as the result of a seven-year plan of fortification.

Raffles did not envisage Singapore as a naval base. He was concerned more particularly with its use as a port for eastern trade routes, and as a centre to stop the activities of the Dutch, who seemed likely to gain pre-eminence over the British in that quarter of the world.

Singapore was founded by Raffles on January 29th, 1819. He was, at that time, Lieutenant-Governor of Fort Marlborough

(Sumatra). Insistent warnings had been sent by Raffles to Lord Hastings, Governor-General of India, of the penetration of the Dutch, who were gradually establishing a complete control over the Eastern Archipelago.

Impressed at last, Hastings sent Raffles to look for a foot-hold in the area which the Dutch were about to seal up. But the Government at home could not make up their mind what action to take, and a few weeks later Hastings had to send a message of recall to Raffles.

Raffles, however, had not lingered. He was off immediately on receipt of Hastings' first instructions, and, by the time a decision had been made to order him back, he had planted the Union Jack on the shore of Singapore with his own hands.

When Raffles returned to England after accomplishing this good work, he found himself in trouble with his employers, the East India Company. There was an accumulation of disputes which made it necessary for him to compile voluminous documents for his own vindication.

At last, in April 1826, the Court passed a formal decision in his favour. At the same time it took care to censure him for "his precipitate and unauthorised emancipation of the Company's slaves !"

After his death the Company made his widow pay £10,000 for certain items which included the cost of his mission to found Singapore.

Born on July 5th, 1781, Raffles was the son of a captain in the West India trade. He was educated at a school in Hammersmith, and at the age of 14 became a clerk in the offices of the East India Company.

His duties were irksome, but he soon secured promotion. During his leisure hours he studied literature and science. He had an extraordinary facility for learning languages.

In 1805 the Company resolved upon the foundation of a new settlement at Penang, or Prince of Wales's Island, and Raffles was appointed assistant secretary of the new establishment. On the way out he learned the Malay language, which gave him an advantage over the other officials, and in 1806 he was made secretary and also registrar to the new court of judicature.

In 1808 he became ill and had to go to Malacca for the recovery of his health. While there he learned a great deal about the trade and resources of the Archipelago. At this time, too, he became acquainted with the Governor-General of India, Lord Minto, who was greatly impressed by the young man.

Then came the turning-point in his career. The East India Company had decided to abandon Malacca, and orders were given to have it dismantled. But Raffles drew up a long report urging the retention of the district. The Penang authorities sent the report to London and a copy to the Governor-General.

Lord Minto immediately gave orders for suspending the evacuation of Malacca, and in 1809 the company finally reversed its own decision.

Years later this matter was considered calmly in the light of subsequent events, and the verdict was arrived at "that Raffles had prevented the alienation of Malacca from the British Crown."

In June 1810, Raffles went to Calcutta of his own accord and was kindly received by Lord Minto. He remained in the city for four months, and finally induced the Governor to undertake the conquest of Java.

Java, which had formerly belonged to the Dutch, was then in the hands of the French.

In August 1811, a British expedition occupied Batavia without fighting. On the 25th of the same month, a battle took place at Cornelis, south of Batavia, which resulted in a British success.

A month later the French commander, General Janssens, capitulated at Samarang, and the island was occupied. Raffles was appointed Lieutenant-Governor of Java.

For five years Raffles ruled this large island. He reformed the departments of revenue, commerce and law, then full of abuses, and ameliorated the conditions of the natives. He abolished slavery, instituted native schools, and opened markets for the free sale of agricultural produce.

He increased the public revenue eight times as much as it had been under the Dutch.

In 1816 there was talk about returning the island to the Dutch. Raffles was recalled to England to find on his arrival that there was considerable misapprehension about the value of Java. He therefore wrote and published in 1817 a history of the island.

In 1805, Raffles had married Mrs. Fancourt, the widow of a Madras surgeon. She died in 1814.

He married, secondly, in 1817, Sophia, daughter of T. W. Hull, of County Down, Ireland, and about the same time was knighted by the Prince Regent.

During his stay in England Sir Stamford Raffles became interested in the formation of the Zoological Museum and Gardens on the model of the Jardin des Plantes at Paris.

In November 1817, he left England and returned to the East, being put in charge of the administration of Sumatra, a post he held until 1823. It was during this period that he founded Singapore as a British possession.

The climate of the East took toll from his health, and his wife, too, suffered from illness. Three of their four children died. In February 1824, he set sail for England for the last time.

They embarked in the sloop *Fame* which, when about 50 miles from land, suddenly broke into flames. The crew of 50 were saved with great difficulty, but all Sir Stamford's papers, including material for a history of Sumatra, Borneo and the islands of the Archipelago, and a map of Sumatra which had taken many months to compile, were destroyed. His own private loss was estimated at £20,000.

He reached England in August 1824, and died suddenly of apoplexy on his birthday, July 5th, 1826. He had just completed his forty-fifth year.

Sir Stamford was a great naturalist, and is regarded as the founder of the Zoological Society.

Edward VI

It is said that when Henry VIII was asked whether he wished his wife's life to be saved, or that of her newly born child, he replied with characteristic bluntness, "The child by all means, for wives can easily be found."

A contemporary poet, probably Thomas Churchyard, has written of the incident. After dealing with the loss of Henry's famous ship, the *Mary Rose*, he concludes :

Being thus perplexed with grief and care,
A lady to him did repair,
And said, "O king shew us thy will,
The queen's sweet life to save or spill?"
"Then as she cannot saved be,
O save the flower though not the tree."
O mourn, mourn, mourn, fair ladies,
Your queen the flower of England's dead.

There is another version of this story, however, which declares that Jane Seymour urged the physicians to save the child rather than herself. She might have survived had she received proper treatment.

Having been shut up in her room a full month before the birth, the Queen had to take part in an elaborate ceremonial of christening three days after.

A procession was arranged, which actually began in the Queen's chamber. Etiquette demanded that she should take part. She was removed from her bed and placed on a pallet emblazoned with the crown and arms of England.

The ceremony took place at midnight in Hampton Court chapel. The two future queens, Mary and Elizabeth—the latter a motherless infant who had been dragged from her sleep—dressed in robes of state, were also there. Seymour, brother of the Queen, carried Elizabeth in his arms, the little princess holding the chrism.

By the side of Princess Mary was Cranmer, who was destined to go to the stake in her reign. The solid silver font was guarded by four baronets, wearing aprons and towels.

The Marchioness of Exeter, who afterwards suffered imprisonment in the Tower, carried the infant prince under a canopy borne by the Duke of Suffolk, the Marquess of Exeter, the Earl of Arundel and Lord William Howard.

The Te Deum was sung, and Edward was baptized, Garter King of Arms proclaiming his title thus: "God, in his Almighty and infinite grace, grant good life and long, to the right high, right excellent, and noble prince Edward, Duke of Cornwall and Earl of Chester, most dear and entirely-beloved son of our most dread and gracious lord Henry VIII."

The baptismal presents included a gold cup from Mary,

three bowls and two pots from Cranmer, similar offerings from the Duke of Norfolk.

The little Edward was carried back in solemn state to his mother's chamber, trumpets sounding a fanfare.

Henry remained by the pallet of the Queen during the three-hour ceremony. She was in a highly nervous state. The "goodly noise" of the trumpets did not improve her condition.

On the following day she was ill, and on Wednesday she was in such a condition that she received the last rites of the Catholic church. Official documents are in existence proving that she was a Catholic.

One giving an account of her last days records :

Her confessor hath been with her grace this morning, and hath done that which to his office appertaineth, and even now is about to administer to her grace the Sacrament of Unction. At Hampton Court this Wednesday morning, eight o'clock.

The Queen, however, improved. On October 24th, twelve days after Edward's birth, she was still alive, as is shown by a letter from Sir John Russell to Thomas Cromwell, in which he states that Jane "is somewhat amended." But she died the same night.

According to a work by Leland published in 1543 :

On Thursday, October 25th, she was embalmed ; and wax-chandlers did their work about her. The next day, Friday 26th, was provided in the chamber of presence, a hearse, with twenty-four tapers, garnished with pensils and other decencies.

Also, in the same chamber, was provided, for mass to be said, richly apparelled with black, garnished with the cross, images, censers and other ornaments. And daily masses were said by her chaplains, and others. This done, the corpse was reverently conveyed, from the place where she died, under a hearse, covered with a rich pall of cloth of gold, and a cross set thereupon.

Lights were burning night and day ; with six torches and lights upon the altar all divine service time. All ladies were in mourning habits, with white kerchiefs over their heads and shoulders, kneeling about the hearse all service time, in lamentable wise, at mass forenoon, and at dirge after.

On November 12th, the Queen's funeral procession set out from Hampton Court to Windsor.

Mary was chief mourner, and the body of the dead Queen was buried in the midst of the choir in St. George's Chapel. According to some authorities the following lines were engraved on her stone :

> *Here a phoenix lieth, whose death*
> *To another phoenix gave breath :*
> *It is to be lamented much*
> *The world at once ne'er knew two such.*

The young "phœnix" was a sickly child. Yet all accounts agree that he was amiable and pious. His father died when he was ten, and his uncles, Sir Thomas Seymour and the Duke of Somerset, who had been appointed Protector, conspired for each other's downfall. Finally Somerset won, and Seymour was executed.

Throughout his brief reign Edward was the puppet of others, and he surrendered himself to their authority. His only consolation seems to have been his Protestant religion. We find him reproving his sister, Mary, for permitting the mass. There were rebellions, a war with France, and the final overthrow of Somerset.

A war with Germany was threatened because Edward condemned Mary's religious views. It was only when his religious zeal was aroused that Edward resisted those who happened to be his counsellors at the time. It was with difficulty that he was induced not to accept the challenge of Germany.

Late in the year 1552 Edward caught a chill while playing tennis. By the following June it was evident that he was dying.

It is believed that his death was hastened by the lack of skill of a woman physician. He breathed his last on July 6th, 1553. He had reigned four years, and was still less than 16 years of age.

Peter the Hermit

There is no more amazing character in medieval European history than Peter the Hermit. He it was who stirred countless thousands of rich and poor alike to risk their all in the fruitless attempt to wrest Palestine from the Turk.

His fanatical enthusiasm was contagious. When he stood up and preached, holding aloft his cross, all minor passions were subordinated to the dominant passion of crusading. Everyone who had a spark of religious feeling hastened to obey the urgent appeal of this anchorite.

The feudal chief forgot to impose upon his serfs; the serfs forgot to complain; the robber left the haunts of his depredations; kings and princes delegated their powers and threw in their lot with the common people.

"To the Holy Sepulchre!" was the cry on every hand. Like migrating ants from an anthill, people of all classes left their homes and began the long trek to Jerusalem.

France was chiefly affected by this fanaticism. Tents were erected around the castles to house the vassals who were to join their lords and fight under their banner.

The meadows, too, were covered with tents, and thousands of booths and huts were constructed near the towns as a preliminary to their occupants joining some popular leader of the crusade.

Everywhere there was excitement which no one attempted to suppress. Those who took part in the expedition were assured of eternal life. Licentiousness, gluttony, drunkenness and debauchery reigned supreme. In and around the canvas townships the courtesan plied her trade with a red cross emblazoned on her shoulders.

Who was this Peter the Hermit?

Of his antecedents little is known. But he was one of those many thousands of people who, having gone to the Holy Land on a pilgrimage, saw the cruel persecutions of the Christians by the Saracens. He was a monk of Amiens, and before entering the priesthood had served as a soldier. He is said to have been short in stature and unattractive in looks.

Returning home to France, he stampeded Europe with an eloquent story of the wrongs of the pilgrims.

It was while in Palestine that Peter conceived the idea of

arousing Christendom to rescue the Christians of the East from the power of the Mussulmans, and to wrest the Holy Sepulchre from the hands of the unbeliever.

On the way home he asked for an interview with the Patriarch of the Greek Church at Jerusalem, who wrote letters to the Pope and the European monarchs detailing the agonies of the faithful.

Peter interviewed the Pope, Urban II, who gave the Hermit full powers to preach the Crusade.

France, Germany and Italy listened to the pleading voice and became frantic in their desire for revenge. The people reverenced the Hermit. They plucked hairs from the mane of his mule as relics. While preaching he wore a rough tunic and a dark-coloured mantle that reached to his heels. His arms and feet had no covering, and he ate only fish and drank only wine. ·

His starting-point is not known, but, says an old chronicler, "we saw him passing through the towns and villages, preaching everywhere, and people surrounding him in crowds, loading him with offerings and celebrating his sanctity with such great praises, that I never remember to have seen such honours bestowed upon anyone."

There were many leaders, and many banners. But the great concourse of people that followed Peter the Hermit was the most important.

Many others joined the intrepid adventurer Walter the Pennyless, said to have belonged to a noble family and have learned the art of war. Another multitude enlisted under the command of a monk named Gottschalk, who hailed from Germany.

In these three bands there were about 300,000 people, including the scum of Europe.

In the spring of 1096, Walter the Pennyless began his trek to Jerusalem. His host rolled through Germany, being received with enthusiasm. They crossed the frontier into Hungary, where they ravaged town and countryside, raided mansions, and plundered the dwellings of the poor. At Semlin the Hungarians attacked the rear of the Crusaders, killed many, and captured their crosses, which they attached to the walls of the city.

Close upon the heels of Walter came the Hermit, with a rabble that was, if anything, worse than Walter's. But they had neither money nor provisions, and were reduced to pillage.

They reached Semlin, and there they saw the crosses that had been nailed to the walls. This infuriated the Crusaders. They rushed the city, and by weight of superior numbers gained access. Terrible scenes of massacre occurred.

At last the King of Hungary appeared on the scene with an army, and the Hermit, who had tried in every possible way to restrain his followers, retreated to the Danube. He was met by a party of Bulgarians, who harassed his band, and he lost thousands of his fighting strength.

At length Peter and his army were separated. He took refuge in a forest near Nissa. The leader of a hundred thousand had become an outcast.

Two or three of his bravest knights collected about five hundred of the stragglers and eventually found the Hermit. It was decided to try and gather the remnants of the army. Twenty thousand were collected ; the bodies of the remainder rotted in the forests of Bulgaria.

They arrived at Constantinople where they found Walter the Pennyless. Here again the Crusaders indulged in rapine and plunder. The Hermit had no power over them. Public buildings were burned, lead was stripped from the roofs of the churches, and other damage done.

Disputes arose between the two armies of Crusaders. Peters' band chose another leader, Reinaldo. They crossed the Bosphorus. Peter deserted them and returned to Constantinople.

The Crusaders were besieged in a fortress by the Sultan Soliman. Reinaldo agreed to become a Mohammedan, delivered up the fortress into the hands of the Sultan, and the Christians were eventually put to the sword.

Other large crusading bands, however, were on the way, and Peter found himself at the siege of Antioch in 1097. He accompanied the Christian army to Jerusalem, and is said to have preached on the Mount of Olives. Returning to Europe, he founded a monastery near Huy, in the diocese of Liége, and there he died on July 7th, 1115.

Edmund Burke

Samuel Johnson was being shown over Edmund Burke's estate at Beaconsfield, Bucks.

Said Johnson : "I do not envy, I am only astonished." But he added a little more significantly : "I wish you all the success which can be wished—by an honest man."

It is clear from this that Johnson did not believe Burke had come by his estate honestly. And, in fact, there *was* a mystery connected with it.

Writing in 1853, an author suggested that Burke made the money to buy his property by speculating in India stock. In the ordinary course there could not have been anything reprehensible in this. But, according to Macknight in his *The Life and Times of Edmund Burke,* he went into his speculations with somewhat grubby hands.

This is what Macknight says :

In 1767, when Lord Rockingham refused to return again to office, and Burke, though in very straitened circumstances, adhered faithfully to his noble leader, it then occurred to the Màrquis that it was incumbent on him to do something for the fortune of his devoted friend.

He advanced £10,000 to Burke on a bond that, it was understood, would never be reclaimed. With those £10,000, £5,000 raised on mortgage from a Dr. Saunders in Spring Gardens, another £8,000 doubtless obtained from the successful speculations of William and Richard Burke, his brothers, in Indian stock, Burke purchased the state of Gregories. After the reverse of his relatives in the year 1769, all the money they had advanced to him was required. Lord Rockingham again came forward.

From that time, through many years of opposition, as Burke's fortune, so far from increasing, actually diminished under his unvarying generosity and the requirements of his position, this noble friend was his constant and unfailing resource.

Burke had an agency for a New York firm through which he received £1,000 a year. When this was lost, Rockingham came forward with further loans. It is estimated that at the time of the latter's death Burke had received from him £30,000. Burke always insisted on giving bonds, which Rockingham, however, never required.

It will thus be seen that Burke kept up his position through the generosity of his friend. He had a splendid mansion, beautiful vineries, exquisite statuary, a four-horsed carriage.

The obvious interpretation of this is bribery.

Burke's sudden rise to affluence created a mild sensation in the House of Commons. It is clear that he had no money at first, and was compelled to write for his bread, as was usual with penniless Irishmen of his day.

At length, becoming private secretary to Lord Rockingham, and entering Parliament for a small English borough, he almost immediately bought his estate for £23,000, and appeared as a man with a large and independent fortune.

Burke's parliamentary colleagues were always anxious to get an invitation to Beaconsfield out of sheer curiosity. Some of them did, and they returned with strange stories of the madness of Burke. He was said to wander about his grounds kissing his cows and horses.

When his niece drew his attention to the rumour that he was insane, Burke replied, "Some part of the world, my dear— I mean the Jacobins, or unwise part of it—think, or affect to think, that I am mad; but, believe me, the world, twenty years hence, will, and with reason, too, think from their conduct that they must have been mad."

The French Revolution was Burke's sore point. He condemned the revolutionaries on every convenient occasion, in Parliament and out.

At the height of the Terror, having to speak on the second reading of the Alien Bill, he called at the office of Sir Charles M. Lamb, Under-Secretary of State.

Three months had passed since the massacre in Paris, and England was still suffering from its repercussion. There was a firm belief in the country that a revolutionary party was in existence whose object was to change the constitution as the French had done.

The story had got round that a member of this party had sent a dagger to a Birmingham manufacturer, asking him to supply a large quantity of the same pattern. The weapon had a foot-long blade and was coarsely fashioned, and could be used as a stiletto or as a pike-head.

The Birmingham manufacturer did not like the order. He brought it to London, called at the Under-Secretary's office, and, in effect, said, "What about it?"

Burke saw the weapon on his visit, and pleaded to be allowed to take it with him to the House of Commons.

It was a good opportunity for Burke to begin with a tirade against the French revolutionaries. There were elements in England at that moment, said he, who were conspiring to follow their example.

At the appropriate moment, when his own friends were lost in admiration of Burke's eloquence, and his opponents were laughing at his apparent fanaticism, he produced the dagger from his bosom and, with a dramatic gesture, cast it on the floor, insinuating that before long those present might be expected to find the point of one of these weapons at their throats.

Of course there were many who showed signs of alarm when Burke revealed the history of the dagger, but there were far more who laughed him down.

It is doubtful whether Burke ever got any satisfaction out of this dramatic attempt to stir up hatred against the Jacobins, for the affair was taken up by Gillray, the caricaturist, who produced a picture that made Burke more ludicrous than ever.

Burke is described by many people as a reckless, haphazard talker. One evening he was at Sir Joshua Reynolds's. He let his tongue slip away in extolling the beauty of some island in the West Indies. A certain widow, named Mrs. Horneck, impressed by Burke's eulogy, lost no time in buying some land there. She finally lost a large part of her slender capital.

"Dear sir," said Mrs. Piozzi to Burke some time later, "how fatal has your eloquence proved to poor Mrs. Horneck."

"How fatal her own folly," retorted Burke. "Odds ! my life, must one swear to the truth of a song ?"

Despite Burke's eccentricities, Johnson was honest in saying of him, "You could not meet Burke for half an hour under a shed without saying he was an extraordinary man."

He died on July 8th, 1797.

James Whistler

"For Mr. Whistler's own sake, no less than for the protection of the purchaser, Sir Coutts Lindsay ought not to have
admitted works into the gallery in which ill-educated conceit
of the artist so nearly approached the aspect of wilful impos-
ture. I have seen, and heard, much of Cockney impudence
before now, but never expected to hear a coxcomb ask two
hundred guineas for flinging a pot of paint in the public's
face."

This criticism by John Ruskin of one of Whistler's noc-
turnes exhibited in the Grosvenor Gallery soon brought a
reply from the painter. It was in the form of a writ. There
was a long trial, and Whistler was at length awarded a farthing
damages.

Then Whistler attacked Ruskin in the following lampoon :

We are told that Mr. Ruskin has devoted his long life to art,
and as a result—is "Slade Professor" at Oxford. In the same
sentence we have thus his position and its worth. It suffices not.
Messieurs, a life passed among pictures makes not a painter—else
the policeman in the National Gallery might assert himself.

As well allege that he who lives in a library must needs die a
poet. Let not Mr. Ruskin flatter himself that more education
makes the difference between himself and the policeman when both
stand gazing in the Gallery.

There they might remain till the end of time ; the one decently
silent, the other saying in good English many high-sounding empty
things, like the crackling of thorns under a pot—undismayed by
the presence of the Masters with whose names he is sacrilegiously
familiar ; whose intentions he interprets, whose vices he discovers
with the facility of the incapable, and whose virtues he descants
upon with a verbosity and flow of language that would, could he
hear it, give Titian the same shock of surprise that was Balaam's,
when the first great critic proffered his opinion.

Whistler's examination during the trial caused widespread
interest. One answer to a question was typical of his sharp
tongue and arrogance. He was asked how long it took him
to execute a certain picture. He replied, "All my life."

Whistler quarrelled with many other people. He accused
Oscar Wilde of plagiarism. Wilde retorted, "With our James

vulgarity begins at home, and should be allowed to stay there."
Whereupon Whistler concluded with : "A poor thing, Oscar,
but for once, I suppose, your own."

The painter also had a dispute with Mr. Frederick Leyland,
the shipowner and art patron, which brought an end to a close
friendship. Eventually Whistler painted Leyland's portrait
in life-size as a devil with horns and hoofs.

Whistler was most eccentric in his dress, and this, combined
with a caustic wit, brought him notoriety.

Following his quarrel with Ruskin he published a satirical
pamphlet entitled *Whistler* v. *Ruskin* : *Art* v. *Art Critics*, and
some years afterwards he produced *The Gentle Art of Making
Enemies*. In these flippant publications he insisted that the
artist could do what was right in his own eyes, and asserted
that the critics and the public had no ideas about art.

Later in life he had a quarrel with Sir William Eden.
Whistler had painted his wife and refused to hand over the
finished work. The dispute came into the Paris courts, and
although the painter was allowed to keep his picture he had
to pay damages.

Whistler—his full Christian names were James Abbott
McNeill—was an American. He was born at Lowell, Massachusetts, on July 10th, 1834. His father was a major.

He was first heard of when he was about 23, when his early
etchings, known as "The French Set," secured him the notice
of a certain art circle, but these works had a small circulation.

He continued to etch and he came to London in 1859,
where he immediately began to portray the quaint riverside
buildings and the craft on the Thames. Within a few months
he produced the Thames series of sixteen etchings. Among
his famous river pictures are "The Pool," "Thames Police,"
and "Black Lion Wharf."

For several years afterwards Whistler did little etching,
but in 1870 he entered what has been called by art critics as his
"Leyland period." This was his association with Mr.
Frederick Leyland, in whose house at Prince's Gate was
Whistler's famous "Peacock Room," painted in 1877.

Among his most notable productions at this time are the
"Model Resting" and "Fanny Leyland." A little later came
the pictures of Battersea and Putney Bridges and "The Adam
and Eve"—a picture of the river-front of old Chelsea.

In 1879, at the suggestion of the Fine Art Society, Whistler made a journey to Venice, and here he began the set of prints called the "Venice Set" and also the "Twenty-six Etchings," some of which also dealt with Venice.

Altogether there are nearly 300 of Whistler's etchings.

About a hundred lithographs have also been catalogued ; some of them are slightly draped figures, some are of Thames subjects, including a Limehouse "nocturne," and other churches in Soho. There are a few oil pictures, including the "Portrait of the Painter's Mother," now in the Luxembourg, and the "Portrait of Carlyle," now at Glasgow.

Whistler's etchings have been described by Frederick Wedmore who, like Ruskin and Oscar Wilde, came in for some sarcasm from the painter. Wedmore had criticized Whistler, and the painter had replied by misquoting a statement made by Wedmore. The latter complained of this pointing out that Whistler had defended himself by turning the words "did not wish to understate Mr. Whistler's merit" into "did not wish to understand it."

The argument concluded by Whistler writing to the *World* in 1883, in the following strain :

Mr. Frederick Wedmore—a critic—one of the wounded—complains that by dexterously substituting "understand" for "understate," I have dealt unfairly by him, and wrongly rendered his writing. Let me hasten to acknowledge the error and apologize. My carelessness is culpable, and the misprint without excuse ; for naturally I have all along known, and the typographer should have been duly warned, that with Mr. Wedmore, as with his brethren, it is always a matter of understating, and not at all one of understanding.

During the latter years of his life, Whistler lived mainly in Paris, but in 1902 he returned to live in London. In 1888, he had married Mrs. Goodwin, widow of E. W. Goodwin, the architect, and daughter of J. B. Philip, the sculptor. She died in 1896. There were no children of the marriage.

In 1886 he became President of the Royal Society of British Artists. It is said that afterwards he referred to the title in a derogatory way. He was also the first President of the International Art Society, which he took a leading part in establishing.

After his death the National Art Collection Fund presented his "Nocturne in blue and silver" to the National Gallery.

Whistler died on July 17th, 1903.

Robert Stevenson

Many people will recall Southey's poem, *The Inchcape Rock*. It tells the story of how the good Abbot of Aberbrothock—a name which rhymes fortuitously with Rock—placed a warning bell on the Inchcape to assist mariners.

Then came the wicked Sir Ralph the Rover, who removed the bell and thus brought about his own destruction, for he himself was wrecked on the Rock.

The Bell Rock lies off the east coast of Scotland, off the Firth of Tay, and about 10 miles from Arbroath and 24 miles east of Dundee harbour. It is in the track of all vessels making for the estuaries of the Forth and Tay.

From a very early period it was the scene of many shipwrecks. The top of the rock was visible only at low water.

In 1799 about 70 vessels were wrecked on the coast of Scotland in a terrific storm, and the necessity of building a lighthouse on the rock was at last recognized.

The Commissioners of the Northern Lighthouses, who were responsible for the lights on the coast of Scotland, put the matter in the hands of their scientific engineer, Robert Stevenson, not to be confused with Robert Stephenson, son of George, the railway engineer.

Robert Stevenson, who was born on June 8th, 1772, was the son of a West India merchant. At the time of his birth the family were in difficulties. When he was 15 his mother married for the second time, her husband being Thomas Smith, of Edinburgh, engineer to the Board of Commissioners of the Northern Lighthouses, to whom Stevenson became an apprentice and afterwards an assistant.

He superintended the works of the Little Cumbraè lighthouse in the Firth of Clyde when he was still only nineteen.

Stevenson subsequently became Smith's partner, and in 1799 married Smith's eldest daughter. Finally he became his successor as engineer to the Northern Lighthouse Board.

His greatest work was the Bell Rock lighthouse, which, it is agreed, was a much more difficult job than the building of the Eddystone lighthouse.

In the course of his work as engineer of the Board, Stevenson prepared designs for a stone tower on the lines of Smeaton's Eddystone. At that time the latter was the only specimen of the kind, and Stevenson had only Smeaton's book on the subject.

But Stevenson did not follow entirely the designs of Smeaton. For one thing, his tower was 100 feet, against the 68 feet of the Eddystone. His base had to be deeper because of the tide, and he made it 21 feet above high water as compared with 11 feet of the other lighthouse.

There were many other details which varied from Smeaton's design.

In 1806 an Act of Parliament was passed authorizing the building of the lighthouse. The Board had considered Stevenson's designs and become uneasy. There were unusual features which the members were afraid at first to adopt, particularly as Stevenson was still a young man and had not had the experience of many other engineers.

The members of the Board gazed at the model which Stevenson had produced and which lay on the table. The matter was considered for a long time. Finally the Board decided to call in John Rennie to consult with their own engineer. He confirmed every detail of Stevenson's.

In constructing the lighthouse it was possible to work only at low tide, which meant an hour or two at a time. In the first season, for instance, it was found impossible to work more than 13½ days of ten hours. In the second season the aggregate was 22 days.

At the outset a ship was taken out to the rock to serve both as a lightship and as quarters for the men. A timber beacon was then built on the rock. It was a two-storey building in which the employees could take refuge during inclement weather.

The preliminary work was begun in 1807, and the construction of the lighthouse in 1808. In 1809 the tower had been raised 17ft. above high water. Next year the whole was finished and the light placed therein.

All the stones were shaped and prepared at Arbroath, and the courses were dovetailed and cemented together. Thus, when complete, the tower seemed welded into one solid mass. The entire height of the tower was 115-ft., and the cost £60,000.

During stormy and foggy weather the machinery which caused the reflectors to revolve, was made to ring two large bells, each weighing about 12 cwt., which warned mariners of their nearness to the rock.

An interesting story is told of an experience of Stevenson while he was visiting other lighthouses on the coast before preparing his design for the Bell Rock. He had visited several erections in Cornwall, and was on his way to join his coach when he was stopped by a party of Cornishmen, who took him in charge and conducted him to the nearest magistrate.

Stevenson, it appears, had aroused suspicion. England was at war with France, and the spy mania obsessed the coast folk. They took Stevenson for a French spy.

Stevenson produced his papers before the magistrate, but the latter was too nervous to take the responsibility of releasing him. He was thus taken to the nearest town, appeared before a bench of magistrates. At length he was liberated with many apologies from the justices.

In 1815 Sir Walter Scott visited the Bell Rock lighthouse, and in the album which was kept there he wrote :

> *Far on the bosom of the deep,*
> *O'er these wild shelves my watch I keep ;*
> *A ruddy gem of changeful light,*
> *Bound on the dusky brow of Night ;*
> *The seaman bids my lustre hail,*
> *And scorns to strike his tim'rous sail.*

A curious story is told of the Bell Rock lighthouse in a mid-eighteenth century work as follows :

One horse, the property of James Craw, a labourer in Arbroath, is believed to have drawn the entire materials of the building. This animal latterly became a *pensioner* of the Lighthouse Commissioners, and was sent by them to graze on the island of Inchkeith, where it died of old age in 1813.

Dr. John Barclay, the celebrated anatomist, had its bones collected and arranged in his museum, which he bequeathed at his death to the Royal College of Surgeons (Edinburgh), and in their museum the skeleton of the Bell Rock horse may yet be seen.

Between 1835 and 1844 a tower similar to the Bell Rock lighthouse was built on the rock called Skerryvore in the Hebrides, by Alan Stevenson, son of Robert. The construction of this lighthouse involved even greater dangers than that of the Bell Rock. Both Robert and his son, Alan, wrote a comprehensive treatise on their works.

Robert Stevenson also designed and executed several important engineering works, such as Hutcheson bridge at Glasgow, the Regent's bridge at Edinburgh, and various road and harbour works. He was one of the first, if not actually the first, to suggest the use of long wrought iron rails for railways.

His sons, Alan, David, and Thomas succeeded him in his business.

Robert Stevenson died at Edinburgh on July 12th, 1850.

Bertrand du Guesclin

Chivalry has no greater name than Bertrand du Guesclin, Constable of France. Yet he was born of a poor family in Brittany and could never read nor write.

"There is not such a bad boy in the world," was his mother's complaint. "He is always wounded, his face disfigured, fighting or being fought; his father and I wish he were peaceably underground."

Tutors could do nothing with young Bertrand. He would have none of their lessons and they at last gave it up as a bad job. Fighting was all he cared about.

A tourney was held one day in the vicinity. Bertrand's father went to see if he could win anything in the lists. His son followed him on decrepit pony.

Bertrand hitched the animal to a post and sat down despondently in the local hostelry. Soon came the first knight who had retired from the lists. Bertrand clutched him by the knees and pleaded to be allowed to use his horse and lance.

The knight, in a bad humour because of his lack of success, was inclined to deride the lad. But Bertrand was so persistent that at length his request was granted.

The knight watched him go out with a smile.

Du Guesclin that day overcame fifteen adversaries. No one knew who he was. But when Du Guesclin senior offered to run a course with him Bertrand threw down his lance and raised his visor.

The astonished father embraced him tenderly. Hitherto he had taken little notice of his son; now he took every possible means to ensure his advancement.

Bertrand entered the French army and took part in the campaign against the English in 1359. His exploits were known all over Europe, and he was feared by the English army.

In 1367 occurred the Battle of Navarete in Spain. The French army under Du Guesclin had come to the aid of Henry of Castile against his brother Don Pedro, the reigning monarch. Pedro was deposed and Henry substituted. The English Black Prince decided to help Pedro. At Navarete, where Henry was defeated and barely escaped with his life, Du Guesclin was taken prisoner.

He was kept in confinement for some time until it pleased the Black Prince to call him in front of him.

The Prince inquired after his prisoner's health.

"My lord," replied Du Guesclin, "I was never better. Indeed I cannot be otherwise than well, for I am, though in prison, the most honoured knight in the world."

"How so?" asked the Black Prince.

"Why, they say in France that you are so much afraid of me that you dare not set me free, and for this reason I think myself so much valued and honoured."

"What," exclaimed the Black Prince, who seemed too dull to understand the crafty game Bertrand was playing, "do you imagine that we keep you a prisoner for fear of your prowess? By St. George it is not so; for, my good sir, if you will pay one hundred thousand francs you shall be free at once."

Du Guesclin intimated that he would pay the ransom.

"But where will you get it?" asked the Black Prince, who had expected the other to argue about the price.

"The King of France, the Pope and the Duke of Anjou will lend it to me, and were I in my own country the women would earn it with their distaffs."

Both the Prince and his wife were charmed with Du Guesclin's directness, and he was invited to dinner, the Princess herself offering to pay twenty thousand francs towards the ransom.

Bertrand fell on his knees before the Princess. "Madam," said he, "I believed myself to be the ugliest knight in the world, but now I need not be so displeased with myself."

Many of the English knights offered him their purses, and Du Guesclin set off to raise the remainder of the money. On the way he met many of his soldiers who had been dispersed by the Black Prince's army, and, pitying their distress, he distributed all his money among them.

He arrived home and asked his wife for one hundred thousand francs which he had left with her for safe custody, but she had also spent the money in relieving the wants of soldiers, a proceeding which Du Guesclin appears to have readily approved.

Bertrand now went to the Duke of Anjou and the Pope and obtained from them forty thousand francs. But on his way back to Bordeaux he could not resist dispensing the whole of the money.

As he had now exhausted the means for raising the ransom he returned to the Black Prince and offered himself as his prisoner.

"Have you brought the ransom?" said the Prince of Wales.

"No," replied Bertrand, "I haven't a doubloon."

"You do the magnificent," said Edward. "You give to everybody and have not what will support yourself; you must go back to prison."

Du Guesclin was about to be led away when a messenger arrived from the King of France prepared to pay the full sum required.

This reads like a fairy tale; and it probably is. But contemporary chroniclers recite this story with every appearance of veracity, and there may be some foundation in fact.

The career of Bertrand du Guesclin was not finished. In a subsequent campaign he captured the city of Limoges from the English, to the annoyance of the Black Prince.

The latter was ill when he heard the news, and although unable to mount his horse, he swore he would regain the city. He did, and the place was ransacked by the English.

When the King of France was told of this conquest he summoned his council and told them that he intended to elect a chief commander to be called Constable of France. The council immediately chose Du Guesclin.

At that time Bertrand was in the vicinity of Limoges, where he was busy reducing castles and forts. As soon as he received the message from the King he rode to Paris and endeavoured to excuse himself, arguing that he was not fit for the high post.

"I am a poor knight compared with the great lords and

valorous men of France, however fortune may have favoured me."

But the King had made up his mind and Bertrand was invested with the office.

The whole nation approved of the King's choice.

Yet, a few years later Du Guesclin lost the confidence of the King. There were many who were jealous of his promotion, and soon the King was inundated with complaints about the inefficiency of the knight and his infidelity. The King wrote a letter to Bertrand couched in offensive terms. Whereupon Du Guesclin immediately sent back his Constable's sword.

The French nation, however, would not stand for it. At length, in face of the outcry, those who had traduced him admitted their "error," and Charles of France graciously apologized and sent the Dukes of Anjou and Bourbon to return the sword. Du Guesclin was appointed to the army in Auvergne, where the English were busy pillaging the country. Bertrand besieged the castle of Randan, but was smitten with disease and died on July 13th, 1380.

The French camp resounded with the moans of the soldiers. Even his enemies paid homage to his memory. The English had promised to surrender on a certain day if they were not relieved. Hearing of the death of Du Guesclin, the commander promptly marched out of the fortress at the head of his men and, kneeling beside the bier on which lay the dead Frenchman, placed the keys of the castle beside the body.

Charles of France ordered Du Guesclin to be buried at St. Denis by the side of the tomb which he had prepared for himself.

As the funeral *cortège* passed through village and town the people came out in their thousands. Great was the lamentation in France.

An appropriate epitaph was placed on his tomb, giving the circumstances of his death, and concluding with "Pray God for him."

Father George Tyrrell

In Storrington Churchyard, Sussex, there is a gravestone which bears the following inscription : "Of your Charity Pray for the soul of George Tyrrell, Catholic Priest, who died July 15th, 1909. Aged 48 years. Fortified by the Rites of the Church. R.I.P."

It is said that he was not buried with the rites of the Roman Catholic Church, although he was "fortified" with such.

At first sight this appears paradoxical. The truth was, however, that Tyrrell, a priest and a member of the Society of Jesus, was excommunicated from his Church for advocating Modernism.

The last Sacraments in his case were administered after he had received what is known as "conditional absolution."

According to the biography of Father Tyrrell, by Mr. H. D. A. Major, in *Great Christians*, Tyrrell was in a semi-conscious condition at the time. Present at the bedside was Baron von Hügel, the dying man's friend.

To an inquiry by the confessor about Tyrrell's spiritual state, Von Hügel gave it as his opinion that his friend would most certainly wish to receive the Sacraments. He would, moreover, have been ready to profess repentance of his sins ; but the Baron felt sure that Tyrrell would not have retracted his Modernist views as a condition of receiving the Sacraments.

Between the day of his death and that of his burial, letters appeared in the Press explaining what had occurred during his last hours. As a result, Tyrrell was denied a Roman Catholic burial, in accordance with the encyclical letter, known as the "Pascendi Gregis," issued by Pope Pius X.

The interment took place in Storrington Churchyard, but a moving funeral oration was given over his grave by his friend, the Abbé Bremond.

To understand Modernism and its relation to the Roman Catholic Church, it is necessary to go back to the days of the great Pope Leo XIII, who reigned from 1878 to 1903. During those years, certain liberal tendencies had crept into the Roman Catholic Church which apparently Leo did not condemn.

His successor, Pius X, however, was strongly against the movement, and in 1907 he published his "Pascendi" *On the Doctrines of the Modernists*, in which he declared that they were "the synthesis of all heresies."

Certain "remedial measures" were prescribed to stop the movement. Professors in colleges holding these views were to be removed and periodical literature was to be censured. Priests were forbidden to discuss theological subjects in congresses.

Tyrrell was the most noted of the British modernists. Born in Dublin in 1861, he was the son of a journalist who died before George was born. The family were left in poor circumstances, and George was sent to various schools, his last being Rathmines College. He became a teacher at Wexford, and in 1878 matriculated and attended lectures at Trinity College, Dublin, but never graduated.

He had been brought up as a Protestant but, like a great many other young men who have afterwards made their mark in life, Tyrrell went through a period of spiritual doubt. Protestantism did not appeal to him, and at one time he was even a professing atheist.

At length the traditions and form of worship of the Roman Catholic Church attracted him. He came to London and stayed with his friend, Robert Dolling, an Anglo-Catholic priest. Later he secured an introduction to the English Jesuits, and was admitted as a novice into the Society.

At this period he was in a maze of doubt, as is shown by his statement : "I drifted into the Church for a thousand paltry motives and reasons, some good, some bad, some true, some false or fallacious.

The English college was opening a branch in Cyprus, and it was suggested that Tyrrell should join that establishment as an usher to assist in teaching English. There he was to remain a year, and, if at the end of that time he was still desirous of entering the Society, he could do so.

He completed his year of probation and then returned to England and entered Manresa House, a Jesuit establishment at Roehampton.

For three years he taught at Malta. In 1888 he studied theology in North Wales. In 1891 he became a priest, and in 1893 was given a district at St. Helens.

Meanwhile he had contributed articles to the periodical

called *The Month*, and in 1897 published his book *Nova et Vetera*, which brought him into contact with Baron von Hügel and his Modernist views. So far the Jesuit authorities had not taken him to task, but in 1900 he wrote an article for a review in which he criticized the Roman Catholic authorities. He was openly complimented for this in the *Nineteenth Century*. In the same year Catholic Liberalism was condemned by the Roman Catholic Bishops.

During the next five years Tyrrell lived at Richmond, Yorkshire, and published a number of works. One, which was written in 1903 caused his expulsion from the Jesuit Society. It contained the words : "I think you should be slow to take theology as seriously as theologians would have us take it."

In a letter to Baron von Hugel he wrote :

I am still young and inexperienced enough to marvel at the blindness that makes Rome devour her most serviceable children, not in exceptional deliria of puerperal fever, but steadily and systematically.

When he left the Jesuit Society, he decided to try and obtain work as a secular priest. But he could get none.

In September 1907 came the "Pascendi." He criticized this document publicly, and at last he was notified that he was excommunicated. He had to leave the monastery at Storrington where he was staying, but he refused to leave the district.

At times he turned his eyes to the Anglican Church, and it is believed that he had intentions of returning to that communion, for other Modernist Roman Catholic priests were admitted into the Church of England at that time.

But on July 6th, 1909, he became seriously ill, and on the 15th he died.

The question as to whether Tyrrell received the full rites of his Church has often been debated. Less than ten years ago the controversy was still going on, as is shown by a pamphlet published in 1928 entitled *An Open Letter from a Catholic Layman to a Catholic Bishop*. It contained the following severe comment :

Since the days of Bruno there has been no more disgraceful exhibition of clerical intolerance, bigotry, cruelty, and I will add stupidity, than was shown by our ecclesiastical authorities in the Tyrrell case.

We laymen are not all fools, my Lord. We have known drunken priests, dishonest priests, evil-living priests—they are few, very few, and far between—but they are there, from time to time. And we have known that as long as they kept their vices quiet, and gave no open scandal, and did their work they were left alone, and when they eventually died were buried with the privileges of the good.

But in George Tyrrell's case we had the unseemly spectacle of a French priest and an English laywoman—all honour to both ! —hurrying from one Catholic bishop to another to beg for what each sternly refused. Christian burial for a great man whose life was beyond reproach, who loved the Church better than she knew, whose sole desire was to serve her.

St. Arsenius

No one at the Court of Theodosius the Great had richer apparel than Arsenius. No one had a more numerous train of servants ; there were a thousand of them, more sumptuously clad than the attendants of the Emperor himself.

The position of Arsenius in the palace was merely that of tutor to the children of Theodosius ; but he had made such an impression on his master that he was treated like a prince, and had been elevated to the rank of senator.

One day Theodosius came to see his children at their studies. He found them sitting down, while Arsenius was standing up. He was so displeased at this that he ordered his children to stand in future, and Arsenius to sit down.

Thus it will be seen that in the Constantinople Court there was no one higher than Arsenius but the Emperor himself.

With all these good things in life one would have expected Arsenius to be content. But, according to the ancient writers, Arsenius pined for a quiet life. He had a great fortune that had become an encumbrance. Titles and honours, we are told, were burdensome to him. As the days passed the urge to get away from it all became more imperative.

At length, about the year 390, he made up his mind. Arcadius, the young son of Theodosius, had become intractable. Arsenius gave him a sound whipping, and then caught a vessel sailing to Alexandria.

Proceeding to the desert of Sceté, he took to the life of an anchorite. He was now in his fortieth year, and had been at the Court of Theodosius for eleven years.

He was praying one day when he heard a voice urging him to a more rigid mode of living if he would obtain salvation. Obeying the injunction he chose for himself a cell that was remote from all civilization. He would have no visitors, and when he went to church, which was over thirty miles away, he would hide himself behind one of the pillars so that he never saw, nor was seen, by anyone.

The Emperor Theodosius sought him far and wide. But they never met again, for the Emperor died in 395.

Arcadius, who had now succeeded to the throne, bore Arsenius no malice for the whipping, and he, too, was anxious to get him back to the Court. Ascertaining his whereabouts, he wrote to Arsenius beseeching him to come and take over the Egyptian tribute and use it for the provision of monasteries and the poor.

But even this opportunity for helping his fellow men did not appeal to Arsenius.

Instead he went on to earn his saintly diadem by becoming even more of a recluse. Thus the immense Egyptian tribute was allocated to secular uses.

Arsenius went through some extraordinary experiences in striving for the needful humility. When he applied to be admitted to the order of the monks of Sceté, they treated him contemptuously until they knew what a great man he had been in Constantinople.

They made him kneel on the floor and eat mouldy bread, and he was subjected to other indignities.

But when they learned of his great distinctions they were disposed to forgive him for his lapses. They were afraid to chide such a great man, and adopted subtle ruses to draw his attention to such faults.

Arsenius had a habit of sitting cross-legged, or of putting one knee over the other. This was forbidden in the rigid establishment of the monks. So the abbot agreed with another of the monks that he should sit with his legs crossed. The monk was severely rebuked for his immodesty and Arsenius, seeing that this was really meant for him, never sat in such a posture again.

A great source of worry to Arsenius was his former

magnificence at the Emperor's court. To atone for this, he became one of the most meanly dressed of all the monks. On working days he employed himself making palm leaf mats. He always carried a handkerchief to wipe away the tears that fell incessantly from his eyes.

He never changed the water with which he damped his palm leaves. When questioned about this, he replied : "I ought to be punished by this ill smell for the sensuality with which I formerly used perfumes when I lived in the world."

One day there came a messenger from Constantinople bringing with him the will of a relative who had left him a large estate. The saint took the will, and was about to tear it to pieces when the messenger begged him not to do so, as such an accident would expose him to be tried for his life.

But Arsenius refused the bequest, saying : "I died before him, and cannot be made his heir."

Arsenius never met the other monks except at spiritual conferences. The abbot once asked him why he shunned their society. He replied : "I dearly love you all ; but I cannot be both with God and with men at the same time."

The ancient writers emphasize the tears of Arsenius. "The source from which they sprang," says one writer, "was the ardour with which he sighed after the glorious light of eternity and the spirit of compunction with which he never ceased to bewail the sins of his life past and the daily imperfections into which he fell."

He was 40 when he left the Court, and he lived as an anchorite for fifty-five years. He spent forty years in the desert of Sceté, except for a short time about the year 395, when the district was overrun by barbarians from Libya. When the plunderers had gone, Arsenius returned to his cell.

He stayed here three years and then left because his hiding-place was too near the city, and he was visited by curious-minded people. He returned to his former cell near Memphis. After two years he died.

Feeling his approaching end, he said to one of his disciples : "One only thing I beg of your charity, that when I am dead I may be remembered in the Holy sacrifice. If in my life I had done anything that is accepted by God, through his mercy, that I shall now find again."

A second incursion of these people, in which they killed several hermits, caused him to vacate his abode in 434.

He then retired to a rock near Memphis, and ten years later he took up his residence at Canopus, near Alexandria.

They were grieved to hear him speak thus. "My hour is not yet come," he said. "I will acquaint you of it. But you shall answer at the tribunal of Christ, if you suffer anything belonging to me to be kept as a relic."

When they asked what they should do in regard to a funeral procession, he answered simply, "Tie a cord to my feet, and drag my carcass to the top of the mountain, and there leave it."

Arsenius died about the year 449. The then abbot was present at his death.

He is given a place in Roman martyrology on July 19th.

Sir Richard Wallace

There has always been a mystery about the birth of Sir Richard Wallace, whose wife bequeathed the famous Wallace art collection to the nation.

He is said by some to have been the natural son of Maria, Marchioness of Hertford, wife of the third Marquess, who made herself responsible for his education.

Others declare that he was a son of the fourth Marquess, and this was generally supposed to be the case during Wallace's life. The fourth Marquess would have been 18 years of age at his birth.

The Hertford line had always been distinguished for its patronage of the arts. The nucleus of the collection was formed by the first Marquess (1719-1794). It was considerably improved by the second Marquess, but, in contrast to his predecessor, who had specialized in French art, he preferred contemporary English portraiture.

Francis Charles Seymour-Conway, the third to hold the title, was an even greater connoisseur. He was a great friend of the Prince Regent, whom he helped to form the collection of pictures at Buckingham Palace and Windsor. He bought for the Prince Van Dyck's famous picture containing three heads of Charles I.

He it is who figures in Thackeray's *Vanity Fair* as the Marquess of Steyne. His wife, Maria, was the daughter of the Marchesa Fagnani. Both the Duke of Queensberry (Old

Q.) and George Selwyn, the wit, claimed to be her father. When the Duke died he left her £150,000. The Marquess of Hertford died leaving nearly £2,000,000.

Hertford House, the home of the Wallace Collection, was formerly known as Manchester House. It was acquired by the third Marquess on the death of the Duke of Manchester, and here he lived with his Marchesa, as she was called.

The Prince Regent was a frequent visitor to Hertford House, and it was alleged that the Marchioness was the attraction. Moore, eulogizing her as the reigning beauty of the day, refers to her :

> *Or who will repair unto Manchester Square,*
> *And see if the lovely Marchesa be there ?*
> *And bid her to come, with her hair darkly flowing,*
> *All gentle and juvenile, crispy and gay,*
> *In the manner of Akerman's dresses for May.*

The fourth Marquess had a mansion known as Hertford House, in Piccadilly. He built it in 1850 from the designs of a Polish or Russian architect. He would not, however, reside in it, because the parishioners of St. James's refused to allow him to pave the street in front of it according to his own ideas. The house contained a fine collection of works of art, and he left it all to Richard Wallace.

The eccentric fourth Marquess also had a passion for French art. He spent his later years in Paris, and he died in 1870 at Bagatelle, in the Bois de Boulogne.

He never married. At the time of his death the English newspapers noted it by printing a few flattering sentences, and a few that were decidedly unflattering. He was charged with being unpatriotic because he had lived so long abroad.

Richard Wallace was educated mainly in Paris, where he became well known in society. He became a collector of all kinds of objects of art, but in 1857 these were sold, and he devoted his time to assisting the fourth Marquess to acquire a magnificent collection of the best examples of painting, armour, furniture, and bric-à-brac.

When the Marquess left England to reside in Paris, Hertford House, Manchester Square, was closed. When he died Wallace sent many of the best of the pictures collected in Paris to this mansion, which was transformed in order to receive them.

During the siege of Paris in 1870 Wallace was particularly active on behalf of the besieged. He equipped several ambulances, founded the Hertford British Hospital, and spent many thousands of pounds on relief work. These benevolent activities made him immensely popular in Paris, and in 1871 he was created a baronet.

From 1873 to 1885 Sir Richard had a seat in Parliament, but he lived mostly in Paris. In his villa in the Bois de Boulogne he had a collection of art treasures that was only a little inferior to those at Hertford House.

He died on July 20th, 1890.

The house in Piccadilly, which Wallace had received with the remainder of the estate of the Marquess, was sold to Sir Julian Goldsmid, after whose death it became the home of the Isthmian Club, which vacated it in 1920.

The collection in the house in Manchester Square was bequeathed to the nation in 1897 by the widow of Sir Richard Wallace on condition that the Government bought a museum to contain it. Hertford House was accordingly bought and reconstructed for that purpose at a cost of £100,000, and opened to the public in 1900.

Nine years later further structural alterations were made. The actual lines of the mansion were preserved, but it was found necessary to make some changes to enlarge the picture galleries.

When the collection was taken over for the public certain necessary weeding out had to be done. But the committee of four who took the matter in hand were compelled to leave the walls over-weighted with pictures, and it was a long time before the exhibits could be displayed satisfactorily, and an informative catalogue produced.

The portrait of the second Marchioness, who drew all London to her assemblies, is displayed there, as well as two of the Prince Regent in his yellow chariot. A portrait by Lawrence of the third Marquess had gone astray, as well as Gainsborough's picture of his wife, Maria Farnani. But there is still the portrait of "Old Q."

In the museum collection is a seventh century Irish bell. With this is associated a tradition that its hereditary keepers produced magical drinks from it which they gave to the lasses of the countryside.

In the collection is François Boucher's famous portrait of

the Marquise (Madame) de Pompadour, in which she is wearing one of the most beautiful dresses ever worn by woman.

The work entailed in gathering this collection must have been enormous. One can picture the anxiety of these noble connoisseurs to obtain the best that was available, and the industry of Sir Richard Wallace in trying to satisfy the demands of the fourth Marquess.

The first Marquess of Hertford received his title in 1794. But long before this time there had been earls and marquesses of Hertford.

The first earls were members of the great Clare family, who held the earldom until 1314. In 1537 the Seymours became connected with the title. Edward Seymour, afterwards the protector Somerset, was made an earl, and the title passed to his son Edward, who lost it, and regained it in 1559.

William Seymour, his grandson, was made Marquess of Hertford and Duke of Somerset, and the two titles remained united until the fourth Duke of Somerset died in 1675. The title then became extinct until 1794.

In some respects it is a pity that the Hertford name is not more closely associated with the Wallace collection. One would like to think that the fourth Marquess gave some indication that he hoped his collection would eventually become the property of the nation.

Peter Thellusson

In the days of George III there were six very rich bankers in London. None of them was a Rothschild, for Meyer Anselm was still a little broker in Jew Lane, Frankfort.

These great bankers were Thomas Coutts, Joseph Denison, Francis Baring, Henry Hope, Lewis Tessier and Peter Thellusson. The last-named was the leading figure in an extraordinary will case.

Thellusson was of French extraction. His family had held enormous estates in France up to the time of the Massacre of St. Bartholomew. Only one of the family survived that dreadful night. He was the ancestor of Peter.

Peter came to London as a young man and established a banking business. He seems to have had one obsession—to make a huge fortune. That is not an uncommon aspiration, but with Peter it was the one thing he lived for.

He had children, but he troubled little about them. He became wealthy but still yearned for more money. He eventually acquired £600,000 in hard cash and a rent roll of £4,500 a year. He had, too, one of the principal banking-houses in the City.

Thellusson is described as a man of "great sagacity and extraordinary perseverance, coupled with a desire of making money which amounted to an all-absorbing passion."

Approaching the age of 60, Thellusson began to wonder what would happen to his money when he was dead. True, he had three sons, but, thought the miserly banker, if he directed that his fortune should be divided between them, the name of Thellusson would probably not be perpetuated as being associated with one of the world's greatest fortunes.

On the other hand, he could not leave it to his eldest son, Peter Isaac, for although Peter was the mainspring of his business there was no assurance that he would be able to increase the capital.

Thellusson had founded a family ; but that was not enough. He visualized some of his descendants marrying into the peerage. Money, and plenty of it, was the only way to ensure a title, and the more Thellussons with huge fortunes, the more chances of coronets.

And this is how this man of "great sagacity and extraordinary perseverance" attempted to solve the difficulty.

He took legal advice and made a will. He left £100,000 to his wife, his three sons and three daughters.

This bequest, he considered, was enough to save him from the stigma of having left his family destitute.

The remainder of his fortune, amounting to more than £600,000, was conveyed to trustees, who were instructed to allow it to accumulate at compound interest until three generations of Thellussons had died out.

When that point had been reached, the greatly increased wealth was to be given to the nearest male descendants who bore the name of Thellusson. It was conceivable, of course, that there might be as many as a dozen or more of these lucky beneficiaries, but by that time, say 100 years from his own death, the money would have increased to something like £30,000,000.

So thought Thellusson. Yet it was by no means a certainty. It looked good on paper ; in practice, it was a different matter.

The truth was that Peter Thellusson had left out of calculation an institution called the Court of Chancery.

When Peter died on July 21st, 1797, the Thellussons naturally contested the will. It cost them nothing to do so, for the law costs came out of the estate.

Here was a lucky break for the bewigged gentlemen of the Chancery Court. They proceeded to pare and even to carve up the Thellusson fortune. Leaders and their juniors, solicitors and their clerks, and even the ushers of the Court had their pickings.

There were suits and cross-suits ; there were injunctions and motions by the hundred. To use the words of a mid-eighteenth century chronicler, the Chancery gentry so "clipped and pollarded Peter Thellusson's oak that it was not much larger than when he left it."

There was a Chancery suit to set aside the will, but there was also a cross-suit to have the trusts of the will performed under the direction of the Court of Chancery ! This latter case lived longer than had Peter Thellusson himself, for at the age of 60 it was still going strong.

But there were many other suits. Some dealt with post-testament acquisitions, others about advowsons. All of these took longer than the average Chancery case.

Everyone who was not busy helping himself to a piece of the fortune declared that the will was unwise, and, moreover, illegal. But in 1799, two years after the death of Peter, Lord Chancellor Loughborough pronounced the will valid. There was an appeal to the House of Lords, who unanimously upheld his decision.

But the absurdity of the whole thing was tacitly admitted by the Government when in the following year an Act was passed rendering null all bequests for the purposes of accumulation for longer than 20 years after the testator's death.

Peter Thellusson's last grandson died in 1856, whereupon the Thellusson case had a new lease of life, and bid fair to go on interminably like Jarndyce v. Jarndyce.

A dispute arose about whether Thellusson's eldest

descendant, or the grandson of Thellusson's eldest son should inherit. It seemed perfectly clear to anyone but lawyers that the latter was the legatee. But the case took three years to reach the House of Lords, who finally·decided the matter in the way that any common sense person would expect.

The descendant of Thellusson who at last inherited was Charles S. Thellusson, who instead of the many millions calculated by old Peter, received about £600,000—less than the original fortune.

Peter Thellusson's wife, before her marriage, was a Miss Woodford, the daughter of Mr. Matthew Woodford, of Carlby, at one time member of Parliament for Evesham. She derived very little satisfaction out of the comparatively small fortune that her husband left her. She is said to have exclaimed : "True happiness is not to be found in money-bags."

Although Peter miscalculated the drift of his fortune, he would have been gratified, had he lived, to know that at least one peerage fell to the Thellusson family. All three sons obtained seats in the House of Commons. In 1806 the Irish barony of Rendlesham was conferred on Peter Isaac. Three of his sons held the title in succession. The present Lord Rendlesham is the sixth Baron.

The Act passed by Parliament which prevented any similar bequests as that of Peter Thellusson was known, and still is known, as the Thellusson Act.

The Thellussons trace their descent to at least the fourteenth century. The first of the family about whom much is known, was Frederick de Thellusson, Seigneur de Flescheres and Baron de Saphorin, one of the nobles who assisted Philip VI of France in his expedition.into Flanders. The family still held their estates to the time of the Massacre of St. Bartholomew.

Sir Henry Percy (Hotspur)

When Henry Percy, the redoubtable Hotspur, scion of the House of Northumberland, heard the prophetic words of the aged seer that he would meet a violent death soon after he had seen Berwick, he laughed with the abandon of a man who fears neither man nor devil.

But when he was girding himself for the Battle of Shrewsbury, his men saw that he was not quite himself.

Said he : "Bring me my sword."

To which his esquire replied : "Sir, you left it at Berwick last night."

"So that was the name of the village where we lay," said Hotspur. "Methinks I now know the cause of my uneasiness. Alas ! Then my death is near at hand, for a wizard once told me that I should not live long after I had seen Berwick. But I thought he meant the town on the Border. Yet will I not be cheaply won."

Nor was he. In the great fight of Shrewsbury in which Scot met Scot and Englishman met Englishman, there was not a braver man than Hotspur. The seer's words were forgotten in the heat of the battle.

The afternoon of July 22nd, 1403, was well advanced when Henry of Lancaster, usurper of the throne of Richard II, rode through the silent ranks of dead.

It was gratifying to him that he had removed from his path the heir of the Northumberlands and the Scottish Earl of Douglas. Somewhere on the field Hotspur lay dead ; Douglas, wounded, had been captured.

Soon word was brought that his enemy's body had been found beneath a heap of slain.

So died one of the illustrious family that had placed Henry on his throne. In the days of Henry of Lancaster's distress they had been his constant friends.

They had stuck to him even when he had become a tyrant and his popularity had waned. They stood by him when Owen Glendower, the Welshman, had revolted. They had fought for him against the Scots and several times saved his crown, when the Earl of Douglas had made his impetuous raids into England.

Percy was the man of whom Shakespeare makes Henry IV say :

> "O that it could be proved
> That some night-tripping fairy had exchanged
> In cradle-clothes our children where they lay,
> And called mine Percy, his Plantagenet !
> Then would I have his Harry and he mine."

Hotspur's quarrel with the King discloses a typical arrogance in the latter.

It was customary in those days for a victorious leader to

admit to ransom his illustrious prisoners. The Percies of Northumberland, assisted by the Earl of March, had scored a victory over the Scots and captured some of their bravest knights. Immediately the King heard of the victory, he dispatched a messenger commanding his leaders not to allow ransom, but to hold their captures.

Henry had a reason for this. He wanted to keep Scotland quiet by retaining her leaders in this country. But his peremptory command gave offence to Percy and March.

Their most important prisoner was the Earl of Douglas, who had led the Scots. Douglas had been wounded in five places and had lost an eye as the result. His ransom would amount to a considerable sum.

But Henry was adamant, and Hotspur made preparations to oppose him.

He first demanded that Sir Edmund Mortimer, his brother-in-law, and Mortimer's nephew, the Earl of Marche (not to be confused with the Earl of March), who had been taken prisoner by the Welsh rebel Owen Glendower, should be ransomed, Hotspur himself offering to find the money.

As the Mortimers were the real heirs to the throne of England it was hardly to be expected that Henry would agree, and he refused.

The next move on the part of the Percies was a demand by the Earl of Northumberland, Hotspur's father, for payment of large sums of money due to him for the costs of the Scottish war.

Money was a distasteful subject to Henry, for he was always short himself. Instead of paying Northumberland in hard cash, the King gave to him the lands of Douglas, which would naturally require a lot more money to defend against the ravages of the infuriated Scots.

Northumberland, who had come to London to see Henry, returned in high dudgeon, and preparations for the revolt went on rapidly. The Earl was joined by the Earl of Westmorland, his brother, and they had the blessing of Scrope, Archbishop of York.

The Archbishop advised them to depose Henry of Lancaster and substitute the Earl of Marche on the throne.

Edmund Mortimer managed to free himself from the clutches of Glendower, and with his twelve thousand men joined the confederacy.

There was now a powerful force against Henry of Lancaster.

Meanwhile the Percies and the Earl of March agreed to release the Earl of Douglas on condition that he joined the enterprise with his Scottish knights.

The Percies and March feigned an attack on Scotland to conceal their real enterprise from Henry IV. They even applied for troops and solicited Henry for money.

But there were few craftier men than Henry of Lancaster. He had seen through this solemn farce, and intimated that he proposed to come north to assist in the campaign. This startled the insurgents. They dropped their Scottish enterprise and said that they intended to march against Owen Glendower.

It was a cleverly conceived plan, and if it had been carried out according to schedule Henry of Lancaster would have lost his crown.

The ultimate failure of the enterprise was due to two factors. Hotspur was too impetuous, and his father, the Earl, was too timid. The old Earl fell ill, or, as some historians declare, grew afraid and refused to march.

Hotspur now had to effect a junction with Glendower before Henry could overtake him. With Douglas and his Scottish knights, and the Earl of Worcester, they collected a further force at Chester, but with the defection of the Earl of Northumberland and lack of support from the Scots belonging to other Highland chiefs, they mustered only 14,000 men.

Henry of Lancaster reached Shrewsbury by forced marches, just as the advanced guard of Hotspur and Douglas were trying to gain that city. The insurgents were forced to withdraw to Hartley Field, a short distance from the city.

Early in the morning of July 22nd, 1403, the two armies faced each other. There were fourteen thousand on each side.

Once more Henry of Lancaster out-manœuvred Hotspur by craft. Knowing that he would be the object of the rebels' attack, he put on plain clothes, and had several knights dressed in royal armour.

Time after time Hotspur's army broke through the loyal ranks. Whenever they saw a royally-dressed and mounted champion they attacked and slew him. Douglas himself is said to have killed three of these sham kings with his own hand.

Once he exclaimed to the real King : "Where the devil do all these kings come from ?" and proceeded to attack the plainly-dressed Henry as he had those who wore the royal armour.

They threw down the standard-bearer and standard, killed the Earl of Stafford and two other knights, and would have dispatched the King but for the arrival of his son, the young Prince Henry, who beat them back.

The battle raged for three hours. Then Hotspur was shot through the head by an arrow. This settled the issue.

The body of Hotspur was placed between two millstones in the market place of Shrewsbury, quartered, and hung upon the gates.

Baron von Trenck

Because Baron von Trenck was indiscreet in his love affairs he was incarcerated for twenty years in German prisons.

All might have been well had he not chosen Princess Amelia, sister of Frederick the Great, for one of his affairs. He could even have continued this intrigue if he had been circumspect, but, after the war between Austria and Prussia, in which he served and received the Order of Merit, he seems to have cast discretion to the winds.

A lieutenant of the Foot Guards twitted him about his mistress. Trenck replied angrily. The officer challenged him. They met with swords, and the challenger was wounded.

On the following Sunday, when Trenck was on the parade ground, the King made the somewhat cryptic remark : "The thunder begins to roll and the bolt may fall. Beware !"

Trenck ignored the warning. A few days later he was a little late on the parade ground. Frederick made this a pretext to send him under guard to Potsdam.

Three days before the Prussian army marched on the second campaign against Austria Trenck was released, but during the campaign itself a new excuse was made for his arrest.

It was alleged that he had been corresponding with a cousin in the Austrian army. This may have been true, but many others were doing the same.

Trenck was sent to the fortress of Glatz and lodged in a chamber belonging to an officer of the garrison. He was allowed his own servants.

His first care was to open up a correspondence with the Princess Amelia, and she sent him large sums of money. With this he attempted to bribe some of the officers of the garrison, but his plan was betrayed by a prisoner.

He was now closely confined, and was guarded with more caution, which made him impatient to escape.

His window looked towards the city, but was 90 ft. from the ground. With a notched pen-knife he sawed through three bars of the window ; with a file procured through bribery he cut through five more.

He then cut his leathern portmanteau into shreds, sewed them together, and with the sheets from the bed, he escaped to the ground. It was a dark night and he sank up to his waist in the mud of the moat. At last he was obliged to call the guard to save himself from death.

A subsequent attempt also proved a failure, and a plot in which he tried to bribe the officers only secured him more severe surveillance. His money was now gone, and the princess intimated that she dare not do anything further for him.

Abandoned to his own resources, and blackened with the stigma of treason, Trenck borrowed money from a friend at Schweidnitz. He prevailed upon one of the junior officers, a Lieutenant Schell, to escape with him.

Schell set him free from his prison, and the two men, after some rousing experiences, succeeded in gaining the mountains. Schell, who had sprained his ankle jumping from the wall of the fort, had to be carried by Trenck.

They stole two horses belonging to a peasant and at length set out for Russia with the intention of joining the Imperial army. On the way they encountered a party of Prussian soldiers who had been sent to capture them. They killed two and got away.

Trenck received a letter from his mother advising him not to enter the Russian service. Accordingly the two men went to Vienna. There they parted, Schell having obtained a commission in the Austrian army.

At Vienna Trenck unluckily became involved in a fray with two Austrian officers, and had to quit. He joined the Russian army, and after the peace of 1748 was well received at the Russian Court.

Everything now seemed favourable to advancement, when

news was brought to him that his cousin had died, and left him his large estate on condition that he joined the Austrians.

He therefore returned to Vienna to find that the fortune was not nearly so large as he had expected. He was able, however, to buy a small estate in Austria.

In March 1754, his mother died, and he went to Dantzig to settle her estate. Here he was betrayed to the Prussian authorities, and taken to Madgeburg and thrown into a dungeon.

"This dungeon," says Baron Trenck, in relating his experiences, "was built in a casement, ten feet long and six feet broad. . . . The light came through a window, at the opening of the arch of the vaulted roof, and went through a wall seven feet thick.

"Though it gave light enough, it was placed in such a manner that I could see neither heaven nor earth ; I could only perceive the roof of the magazine.

"On the inside and outside of this window were bars of iron, and in the substance of the wall between them a grate of wire, worked so close together, that it was impossible to distinguish any object either within or without."

There were palisades outside to prevent the sentinels approaching and giving him assistance. His furniture was a bedstead, fastened to the floor, a mattress, a small stove and a box attached to the wall for him to sit upon. His food allowance for twenty-four hours was a pound of mouldy bread and a jug of water.

Yet Trenck nearly escaped from this apparently hopeless situation. As a result he was placed in an even worse dungeon, water dripped from the ceiling, and Trenck records that for three months he was never dry.

He made several attempts to break out of his prison and was caught only in the nick of time. His gaolers were mystified how he got various implements such as saws and files, and when asked about this he replied, "Beelzebub is my best friend. He brings me everything I want, supplies me with light. We play whole nights at piquet, and guard me as you please, he will finally deliver me out of your power."

They searched Trenck and they searched the cell, but they could never find where he hid the articles. To annoy them still more, he would produce money and defy them to find out where he got it. In course of time they really did believe that he was allied with the devil, and they invited citizens to come to the prison and gaze at him on payment of fifty dollars.

To make it doubly certain that he should not escape, they attached irons to his neck and waist and put him in handcuffs. His only occupation was engraving with nails on pewter cups. His first attempts were crude but, after a time, he became expert. These cups were sold by the officers of the fort for large sums. Many of them found their way into the royal family of Prussia.

One day, in attempting to escape by burrowing under the wall of his prison, a fall of stone buried him and it was not until the early hours of the morning that he was able to get back to his cell and cover up the traces of the hole.

He now trained a mouse to do tricks. It would run up to his shoulder and dance and eat out of his mouth. Even this little companion was denied him when the governor of the prison heard what was going on.

At length, when he had been in various prisons for twenty years, and he was about forty years old, he was released through the good offices of the Austrian ambassador.

He went to Aix la Chapelle, where he married the daughter of a former burgomaster. He began business in wines, but spent much time writing.

Many of his works dealt with the alleged deceit of the Jesuits and monks, who tried to drive him out of the city. They arranged to burn his books before his house, and to raze the house itself to the ground. Trenck appeared at the window with eighty-four loaded muskets. His enemies thought better of it and departed.

In 1780 the Baron moved to Vienna with his family, and was received with favour by Maria Theresa. She allowed him a pension, but her successor revoked it. Then Frederick the Great died and Frederick William II sent him a passport to Berlin.

Accordingly, he proceeded to that capital and there he met Amelia. Hardship and misfortune had changed the handsome man into a wreck in forty years, and they parted in mutual disgust.

Frederick William allowed Trenck a pension of twelve hundred dollars.

But the Baron's career was not yet finished. In 1789 he

went to Paris and received an extraordinary reception from the French society. The streets were decorated and fêtes and entertainments given in his honour.

In the ensuing years he wrote a number of works which upset Frederick William, who stopped his pension. Trenck incited a rebellion in Hungary and was thrown first into prison and then a madhouse. Again he was in trouble with the Jesuits after his release.

He died on the 25th of July in 1797, leaving a family of eight children.

Thomas Osborne, Duke of Leeds

It was a pleasant summer morning during the reign of Queen Elizabeth.

The maid employed by Dame Hewitt, wife of Sir William Hewitt, Lord Mayor of London, leaned out of the lattice window of the house on London Bridge, little Mistress Anne in her arms.

No doubt she had often looked out as the barges passed through the arch beneath. Perhaps she had amused the child in this way before.

On this occasion, however, a terrible thing happened. Little Mistress Anne slipped through her arms and plunged headlong into the river.

The distracted nurse shrieked. Fortunately it was high tide, so that the child's fall was merely a matter of ten feet. But the water was deep and there was a strong ebbing tide.

Anne was carried through the arch of the bridge. She would certainly have been drowned had not the nurse's cries attracted the attention of young Edward Osborne, Sir William's apprentice. He rushed to the window, saw what had happened, threw off his shoes and surcoat and dived to the rescue.

Osborne was a good swimmer and he reached the child with little difficulty. He caught her by the hair, and taking her is his arms, waited for the barge that was passing sluggishly through the arch.

Both were taken aboard by the crew and landed at the steps at Fish Street Hill. Osborne then carried the child home to her parents.

Of course, like all good fairy tales, the matter could not possibly end there. Sir William complimented the lad on his pluck; Dame Alice wept on his shoulder.

A few years passed away and Edward Osborne had become Sir William's righthand man. The old man had no sons, and in time it became tacitly understood that Edward Osborne would get a considerable portion of Sir William's fortune.

Moreover, there was nothing in the way of the romance that had been gradually developing. Mistress Anne had often cast furtive glances at the handsome young apprentice as they sat at table. And Edward was not oblivious of Anne's attractive features and luxuriant brown curls.

Thus everything fell into its proper groove. The parental blessing was given, and Sir William intimated that he proposed to make Edward his heir.

There was a family talk, and, within a fortnight, the banns of "Edward Osborne, bachelor, and Anne Hewitt, spinster," were put up in their parish church.

A few weeks later—a sunny morning in August—the City bells rang out a merry peal for the marriage of the apprentice and his master's fair daughter.

Edward Osborne was an expert with the longbow. In winter he was the best skater and curler of the City's young men. He could sing a good song, could appreciate good wine and was in every way an eligible husband for Mistress Anne.

But his eligibility did not stop there. Osborne belonged to an illustrious family whose lineage went back through the mists of antiquity.

There was a John Osborne, esquire, living at Ashford, in Kent, in the days of Henry VI, for it is on record that he took the oath of allegiance with the other local gentry. By the time of Edward Osborne, the family had become financially embarrassed. Hence Edward had to begin at the bottom of the ladder and become a City apprentice.

The union of the Osbornes and the Hewitts, however, introduced a new aspect, for it founded the ducal house of Leeds.

In the seventeenth year of the reign of Elizabeth, Edward Osborne became one of the Sheriffs of London and Middlesex. Eight years later he was raised to the Civic chair, and soon afterwards was chosen as one of the City's representatives in Parliament.

He died, universally respected, in the year 1591, and was buried in the church of St. Dionis Backchurch, where a monument recorded his activities as London's chief citizen and eulogized his virtues.

A word about Sir William Hewitt. He was charitable and benevolent, a benefactor to a number of hospitals in London and to the poor of various parishes.

He was vice-president of St. Thomas's Hospital, Southwark, and the hospital records testify that he gave £20 and 4s. 8d. to every poor maiden that should be married within a year of his death in two parishes in Yorkshire, with which he was connected by family considerations. In his will, dated January 3rd, 1566, he directed that his body should be buried by the side of his beloved wife, Dame Alice Hewitt, in St. Martin's Church, Candlewick-ward.

Hewitt's money came to the Osbornes at a critical time. It enabled the ancient house to re-establish its fortunes.

Edward was discreet. He did not despise the mercantile career on which he had embarked. He had a son and two daughters. The girls married into the Offley and Peyton families. His son entered the army, and fought in the Irish rebellion under the Earl of Essex and received a knighthood.

Sir Hewitt, as he was named, married Joyce, daughter of Thomas Fleetwood, Master of the Mint, and sister of Sir William Fleetwood, of Cranford, Middlesex.

He had a son, Edward, who was knighted and afterwards created a baronet by Charles I. He was appointed Vice-President of the Council for the North of England, and, on the outbreak of the Civil War, became Lieutenant-General of the Royal forces in the north.

His son and successor was Sir Thomas Osborne who took a leading part in bringing about the Restoration of Charles II. He was appointed Treasurer of the Navy, and Lord High Treasurer of the Kingdom. Finally he was raised to the English and Scottish peerage as Lord Kiveton, Viscount Dunblane and Earl of Danby.

When James II skipped the country in 1688, Danby was on the board of commission which declared the throne of Britain vacant, and keenly supported the accession of William and Mary.

He was rewarded with the elevation to the Marquessate of Carmarthen, and five years later to the Dukedom of Leeds.

But Danby had by no means a peaceful career. He objected to King Charles's leniency to the Roman Catholics, nor did he like Charles's subservience towards France. He urged the abandonment of this policy and advised the King to put his trust in those who had contrived his restoration.

His advice was not taken, though he managed to keep in office, despite rebuffs from Parliament. Naturally, Louis XIV of France had an intense dislike for him, and he sought by every means to bring about his downfall.

At length Danby was impeached, and so determined were the Commons to punish him, that when the impeachment hung fire, a Bill of Attainder was introduced which sent him to the Tower in 1679.

He was released in 1684 and managed to steer himself safely through the maze of internal politics until he became the chief adviser to William III.

But in 1695 he was again impeached, this time for corruption. Although the charge was not pressed, it brought an end to his official career. He died on July 26th, 1712.

Since the days of Edward Osborne, the apprentice, the ducal house of Leeds has absorbed into its line representation, in part or entire, of the houses of Conyers, D'Arcy and Godolphin as well as many of the descendants of the Royal Plantagenets.

Not withstanding this, Edward Osborne, the founder of the Leeds fortune, is worthy to rank with the others.

George Borrow

There is still a circle of literary critics whose adherents believe that George Henry Borrow was a "consummate liar."

He claimed, or it was claimed for him, that before he was 18 he had a knowledge of twelve languages—English, Welsh, Erse, Latin, Greek, Hebrew, German, Danish, French, Italian, Spanish, and Portuguese. In later years he acquired others, and we have the evidence of his translations from the Danish, the Russian, the Polish, the Turkish, and the Cambrian British.

But how he could contrive to translate the Danish *Romantic Ballads* and publish them in 1826 when, all the previous summer, he was experiencing extraordinary adventures, pretending to be a travelling hedge-smith, and consorting with gipsies, is a mystery, particularly when it is remembered that in the year of his vagabondage (1825) he translated from the German *Faustus, His Life and Death.*

The question arises : Does *Lavengro* purport to be a true autobiography ? In his preface to his work, Borrow declares :

In the following pages I have endeavoured to describe a dream, partly of study, partly of adventure, in which will be found copious notices of books and many descriptions of life and manners some in very unusual form.

The story was told in 1850 of events that occurred in 1825. He could not be expected to remember all the incidents that took place twenty-five years before.

The romance of the magnificent road-girl whom he calls Isobel Berners, who was born in Long Melford workhouse, is mainly a product of Borrow's imagination. At their first encounter the girl speaks the language of the road ; within a few hours her speech is correct and elevated.

The episode of the gipsy girl who tried to poison him with doped cake is no doubt also a part of his "dream."

The extent to which *Lavengro*, and its sequel *Romany Rye*, are autobiographical will never be known. But the principal events of Borrow's life are clearly defined.

He was born at East Dereham, Norfolk, on July 5th, 1803, and belonged to a Cornish family not richly endowed with worldly goods.

At the age of 13 he went to Norwich Grammar School. There he remained for three years with—according to Theodore Watts-Dunton—"no great profit." He was then articled to a firm of Norwich solicitors, where he neglected his law studies and gave instead attention to languages.

In the early pages of *Lavengro*, Borrow gives a pen picture of the "respectable" senior partner of the firm, named Simpson. "God bless him !" says Borrow. "I think I see him now with his bald shining pate, and his finger on an open page of *Preston's Conveyancing.*

On the death of his father in 1824 Borrow went to London

with an optimism reminiscent of the ill-fated Thomas Chatterton. He intended "to be stared at, lifted on people's shoulders." He was engaged by Sir Richard Phillips as a hack writer at low wages, with the resultant descent into the doldrums.

Borrow describes his encounters with this radical alderman and sweater. He records how his money was getting short, and one day he asked the publisher for some money.

"Sir," said the publisher, "what do you want the money for ?"

"Merely to live on," replied Borrow. "It is very difficult to live in this town without money."

"How much money did you bring with you to town ?"

"Some twenty or thirty pounds."

"And you have spent it already ?"

"No, not entirely ; but it is fast disappearing."

"Sir," retorted the publisher, "I believe you to be extravagant ; yes, sir, extravagant !"

"On what grounds do you suppose me to be so ?" asked Borrow.

"Sir," replied the publisher, "you eat meat."

"Yes, I eat meat sometimes ; what should I eat ?"

"Bread, sir—bread and cheese."

A year of slavery and Borrow gave it up.

There could never have been a more picturesque vagabond than George Borrow when he set out on an afternoon in May with bundle and stick to tramp the roads.

He was 6 feet 3 inches in height, a well-trained athlete, and had a striking face—partly Greek, partly Hebrew.

He took a course for the south-west and eventually arrived on Salisbury Plain, where his extraordinary adventures began. He became a travelling hedge-smith, made the acquaintance of the waif Isobel Berners, fell in with gipsies and the "Man in Black."

Borrow appears to have made a deep impression on his gipsy friends ; no doubt this was due to his singular appearance, which reminded them of a ghost.

Seven years after the events recorded in *Lavengro* and *Romany Rye*, Borrow secured a post as agent to the Bible Society. He visited St. Petersburg for the Society and remained from 1833 to 1835, publishing a collection of translations. During the next four years he travelled Spain, Portugal, and

Morrocco, and from 1837 to 1839 he was correspondent for the *Morning Herald*.

In 1841 he published his *Gipsies in Spain*, and two years later appeared his *Bible in Spain*. It was the latter work which gained Borrow his reputation. He woke to find himself famous at last.

In 1840 Borrow married Mary Clarke, the widow of a naval officer, who was several years his senior. She had a daughter by her first husband. The family went to live at Oulton Broad, near Lowestoft, and here Borrow began to write again.

It was the success of *The Bible in Spain* that induced Borrow to write *Lavengro*. He anticipated another success ; but he was disappointed. He was much annoyed at this and he stigmatized the critics as "lacqueys, sycophants, and foaming vipers."

Soon afterwards the Borrow family moved to Yarmouth, but whenever possible George rambled in Cornwall. In 1864 he travelled in Wales with his wife and his step-daughter, and next year he visited the Isle of Man. In 1857 he was again in Wales.

In 1860 the family went to live in Hereford Square, Brompton, London, and here Mrs. Borrow died in January 1869. In his *Wild Wales* Borrow has described his wife as a paragon.

In 1874 he returned to Oulton, and here he was often to be seen wandering in the lanes or moping in his summer-house.

The author had become an ogre to the children in the vicinity. He was often met with the cry of "Gipsy !" or "Witch !" for his long white hair and brown eyes which glared at passers-by were enough to inspire terror in the juveniles.

One of Borrow's proudest boasts was his tramp from Norwich to London in 1832. He accomplished the distance of 112 miles in 27 hours and spent only 5½d. on the way.

In his early days he had a great partiality to beer, which he has eulogized in the pages of *Lavengro*. But as he grew older he drank less old ale and more water.

Occasionally he paid visits to Norwich and stayed there for short periods. He died, however, in his own summer-house on July 26th or 27th. A date in August is also given for his death by some authorities.

Thomas Cromwell, Earl of Essex

The town of Boston (Lincs.) wanted to obtain from Pope Julius II a renewal of certain privileges, known as the great and lesser pardons.

Accordingly two men were sent to Rome, to interview the Pope.

It should have been a simple matter, for these privileges had been repeatedly confirmed by the Pope's predecessors.

But the messengers did not relish their task, for Julius had a reputation for irascibility.

At Antwerp they met Thomas Cromwell, admitted a lack of their own qualifications for such important business, and prevailed on him to accompany them to Rome.

Cromwell had rambled over France, Germany, and Italy, and had acquired a knowledge of the language of those countries.   He was thus better equipped than the others, though he admitted that the task was no light one.

They came to Rome and, hoping to get the job over quickly, Cromwell began to consider how best to get on the right side of Julius.

"At length," [says Foxe, in his *Acts and Monuments*] "having knowledge how that the Pope's holy tooth greatly delighted in new-fangled strange delicates and dainty dishes, it came in his mind to prepare certain fine dishes of jelly, after the best fashion, made after out country manner here in England, which to them of Rome was not known or seen before."

Cromwell awaited his opportunity, and when the Pope returned from the hunt, he and his two friends began to sing what Foxe describes as a "three man's-song." In these days we should call it a trio.

The strangeness of the song attracted the attention of Julius. Making inquiries, he learned that they were Englishmen, and, moreover, they had not come empty-handed.

Cromwell and his companions were ordered into his presence. The "fine dishes of jelly" were produced, Cromwell remarking that only kings and princes ate such delicacies in England.

Julius was immensely gratified. "And thus," adds the

somewhat unreliable martyrologist, "were the jelly pardons of the town of Boston obtained, as you have heard, for the maintenance of their decayed port."

It was by enterprise such as this that Thomas Cromwell became the leading man in the country. It was by the same kind of enterprise that he found his way to the scaffold on Tower Hill.

Cromwell's rise was meteoric. Returning from the Continent at the age of 26, he was taken into the employment of Cardinal Wolsey. He is then stated to have obtained a seat in the House of Commons. To his honour it is recorded that when Wolsey was charged with high treason, he defended his master with wit and eloquence.

"And, on this honest beginning," says Lord Herbert, in his *History of the Reign of Henry VIII*. "Cromwell obtained his first reputation."

It was about the year 1530, or early in 1531, that Cromwell gained the confidence of Henry by proposing to him that, in order to get rid of the difficulties about his divorce from Queen Catherine, he should throw off the yoke of the Pope, and assume the supremacy of the Church himself.

He is said to have made this proposal at an audience which he requested and obtained, and to which he went vowing that he would either make or mar his fortunes.

The scheme met with Henry's immediate approval. Thus it would seem that Cromwell has a better right than anyone to be considered the author of the Reformation in England.

In 1531 Cromwell was made a Privy Councillor, and Master of the Jewel House. Soon after, he became Chancellor of the Exchequer. In 1534 he was raised to the posts of the Master of the Rolls and Principal Secretary of State. In the following year he was commissioned to superintend the suppression of the monasteries with the title of Visitor General.

In 1536 he became Lord Privy Seal, and within a few days was made a peer with the title of Lord Cromwell of Okeham. The same year he was constituted Vicar General and Viceregent over all the spirituality under the King, and attended convocation as the King's representative, over both archbishops. Finally, he became Lord High Chancellor of England.

During all this time he was the ruler of the kingdom.

As to the real character of Cromwell, it is difficult to give an unbiased opinion. He has been condemned and praised according to the religious principles of his biographers. There is little doubt, however, that he was ambitious, rapacious and wielded his power like an autocrat. Yet there was another side to his character, for Foxe gives numerous instances of his benevolence.

The following is characteristic.

"In the year of our Lord 1538," [says Foxe] "Sir William Forman being Mayor of the City of London, three weeks before Easter, the wife of one Thomas Freebairn, dwelling in Paternoster Row, being with child, longed after a morsel of a pig, and told her to mind to a maid dwelling in Abchurch Lane, desiring her, if it were possible, to help her unto a piece."

The "maid" told her husband, who, after some difficulty, obtained the pig, which was delivered ready dressed to the home of the Freebairns. But someone gave the Freebairns away. They were visited by Garter King-of-Arms, who demanded if anyone were sick in the house.

The husband admitted that there was not, but that his wife had hungered for a slice of pig.

Freebairn was brought before the Bishop, and on the following day appeared before the Lord Mayor at Guildhall on a charge of eating flesh during Lent. He was sentenced to stand the following Monday in the Cheapside pillory "with one half of the pig on the one shoulder, and the other half on the other."

Freebairn's wife pleaded that she might stand in the pillory instead of her husband. This was not granted, and the pig was tied to Freebairn's back by a ribbon and he was marched into Cheapside.

She now appealed to Cromwell, going to his house for the purpose. Cromwell sent for the Lord Mayor. What passed between them is not known, but Freebairn was set at liberty.

Lord Cromwell's house stood on the north side of Throgmorton Street. It was a magnificent building which he had erected in the early days of his power.

Old accounts testify to the generosity of Cromwell to those who had helped him in the days of his obscurity and poverty. Among the stories one is told of a certain Florentine merchant, Francesco Frescobaldo, who once helped a starving young Englishman (Cromwell) when he applied to him for alms.

Frescobaldo was a frequent visitor to England. He was accidentally seen in the street by Cromwell, now the greatest man in the land. The Chancellor dismounted from his horse and, to the surprise of the Florentine, embraced him. Frescobaldo could barely remember the incident which Cromwell described. It is said however, that the visitor lodged in Cromwell's house all the time he was in England.

It was towards the end of the year 1539 that Cromwell made his one great mistake—the negotiations of the marriage of Henry VIII with the plain Anne of Cleves. Henry never forgave him for producing such an undignified-looking woman for his spouse.

This fall in the graces of his master gave an opportunity to Cromwell's enemies further to disparage him in the mind of Henry.

On the morning of June 10th, 1540, he appeared in his place at the House of Lords as usual. At three o'clock in the afternoon he was arrested by the Duke of Norfolk, as he sat at the Council, on a charge of high treason.

The worst stain on Cromwell's memory was to induce Parliament to proceed against Margaret, Countess of Salisbury, the mother of Cardinal Pole, who was eventually executed without being brought to trial.

Cromwell was treated in the way he had treated the Countess. A Bill of Attainder was quickly carried. He lay for six weeks in the Tower, and was then beheaded on Tower Hill on July 28th.

Robert Schumann

There is not a more pathetic figure in music than Robert Schumann.

The latter part of his life of 46 years was a long nightmare. He was sane one day and mad the next, and always subject to gloomy reflections.

Yet when a complete edition of his works was published it took thirty-four volumes.

Schumann appeared to be a man with an excellent constitution. He was well-built and good-looking, but he had an extraordinarily sensitive nervous system.

As a youth at college he was frequently to be found reading emotional works, particularly those of Jean Paul. At the age of 18 he admitted that these poems often drove him to the verge of lunacy. A youth of stronger character would have dropped these studies when he discovered their danger, but Schumann allowed them to influence him throughout life.

Then there was the anxiety of his courtship of Clara Wieck, whose father refused to countenance his marriage to his daughter. This, more than anything else, brought terrible anguish and many days of helpless melancholy.

Obsessed by what might happen on the morrow, he once wrote to a friend : "Man must work while it is yet day." In 1837, when he was still only twenty-seven, he wrote : "I often feel as if I should not live much longer, and I should like to do a little more work."

His marriage to Clara Wieck in 1840 brought much consolation and a period of happiness, but within four years he was again a prey to serious nervous trouble. For a time he had to give up all work and even to avoid hearing music of any kind.

Then came improvement, then relapse. For a short time he was able to work at his compositions, and then had to abandon them.

In 1851, his strange conduct betrayed the state of his mind. He was deluded into the belief that he could hear a musical note indefinitely prolonged. Whispering voices and strange harmonies buzzed in his ears. Once he got up in the night in obedience to the spirits of Schubert and Mendelssohn, and proceeded to note down a musical piece which they had brought him.

Between these attacks Schumann got down to work in full possession of his faculties. But relapse after relapse made him wish to go into an asylum.

A peculiar phase of this nervous disability made him suppose that all musical performances were too quick, and this absurd fancy caused him much emotion, so that at times he could not bear to hear music at all.

He was subject to fits of abstraction that made it difficult for his friends, whom he was always glad to see. He would sit for hours without saying a word.

On February 27th, 1854, he had thus been sitting for some time, when he suddenly rose and, without uttering a word, left his companions. He left the house without being observed, went to the bridge which spanned the Rhine and threw himself into the water.

Some boatmen went to his rescue. He was dragged into their boat and carried home.

It was now imperative to place him under restraint, and he was accordingly taken to an asylum in Endenich. He never regained his sanity, except perhaps a few hours before his death on July 29th, 1856, when he appeared to recognize some of his friends.

Robert Alexander Schumann was born at Zwickau, Saxony, on June 8th, 1810. His father was a bookseller.

Robert evinced a liking for music at a very early age, and without any instruction in harmony composed several choral and instrumental pieces in his eleventh year, for performance by his schoolmates.

He wanted to adopt music as a career, but his parents were insistent that he should become a lawyer, and he went to Heidelberg where, at a students' concert, he made his only public performance on the pianoforte.

He had taken lessons on this instrument while at school at Leipzig. His tutor, Wieck, finally succeeded in persuading Robert's mother—his father having died—to withdraw her objection to her son following the musical profession.

Fortunately for Schumann, his father had left him enough money to make him independent, but he was at a disadvantage in that he had delayed his systematic study of the piano. To overcome this he devised some mechanical means for giving agility to the fingers, and so lessen the time of practical exercise.

He said nothing about this instrument for a long time. But it was ultimately disclosed through an injury which it caused to the third finger of his right hand. He lost the use of this finger permanently.

In 1831 he began the study of composition under Dorn, the *kapellmeister* in Berlin.

Schumann's nervous disease appears to have been hereditary, his eldest sister having lost her reason. Other members of the family were affected in a smaller degree. His first attack was in 1833, induced, it is believed, by grief for the death of his brother's wife.

During this lapse he attempted to throw himself from his

bedroom window on the fourth storey, but was prevented just in time. When he recovered his sanity, the knowledge of what had occurred was a ceaseless source of terror to him, and he would never afterwards sleep in a room above the ground floor.

In 1834 he began the publication of the *Neue Zeitschrift für Musik*, of which journal he was ten years the editor and principal writer. He contributed many brilliant articles, regarded as some of the best examples of musical criticism, and they obtained for him a great reputation entirely apart from his genius as a composer.

These articles are signed "Florestan and Eusebius." His first musical compositions were also printed under this pseudonym. It would seem, therefore, that Schumann wanted to find his feet before he acknowledged his work.

His attachment to Clara Wieck forms one of the most important features in the life of Schumann. Her father— Schumann's pianoforte teacher—long refused to allow the couple to marry. Schumann argued that he had a sufficient income to keep them, but Clara had already achieved a reputation as a performer. Ultimately they were married, but not until Schumann had taken Wieck to court to show cause why the marriage could not take place.

Clara Schumann after the union greatly extended her reputation, and added much to that of her husband by the performance of his music.

In order to prove his worthiness to marry Clara Wieck, Schumann applied to the University of Jena for the degree of Doctor of Music, and offered to write either a literary essay or a musical composition as the preliminary test. But the University decided this was not necessary, and Schumann got his diploma on the strength of the work he had already done.

Schumann left Leipzig in 1844 to undertake the direction of a vocal society in Dresden. In 1850 he removed to Dusseldorf, where he became musical director, but he never made any success as a conductor, presumably because of his malady.

It is impossible to enumerate all the works of Schumann, but it may be stated that his *Symphony in B Flat* was first played at his wife's concert in Leipzig in December 1841. The *Scherzo and Finale in E* was written in the same year. The *Symphony in C* was written in 1845-46, and that in *E Flat* in 1849. The *D Minor* appeared in 1851.

His cantata *Paradise and the Peri* was composed in 1843 at the suggestion of the German translator of Moore's poem, and was first performed at Leipzig. Among his other cantatas are *Der Rose Pilgerfahrt, Hermannund Dorothea, Der Königsohn,* and *Des Sangers Fluch,* and also a mass and requiem.

The opera *Genoveva* was performed at Leipzig in 1850, and his overture and incidental music to Byron's *Manfred* at Weimar in 1852. The music for Goethe's *Faust* was written at four different periods.

William Penn

Rex *v.* William Penn and William Mead.

Before John Howell, Recorder of London, and Samuel Starling, Lord Mayor.

Charge : Causing a riot through preaching in Gracechurch Street, London.

This trial is one of the most important in the history of British Courts, for it emphasized the right of trial by jury.

Both Penn and Mead made such a remarkable defence that the Recorder, ignorant of the law, had to take refuge in systematic browbeating of prisoners and jury.

At the opening of the proceedings the accused demanded to know on what law the indictment was based.

The Recorder : The Common Law.

They asked to be shown it.

The Recorder flew into a passion. "Think ye I carry the Common Law on my back !" he exclaimed.

He pointed out—or tried to do so—that this particular case was founded upon hundreds that had already been judged. He then admitted that some of the leading lawyers could scarcely tell what it was.

"If it is difficult to produce it cannot be *common* law," retorted Penn. He continued to press for the production of the appropriate law.

The Recorder : "It is *lex non scripta*, that which many have studied thirty or forty years to know, and would you have me tell you in a moment ?"

Penn : "Certainly ; if the common law be so hard to be understood, it is far from being common."

Penn then proceeded to tell the court more about the law

than they knew themselves. He told them that the rights of prisoners were secured by the Acts of Parliament of Henry III and Edwards I and II.

The Lord Mayor and the Recorder consulted together, and then the former said audibly : "My lord, if you take not some course with this pestilent fellow, to stop his mouth, we shall not be able to do anything to-night."

The prisoners persisted in their demand to be shown the law and reiterated the illegality of the whole business.

Prevented from charging the jury by Penn's numerous interruptions, the Recorder and Lord Mayor decided to remove the prisoners to the bail-dock.

Here, however, the prisoners could just hear what was going on. The Recorder was making gross misstatements, and Penn called out that there was no law by which a jury could be charged in the absence of the prisoners.

He then addressed the jury and told them they were his judges, and that they could not consider a verdict until they, the accused, had been heard.

"Pull that fellow down ; pull him down !" shouted the Recorder.

He finished his charge to the jury and then asked them for their verdict.

"Guilty of speaking in Gracechurch Street," said the foreman.

"Is that all ?" demanded the Recorder. "You mean guilty of speaking to a tumultuous assembly."

"My lord," replied the trembling foreman, "that is all I have in commission."

The Lord Mayor sent back the jury to amend their verdict. Both he and the Recorder were in an explosive state.

When again called into court the jury brought in the verdict in writing with all their signatures appended. The only words they had added to their previous verdict were "or preaching to an assembly." That, of course, was no crime. What the justices wanted was the addition of the word "riotous."

The court again flew into a rage and ordered the jury to be shut up all night without meat, drink, fire, candles or tobacco.

"Stand firm !" advised Penn. "Do not give away your right !"

"We will not relinquish our right," replied Edward Bushell, one of the jurymen.

When the court resumed next day, the jury declared that they could bring no other verdict. The Mayor and Recorder now lost patience, and vowed that they would starve the men into a verdict.

Bushell argued that they had returned a verdict according to their consciences.

"That conscience of yours would cut my throat," cried the Lord Mayor, while the Recorder, addressing Bushell, added, "You are a facetious fellow. I will set a mark upon you, and whilst I have anything to do in this city, I will have an eye upon you."

The Lord Mayor surveyed the jury contemptuously. "Have you no more wit than to be led by such a pitiful fellow ?" he demanded. "I will cut his nose !"

Penn now took up the cudgels on behalf of the jury. "Unhappy are these juries who are threatened to be starved, fined, and ruined if they give not in their verdict contrary to their consciences," he said.

"My lord," interrupted the Recorder, "you must take a course with this fellow."

"Stop his mouth !" shrieked the Lord Mayor. "Gaoler, bring fetters and stake him to the ground !"

"Do your pleasure," said Penn. "I matter not your fetters."

"Till now," exclaimed the Recorder, in a fury, "I never understood the reason or the policy of the Spaniards in suffering the Inquisition among them, and certainly it will never be well with us till something like the Spanish Inquisition be in England."

Once more the jury were shut up all night without food or conveniences. They refused to budge from their verdict. If anything, they made it less equivocal by pronouncing the plain decision "Not guilty !"

Defeated by this collection of honest men, the exasperated court proceeded to fine every member of the jury forty marks for refusing to do as they were required. They were also committed to prison until such time as the fines were paid.

Penn was fined for contempt of court because he had refused to remove his hat, and he went to prison in default of payment. Mead was also fined for contempt, though the grounds were vague.

But the jury had shown the stuff of which they were made, and they did not intend to sit down quietly. They immediately brought the case before Chief Justice Vaughan, who decided that the whole affair was illegal.

The Chief Justice sealed his judgment with a peroration from the bench in which he expressed his views on the law concerning the rights of juries.

Penn was 26 at this time. Next year, 1671, he was again arrested for preaching in Wheeler Street, and he was imprisoned for six months.

It was about this period that he became interested in American affairs. In return for a debt which the Crown owed his father, Admiral Penn, he was granted a stretch of land which he proposed to call "Sylvania," but Charles II added the word "Penn" in honour of the Admiral.

In 1682 Penn left England with his family and sailed with a hundred comrades from Deal. Stories of the persecution of Quakers in England brought Penn back. Five months after his arrival Charles II died, and Penn found himself with considerable influence, as he had been friendly with James II while the latter was Duke of York.

Macaulay credits him with some dirty work on behalf of James, particularly at the time of the Monmouth Rebellion, but there is good reason to believe that Macaulay was actuated by motives of revenge, for it is an historical fact that his grandfather was dismissed from the Society of Friends, while he himself lost the representation of Edinburgh through the activities of that Society.

Penn died on July 30th, 1718.

Dorothy Jordan

An old chronicler, telling the story of how Mrs. Dorothy Jordan got her name, remarks : "Her *maiden* name—in the significant sense of maidenhood—was Bland. When she went on to the stage she changed to Miss Francis. Before long, however, her mother wrote to request another change, and she took that of Mrs. Jordan. The *Mrs.* was prefixed, we are told, to keep frivolous suitors at bay."

Miss Bland (or Francis) had a sense of humour. An amusing story is told of her choice of the name "Jordan."

She came from Ireland and thus had crossed the Irish Sea. Consulting with old Tate Wilkinson, the actor, on her proposal to become a *Mrs.*, he suggested : "You have crossed the water, my dear, so I'll call you Jordan."

"And by the memory of Sam !" says Wilkinson, "if she didn't take my joke in earnest and call herself Mrs. Jordan ever since."

The expression "frivolous suitors" did not apparently apply to the Duke of Clarence, afterwards William the Fourth, for she became his mistress, and was the mother of ten children by him.

There is a great difference between the carefree days of her popularity as one of London's leading actresses and her death in France comparatively poverty-stricken.

The heroine-worship of London Society during Mrs. Jordan's palmy days may be gathered from a eulogy by Sir Joshua Reynolds. Said he to a friend : "She vastly exceeds everything that I have seen, and really *is* what others affect to be."

"What, Sir ! greater than your friend, Mrs. Abington ?"

"Yes, sir," replied Reynolds, "greater than Mrs. Abington, wherever she challenges comparison."

"But," said the other, "you must not forget the more extended range of Mrs. Abington—her fine lady."

"I do not forget the fine lady of Mrs. Abington," replied Sir Joshua ; "it is never to be forgotten—I spoke of the two actresses where they challenged comparison. But as to more extensive range, I do not know that you can make out your point ; for opposed to these fashionable ladies you have the fashionable *men* of Mrs. Jordan, and the women who would pass for men, whether Wildairs or Hypolitas in comedy and the tender and exquisite Viola of Shakespeare, where she combines feeling with sportive effect, and does as much by the music of her melancholy as the music of her laugh."

Mrs. Jordan's smile made everyone laugh ; her vivacity inoculated the stalls with a new outlook on life. She bewitched the public.

C. R. Leslie, in his *Life of Reynolds*, remarks :

I went a short time ago to see Mrs. Jordan in *As You Like It*, and was quite as much pleased with her as I expected; indeed more so, for I had been taught to expect an immensely fat woman, and she is but moderately so.

Her face is still very fine; no print that I ever saw of her is much like. Her performance of Rosalind was, in my mind, perfect; though I am convinced the character from its nature, did not call forth half Mrs. Jordan's powers.

As Rosalind, Mrs. Jordan was the equal of Mrs. Siddons. She was naturally a romp, a hoyden, a little too vivacious for some of the critics, but as Thomas Campbell says: "Shakespeare himself, if he had been a living spectator, would have gone behind the scene and saluted her for her success."

She was as charming in private life as in her work. She had beautiful curls which she knew how to conceal or display as occasion warranted.

"Her smile had the effect of sunshine, and her laugh did one good to hear it," says Hazlitt, "her voice was eloquence itself—it seemed as if her heart were always at her mouth. She was all gaiety, openness and good nature; she rioted in her fine animal spirits, and gave more pleasure than any other actress, because she had the greatest spirit of enjoyment in herself."

All London knew of Mrs. Jordan's connection with the Duke of Clarence. No one was surprised. Least of all could George IV object; he himself had sown his wild oats and was reaping tares. He smiled to himself and watched with equanimity the growing family of his brother.

Long before William IV came to the throne, Mrs. Jordan had been forgotten. Fifteen years is a big slice out of a human life, and by that time (1831) he had become a respectably married man, for Mrs. Jordan died in 1816. Two years after her death the Duke married Adelaide of Saxe Meiningen.

Little is known of the early life of Mrs. Jordan. She was born at Waterford about 1762. Her mother, Mrs. Bland, was then an actress. In 1777 she appeared for the first time in Dublin under the name of Miss Francis. After an engagement at Cork, she went in 1782 to Leeds, in Yorkshire, where she was engaged by Tate Wilkinson, who had once played with her mother.

She came to London in 1785 and obtained an engagement at Drury Lane, London, where she very soon earned great applause. She did, in fact, usurp the position previously held by Mrs. Abington, where, to quote Leslie again :

It must have been gall and wormwood to the jealous and domineering temper of Mrs. Abington to see the throne she had held so long taken by this raw young actress-of-all-work, who dressed carelessly, moved as the whim prompted her, thought nothing of cadences or points, and, in short, was as completely the ideal of natural charm as Mrs. Abington of artificial.

She played both in tragedy and comedy, appearing one day as Viola in *Twelfth Night*, and on the next as Imogen in *Cymbeline*. Unquestionably, however, she was better in comic parts, in which she showed real genius.

It was in 1790 that the Duke of Clarence wooed and won her. They formed a domestic connection that lasted for twenty years. She remained, however, on the stage. Her prodigal expenditure often got the Duke into pecuniary difficulties, for his income was limited.

In 1811 the pair separated at the Duke's request for reasons that have never been explained. It is fairly certain, however, that he was beginning to realize the probability of his succeeding to the Throne. At that time, Prince George, his brother, was acting as Regent.

It was generally believed that Mrs. Jordan saved a large sum of money from her allowance from the Duke. This does not, however, appear to be substantiated by her subsequent misfortunes.

She is said to have been allowed £4,400 a year, with the provision that if she returned to the stage the care of the Duke's four daughters, together with £1,500 a year, should revert to them. She did return to the stage, and the children and the money were surrendered to the Duke.

Very soon, however, she had to quit acting and went abroad to live on the remainder of the allowance. She could not keep free from debt, and she died in comparative poverty at St. Cloud, France. The date of her death is variously stated as July 5th, July 3rd, and July 31st, 1816.

The eldest son of William IV by Mrs. Jordan was created Earl of Munster. He married Miss Wyndham, one of the natural daughters of Lord Egremont, from whom he had a fortune of £40,000. He was appointed Constable of Windsor

Castle, a position which was confirmed to him by Queen Victoria.

Before his elevation to the peerage he was known as Colonel Fitz-Clarence, and showed great bravery and energy in arresting the leaders of the Cato Street conspiracy. On his father's accession to the throne he received his peerage. In 1842 he committed suicide.

Frederick William III of Prussia

Up to the time of Frederick William III, it had been customary to give Prussian heirs-apparent a one-sided education. They were taught very little more than military strategy.

With Frederick William they tried an innovation and instructed in philosophy and humanitarianism without, of course, neglecting the military side.

It proved a happy combination, and he is renowned in history for the able administration of his country, and a conspicuous common sense during the greatest of European upheavals, brought about by the ambitions of Napoleon.

He was fortunate in the choice of his first wife, Princess Louise of Mecklenburg-Strelitz, who had a great influence on his character and activities.

Born at Berlin on August 3rd, 1770, Frederick was not allowed to make a social appearance until he was 21, when he accompanied his father, Frederick William II, to the diplomatic conferences of the German powers at Dresden.

In June of the following year he joined the army, then on the frontiers of France. Passing through Frankfort-on-Maine he met Princess Louise, and within a year they were married.

Frederick William ascended the throne on November 16th, 1797, and in the spring of the following year he and his queen visited the principal towns of Prussia with a view to obtaining a first-hand knowledge of the conditions of his people. No monarch was ever received with greater enthusiasm.

The result of this tour was soon seen in a series of decrees. Monopolies of all kinds were abolished, taxation was reduced, and the finance of the country put on a sounder footing.

To encourage economy the King himself reduced the expenses of his household to the narrowest limits. His predecessor had been prodigal in his court expenditure, and Frederick William made a clean sweep.

During the last reign Prussia had been almost continually at war, and when Napoleon loomed on the horizon the King would gladly have kept out of the struggle, for the country was in no condition for exploits. But circumstances ruled otherwise.

He kept out for a time as a result of the Treaty of Basle, but when the peace of Luneville of February 9th, 1801, took some Rhine provinces from Prussia with inadequate compensation Frederick William began to consider more drastic measures.

Czar Alexander I made a personal visit to Berlin and induced Frederick William to join the coalition against France. But the Battle of Austerlitz stopped any demonstration by Prussia, who secured Hanover as a result of a separate treaty.

Frederick William was about to take possession of Hanover in April 1806, when England entered a protest and followed it up by a declaration of war.

In a few months an arrangement was made whereby Prussia retained Hanover, and agreed to declare war on France again. The French army, however, moved with extraordinary rapidity and the King was quickly defeated at Saalfeld (where Prince Louis of Prussia was killed), at Jena, and at Auerstadt.

Before long the King was driven to the northern part of his country, and it was only through the courageous action of his queen, who personally pleaded with Napoleon, that he retained even a fraction of his dominions.

The conditions of the Treaty of Tilsit, in July 1807, reduced Prussia to the size of a minor German state. Despite this, Frederick William immediately began to make the best of what he had left. He issued a series of wise decrees, proclaiming free trade, introduced a new constitution, abolished the privileges of the nobility, and, in a short time, his little state was flourishing.

In July 1810, Queen Louise died, a bereavement from which Frederick William did not recover for years.

When Napoleon demanded from Frederick William a levy of ten thousand men for his Russian campaign, the King had to make an awkward decision. He was on good terms with the Czar, but he dare not refuse Bonaparte. He took refuge in strategy. He provided the men, but he put them under the command of General York, an officer well known for his anti-French sentiments.

His ruse was justified, for, when Napoleon was in retreat

from Moscow, York made a treaty with the Russian commander to secure the safety of the Prussian troops.

The King ratified the treaty in an order of the day, and by a further proclamation within a week called his people to arms against Napoleon.

Volunteer bands were raised with great rapidity. In less than a month the King was able to take the field.

The first events of the war were unfavourable to the Prussians. But when the young recruits improved, the French frontier was gained and Paris occupied by the allies.

In June 1814, Frederick William, with Czar Alexander, paid a visit to England. On returning to his country he made a solemn entry into Berlin.

Later he went to Vienna for the assembly of the nations. He promoted the so-called Holy Alliance, and directed from a distance the movement of Blücher and his troops which led to the victory of Waterloo.

He returned to his capital in October 1815, and three days later celebrated the 400th anniversary of the reign of the Hohenzollerns in Brandenburg.

By the Treaty of Vienna Prussia recovered her lost territory and population, and Frederick William employed his time in consolidating into one State the whole of his realm.

Prussia now considered of a territory of over five thousand square miles, with a population of twelve millions. Before his death Frederick William subdivided the country into ten parts, each with a governor, and when this was accomplished the army was reorganized, and it became a fundamental law of the State that every man should serve in the Forces.

For some reason or other a sudden change took place in the character of Frederick William. Having promised a new and liberal constitution he went back on his word. There was a desperate struggle between him and his people which continued to the time of his death.

Thus the lustre of his career was dimmed by his acts of later years.

But there was a long peace following the Congress of Vienna and much wise legislation was passed.

In 1818 he founded the University of Bonn, and increased the money available for education throughout the country. He made several attempts to bring about a union between the Lutheran and reformed churches, but without success.

At this time was established the German Zollverein which brought about a new impulse in commerce. All kinds of industrial undertakings were encouraged to an extent never before seen in Prussia.

Frederick William was fond of the society of the eminent thinkers, and he called to Berlin Fichte, who, having been pronounced an atheist, was sent away from the University of Jena.

In November 1824 the King married morganatically the Countess Augustine von Harrach, who was only 24. She was the opposite in character to his Queen, and is said to have been a bad influence on Frederick William.

The King died on June 7th, 1840, aged 70. He enjoyed good health almost to the last moment.

He was a man of regular habits, always ate and drank moderately, and slept on a hard straw mattress. He dressed mostly in a long blue coat, buttoned up to the neck, without ornament of any kind.

The Duke of Sussex

"The most unfortunate of all Acts."

In this way, Brougham, afterwards Lord Brougham, stigmatized the Royal Marriage Act, fifty-two years after the measure had become law.

The great Wilberforce, too, was of the opinion that it was "the most unconstitutional Act that ever disgraced the statute book."

This statute, passed at the request, and almost at the command, of George III, went a long way towards alienating the King from the affections of his family. His ministers prophesied all kinds of difficulties.

But the most tragic result of the Act, which provided "that no descendant of his late Majesty, George II, shall be capable of contracting matrimony without the previous consent of his Majesty," was the breaking up of the home life of the third George's son, Augustus Frederick, Duke of Sussex.

George III had peculiar notions as to the dignity of the royal prerogative. Two of his brothers had actually had the audacity to marry two English ladies. In his opinion this was not maintaining the regality of the British throne.

He had apparently forgotten his own affair fifteen years before with the "Fair Quakeress" of St. James's Market, for George III is said to have been married to Hannah Lightfoot in Kew Church in 1759, or at Curzon Street Chapel by the notorious Parson Keith.

Augustus Frederick, the sixth son and ninth child of George III, was the most amiable of all the princes. It was while travelling in Italy that he formed an attachment for Lady Augusta de Ameland, daughter of John Murray, 4th Earl of Dunmore.

The earl himself was not in Italy at the time, but it is said that Lady Dunmore consented to a private marriage of her daughter with the prince, who was then 22 years of age.

It is impossible to believe that the Duke of Sussex was ignorant of the Royal Marriage Act, nor is it believable that Lady Dunmore was unaware of the statute.

The lapse of twenty years since the passing of the Act may have induced them to believe that George III would look upon the union with a more benevolent eye.

The young couple lived in Rome for several months, and then came to England. Lady Augusta's family now desired that the marriage should be regularized in England, and the Duke consented.

They took lodgings in the house of a coal merchant in South Molton Street, Mayfair, so that, after the expiration of a month, they could be married at St. George's Church, Hanover Square.

The banns were callèd, and on a cold morning in December 1793 the contracting parties presented themselves at the church. They were married under the names of Augustus Frederick and Augusta Murray, the only witnesses being the coal merchant and his wife and another.

It was an exceedingly anxious moment for Lady Augusta. By this time the couple must have been aware of George III's attitude to the Italian marriage. Moreover, she was about to become a mother.

If, however, they expected George III to look upon this second ceremony as legal, they were disappointed. The King declared that he would never recognize it. He went further and declared that he would never forgive his son.

He immediately instituted a suit against his son in the Court of Arches for a nullity of the marriage, thus showing his own personal spite.

Within a week after the confinement of Lady Augusta a notice was served on the Duke requiring him to answer the charges.

The various phases of the suit were prolonged. George III, despite his legal advisers, was at a loss to know how to proceed. There were many costly investigations with the object of proving that the St. George's Church ceremony had never taken place.

The Privy Council were instructed to do their worst. They took the testimony of the mother and sister of Lady Augusta, of the coal merchant and his wife, and of the clergyman who officiated.

The clergyman declared that so far as the church was concerned it was a perfectly legal marriage.

But there was no mistaking the terms of the Royal Marriage Act, and on the 9th of August, 1794, after the young couple had been kept in suspense for several months, they were told that the marriage was not a marriage according to English law. They were further informed that the son who had been born to Lady Augusta was not legitimate.

The result of this unhappy union were a son, Colonel Sir Augustus d'Este, born January 13th, 1794, and a daughter, Ellen Augusta d'Este, both of whom survived their parents. Soon after the birth of the girl the prince and Lady Augusta finally separated.

Later monarchs endeavoured to alleviate the misery that had been caused to the noble family of Dunmore by giving a certain degree of rank and position to those who had been ostracized from the royal circle.

The decision in this particular case was held by many lawyers to be unsound because of its special circumstances.

Lady Augusta, writing to a friend in 1811, said :

Lord Thurlow told me my marriage was good in law ; religion taught me that it was good at home ; and not one device of my powerful enemies could make me believe otherwise, nor ever will.

Out of an allowance which the Duke of Sussex received from Parliament, an income was provided for Lady Augusta. But the king, during the remainder of his life, did his best to prevent his son from securing any office which might augment his resources.

After a separation of some years Lady Augusta died on March 5th, 1834.

The Duke of Sussex was less in the hands of politicians than his brothers. At an early age he adopted liberal principles to which he adhered steadfastly to the last. He made speeches in Parliament in support of the abolition of slavery and of the slave trade, and the removal of the Roman Catholic and Jewish disabilities, and was always on the side of tolerance in religion.

He took an active part in the passing of the Reform Bill and of the laws for the establishment of free trade.

In 1810 he was elected Grand-Master of the Freemasons of England, and in 1816 President of the Royal Society, an office which he held until 1839.

Some years before his death he married Lady Cecilia Letitia Buggin, widow of Sir George Buggin. She was the daughter of Arthur Saunders Gore, 2nd Earl of Arran.

It has been a matter of dispute as to whether this marriage, too, was a contravention of the Royal Marriage Act. But it would appear that William IV, who was then reigning, gave his consent and thus validated the union. At all events, the Duke's wife was raised to the rank of Duchess of Inverness.

The Duke of Sussex was connected with many benevolent institutions, and he subscribed liberally considering his poor income. In private life he was unostentatious and avoided a display of rank. He left one of the largest private libraries in the kingdom. A collection of these works was published, and it appeared under the title of *Bibliotheca Sussexiana*. Twelve thousand of the fifty thousand volumes dealt with theological matters.

The Duke died on April 21st, 1843, leaving no issue of his second marriage.

James Wilson

Until the middle of the nineteenth century the Government of Great Britain was preponderatingly aristocratic.

The people had clamoured for the Reform Bills, but, having got their way, they generally elected men with blue blood in their veins. Men without fortune were not encouraged to aspire to office, so that the clever but poor individual found the going hard.

One who succeeded in breaking the tradition was James Wilson, the son of a Quaker, who began life as a hat manufacturer, first in his native town of Hawick, Roxburghshire, and afterwards in London.

A hobby will often take a person farther along the road of fame than his ordinary business. Such was the case with Wilson. Spending his leisure time in studying political economy, he, in time, began a weekly paper called *The Economist*, entered the House of Commons, and rose to the office of Financial Secretary of the Treasury.

Wilson entered Parliament as Member for Westbury at a time when the country was disturbed by the conflicting questions of tariffs and free trade. He had founded *The Economist* in 1843, and his contributions on economics had displayed an original and penetrating mind.

He had more original ideas on the subject of tariffs than Cobden. The latter's advocacy of free trade was based upon the struggle between the classes, which naturally brought a stubborn opposition from landlords and moneyed interests.

Wilson, on the other hand, argued that protection was disadvantageous to all classes, since all classes had one interest. A man who had made a success in his own business was worth listening to, and Wilson thus added great force to the cause of free trade.

Wilson's financial ability did not stop at internal politics. As early as 1848 he was taking part in the debates on India. Disraeli, writing to Lord John Manners on February 5th, said :

The West India debate terminated last night at two o'clock in the morning, and was without exception the best supported debate by our friends that has occurred since we were a party. . . .

G.B. (Lord George Bentinck) made his exposition in a speech of three and a half hours, which never for an instant flagged. After him the Chancellor of the Exchequer. Then, next night, Wilson, who is a great accession to the House, and delivered one of his best essays. He was followed by Tom Baring from our red box, sitting between G.B. and myself, with a vigour, an earnestness and a freshness which were quite captivating and which wonderfully took.

By 1859 there were prospects of Wilson soon becoming

a member of the Cabinet, for it was agreed by all parties that he had never sacrificed honour for ambition.

But at this time the affairs of India, particularly in regard to finance, were in a desperate state, and, looking round for someone to put things right, the Government fastened on Wilson.

He was induced to go to India as financial member of the council. There he was faced with a big deficiency in the budget and an increase in public debt. He imposed an income-tax on incomes above 200 rupees, with a reduction for those not exceeding 500 rupees. He introduced paper currency with notes for five up to 1,000 rupees, and effected a revolution in the system of keeping public accounts.

James Wilson was born in 1805 and was the third son of a family of fifteen. From 1816 to 1819 he was at school at Ackworth conducted by the Society of Friends. He then spent six months at school at Earl's Colne, Essex. At an early age he had a taste for books, and wanted to be a schoolmaster.

At the age of 16, however, he was apprenticed to a hat manufacturer at Hawick. At night he continued to study.

His father bought the hat manufacturer's business and handed it over to James Wilson and his elder brother, William. The firm prospered, and they soon found their native town too small for their enterprise. Thus in 1824 they came to London and began business with a partner under the title of Wilson, Irwin and Wilson. The firm was dissolved in 1831, though successful, and James Wilson continued as Wilson and Co.

On January 5th, 1832, Wilson married Elizabeth Preston, of Newcastle, and gave up his membership of the Society of Friends.

He lived at Dulwich, then a secluded village, four miles from the City, where he entertained his friends and discussed politics.

For twelve years his business prospered, but in 1836 he was induced to speculate in indigo, and in the space of three years his capital was almost exhausted. He called his creditors together and made a proposal to them which was accepted.

In later years, when Wilson had risen to eminence, there were enemies who declared that he had never made an attempt to pay his creditors. This was afterwards proved to be untrue. Out of his own personal means he discharged half the deficiency and the plant of the concern was accepted in settlement of the remainder.

This arrangement turned out less favourably than was anticipated, and, there still being a deficiency, Wilson made good the difference.

In 1844 Wilson retired from business and began to write regularly. In 1839 he had already published *Influences of the Corn Laws* and, in the following year, *Fluctuations of Currency, Commerce and Manufactures*.

In 1843 he wrote leaders for the *Morning Chronicle*, and for several years afterwards contributed to the *Examiner*.

A consultation with Cobden and Villiers, leaders of the Anti-Corn Law League, resulted in the production of a weekly paper devoted to financial and commercial matters. He named it *The Economist*. In it he invested part of his capital and obtained the remainder of the money from Lord Radnor, a prominent free-trader.

The Economist began to be recognized as a power in the newspaper world, and has maintained its position. Wilson wrote nearly the whole of the paper during the early days of its existence.

One day Lord Radnor suggested that Wilson should enter Parliament. Up to this time such a move had never occurred to him. In the election of 1847 he stood as a Tory candidate for Westbury, and was elected by 170 votes to 149. His opponent on that occasion was Matthew James Higgins, who was known as "Jacob Omnium." In 1852 Wilson was re-elected by only six votes.

From 1857 to 1859 Wilson represented Devonshire.

His first speech was on a motion for a Committee of Inquiry into the commercial depression which existed, and he obtained considerable influence by his brilliant arguments.

Within six months of his election to the House of Commons he was offered office and he became one of Lord John Russell's joint secretaries of the Board of Control.

In the Aberdeen administration he became Financial Secretary to the Treasury, and under Lord Palmerston, in 1859, was made vice-president of the Board of Trade. In the same year he was made a Privy Councillor.

Wilson's work in India secured the approbation of all parties.

The climate, however, did not suit him. He was subject

to attacks of dysentery. On August 2nd, 1860, he had a relapse. He took to his bed, and on the evening of August 11th he was found dead.

Calcutta went into mourning. A monument was erected to his memory in the Calcutta cemetery.

His widow died in England in 1886 and was buried in Curry Rivel churchyard, Somerset.

He left six daughters. One of them married Walter Bagehot, who succeeded Wilson as editor of *The Economist*.

From the time of the death of Wilson to about nine years ago *The Economist* was held in trust for his six daughters. In 1928 the periodical was sold with the approval of the Court and came under new management.

St. Radegundes, Queen of France

When Clotaire I, King of Soissons, raided Thuringia he brought home to France, as a captive, the beautiful Radegundes, 12-year-old daughter of the dead Thuringian monarch, Bertaire.

Desirous of making this girl his queen, he had her educated, instructed in the Christian religion and baptized. It was a bad move for the purpose of his scheme, for Radegundes was a willing learner, and impressionable.

From the moment of her baptism she decided upon a cloistered existence. Clotaire watched her, and noted how she kept long fasts and that during Lent she wore a hair-cloth beneath her rich garments.

The king himself professed Christianity with as much enthusiasm as any of the continental rulers, and, at first, he was quite content to see the way in which her character was being modelled.

She cut down her own meals to feed the poor, whom she fed with her own hands, and indulged in other austerities to the gratification of Clotaire.

But when the time arrived for Radegundes to become queen he soon discovered whither all this piety was leading, for she declared that she had no desire to marry.

Clotaire flew into a rage, and the girl had to give way to the king's desire to marry her. Having become queen, however, she abandoned none of her prayers and humiliations; she intensified them.

"Have I married a nun?" demanded Clotaire, who complained that his court had been turned into a monastery. "Remember you are a queen, and I expect you to act as such."

Radegundes replied that she had never failed in her regal duties, and continued her religious devotions.

At length Clotaire's patience was exhausted. He retaliated by causing his wife's brother to be murdered, and then seized his dominions in Thuringia.

Whereupon the queen insisted on leaving the court entirely. She went to Noyon to take the veil, but the bishop refused at first to give his permission on the grounds that she was a married woman.

In those days it was permissible for a husband or wife to enter holy orders if the other party consented. To Clotaire's credit he gave the necessary permission, though it involved his remaining unmarried during his wife's lifetime.

The prelate was thus prevailed upon to consecrate Radegundes a deaconess.

She withdrew to an estate at Poitou which the king had given her, and spent her whole income on charitable works. She lived on rye and barley bread, and slept upon a bed of ashes covered with sackcloth.

She built a monastery at Poitiers, the cost of which was defrayed by Clotaire, who, after his wrongdoings, was now concerned for his immortal soul.

This renewal of piety on the part of the king, however, lasted only a short time. He suddenly determined to descend upon Poitiers and carry his wife back to court.

In some manner Radegundes learned of her husband's design. She wrote to Germanus, Bishop of Paris, who sought an audience of the King and induced him to relinquish his intention.

In 566 a Council of Tours confirmed the foundation of her monastery, and Radegundes proceeded to enrich her church with relics of the saints.

Desirious of obtaining a piece of the true Cross, she sent a mission to Constantinople to the Emperor Justin. The emperor, it is said, "readily sent her a piece of that sacred wood adorned with gold and precious stones; also a book of the four Gospels beautified in the same manner, and the relics of several saints."

The Archbishop of Tours deposited these treasures in the monastery church.

In the year 560, Clotaire, who was the fourth son of Clovis King of the Franks, became King of France, his three brothers having died. In the last year of his reign he went on a pilgrimage to the tomb of St. Martin at Tours, taking with him rich gifts.

Kneeling on the penitent stool, Clotaire confessed the whole of his sins and with "deep groans" besought forgiveness through his confessor.

He gave indication of a sincere repentance by founding St. Medard's Abbey at Soissons. But on his death bed his sins overwhelmed him. He exclaimed in his last moments : "How powerful is the Heavenly King, by whose command the greatest monarchs of the earth resign their life !"

Clotaire died in 561, after a reign of fifty years.

Soon afterwards France was rent by civil war. His four sons had divided the kingdom between them. Charibert reigned at Paris, Chilperic at Soissons, Gontran at Orleans and Sigebert in Austrasia, which included Lorraine, Champagne and Auvergne and some German provinces.

Charibert lived a short time. Then a civil war began between Sigebert and Chilperic to the distraction of all France. Finally, Childebert, son of Sigebert, became King of Austrasia, Orleans and Paris, and, as his father had done, continued as protector of Radegundes and her monastery of the Holy Cross.

Here she had about two hundred nuns, many of whom were of noble birth and some of royal blood.

During the strife of the civil war the monastery was not molested.

In the records of the Roman Catholic Church, Radegundes is regarded as one of the most illustrious of woman saints. She is renowned for the efficient way in which she conducted her establishment.

She insisted that her nuns should give alms to the utmost of their abilities, and she demanded unusual austerities, obedience and discretion.

She prescribed that every nun should learn the psalter by heart, and be able to read. She condemned familiarity and friendships. Not satisfied with the rules she had made herself, she took her Abbess, Agnes, to the ecclesiastical authorities at Arles, to ascertain if she had forgotten anything in regard to discipline.

Radegundes died on August 13th, 587, and her memory is honoured by the Church to-day.

Upon receiving news of her death, Gregory, archbishop of Tours, went to Poitiers, and performed the funeral office at her burial.

Among the miracles which brought the crown of a saint to Radegundes, was one which concerned the restoration of sight to a blind man at her funeral. In later years many other miracles are said to have been performed at her tomb.

Her relics were kept in the church of Our Lady at Poitiers until they were dispersed by the Huguenots in the sixteenth century.

Letitia Elizabeth Landon

It was a wild night. Rain fell in torrents. The little party of half a dozen who stood beside the open grave in the court-yard of Cape Coast Castle hugged themselves in their cloaks.

Inadequate illumination from flickering torches cast grotesque shadows on the castle walls.

The funeral service was read hastily, for none wanted it prolonged. The drenched workmen, who had just finished their task of digging the grave, fidgeted impatiently. They had little sympathy with the business, for what right had a woman to risk her life in this fever-stricken solitude ?

The order of committal over, the mourners hurried away, the clay falling with a hollow thud upon the coffin of one of England's illustrious poetesses, Letitia Elizabeth Landon.

She had arrived at the miserable town of Cape Coast on August 15th, exactly two months before. An hour or two before her burial a coroner's jury had returned a verdict of "Death from having incautiously taken a dose of prussic acid."

Did a mystery surround the death of Letitia Landon ?

Many of her numerous friends in England thought so. On the very morning that she died she wrote in a letter:

The solitude, except an occasional dinner, is absolute. From seven in the morning to seven in the evening when we dine, I never see Mr. McLean (her husband) *and rarely anyone else.*

Previously she had written :

He expects me to cook, wash and iron, in short, to do the work of a servant. *He says he will never cease correcting me until he has broken my spirit, and complains of my temper, which you know was never, even under heavy trials, bad."*

Before her marriage Letitia Landon had been the idol of society, and no one could understand her motive in marrying the Governor of the Gold Coast, a settlement which in those days, was known as the "White Man's Grave."

In one of her poems she had predicted—though at the time referring to someone else :

> *Mine shall be a lonelier ending,*
> *Mine shall be a wilder grave ;*
> *Where the shout and shriek are blending,*
> *Where the tempest meets the wave.*
> *Or perhaps a fate more lonely,*
> *In some drear and distant ward,*
> *Where my weary eyes meet only*
> *Hired nurse and sullen guard !*

The spot chosen for the grave of Letitia Landon could not have been more inappropriate. Nothing distinguished it from the graves of military men but a few tiles. These had no significance in the eyes of the soldiers who daily performed their evolutions on the parade ground.

One can understand the doubt that existed in the minds of the friends of Letitia Landon. On the eve of her departure for the Gold Coast—she had then been married a little over a year—a farewell party was held in her honour. A speaker referred to the affection with which she was regarded. It was such a striking speech that some shed tears.

Her husband rose to thank them for the kind things they had said, but cast a damper on the proceedings with his words : "If Mrs. McLean has so many friends, I wonder they allow her to leave them."

Lady Blessington instructed Dr. Madden, who lived for a short time at Cape Coast Castle, to erect at her cost a monument over the remains of Letitia Landon. He found, however, that Mr. McLean had ordered from England a mural slab with an inscription. This had been lying for some time in the store of the Castle. A few days afterwards the slab was placed in position in the castle wall.

Madden records a singular dream which he had while sleeping in the room in which Letitia Landon had died. It was a "half-waking, half-sleeping sort of hallucination, in which I fancied that the form of Mrs. McLean, clad in a white dress, was extended lifeless before me on the floor on the spot where I had been told her body had been discovered. This imaginary white object lay between my bed and the window, through which the moon was shining brightly, and every time I raised myself and examined closely this spot, on which the moonbeams fell in a slanting direction, the imaginary form would cease to be discernible ; and then in a few minutes when I might doze, or fail by any effort to keep attention alive, the same appalling figure would present itself to my imagination."

Letitia Landon was a fascinating woman. At the time of her marriage she was 36. It was said that she had an affair with the notorious Dr. Maginn, whose wife had a good deal to say on the matter. He used to visit her, and she wrote him some flattering letters, which Mrs. Maginn construed as a liaison.

In a letter to a friend she denied that there was a love affair. "A note of mine that would pass for a love-letter must either have been strangely misrepresented or most strangely altered," she declared.

For a long period the poems of Letitia Landon, who wrote above the initials L. E. L., were the rage of London and, indeed, the country. She was barely 15 when those initials first appeared with a poem in the *Literary Gazette*, and when it was discovered that the author was still in her teens, she became famous at once.

She was courted and flattered. Of this popularity she wrote :

> *I well remember how I flung myself,*
> *Like a young goddess on a purple cloud*
> *Of light and odour.*
> *And I—I felt immortal, for my brain*
> *Was drunk and mad with its first draught of fame.*

In her 18th year she published a volume of poetry which included the "Fate of Adelaide," a romantic tale of Switzerland.

Then in the *Literary Gazette*, she began a series of poetical sketches with her initials attached.

She was born in Hans Place, Chelsea, on August 14th, 1802, where, except for a few brief intervals, she spent the whole of her life.

"Childishly untidy" is the description applied to her in her youth, but at the zenith of her fame her appearance was highly attractive, and she was brilliant in society.

In 1824 was published *The Improvisatrice, and other Poems*, which met with a triumphant reception. Sometimes, however, her works are defective through a want of care and time spent on them.

Another characteristic of her poetry is its gloominess.

She also wrote three novels, *Ethel Churchill*, *Francisca Carrara*, and *Romance and Reality*.

From 1831 to 1837 she edited *Fisher's Scrap Book*.

In June 1838 she married Mr. McLean, and, according to some reports, they lived happily together for just over twelve months.

It has been assumed that she took prussic acid because of neuralgic pains.

Frederick, Duke of York

When Frederick, Duke of York, son of George III, was commander-in-chief of the Army his mistress sold commissions to the highest bidder.

To what extent the Duke was involved in these scandalous transactions is not certain, but she is known to have inserted names in the commission lists which were signed by the Duke without question.

The name of this woman was Mary Ann Clarke. Her antecedents are obscure.

According to the *Reminiscences* of Captain Gronow, she was introduced to the Duke when she was a "sweet, pretty, lively girl of sixteen."

She was walking one day across Blackheath, near her home, when she met a cavalier. He saluted her; she returned the salute. He introduced her to his friend, and she and the friend became acquainted.

Mary accompanied the young man to a theatre, knowing nothing of his standing in society.

They occupied a private box and attracted much notice. The girl took these acknowledgments as a testimony to her beauty. They went again, and on this occasion Mary Ann Clarke was addressed as Her Royal Highness. She then discovered that her lover was the Duke of York, who had recently been married. Mary had been taken for his wife.

But there is a different version as to the antecedents of Mary Ann Clarke. She was born, it is said, about 1777, and was the daughter of a journeyman printer, named Farquhar, who lived in one of the small courts at the back of Fetter Lane, London.

Before she was thirteen, a young compositor named James Day began to send her love sonnets. Instead of returning the affection of Day, however, she eloped with Joseph Clarke, a builder's son. She lived with him for three years on Snow Hill, and then married him. The couple had several children.

This story of Mary Ann Clarke does not explain how she became acquainted with the Duke of York, but it would appear that she was living openly with him at No. 31, Tavistock Place, about the year 1802. She then moved to Gloucester Place, Portman Square, where she kept up an elaborate establishment which included two carriages, eight horses, and nine menservants. She received an allowance of £2,000 a year from the Duke.

She was courted by military men, and was popular with persons of rank. The Duke was gratified with the attentions paid to her, and he did not attempt to restrain her extravagances.

Soon she became embarrassed and induced the Duke to give her Army commissions so that she could dispose of them at a good price. This traffic also extended to preferments in the Church. If the Duke knew what she was doing with these commissions he said nothing.

Some suspicion having arisen, Colonel Wardle, Radical M.P., ingratiated himself with Mrs. Clarke, and ascertained from her names of men who had paid her for commissions.

On one occasion he was visiting her when the Royal carriage drove up at her door. The Colonel immediately took refuge under a sofa. It proved, however, to be not the Duke but one of his aides-de-camp. The Colonel, from his hiding-place, was able to listen to a conversation relating to commissions which passed between Mrs. Clarke and her visitor.

In 1809 the matter was inquired into in Parliament at the instigation of Colonel Wardle. By this time the Duke had "thrown over" Mrs. Clarke, and she was only too glad to be called as a witness.

The country was split in two by the controversy.

The Duke denied any corruption, and he was exonerated by a majority of eighty in the House of Commons. Nevertheless, the country clamoured for his resignation as Commander-in-Chief, and he gave up the post.

The matter was never cleared up to the satisfaction of all concerned. But it transpired afterwards that a year before the Parliamentary inquiry Colonel Wardle furnished a house for Mrs. Clarke in Westbourne Place, Sloane Square, which was understood to be a reward for her evidence against the Duke.

Colonel Wardle denied the agreement, and this led to an action against him for the recovery of nearly £2,000, representing an upholsterer's bill.

For about six years little was heard of Mrs. Clarke. Then she broke her silence with a libel on the Irish Chancellor of the Exchequer. For this she was sentenced to nine months' imprisonment.

Her next move was to write her *Life and Adventures*. She went to John Galt, the novelist, for advice. "I told her point-blank," says Galt, "that she was in want of money and that this was an expedient to raise the wind. She confessed the truth, and also that her debts had been paid to the amount of £7,000, and an annuity of £400 granted to her on condition that she should not molest the Duke of York."

Galt declared that the "history" was not fit for publication, and he induced her to drop the idea.

But 10,000 copies had already passed through the press, and the printer demanded reimbursement of his expenses. A settlement was eventually made on condition that the books were burned and the manuscript delivered up to interested parties.

For three successive days there was a bonfire on the premises of the printer in Salisbury Square. The smell of burning paper caused considerable excitement in the neighbourhood of Fleet Street.

Mrs. Clarke still nursed a grievance against the Duke of York, and she next threatened to publish his love-letters.

Some of the letters were not complimentary to other members of the Royal Family. At length she was offered a large sum of money and a pension to leave England.

She went to the Continent and finally settled down in Paris, where she died.

Mrs. Clarke was of lively disposition and noted for her wit. It is said that she used to provide the Duke with dinner-table anecdotes of the Royal Family and people in society. Next morning she would say : "Well, Dukey, how did the story go off ?"

Galt declares that Mrs. Clark was not a beauty, but was, nevertheless, fascinating ; although, according to him, "she did not possess that extraordinary fascination which posterity may suppose from the incidents in which she was engaged."

On one occasion, while being examined in the King's Bench Court, Lord Ellenborough, who presided, asked sarcastically, "Under whose protection are you just now ?"

"Your Lordship's," retorted Mrs. Clarke.

Wilberforce described Mrs. Clarke as "a low, vulgar woman," but certain writers, notably Cyrus Redding, have tried to disprove the stories of her obscure origin.

"Not one paper stated the truth about her," declares Redding. "I accidentally had twenty or thirty of her letters before me at one time. I read them, and they fully proved she was a woman who had been well educated. . . .

"Mrs. Clarke was the daughter of Colonel Frederick, and grand-daughter of Theodore, King of Corsica, whose melancholy fate, as well as that of his son, need not be repeated here. She had a son, and, I believe, two daughters. . . .

"As the daughter of Colonel Frederick, Mrs. Clarke had been noticed by the Prince of Wales, Lady Jersey, and several persons of distinction before the Duke of York knew her, and she received money from them in consideration of her misfortunes. Perhaps his knowledge of her arose in that way. One lady who died left her a hundred guineas in her will, in addition to former gifts."

Frederick, Duke of York and Albany, was born on August 16th, 1763. He held the title of Bishop of Osnaburg, became Field Marshal, and eventually Commander-in-Chief of the Army. In September 1791 he married Frederica, Princess Royal of Prussia, daughter of Frederick William II. He died without issue on January 5th, 1827.

The Princes in the Tower

Who *did* murder the Princes in the Tower of London ?
Was it Richard III, Henry VII, or some other person
so far unsuspected ?

The chief accuser of Richard III is Sir Thomas More.
Here is the story as told by him.

Richard III was crowned on July 6th, 1483, in Westminster
Hall. He began his reign auspiciously, with acts of clemency
and mercy. Hitherto he had had the support of the Duke of
Buckingham, who now suddenly turned upon him and led an
insurrection of the people of Kent, Essex, Sussex, Berkshire,
Hampshire, Wiltshire and Devonshire.

To check this movement, Richard is said to have
immediately contemplated the murder of the young Edward V
and his brother, the Duke of York.

Richard's excuse for usurping the throne was that Edward
V was illegitimate. The child was born in the Sanctuary,
Westminster, on November 2nd, 1470, his mother being
Elizabeth Widville, who had taken refuge there while her
husband, Edward IV, was fighting the Lancastrians.

In Richard's confidence was a man named John Greene.
It is alleged that the King sent this man to Sir Robert Brackenbury, constable of the Tower, with a letter and credentials
ordering Sir Robert "in any wise" to put the children, who
were under his care, to death.

Brackenbury refused, though his refusal was bound to
incur the wrath of Richard. Whereupon Richard said to one
of his pages : "Whom shall a man trust !"

"Sir," said the page, "there lieth one in the pallet-chamber
without that I dare well say, to do your Grace pleasure the
thing were right hard that he would refuse."

By this the page meant Sir James Tyrrel.

According to Sir Thomas More, Richard approached
Tyrrel, and the latter "devised that they should be murdered
in their beds and no blood shed : to the execution whereof
he appointed Miles Forrest, one of the four that before kept
them, a fellow fleshbred in murder beforetime ; and to
him he joined one John Dighton, his own horsekeeper, a big,
broad, square and strong knave."

More then proceeds as follows : "Then this Miles Forrest

and John Dighton, about midnight, came into the chamber, and suddenly wrapped them up amongst the clothes, keeping down by force the featherbed and pillows hard upon their mouths, that within a while they smothered and stifled them, and their breaths failing, they gave up to God their innocent souls into the joys of heaven, leaving to their tormentors their bodies dead in bed ; after which the wretches laid them out upon the bed, and fetched Tyrrel to see them. And when he was satisfied of their death he caused the murderers to bury them at the stair-foot, meetly deep in the ground, under a great heep of stones."

Now, Thomas More, who was almost contemporary with this period, has come down in history as a man of honour and conscience. What advantage could he have reaped by mis-representing the story of the murder of the princes ?

That his tale is circumstantial is shown by the fact that in 1674 the reputed bones of the boys were found beneath a circular flight of stairs leading to the chapel of the White Tower. They were removed by order of Charles II to Henry VII's chapel at Westminster.

More, of course, was a mere boy in 1483. He was brought up in the household of Cardinal Morton, who would probably be in a position to know the facts, and it is assumed that Sir Thomas obtained his information from him.

Accepting More's story, historians have placed the date of the murder of the princes between the end of July and the beginning of September, 1483. August 7th, August 15th and August 17th are suggested dates. At this time Richard III was at Warwick, and More declares that he sent Tyrrel from that town to London to arrange for the murder.

If one is to disbelieve More, the only certain fact remaining is that the princes disappeared from history in June 1483, after the elder, Edward V, had reigned for about ten weeks.

As recently as 1933 the bones believed to be those of Edward V and the Duke of York were examined. They were exhumed from their grave in Westminster Abbey before distinguished witnesses, including the Dean of Westminster.

In addition to human bones were found chicken bones and bones of the patella of an ox. It was concluded after careful examination by surgeons that the human bones were those of brothers about 9½ and 12½ years of age.

Some confirmation of the story that they were smothered

was found in certain stains on the cheek bones, caused, it was said, by the congestion of blood in the face, typical of this type of death.

It was further decided that death must have occurred in 1483 when Richard III was King, and that Henry VII could not, therefore, have been guilty of the crime.

But this does not place the guilt on Richard III without quibble.

Since the examination of the bones a document has come to light, purporting to be signed by "Richard Gloucestre" and the Duke of Buckingham commending Tyrrel for his foul dead and promising that he would be remembered for it. It would appear that this document can be dismissed as bogus, for at that time Richard and the Duke were enemies.

In defence of Richard it has been further suggested that the Duke of Buckingham was the murderer, but what he would gain by the crime is problematical.

Richard III had some grounds for believing that the two princes were illegitimate. On October 1st, 1470, after the flight of her husband, Edward IV, Queen Elizabeth Widville, with her three daughters, fled from the Tower on the approach of Warwick, the King-maker, and hurried to Westminster for sanctuary.

According to tradition she lived in the Abbot's house, and on November 2nd she gave birth to a son, Edward. The chronicles disagree as to the exact date, but in the Patent Roll for 1472 announcing the grant of the revenues of the Duchy of Cornwall to the Prince, he is said to have been born on November 2nd.

The date of the birth of Richard, Duke of York, is not so easy to ascertain. He was born at Shrewsbury, but there has been dispute about the year. Official records seem content with the date August 17th, 1473.

Assuming, therefore, that the princes were murdered on August 17th, 1483, the young Duke of York was done to death on his birthday and was exactly ten years of age.

Henry VII seems much less likely to have been the murderer of the princes than Richard III ; for until he, Henry of Richmond, was chosen by the chiefs of the English nobility to cope with Richard he could have had little hope, or even ambition, to become King of England.

Furthermore, it was not until he agreed to marry Elizabeth,

eldest daughter of Edward IV, who was the rightful Sovereign of England, that the nobles chose him.

Richard was killed at the battle of Bosworth, August 1483, and Henry became Sovereign. If the murder of the princes had taken place after this date, Edward would have been 14 years of age and the Duke of York about 12.

The surgeons who examined the remains after the exhumation in Westminster Abbey were satisfied, however, that the bones belonged to younger children.